SKILLS · FOR · FLIGHT

Air Law

International Air Law – UK Air Law – Operational Procedures

1

Oxford
aviation academy

This book has been produced by Oxford Aviation Academy.

Production Team

Subject Specialists - Air Law:
Nick Mylne, Keith Boxall

Subject Specialist - Operational Procedures:
John Hooper

Contributors:
Les Fellows, Rhodri Davies, Steve Partridge, Glyn Rees, Lesley Smith

Created and Compiled by:
James Kenny

Editor:
Rick Harland, Lesley Smith

Cover Design by: Chris Hill
Cover Photograph by: AirTeamImages.com

First Published by: Oxford Aviation Academy, Oxford, England, 2007

Printed in Singapore by: KHL Printing Co. Pte Ltd

Contact Details:
OAAmedia
Oxford Aviation Academy
Oxford Airport
Kidlington
Oxford
OX5 1QX
England

Tel: +44 (0)1865 844290

Email: **info@oaamedia.com**

Innovative learning solutions for

www.oaamedia.com   ISBN 978-0-9555177-0-9   www.oaa.com

<u>GENERAL</u>

FOREWORD   v

TO THE PILOT   xiii

<u>AIR LAW</u>

CHAPTER 1: INTERNATIONAL AIR LAW   1

CHAPTER 2: RULES OF THE AIR (ICAO)   21

CHAPTER 3: REGISTRATION (ICAO)   59

CHAPTER 4: AIRWORTHINESS (ICAO)   67

CHAPTER 5: AIRSPACE DIVISION AND AIR TRAFFIC SERVICES (ICAO)   77

CHAPTER 6: FLIGHT PLANS AND CLEARANCES (ICAO)   113

CHAPTER 7: AERONAUTICAL INFORMATION SERVICES (ICAO)   125

CHAPTER 8: SEPARATION (ICAO)   131

CHAPTER 9: AERODROMES   141

CHAPTER 10: UNITED KINGDOM AIR LAW INTRODUCTION   171

CHAPTER 11: UNITED KINGDOM RULES OF THE AIR   175

CHAPTER 12: AIRCRAFT REGISTRATION IN THE UNITED KINGDOM   203

CHAPTER 13: AIRWORTHINESS IN THE UNITED KINGDOM   211

**CHAPTER 14: AIRSPACE DIVISION AND
AIR TRAFFIC SERVICES IN THE UK**   221

CHAPTER 15: FLIGHT PLANS AND CLEARANCES IN THE UK   261

CHAPTER 16: AERONAUTICAL INFORMATION SERVICES IN THE UK   277

CHAPTER 17: SEPARATION (UK)   293

CHAPTER 18: OBSTACLES (UK)   305

CHAPTER 19: ALTIMETER SETTINGS (UK)   321

ANNEX A GENERAL LIGHTS AND SIGNALS   345

ANNEX B THE JAR - FCL PRIVATE PILOT'S LICENCE   375

ANNEX C AIR LAW DEFINITIONS   397

ANNEX D AIR LAW SYLLABUS   411

ANSWERS TO AIR LAW QUESTIONS   415

AIR LAW INDEX   421

FOREWORD TO THE SECOND EDITION.

INTRODUCTION.

Whether you are planning to fly microlights, space shuttles, gliders, combat aircraft, airliners or light aircraft, it is essential that you have a firm grasp of the theoretical knowledge which underpins practical piloting skills. This Oxford Aviation Academy "Skills for Flight" series of text books covers the fundamental theory with which all pilots must come to grips from the very beginning of their pilot training, and which must remain with them throughout their flying career, if they are to be masters of the art and science of flight.

JOINT AVIATION AUTHORITIES PILOTS' LICENCES.

Joint Aviation Authorities (JAA) pilot licences were first introduced in Europe in 1999. By 2006, almost every JAA member state, including all the major countries of Europe, had adopted this new, pan-European licensing system at Air Transport Pilot's Licence, Commercial Pilot's Licence and Private Pilot's Licence levels, and many other countries, world-wide, had expressed interest in aligning their training with the JAA pilot training syllabi.

These syllabi, and the regulations governing the award and the renewal of licences, are defined by the JAA's licensing agency, 'Joint Aviation Requirements - Flight Crew Licensing', (JAR-FCL). JAR-FCL training syllabi are published in a document known as 'JAR-FCL 1.'

The United Kingdom Civil Aviation Authority (UK CAA) is one of the founder authorities within the JAA. The UK CAA has been administering examinations and skills tests for the issue of JAA licences since the year 2000, on behalf of JAR-FCL.

The Private Pilot's Licence (PPL), then, issued by the UK CAA, is a JAA licence which is accepted as proof of a pilot's qualifications throughout all JAA member states.

Currently, the JAA member states are: *United Kingdom, Denmark, Iceland, Switzerland, France, Sweden, Netherlands, Belgium, Romania, Spain, Finland, Ireland, Malta, Norway, Czech Republic, Slovenia, Germany, Portugal, Greece, Italy, Turkey, Croatia, Poland, Austria, Estonia, Lithuania, Cyprus, Hungary, Luxembourg, Monaco, Slovakia.*

As a licence which is also fully compliant with the licensing recommendations of the International Civil Aviation Organisation (ICAO), the JAA PPL is also valid in most other parts of the world.

The JAA PPL in the UK has replaced the full UK PPL, formerly issued solely under the authority of the UK CAA.

Issue of the JAA PPL is dependent on the student pilot having completed the requisite training and passed the appropriate theoretical knowledge and practical flying skills tests detailed in 'JAR-FCL 1'. In the UK, the CAA is responsible for ensuring that these requirements are met before any licence is issued.

EUROPEAN AVIATION SAFETY AGENCY.

With the establishment of the European Aviation Safety Agency (EASA), it is envisaged that JAA flight crew licensing and examining competency will be absorbed into the EASA organisation. It is possible that, when this change has taken place, the PPL may even change its title again, with the words "EASA" replacing "JAA". However, we do not yet know this for certain. In the UK, such a step would require the British Government to review and, where necessary, revise the Civil Aviation Act. But, whatever the future of the title of the PPL, the JAA pilot's licence syllabi are unlikely to change fundamentally, in the short term. So, for the moment, the JAA Licence remains, and any change in nomenclature is likely to be just that: a change in name only.

OXFORD AVIATION ACADEMY AND OAAMEDIA.

Oxford Aviation Academy (OAA) is one of the world's leading professional pilot schools. It has been in operation for over forty years and has trained more than 15 000 professional pilots for over 80 airlines, world-wide.

OAA was the first pilot school in the United Kingdom to be granted approval to train for the JAA ATPL. OAA led and coordinated the joint-European effort to produce the JAR-FCL ATPL Learning Objectives which are now published by the JAA, itself, as a guide to the theoretical knowledge requirements of ATPL training.

OAA's experience in European licensing, at all levels, and in the use of advanced training technologies, led OAA's training material production unit, OAAmedia, to conceive, create and produce multimedia, computer-based training for ATPL students preparing for JAA theoretical knowledge examinations by distance learning. Subsequently, OAAmedia extended its range of computer-based training CD-ROMs to cover PPL and post-PPL studies.

This present series of text books is designed to complement OAAmedia's successful PPL CD-ROMs in helping student pilots prepare for the theoretical knowledge examinations of the JAA PPL and beyond, as well as to provide students with the aviation knowledge they require to become safe and competent pilots.

The OAA expertise embodied in this series of books means that students working towards the JAA PPL have access to top-quality, up-to-date, study material at an affordable cost. Those students who aspire to becoming professional pilots will find that this series of PPL books takes them some way beyond PPL towards the knowledge required for professional pilot licences.

THE JAA PRIVATE PILOT'S LICENCE (AEROPLANES).

The following information on the Joint Aviation Authorities Private Pilot's Licence (Aeroplanes); (JAA PPL(A)) is for your guidance only. Full details of flying training, theoretical knowledge training and the corresponding tests and examinations are contained in the JAA document: **JAR–FCL 1, SUBPART C – PRIVATE PILOT LICENCE (Aeroplanes) – PPL(A).**

The privileges of the JAA PPL (A) allow you to fly as pilot-in-command, or co-pilot, of any aircraft for which an appropriate rating is held, but not for remuneration, or on revenue-earning flights.

For United Kingdom based students, full details of JAA PPL (A) training and examinations can be found in the CAA publication, **Licensing Administration Standards Operating Requirements Safety (LASORS),** copies of which can be accessed through the CAA's Flight Crew Licensing website.

Flying Training.

The JAA PPL (A) can be gained by completing a course of a minimum of 45 hours flying training with a training organisation registered with the appropriate National Aviation Authority (the Civil Aviation Authority, in the case of the United Kingdom).

Flying instruction must normally include:

- **25 hours** dual Instruction on aeroplanes.

- **10 hours** supervised solo flight time on aeroplanes, which must include **5 hours** solo cross-country flight time, including one cross-country flight of at least 150 nautical miles (270km), during which full-stop landings at two different aerodromes, different from the aerodrome of departure, are to be made.

The required flying-instructional time may be reduced by a maximum of 10 hours for those students with appropriate flying experience on other types of aircraft.

The flying test (Skills Test), comprising navigation and general skills tests, is to be taken within 6 months of completing flying instruction. All sections of the Skills Test must be taken within a period of 6 months. A successfully completed Skills Test has a period of validity of 12 months for the purposes of licence issue.

Theoretical Knowledge Examinations.

The procedures for the conduct of the JAA PPL (A) theoretical knowledge examinations will be determined by the National Aviation Authority of the state concerned, (the Civil Aviation Authority, in the case of the United Kingdom).

The JAA theoretical knowledge examination must comprise the following 9 subjects: *Air Law, Aircraft General Knowledge, Flight Performance and Planning, Human Performance and Limitations, Meteorology, Navigation, Operational Procedures, Principles of Flight, Communication.*

A single examination paper may cover several subjects.

The combination of subjects and the examination paper titles, as administered by the UK CAA, are, at present:

1. Air Law and Operational Procedures.
2. Human Performance and Limitations.
3. Navigation & Radio Aids.
4. Meteorology.
5. Aircraft (General) & Principles of Flight.
6. Flight Performance and Planning.
7. JAR-FCL Communications (PPL) (i.e. Radiotelephony Communications).

The majority of the questions are multiple choice. In the United Kingdom, examinations are normally conducted by the Flying Training Organisation or Registered Facility at which a student pilot carries out his training.

The pass mark in all subjects is 75%.

For the purpose of the issue of a JAA PPL(A), a pass in the theoretical knowledge examinations will be accepted during the 24 month period immediately following the date of successfully completing all of the theoretical knowledge examinations.

Medical Requirements.
An applicant for a JAR-FCL PPL(A) must hold a valid JAR-FCL Class 1 or Class 2 Medical Certificate.

THE UNITED KINGDOM NATIONAL PRIVATE PILOT'S LICENCE (AEROPLANES).

One of the aims of the United Kingdom National Private Pilot's Licence (UK NPPL) is to make it easier for the recreational flyer to obtain a PPL than it would be if the requirements of the standard JAA-PPL had to be met. The regulations governing medical fitness are also different between the UK NPPL and the JAA PPL.

Full details of the regulations governing the training for, issue of, and privileges of the UK NPPL may be found by consulting LASORS and the Air Navigation Order. Most UK flying club websites also give details of this licence.

Basically, the holder of a UK NPPL is restricted to flight in a simple, UK-registered, single piston-engine aeroplane (including motor gliders and microlights) whose Maximum Authorized Take-off Weight does not exceed 2000 kg. Flight is normally permitted in UK airspace only, by day, and in accordance with the Visual Flight Rules.

Flying Training.
Currently, 32 hours of flying training is required for the issue of a UK NPPL (A), of which 22 hours are to be dual instruction, and 10 hours to be supervised solo flying time.

There are separate general and navigation skills tests.

Theoretical Knowledge Examinations.
The UK NPPL theoretical knowledge syllabus and ground examinations are the same as for the JAA PPL (A). This series of books, therefore, is also suitable for student pilots preparing for the UK NPPL.

THE UNITED KINGDOM FLIGHT RADIOTELEPHONY OPERATOR'S LICENCE.

Although there is a written paper on Radiotelephony Communications in the JAA PPL theoretical knowledge examinations, pilots in the United Kingdom, and in most other countries, who wish to operate airborne radio equipment will need to take a separate practical test for the award of a Flight Radiotelephony Operators Licence (FRTOL). For United Kingdom based students, full details of the FRTOL are contained in LASORS.

NOTES ON CONTENT AND TEXT.

Technical Content.

The technical content of this OAA series of pilot training text books aims to reach the standard required by the theoretical knowledge syllabus of the JAA Private Pilot's Licence (Aeroplanes), (JAA PPL(A)). This is the minimum standard that has been aimed at. The subject content of several of the volumes in the series exceeds PPL standard. However, all questions and their answers, as well as the margin notes, are aimed specifically at the JAA PPL (A) ground examinations.

An indication of the technical level covered by each text book is given on the rear cover and in individual subject prefaces. The books deal predominantly with single piston-engine aeroplane operations.

Questions and Answers.

Questions appear at the end of each chapter in order that readers may test themselves on the individual subtopics of the main subject(s) covered by each book. The questions are of the same format as the questions asked in the JAA PPL (A) theoretical knowledge examinations, as administered by the UK CAA. All questions are multiple-choice, containing four answer options, one of which is the correct answer, with the remaining three options being incorrect "distracters".

Students Working for a Non-JAA PPL.

JAA licence training syllabi follow the basic structure of ICAO-recommended training, so even if the national PPL you are working towards is not issued by a JAA member state, this series of text books should provide virtually all the training material you need. Theoretical knowledge examinations for the JAA PPL are, however, administered nationally, so there will always be country-specific aspects to JAA PPL examinations. 'Air Law' is the most obvious subject where country-specific content is likely to remain; the other subject is 'Navigation', where charts will most probably depict the terrain of the country concerned.

As mentioned elsewhere in this Foreword, this series of books is also suitable for student pilots preparing for the United Kingdom National Private Pilot's Licence (UK NPPL). The theoretical examination syllabus and examinations for the UK NPPL are currently identical to those for the JAA PPL.

Student Helicopter Pilots.

Of the seven book in this series, the following are suitable for student helicopters pilots working towards the JAA PPL (H), the UK NPPL (H) or the equivalent national licence:

Volume 1: 'Air Law & Operational Procedures'; Volume 2: 'Human Performance'; Volume 3: 'Navigation & Radio Aids'; Volume 4: 'Meteorology', and Volume 7: 'Radiotelephony'.

The OAAmedia Website.

If any errors of content are identified in these books, or if there are any JAA PPL (A) theoretical knowledge syllabus changes, Oxford Aviation Academy's aim is to record those changes on the product support pages of the OAAmedia website, at: www.oaamedia.com

Grammatical Note.

It is standard grammatical convention in the English language, as well as in most other languages of Indo-European origin, that a single person of unspecified gender should be referred to by the appropriate form of the masculine singular pronoun, *he*, *him*, or *his*. This convention has been used throughout this series of books in order to avoid the pitfalls of usage that have crept into some modern works which contain frequent and distracting repetitions of *he or she*, *him or her*, *etc*, or where the ungrammatical use of *they*, and related pronouns, is resorted to. In accordance with the teachings of English grammar, the use, in this series of books, of a masculine pronoun to refer to a single person of unspecified gender does not imply that the person is of the male sex.

Margin Notes.

You will notice that margin notes appear on some pages in these books, identified by one of two icons:

a key 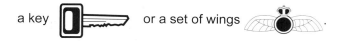 or a set of wings .

The key icon identifies a note which the authors judge to be a key point in the understanding of a subject; the wings identify what the authors judge to be a point of airmanship.

The UK Theoretical Knowledge Examination Papers.

The UK CAA sets examination papers to test JAA PPL (A) theoretical knowledge either as single-subject papers or as papers in which two subjects are combined.

Two examination papers currently cover two subjects each:

- **Aircraft (General) & Principles of Flight**: The 'Aircraft (General) & Principles of Flight' examination paper, as its title suggests, covers 'Principles of Flight' and those subjects which deal with the aeroplane as a machine, 'Airframes', 'Engines', 'Propellers' and 'Instrumentation', which JAR-FCL groups under the title 'Aircraft General Knowledge'.

- **Flight Performance & Planning:** The examination paper entitled 'Flight Performance & Planning' covers both 'Aeroplane Performance, and 'Mass & Balance'.

When preparing for the two examinations named above, using this Oxford series of text books, you will need **Volume 5, 'Principles of Flight'**, which includes 'Aeroplane Performance', and **Volume 6, 'Aeroplanes'**, which includes 'Mass & Balance' as well as 'Airframes', 'Engines', 'Propellers', and 'Instrumentation'. So to prepare for the 'Aircraft (General) & Principles of Flight' examination, you need to take the **'Aeroplanes'** infomation from **Volume 6** and the **'Principles of Flight'** information from **Volume 5**. When you are preparing for the 'Flight Performance & Planning' examination you need to take the **'Aeroplane Performance'** information from **Volume 5** and the **'Mass & Balance'** information from **Volume 6**.

It has been necessary to arrange the books in this way for reasons of space and subject logic. The titles of the rest of the volumes in the series correspond with the titles of the examinations. The situation is summed up for you in the table on the following page:

JAA Theoretical Examination Papers	Corresponding Oxford Book Title
Air Law and Operational Procedures	Volume 1: Air Law
Human Performance and Limitations	Volume 2: Human Performance
Navigation and Radio Aids	Volume 3: Navigation
Meteorology	Volume 4: Meteorology
Aircraft (General) and Principles of Flight	Volume 5: Principles of Flight Volume 6: Aeroplanes
Flight Performance and Planning	Volume 5: Aeroplane Performance Volume 6: Mass and Balance
JAR-FCL Communications (PPL)	Volume 7: Radiotelephony

Regulatory Changes.

Finally, so that you may stay abreast of any changes in the flying and ground training requirements pertaining to pilot licences which may be introduced by your national aviation authority, be sure to consult, from time to time, the relevant publications issued by the authority. In the United Kingdom, the Civil Aviation Publication, LASORS, is worth looking at regularly. It is currently accessible, on-line, on the CAA website at **www.caa.co.uk**.

Oxford,
England

April 2007

TO THE PILOT.

As private pilots exercising the privileges of a JAR-FCL Private Pilot's Licence (PPL), you will be entitled to fly in the sovereign airspace of many nations, notably, of course, in the airspace of the member nations of the Joint Aviation Authorities (JAA) and those nations in which the practice of aviation falls under the authority of the European Aviation Safety Agency (EASA). Wherever you fly, some parts of the airspace you enter will be under the formal control of air traffic control units, while other parts of the airspace will be uncontrolled. But whatever type of airspace you find yourself in, you will be sharing the air with thousands of your fellow aviators. They will be both amateur and professional, and will be flying many different types of aircraft, among which will be balloons, jet-airliners, light aircraft, military fighters, helicopters, gliders and micro-lights.

Like any community, the aviation community is governed by laws and regulations. Air Law, and its associated subject Operational Procedures, covers such areas as Rules of the Air, Air Traffic Regulations, Airspace Classification, Pilots Licences, Distress and Urgency Procedures, and Accident Investigation. In the aviation community, as in any field of human activity, if you are to become an effective, safe and responsible member of that community, you must be familiar with the body of Air Law which is in force in the airspace you fly in, and abide by its teachings.

Because aviation is an activity that is global in scope, Air Law applies internationally, too. Organisations such as the International Civil Aviation Organisation (ICAO) lay down regulations and procedures which, to a very great extent, are enshrined in the national legislation of ICAO's member countries and in that of other multi-national authorities such as the JAA and EASA.

You are, of course, required to comply with the law at all times. But rather than being simply a dry, legal subject, Air Law embodies rules and regulations which are there for a reason. A lot of Air Law reflects common sense, or, to use a better term, good airmanship. So Air Law is a very practical subject, and in mastering Air Law, you will not only be contributing to the efficient and expeditious flow of air traffic, but also ensuring that you do not compromise Flight Safety for yourself or for any other user of the air.

The introduction of the JAR-FCL PPL has brought with it a change in the way Air Law is examined. In the new examination you are just as likely to have to answer questions on ICAO procedures as on procedures applicable to the airspace of your own country, alone. The main development, then, has been to place greater emphasis on testing your knowledge of Air Law so that you are prepared to fly in the airspace of countries other than your own.

You should at all times be aware that Air Law is a living discipline which is constantly evolving. For instance, just before the first edition of this book went to press in March 2007, the UK CAA announced that, in the United Kingdom, a new rule concerning a requirement for transponder-equipped aircraft to continue to select their transponders "on" when operating near the traffic patterns of busy aerodromes was to become effective from 15 March 2007.

The content of the corpus of Air Law is massive and cannot be covered in its entirety in this or any other book. Consequently, this text book does not claim to be anything other than Oxford Aviation Academy's best attempt at providing a guide to Air Law and to your preparation for the JAR-FCL PPL examination in Air Law and Operational Procedures. This book must not be considered as a definitive treatise on Air Law, and the study of this book cannot replace reference to the relevant legal documents produced by national and international aviation authorities.

Remember, as a pilot, you must make it your responsibility to keep up to date with the requirements of Air Law by periodically referring to the latest documents and publications which appear on the subject.

HOW TO USE THIS BOOK - INTERNATIONAL (ICAO) AND NATIONAL AIR LAW.

As we mention above, since the introduction of the JAR-FCL PPL the Air Law & Operational Procedures examination set by national aviation authorities, and notably by the United Kingdom Civil Aviation Authority, is just as likely to ask questions on International (ICAO) Air Law as on Air Law applicable only to a candidate's own country.

In accordance with the spirit of Article 12 of the 'Convention on International Civil Aviation', all ICAO contracting states endeavour to formulate the Air Law prevailing in their country along guidelines which are as uniform as possible, especially where Rules of the Air are concerned. However, all ICAO member states are sovereign states and will, inevitably, elect to pass laws which have force in their country alone. Where this is so, it is the Air Law of the individual state which prevails over International (ICAO) Air Law.

Nevertheless, many elements of International (ICAO) Air Law, especially the Rules of the Air, are common to all countries. When a contracting state's rules differ from the ICAO agreements, that state "files a difference" with ICAO.

International organisations such as the Joint Aviation Authorities (JAA) and the European Aviation Safety Agency (EASA) have undertaken to seek to normalise the aviation regulations of their member states by bringing them into line with ICAO regulations.

While we recognise that many readers of this book will be United Kingdom-based pilots, as this book is a text book for pilots studying for a JAR-FCL pilot's licence, the book is divided into two principal parts: International (ICAO) Air Law and United Kingdom Air Law, in order that readers may know which elements of Air Law are international, and which elements are applicable to the United Kingdom alone. Many elements of United Kingdom Air Law are identical to ICAO Air Law; however, the United Kingdom (UK) has filed several differences with ICAO in respect of the Rules of the Air and some Air Traffic Services.

In the first section of this book, therefore, you will read about International (ICAO) Air Law which will generally be in force, to a large extent, in all ICAO member countries, including the United Kingdom. It is hoped that non-UK based readers will still be able to learn much of value about Air Law from this first section of the book.

UK-based readers will need to study both the International (ICAO) Air Law section and the section on United Kingdom Air Law. UK-based readers should also note that the JAR-FCL PPL examinations for Air Law & Operational Procedures set in the United Kingdom contain questions which are, for the most part, based on International (ICAO) Air Law. There will, however, be questions on Air Law applicable to the United Kingdom alone, these questions being identified in a suitable manner, in the question text.

CHAPTER 1
INTERNATIONAL
AIR LAW

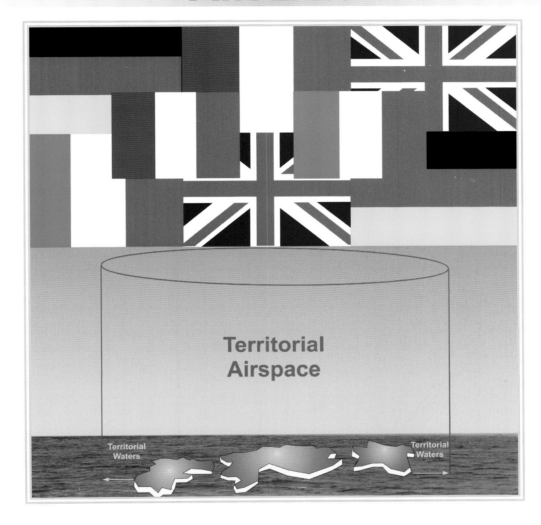

Territorial
Airspace

Territorial
Waters

Territorial
Waters

THE CONVENTION ON INTERNATIONAL CIVIL AVIATION - HISTORICAL BACKGROUND.

The first scheduled international air service began in 1919 which coincided with the first international conference on civil aviation in Paris.

The Second World War saw huge advancements in aviation which forced nations to realise that without a cohesive and international effort to create supra-national laws, further advancement would not be possible.

Consequently, invitations were sent to 55 allied states to meet in Chicago in November 1944.

Figure 1.1 World War II.

The Meeting in Chicago.

The outcome of this meeting was the The Convention on International Civil Aviation (often referred to as the Chicago Convention) in which a number of principles – or Articles - were agreed. It soon became clear that a permanent international body was needed to oversee, implement and administer these Articles. This was achieved in 1947 with the formation of The International Civil Aviation Organisation (ICAO) based in Montreal, Canada.

> *The Convention on International Civil Aviation (The Chicago Convention) created ICAO as a permanent international body to oversee, implement and administer the Articles (Standards and Recommended Practices).*

Figure 1.2 ICAO Headquarters, Montreal.

The following articles and definitions of the Convention on International Civil Aviation must be known by a PPL candidate:

Article 1 – Sovereignty.

States that: *"All Contracting States recognise that every State has complete and exclusive sovereignty over the airspace above its territory"*.

Sovereignty implies the right of a State to impose national law on users of the State's territorial airspace.

Every contracting state has complete and exclusive sovereignty above its territory.

Figure 1.3 Flags of Sovereign Nations.

Article 2 – Definition of "Territory".

Defines "territory" as: *"the land areas and territorial waters adjacent thereto under the sovereignty, suzerainty, protection or mandate of a State"*.

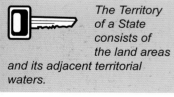

The Territory of a State consists of the land areas and its adjacent territorial waters.

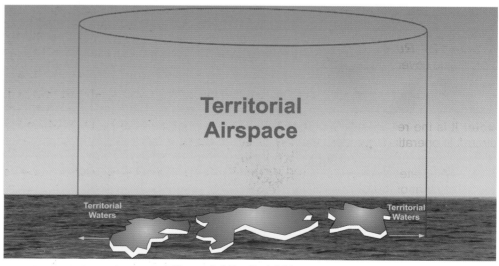

Figure 1.4 Territorial Airspace.

Article 5 – Rights of Non-Scheduled Flights.
3 points are covered by this article with regards to non-scheduled flights:

- Each State must allow non-scheduled flights into or through its territory and to land without prior permission.

- Any State has the right to require an over-flying aircraft to land.

Note: Scheduled flights require permission to overfly another State.

- Each State has the right to require an aircraft which is flying over inaccessible terrain, or in airspace which is inadequately served by navigational aids, to follow prescribed routes or to obtain special permission to conduct such flights.

Only non-scheduled flights are allowed to fly into or through the airspace of another Contracting State without permission.

Article 10 – Landing at Customs Airports.
This article concerns itself with the right of any State to require an aircraft entering its territory to land at a customs airport and to be subject to examination (unless that aircraft has obtained permission to over-fly).

Furthermore, a State has the right to require an aircraft departing its territory to take-off from a designated customs airport.

Article 11 – Applicability of Air Regulations.
Regardless of its nationality, any aircraft operating within a State's territory must obey the rules and regulations of that State.

Figure 1.5 Customs.

Article 12 – Rules of the Air.
This article covers 4 major points:

- All aircraft must obey the Rules of the Air of the State in which it is flying.

Note: It is the responsibility of the State which regulates the airspace in which the aircraft is operating to ensure that this rule is complied with.

- All States must endeavour to keep their Rules of the Air as close as possible to that of the Convention (ICAO).

- Over the high seas the Convention's (ICAO) Rules of the Air shall apply without exception.

- Each Contracting State undertakes to prosecute all persons violating these regulations. Before entering another State's airspace with the intention of landing, the pilot must ensure that:

It is the responsibility of the State which regulates the airspace in which an aircraft is flying to ensure its rules and regulations are complied with.

Before entering another State's airspace with the intention of landing, the pilot must ensure that:

1. *The aircraft is correctly registered.*

2. *The aircraft is airworthy.*

3. *All relevant documentation, including the C of A, is on board.*

- The aircraft is correctly registered.

- The aircraft is airworthy.

- All relevant documentation, including the Certificate of Airworthiness (C of A), is on board.

French Rules of the Air Apply!

Figure 1.6 Rules of the Air.

Article 13 – Entry and Clearance Regulations.

A State's laws and regulations must be obeyed with regards to the entry and departure of any passengers, crew or cargo.

All aircraft entering or departing from a State are required to adhere to the laws and regulations of that State.

These would include laws and regulations concerning:

- Entry.

- Clearance.

- Immigration.

- Passports.

- Customs.

- Quarantine.

Article 16 – Search of Aircraft.

Each State has the right to search, without reasonable delay, the aircraft of other Contracting States on landing and departure. It also has the right to inspect certificates and any other document specified by the Convention.

Article 22 – Facilitation of Formalities.

All Contracting States undertake to adopt measures to expedite the navigation of aircraft between States and to prevent unnecessary delays to aircraft, crews, passengers and cargo, especially in the areas of:

- Immigration.

- Quarantine.

Figure 1.7 Customs.

- Customs.

- Clearance.

Article 23 – Customs and Immigration Procedures.
Each Contracting State shall establish customs and immigration procedures in accordance with the Convention. This does not, however, prevent any State establishing customs-free airports.

Article 24 – Customs Duties.
Aircraft arriving, departing or crossing the territory of another State will be admitted temporarily free of duty.

Fuel, oil, spare parts and aircraft stores plus any regular equipment that is on board an aircraft on arrival shall be exempt from customs duty, inspection fees or similar charges *as long as they remain on board*.

This privilege does not apply to anything that is taken off the aircraft. However, any spare parts that are imported for use by another aircraft from another State will be free of duty.

Article 29 – Documents Carried in Aircraft.
According to the Chicago Convention all International flights of Contracting States must carry the following original documents:

- Certificate of Registration (C of R).

- Certificate of Airworthiness (C of A).

- Crew licences.

- Radio Station Licence – if equipped with a radio.

- Journey log book.

- A list of any passengers together with their names, places of embarkation and destination.

- If applicable, the Cargo Manifest and a detailed declaration of the cargo.

All aircraft on an international navigation flight are required by the Chicago Convention to carry, amongst other documents the C of R, C of A and crew licences.

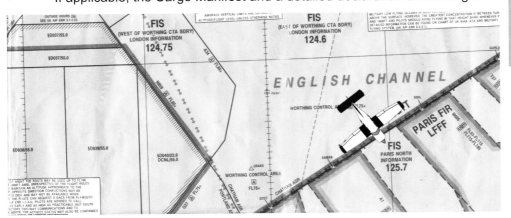

Figure 1.8 All Aircraft must carry the above documents at all times.

Article 30 – Use of Aircraft Radio Equipment.

- Aircraft operating in another State's territory must carry a licence to install and operate radios issued by the state of aircraft registration.

- The use of such radios will be in accordance with the rules and regulations of that State in which the aircraft is being operated.

- Radios may only be operated by crew holding appropriate licences issued by the State of Registration.

The radio licence is issued by the state of registration.

Figure 1.9 Radios may only be operated by personnel with the appropriate licences.

Article 31 – Certificate of Airworthiness.

Every aircraft engaged in international navigation must be provided with a Certificate of Airworthiness issued by the State of aircraft Registration.

The State of Registry is that State or country in which the aircraft is currently registered and in whose register details of the aircraft and ownership are entered.

Figure 1.10 Certificate of Airworthiness.

Article 32 – Licences of Personnel.

Pilots and other operating crew must be provided with licences and certificates of competency issued by the State of aircraft Registration.

However, States reserve the right to refuse to recognise such licences or certificates issued to its nationals by other States for flights over its territory.

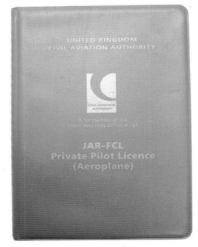

Flying licences are issued by the State of Registration.

Figure 1.11 JAR FCL Private Pilot's Licence.

Article 33 – Recognition of Certificates and Licences.

Certificates of Airworthiness and competency together with licences issued by the State of Aircraft Registration shall be recognised by other Contracting States provided they meet the standards laid down by the Convention, in other words, that they meet ICAO standards.

C of A's and licences issued by one State shall be recognised by another State providing they meet the standards laid down by the Convention.

Figure 1.12 Pilot's Licences.

Article 34 – Journey Log Books.

All aircraft engaged in international navigation shall maintain a Journey Log Book which is to contain particulars of:

•   the aircraft,

•   the crew, and

•   each journey

in the form laid down by the Convention.

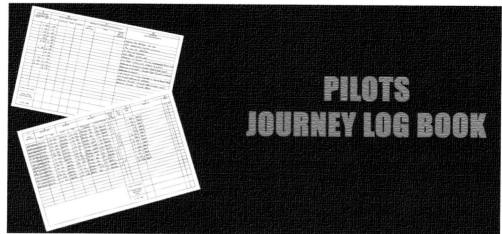

Figure 1.13 Journey Log book.

Article 35 – Cargo Restrictions.

No munitions of war may be carried in or above the territory of a State without permission of that State.

No munitions or implements of war may be carried in or above the territory of a State without the permission of that State.

Each State is to define what constitutes munitions and implements of war in line with the recommendations of the Convention.

All States reserve the right to prohibit the carriage of any other article as long as this prohibition does not jeopardise the safety of the aircraft or its passengers.

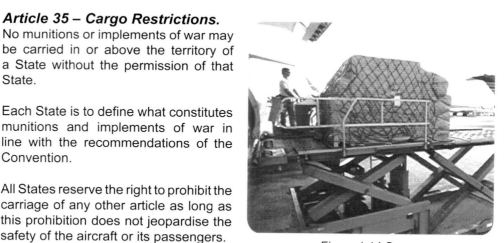

Figure 1.14 Cargo.

Article 36 – Photographic Apparatus.

Each Contracting State may prohibit or regulate the use of photographic apparatus in aircraft over its territory.

Figure 1.15 Photography.

Article 37 – Adoption of International Standards and Procedures.

All States are to undertake to collaborate in order to ensure that there is uniformity of:

- Regulations.

- Standards.

- Procedures.

- Organisation of aircraft and personnel.

To this end ICAO is to adopt and amend Standards and Recommended Practices, (SARPS) as may be necessary dealing with:

- Communication systems, and air navigation aids including ground markings.

- Airports and landing area.

- Rules of the Air and ATC practices.

- Licensing of operating crew and maintenance personnel.

- Airworthiness of aircraft.

- Registration and identification of aircraft.

- Collection and exchange of meteorological information.

- Log books.

- Aeronautical maps and charts.

- Customs and immigration procedures.

- Aircraft in distress and accident investigation.

Eighteen Annexes to the Chicago Convention have been established covering the SARPS mentioned above. These Annexes are listed on Pages 14 and 15.

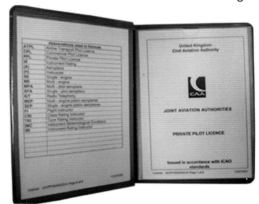

Figure 1.16 JAR - FCL Private Pilot's Licence.

Article 39 – Endorsement of Certificates and Licences.

Any aircraft (or part of an aircraft) which fails to satisfy the standards of airworthiness shall show on its airworthiness certificate complete details of such failure(s). Such an aircraft may enter another state, with permission, but cannot depart unless such failures are rectified.

Any licence holder who does not satisfy the international standards relating to such a licence shall have full details, shown on the licence, of the particulars in which he does not satisfy the conditions.

Figure 1.17 Essential Licences and Certificates.

Article 40 – Validity of Endorsed Certificates and Licences.

No aircraft or person shall participate in international navigation unless licensed to do so - except if permission is granted by the State whose territory is entered.

The use of any aircraft, or certified aircraft part in a State, other than the one in which it was first registered, is permitted only at the discretion of the state into which the aircraft or part is imported.

ORGANISATIONS.

International Civil Aviation Organisation (ICAO).

Created by the Chicago Convention, ICAO is an inter-governmental organisation. The headquarters of ICAO are in Montreal and it provides the machinery to achieve standardisation and agreement between Contracting States in all technical, economic and legal aspects of international civil aviation.

Figure 1.18 ICAO Logo.

Joint Aviation Authorities (JAA).

The JAA represents the civil aviation regulatory authorities of a number of European States which have agreed to co-operate in developing and implementing common safety regulatory standards and procedures.

JAA membership is based on signing the "JAA Arrangements" which were agreed at the Convention of Cyprus in 1990.

Figure 1.19 JAA Logo.

States have the authority to replace the rules and regulations with national laws but they must publish full details in their national Aeronautical Information Publication (AIP).

European Aviation Safety Agency (EASA).

Based in Cologne, EASA will gradually take over the functions of the JAA. EASA will develop common safety and environmental rules at the European Level.

At the time of writing, EASA has legal responsibilities for Certification and Maintenance regulations only. It is expected that the Operational and Licensing functions will continue to transfer from JAA to EASA during 2010.

Figure 1.20 EASA Logo.

MAJOR DOCUMENTATION.

ICAO Annexes.

The rules and regulations (Standards and Recommended Practices) emanating from ICAO are organised into 18 Annexes.

All Contracting States have the option to replace any of these rules or regulations with their own national laws applicable to aircraft within or above their territories. If this is the case, States must publish full details in their national Aeronautical Information Publication (AIP).

The most important ICAO Annexes are as follows:

Annex 1	Personnel Licensing
Annex 2	Rules of the Air
Annex 3	Meteorological Services for International Air Navigation
Annex 4	Aeronautical Charts
Annex 5	Units of Measurement to be used in Air and Ground Operations
Annex 6	Operation of Aircraft
Annex 7	Aircraft Nationality and Registration Marks
Annex 8	Airworthiness of Aircraft
Annex 9	Facilitation
Annex 10	Aeronautical Telecommunications
Annex 11	Air Traffic Services

Annex 12	Search and Rescue	
Annex 13	Aircraft Accident Investigations	
Annex 14	Aerodromes	
Annex 15	Aeronautical Information Services	
Annex 17	Security – Safeguarding International Civil Aviation against Acts of Unlawful Interference	
Annex 18	Transport of Dangerous Goods by Air	

Questions may be asked on the numbering and titles of all Annexes.

The United Kingdom Air Navigation Order (ANO).

This document, enacted by Parliament, is the legal basis of United Kingdom (U.K.) civil aviation. Pilots who contravene its Articles are liable to prosecution. It also concerns itself with the Rules of the Air Regulations.

All U.K. registered aircraft are subject to the provisions of the ANO and the Rules of the Air Regulations at any time wherever they may be.

All U.K. registered aircraft are subject to the provisions of the Air Navigation Order (ANO) and the Rules of the Air Regulations at any time wherever they may be.

U.K. Aeronautical Information Publication (AIP).

This publication, known by many as the "Air Pilot", is the core document laying out essential information regarding all aspects of flying in the United Kingdom. It is subdivided into 3 parts:

The AIP consists of 3 parts: GEN, ENR and AD.

- General Information (GEN).

- En-Route Data (ENR).

- Aerodrome Data (AD).

Representative PPL - type questions to test your theoretical knowledge of UK and International Legislation.

1.   An aircraft entering another contracting state's airspace and proposing to land must:

     a.   Conform to the C of A of the airspace of the state into which it is flying

     b.   Be registered, airworthy and carry all the relative documents required including the C of A

     c.   Carry the C of A and the International Interception Table of Signals

     d.   Ensure it carries an original copy of the flight plan only

2.   Does each state have the right to search, without reasonable delay, the aircraft of other contracting states on landing and departure?

     a.   Yes

     b.   No

     c.   Yes but this applies only to commercial aircraft

     d.   Yes but this applies only to non-commercial aircraft

3.   When an ICAO aircraft lands in another contracting state what items are temporarily exempt from customs duty?

     a.   Aircraft spare parts and items of flight safety

     b.   Only the fuel and oils remaining on board the aircraft

     c.   Fuel, oil, spare parts and aircraft stores plus any regular equipment that is on board the aircraft

     d.   Un-bonded goods under the strict supervision of customs

4.   You are flying a UK registered aircraft over Germany. Whose Rules of the Air must you obey?

     a.   ICAO's

     b.   UK's

     c.   JAA's

     d.   Germany's

5.   When can an ICAO aircraft make flights into the airspace of another contracting state without permission?

     a.   If it is a non-scheduled flight

     b.   If it is a scheduled flight

     c.   Never

     d.   If it is not carrying passengers

6.   When entering into another country's airspace, the licence of the Pilot-in-Command must have been issued by the authority of:

    a.   The state of aircraft registration
    b.   Any JAA member state
    c.   The State of Airworthiness
    d.   Any contracting ICAO state

7.   Which rules of the air govern the entry and departure of international air traffic into and out of a foreign state?

    a.   ICAO's
    b.   The foreign state's
    c.   International Rules and Regulations
    d.   IATA's

8.   A state must recognise as valid the C of A of another member state if the C of A:

    a.   Was issued in accordance with ICAO requirements and standards
    b.   Was issued in accordance with international requirements and standards
    c.   Is valid and current
    d.   Was issued in accordance with the State of Registry

9.   The C of R must be:

    a.   Carried in the aircraft at all times and may be a copy of the original
    b.   Carried in the aircraft at all times and must be in the original form issued
    c.   Signed by the Pilot-in-Command
    d.   Held in safe-keeping at the aerodrome of departure

10.   All contracting states recognise that every state has complete and exclusive sovereignty over the airspace above its territory. Is this statement true?

    a.   Yes
    b.   No

11.   Who has the responsibility to ensure that all aircraft entering a state's airspace obey that state's rules and regulations?

    a.   The state of aircraft registration
    b.   The state issuing the C of A of the aircraft
    c.   The state which regulates the airspace in which the aircraft is operating
    d.   ICAO

12. An aircraft which has failed its C of A but nevertheless has written details of the reasons why it had so failed shall:

    a. Not take part in international navigation
    b. Be allowed to depart another contracting state's airspace but cannot enter it
    c. Be allowed to enter another contracting state's airspace but cannot depart until all the failures are rectified
    d. Not take part in international navigation except with the permission of the state, or states whose territory is entered

13. All UK registered aircraft are subject to the provisions of the ANO and the Rules of the Air Regulations:

    a. Only when inside UK territorial airspace
    b. Only when within the airspace of any ICAO contracting State
    c. Anywhere at any time
    d. Only if they carry a C of A issued by the UK CAA

14. What is the name of the Convention which is commonly known as "The Chicago Convention?"

    a. The Convention of Civil Commercial Aviation
    b. The Convention on International Civil Aviation
    c. The ICAO Convention of Civil Aviation
    d. The Convention on International Civil Transportation

15. According to the Chicago Convention which of the following documents, amongst others, are required to be carried in the aircraft on an international flight?

    a. Certificate of Airworthiness (C of A), Certificate of Registration (C of R) and crew passports
    b. Crew licences and log books, journey log book and, if applicable, Radio Station Licence
    c. Crew licences, journey log book and, if applicable, the cargo manifest and a detailed declaration of the cargo
    d. Passports for all crew and passengers, Certificate of Airworthiness (C of A), Certificate of Registration (C of R)

16. The U.K. Aeronautical Information Publication (AIP) is subdivided into the following sections:

    a. GEN, AGA, ENR and AD
    b. AGA, ENR and AD
    c. GEN, AGA and ENR
    d. GEN, ENR and AD

17.	Can a state search a visiting aircraft from another contracting state without permission?

	a.	No
	b.	Yes
	c.	Only if a crime is reasonably suspected
	d.	Only if it is reasonably suspected that the aircraft is carrying inadmissible passengers

18.	What does ICAO Annex 2 concern itself with?

	a.	Personnel Licensing
	b.	Facilitation
	c.	Rules of the Air
	d.	Aerodromes

19.	What ICAO Annex covers the Airworthiness of Aircraft?

	a.	Annex 8
	b.	Annex 9
	c.	Annex 12
	d.	Annex 14

20.	What organisation will take over the responsibilities and role of the JAA?

	a.	IATA
	b.	ECAC
	c.	EU
	d.	EASA

21.	The Chicago Convention recognises that:

	a.	Every State has sovereignty over airspace above its territory up to FL660
	b.	Every Contracting State has complete and exclusive sovereignty over the airspace above its territory
	c.	Every Contracting State has complete but not exclusive sovereignty over the airspace above its territory
	d.	Every Contracting State has complete and exclusive sovereignty over the airspace above its territorial waters

22.	Under the Chicago Convention, the Territory of a State consists of:

	a.	Its total land area
	b.	Its total land areas and up to 10 miles of its surrounding territorial waters (if any)
	c.	The land areas and its adjacent territorial waters
	d.	Its total land areas and up to 25 miles of its surrounding territorial waters (if any)

23. All aircraft entering or departing from a State must obey the laws and regulations of:

   a. The State of Registry of the aircraft
   b. ICAO
   c. The State in question
   d. The State having jurisdiction over the Customs Laws

Question	1	2	3	4	5	6	7	8	9	10	11	12
Answer												

Question	13	14	15	16	17	18	19	20	21	22	23
Answer											

The answers to these questions can be found at the end of this book.

CHAPTER 2
RULES OF THE AIR (ICAO)

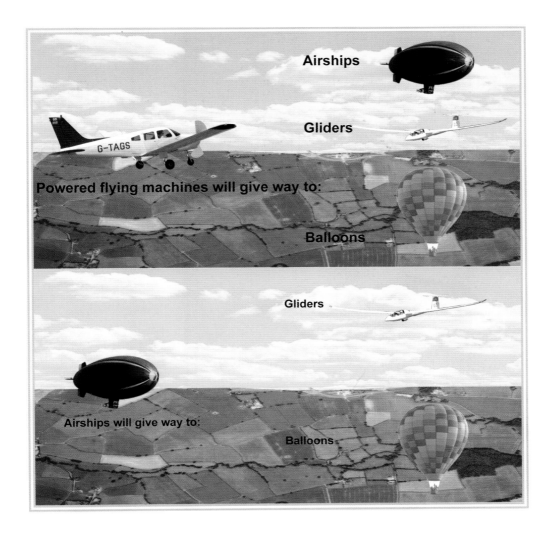

RULES OF THE AIR - (ICAO ANNEX 2).

INTRODUCTION.

Article 12 of the 'Convention on International Civil Aviation', which addresses the issue of Rules of the Air to be applied by ICAO contracting states, stipulates that:

"Every aircraft flying over a state's territory, and every aircraft carrying a territory's nationality mark – wherever it is – must comply with that territory's Rules of the Air. Each state shall keep its own Rules of the Air as uniform as possible with those established under the Convention. The duty to ensure compliance with these Rules rests with the contracting state. Over the high seas the Rules established under the Convention apply."

You may expect, then, that the Rules of the Air which apply in any contracting ICAO state will, in general, follow the internationally agreed ICAO standards for Rules of the Air, as laid down in Annex 2 of the 'Convention on International Civil Aviation', known commonly as ICAO Annex 2. However, you must also note that each ICAO contracting state, while <u>undertaking</u> to endeavour to apply the ICAO-agreed rules, may interpret the ICAO agreements in the context of its own particular requirements.

When a contracting state's rules differ from the ICAO agreements, that state "files a difference" with ICAO.

The Joint Aviation Authorities (JAA) and the European Aviation Safety Agency (EASA) are organisations which have undertaken to seek to normalise the aviation regulations of their member states by bringing them into line with ICAO standards. As this book is a text book for pilots studying for a JAR-FCL pilot's licence, the information on Rules of the Air contained in this chapter deals exclusively with internationally agreed ICAO standards. For the most part, the information in this chapter will apply in all ICAO member states and in all JAA/EASA member states, but it is important that student pilots refer to their own country's aviation legislation to confirm which information is relevant to their country, and to identify where differences may exist.

Furthermore, before flying over the territory of a state, other than his home state, it is the responsibility of the pilot to familiarise himself with any of that state's Rules of the Air which are different from those with which he has been used to complying.

The United Kingdom (UK) has filed several differences with ICAO in respect of the Rules of the Air. Those differences are covered in Chapter 11. UK-based pilots and student pilots should note, therefore, that the information contained in this present chapter, covering the ICAO Annex 2 Rules of the Air, will be relevant to a UK-based pilot's needs, <u>except in those cases where differences are noted in Chapter 11</u>. There are some important differences in the UK Rules of the Air, so Chapter 11 should be studied carefully by UK-based pilots. For instance, in the Rule on collision avoidance between two aircraft on a converging track, the ICAO Rule requires that the aircraft having priority should maintain heading and speed while the UK Rule requires that the priority aircraft maintains course and speed. Therefore, these rules are covered separately in Chapters 2 and 11. On the other hand, the ICAO Rules on aircraft lighting, and avoiding collision in the air by reference to aircraft lights, is the same in the ICAO Rules and the UK Rules. Consequently, these rules are covered in Chapter 2, only.

It should, of course, be a reasonable assumption to expect that all questions asked of a candidate in the theoretical knowledge examination in Air Law will be relevant to the country in which the examination is set. Nevertheless, in the theoretical knowledge examination on Air Law for the JAR-FCL PPL, questions often apply to ICAO Rules of the Air, unless the wording of the question specifically refers that question to a national Rule. So before sitting the theoretical knowledge examination, be sure to seek guidance from your instructor, or your national aviation authority, as to the latest policy on this matter.

As far as the United Kingdom is concerned, the UK Civil Aviation Authority's current policy on this matter (February 2007) is as expressed in the preface to this book. That is: in the current UK Civil Aviation Authority JAR-FCL PPL theoretical knowledge examinations for Air Law & Operational Procedures, the Air Law questions are, for the most part, based on ICAO Air Law. But where UK Air Law differs from ICAO Air Law, these questions are annotated with 'UK Law' at the beginning of the relevant questions.

APPLICABILITY OF RULES OF THE AIR.

Where there is confliction, national rules have precedence over ICAO rules. ICAO Rules apply without exception over the high seas.

The ICAO Rules of the Air apply to aircraft bearing the nationality and registration marks of a Contracting State, wherever they may be, to the extent that they do not conflict with the rules published by the State having jurisdiction over the territory overflown.

Over the High Seas (outside any territorial airspace) the ICAO Rules apply without exception.

Figure 2.1 Cessna over oil rig.

Departure from the Rules.
The pilot-in-command may depart from these rules in circumstances that render such departure absolutely necessary in the interests of safety. These Rules are the General Rules and, in addition to the general rules, the pilot-in-command (PIC), when in flight, is subject to:

Visual Flight Rules (VFR)

and

Instrument Flight Rules (IFR).

GENERAL RULES.

Protection of Persons & Property.
An aircraft shall not be operated in a negligent or reckless manner so as to endanger life or property.

Minimum Heights.
Except for taking off and landing, or when authorised, no aircraft may be flown over congested areas (cities, towns or settlements) unless at a height which permits, in the event of an emergency, a landing to be made without hazard to persons or property on the ground.

Cruising Levels.
The cruising levels at which a flight, or a portion of a flight, is to be conducted shall be defined in terms of:

- flight levels, for flights above the Transition Altitude (TA)

  and

- altitudes, for flights at or below the Transition Altitude.

The cruising levels at which a flight, or a portion of a flight is to be conducted shall be defined in terms of:

a) flight levels, for flights above the Transition Altitude (TA)
and
b) altitudes, for flights at or below the Transition Altitude.

Dropping and Spraying.
Nothing must be dropped or sprayed from an aircraft except when using a method approved by the Authority, and when cleared to do so by Air Traffic Services (ATS).

Towing.
No aircraft or other object must be towed by an aircraft, except in accordance with requirements prescribed by the appropriate Authority, and when cleared to do so by Air Traffic Services (ATS).

Note: The combination of a flying machine** and the glider it is towing is to be considered as a single aircraft under the command of the pilot-in-command of the tug aircraft.

***A 'flying machine' is any power-driven, heavier than air aircraft.*

Figure 2.2 Glider Towing.

Parachute Descents and Aerobatic Flights.

Neither parachute descents nor aerobatic flights are to be made except under conditions prescribed by the appropriate Authority and when cleared to do so by Air Traffic Services (ATS).

Formation Flying.

Aircraft must not be flown in formation except by prearrangement among the pilots-in-command of the aircraft taking part in the flight.

Figure 2.3 Formation Flying.

The following conditions apply:

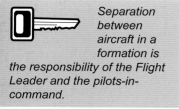

Separation between aircraft in a formation is the responsibility of the Flight Leader and the pilots-in-command.

- The formation operates as a single aircraft with regard to navigation and position reporting.

- Separation between aircraft in the formation shall be the responsibility of the Flight Leader and the pilots-in-command.

- A maximum distance of **1 km (0.5 nms) laterally and 100 feet vertically** must be maintained by each aircraft from the Flight Leader.

Prohibited Areas and Restricted Areas.

Aircraft must not be flown in a Prohibited Area or in a Restricted Area except in accordance with the restrictions or with the permission of the State over which territory the areas are established.

Figure 2.4 Restricted Area.

Operation on and in the Vicinity of an Aerodrome.

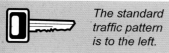

The standard traffic pattern is to the left.

An aircraft operated on or in the vicinity of an aerodrome must, whether or not within an aerodrome traffic zone (ATZ):

- Observe other aerodrome traffic for the purpose of avoiding collision.

- Conform with or avoid the pattern of traffic formed by other aircraft in operation.

- Make all turns to the **LEFT**, when approaching for a landing and after taking off, unless otherwise instructed.

- Land and take off into the wind unless safety, the runway configuration, or air traffic considerations determine that a different direction is preferable.

Signals.
Ground-to-air visual signals are covered in Annex A to this volume.

Time.
Co-ordinated Universal Time (UTC) must be used in a 24 hour format.

A time check must be obtained by pilots prior to operating a controlled flight and, additionally, whenever necessary.

Position Reports by Aircraft Under Air Traffic Control.
Unless exempted by ATC (when ATC uses the phase **"omit Position Reports"**), a controlled flight must report to the appropriate ATSU, as soon as possible, the time and level of passing each reporting point, together with any other required information.

A Position Report should normally contain the following information:

    a.   Aircraft identification **
    b.   Position **
    c.   Time **
    d.   Flight level or altitude
    e.   Next position and time over that position
    f.   Ensuing significant (reporting) point

** Mandatory information

Example:

"London Control, G-ABCD, Honiley 1031, maintaining Flight Level 70, Daventry 1054, Olney next."

In the absence of designated reporting points, position reports must be made at intervals prescribed by ATC. This is normally 30 minutes after take-off and, thereafter, every hour.

AVOIDANCE OF COLLISIONS.

Line of Constant Bearing (LCB).
If two aircraft are converging on a constant relative bearing, they will collide unless avoiding action is taken. Therefore, if a closing aircraft remains in the same relative position in your field of view, a collision risk exists.

However, if the aircraft that you are observing appears to move across your windscreen, vertically or horizontally, then no collision risk exists while both aircraft maintain their tracks.

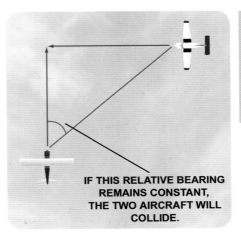

IF THIS RELATIVE BEARING REMAINS CONSTANT, THE TWO AIRCRAFT WILL COLLIDE.

Figure 2.5 Line of Constant Bearing.

REMEMBER!

If another aircraft remains in the same relative position in your field of view, the aircraft will collide, so take early avoiding action!

Proximity.

An aircraft must not be operated in such proximity to other aircraft as to create a danger of collision.

Figure 2.6 An aircraft shall not be operated in such proximity to other aircraft as to create a danger of collision.

RIGHT-OF-WAY – AIRCRAFT IN THE AIR.

Approaching Head-On.

If two aircraft are approaching head-on, both must turn right to avoid collision.

When two aircraft are approaching head-on, or approximately so, and there is danger of collision, each must alter its heading to the right regardless of the type of either aircraft.

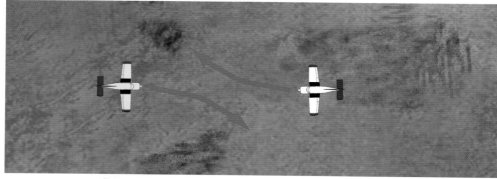

Figure 2.7 Approaching head-on - both aircraft turn right.

Converging.

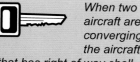

When two aircraft are converging, the aircraft that has right of way shall maintain its heading and speed.

When two aircraft are converging at approximately the same level, the aircraft that has the other on its right must give way. The aircraft having priority must maintain its heading and speed.

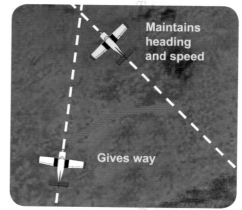

Maintains heading and speed

Gives way

Figure 2.8 Converging.

EXCEPT as follows:

• Power-driven, heavier-than-air aircraft (i.e. flying machines) must give way to airships, gliders and balloons.

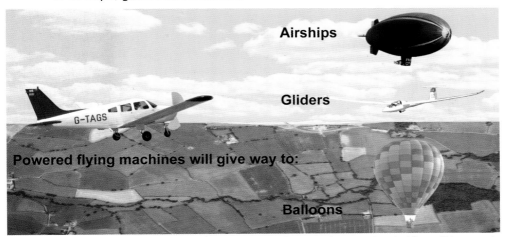

Figure 2.9a A power-driven heavier-than-air aircraft must give way to airships, gliders and balloons.

• Airships must give way to gliders and balloons.

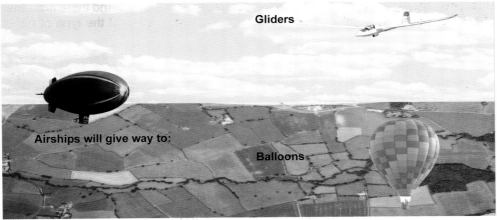

Figure 2.9b Airships must give way to gliders and balloons.

• Gliders must give way to balloons.

Figure 2.9c Gliders must give way to balloons.

• Power-driven aircraft must give way to aircraft which are seen to be towing other aircraft or objects.

The term "flying machine" refers to any heavier-than-air, power-driven aircraft.

The following table summarises the rules concerning right-of-way in the air.

Flying machines	give way to:	Airships Gliders Balloons
Flying machines Airships	give way to:	Gliders Balloons
Flying machines Airships Gliders	give way to:	Balloons

NB: You should note that the term "flying machine" refers to any heavier-than-air, power-driven aircraft.

An aircraft is considered to be overtaking another when the faster aircraft is converging within 70° of the extended longitudinal axis of the slower aircraft.

Memorising the mnemonic **FAGB** may help you remember the right-of-way rules.

Overtaking in the Air.

An overtaking aircraft is a faster aircraft that approaches another from the rear, within a 70° arc either side of the tail.

- An aircraft that is being overtaken has the right-of-way.

- The overtaking aircraft, whether climbing, descending or in horizontal flight, must keep out of the way of the other aircraft by altering its heading to the **right**. However, the overtaking aircraft must not pass over, under or in front of the other aircraft, unless well clear.

- The overtaking aircraft should take into account the effect of wake turbulence.

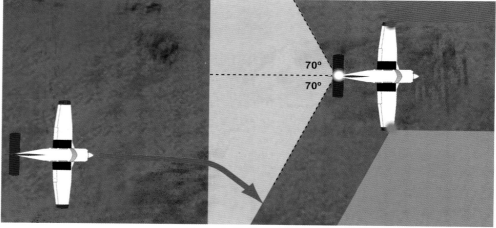

Figure 2.10 Overtaking.

Landing.

An aircraft in flight, or operating on the ground or water, must give way to aircraft landing or in the final stages of an approach to land.

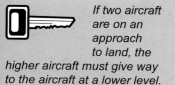

If two aircraft are on an approach to land, the higher aircraft must give way to the aircraft at a lower level.

When two or more heavier-than-air aircraft are approaching an aerodrome for the purpose of landing, aircraft at the higher level must give way to aircraft at the lower level, but the latter must not take advantage of this rule to cut in front of another aircraft which is in the final stages of an approach to land, or to overtake that aircraft.

Figure 2.11 Right of Way on Landing. The lower aircraft has right of way.

Note: Nevertheless, power-driven heavier-than-air aircraft must give way to gliders.

Emergency Landing.

An aircraft that is aware that another aircraft is compelled to land must give way to that aircraft.

Taking Off.

An aircraft taxiing on the manoeuvring area of an aerodrome must give way to aircraft taking off or about to take off.

General.

• An aircraft that has the right-of-way must maintain its heading and speed.

• Nothing shall relieve the pilot-in-command from the responsibility of taking action to avoid collision. Therefore, even if a pilot has the right of way, he is still responsible for ensuring that he avoids the other aircraft.

• An aircraft which is obliged to keep out of the way of another aircraft must avoid passing over, under or in front of the priority aircraft, unless it passes well clear.

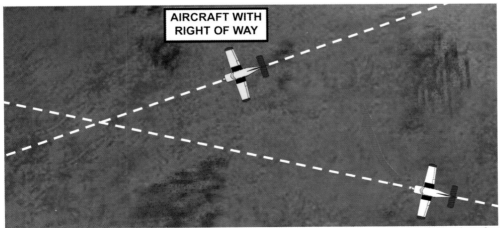

Figure 2.12 An aircraft giving way must avoid passing over, under or in front of the aircraft with right of way.

RIGHT OF WAY ON THE GROUND.

Aircraft with right of way

Figure 2.13 When two aircraft are on a converging course, the one which has the other on its right shall give way.

Surface Movement of Aircraft.

In case of danger of collision between two aircraft taxiing on the movement area of an aerodrome the following rules shall apply:

• When two aircraft are approaching head on, or approximately so, each shall stop or, where practicable, alter its course to the right so as to keep well clear of the other aircraft.

• When two aircraft are on a converging course, the one which has the other on its right shall give way *(see Figure 2.13)*.

• An aircraft which is being overtaken by another aircraft shall have the right-of-way and the overtaking aircraft shall keep well clear of the other aircraft. (**NB**: ICAO rules imply that the overtaking aircraft can pass on either side).

Vehicles and Aircraft.

The following are the rules concerning the rights of way of aircraft and vehicles on the movement area of an aerodrome:

• Flying machines and vehicles shall give way to aircraft which are taking off or landing.

• Vehicles and taxiing flying machines shall give way to vehicles towing aircraft.

• Vehicles which are not towing aircraft shall give way to aircraft.

Figure 2.14 A tug towing an aircraft.

- In any case, an emergency vehicle going to the assistance of an aircraft in distress shall have priority over all other surface movement traffic.

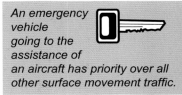

An emergency vehicle going to the assistance of an aircraft has priority over all other surface movement traffic.

LIGHTS TO BE DISPLAYED BY AEROPLANES.

In Flight.

From sunset to sunrise or during any period which may be prescribed by the appropriate authority all aeroplanes in flight must display:

- navigation lights intended to indicate the relative path of the aeroplane to an observer. Other lights are not to be displayed if they are likely to be mistaken for these lights.

- anti-collision lights intended to make an aircraft's presence conspicuous.

Anti-collision lights must be displayed during daylight unless they adversely affect the performance of duties or cause a harmful dazzle to an outside observer.

Navigation Lights.

There are three navigation lights fitted to aeroplanes, one on each wing tip, and the other on the aft parts of the fin. A red light is displayed on the port wing tip, a green light on the starboard wing tip and a white light at the rear of the aircraft.

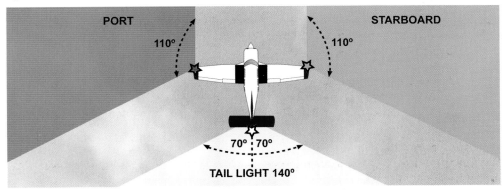

Figure 2.15 Navigation Lights (Top).

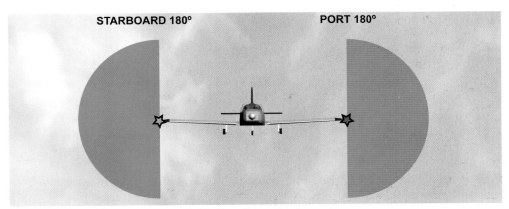

Figure 2.16 Aircraft coming towards you.

The red and green lights are required to be seen from straight ahead through 110° in the horizontal plane and through 90° above and below the aeroplane in the vertical plane. The white light must be able to be seen 70° to the right and left in the horizontal plane aft of the aeroplane and throughout 90° in the vertical plane *(see Figure 2.15)*.

Aeroplanes on the Movement Area.

From sunset to sunrise, or during any other period prescribed by the authority an aeroplane on the movement area, and an aircraft with its engines running, must display:

- When moving, navigation lights intended to indicate the relative path of the aeroplane to an observer. No other lights shall be displayed if they may be mistaken for the navigation lights.

- When moving, lights intended to indicate the extremities of its structure.

- Lights intended to attract attention to the aeroplane (anti-collision lights).

- Lights which indicate the fact that the engine is running (anti-collision lights).

Anti-collision lights must be displayed in daylight hours unless they adversely affect the performance of duties or cause a harmful dazzle to an outside observer.

Colour of Anti-Collision Lights.

Rotorcraft	-	Flashing **RED**
Other Aircraft	-	Flashing **RED** and/or **WHITE**

Switching Off or Reducing Flashing Lights for Safety Reasons.

In the interest of safety, if flashing lights fitted to an aeroplane adversely affect any performance of duty (i.e. reflected flash from cloud at night) or causes harmful dazzle to an observer, the pilot is permitted to switch lights off or reduce their intensity.

Lights must be switched on:

- a. In flight at night.

- b. In flight by day (anti-collision lights).

- c. When taxiing or parked on the Manoeuvring Area at night.

- d. When aircraft are stationary on the apron or Maintenance Area with engines running if fitted by day and by night (anti-collision lights).

Gliders.

Gliders at night must either display standard lights or a steady red light visible from all directions.

Free Balloons.

Free balloons at night must display a steady, red, omni-directional light suspended below the basket.

Airships.

An airship must show standard navigation lights but in addition must display an anti-collision light and a white nose light showing through 110° from straight ahead *(see Figure 2.17)*.

Failure of Navigation and Anti-Collision Lights.

On the ground, if an aircraft suffers a failed light that is required to be displayed at night and which is not immediately repairable, the aircraft must not fly.

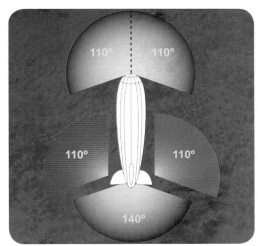

Figure 2.17 Airship Navigation Lights.

If any light fails at night, when airborne, the aeroplane should be landed as soon as is safely possible. The pilot may continue the flight only if authorised to do so by an ATC Unit.

If an anti-collision light fails during the day, the aeroplane may continue its flight providing the light is repaired at the first opportunity.

Collision Avoidance at Night.

A collision risk between aircraft is present if:

    a.   aircraft are operating at or near the same altitude.

    b.   the aircraft are converging and the relative bearing between aircraft is constant.

When the commander of an aircraft observes a light (or lights) of another aircraft at the same altitude, he must decide whether or not a collision risk exists. If there is no risk of collision, no change of heading or speed is needed.

If a collision risk exists, the pilot must first decide which aircraft has right of way in accordance to the Rules of the Air and then take what avoiding action is necessary. A pilot must not insist on his priority if to do so would cause a risk of collision.

Collision Risk & Right of Way.

If a collision risk exists and a pilot has right of way, there is no requirement for the pilot to change heading or speed, but he must watch the other aircraft very closely to ensure that it takes avoiding action.

Remember: A pilot must not fly under or over another aircraft or cross ahead of it unless well clear. Speed or altitude should not be changed unless such action is necessary to avoid immediate danger.

There are a number of simple rules for the pilot to observe, and a number of rhymes which may help him remember the rules:

- If you see a **RED** light on your **RIGHT** and it remains on a constant relative bearing to you, take avoiding action!

  "If to starboard **red** appear, it is your duty to keep clear".

  "**Red** on the right, gives you a fright".

  "**Green** to **red**, you could end up dead".

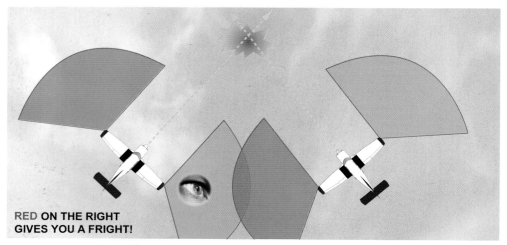

Figure 2.18 Red on the right, gives you a fright!

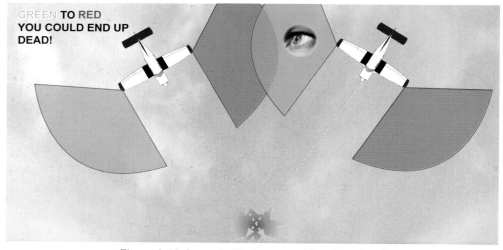

Figure 2.19 Green to Red, you could end up dead!

- If you see a **RED** light to your **LEFT** - Maintain heading and speed.

  "**Red** to **red**, go ahead".

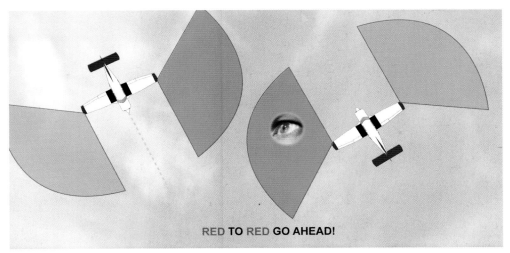

Figure 2.20 Red to Red, go ahead!

- If you see a **GREEN** light to your **RIGHT -** Maintain heading and speed.

  "**Green** to **green**, all serene".

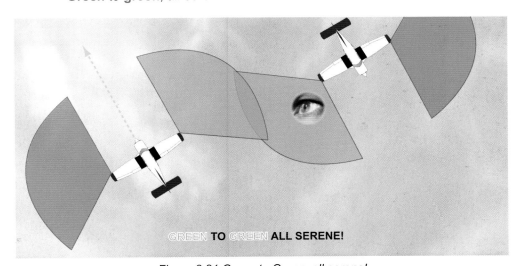

Figure 2.21 Green to Green, all serene!

- If you see a white light ahead which is getting brighter, take avoiding action by turning **RIGHT**.

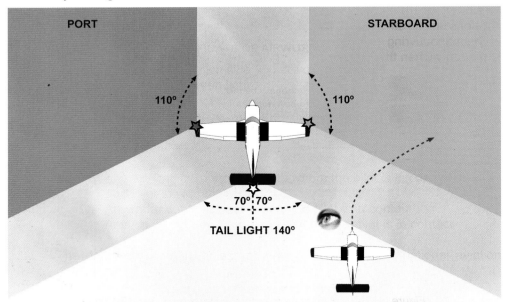

Figure 2.22 A white light ahead getting brighter - you are overtaking.

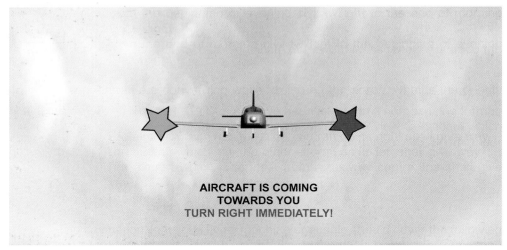

Figure 2.23 Aircraft Head-On!

- **THE ONLY TIME A PILOT WILL SEE A RED AND A GREEN AT THE SAME TIME IS WHEN AN AIRCRAFT IS HEAD ON TO HIM.**

  TURN RIGHT IMMMEDIATELY!

Note: Red/white and green/white can be seen together from 20 degrees aft of the left or right abeam positions respectively - see Fig 2.22.

RUNWAY HOLDING POSITION & STOP BARS.

An aircraft taxiing on the manoeuvring area must stop and hold at all runway-holding positions unless otherwise authorised by aerodrome traffic control. An aircraft taxiing on the manoeuvring area must stop and hold at all lighted stop bars, and may proceed further only when the lights are switched off by ATC. *(See Figures 2.24 and 2.25).*

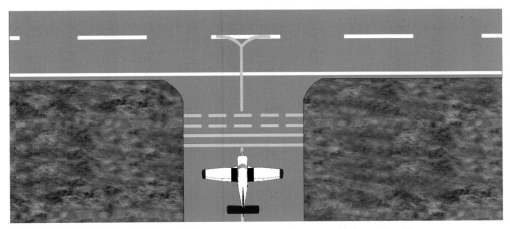

Figure 2.24 An aircraft holding at an 'A' pattern Holding Position.

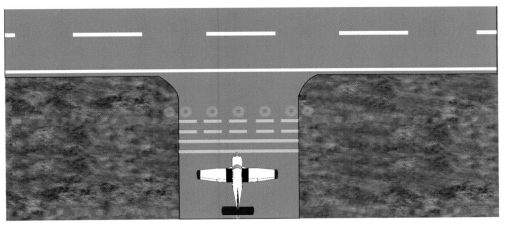

Figure 2.25 An aircraft holding at a Stop Bar.

SIMULATED INSTRUMENT FLIGHTS & PRACTICE INSTRUMENT APPROACHES.

Simulated Instrument Flights.
An aircraft must not be flown under simulated Instrument Meteorological Conditions (IMC) unless:

- The aircraft is equipped with dual controls.

- A qualified pilot occupies a control seat to act as safety pilot for the person who is flying under simulated instrument conditions.

An aircraft must not be flown under simulated IMC unless it is equipped with dual controls and a qualified pilot occupies a control seat.

- The safety pilot has adequate vision forward and to each side of the aircraft.

- In the event of the safety pilot not having an adequate visual field, a competent observer in communication with the safety pilot must occupy a position in the aircraft from which the observer's field of vision adequately supplements that of the safety pilot.

Figure 2.26 Simulated Instrument Flight Conditions.

Practice Instrument Approaches.

A pilot wishing to carry out a practice instrument approach can only do so when:

- In VMC.

- Carrying a competent observer.

- Having received clearance to do so by ATC.

COMMUNICATIONS FAILURES.

A controlled flight must maintain continuous two-way communication with the appropriate ATCU.

Communications Failure in VMC.

In the event of communications failure when flying Visual Meteorological Conditions (VMC) the pilot must:

- Continue to fly in VMC.

- If equipped with a transponder, squawk 7600 and select Mode C.

- Land at the nearest suitable aerodrome.

- Report his arrival by the most expeditious means to the appropriate ATCU.

Communications Failure in IMC:

In the event of communications failure when flying in Instrument Meteorological Conditions (IMC), the pilot must:

The transponder squawk for radio failure is 7600 + Mode C.

- Maintain the last assigned speed and level, or minimum flight altitude, if higher, for a period of 20 minutes (See Notes) following the aircraft's failure to report its position over a reporting point. Thereafter, the pilot shall adjust level and speed in accordance with the filed flight plan.

- If equipped with a transponder, squawk 7600 and select Mode C.

In the event of communication failures the procedure used depends upon whether the conditions are VMC or IMC regardless of whether the aircraft is operating VFR or IFR.

- Proceed according to the current flight plan route to the appropriate designated navigation aid serving the destination aerodrome.

- When required, hold over the navigation aid until commencement of descent.

- Commence descent from the navigation aid as close as possible to, the Expected Approach Time (EAT), if the pilot has received one. If no EAT is received, the pilot should commence the decent as close as possible to his flight planned Estimated Time of Arrival (ETA).

- Complete a normal instrument approach procedure.

- Land, if possible, within 30 minutes after the ETA or EAT, whichever is the later.

- Report arrival by the most expeditious means to the appropriate Air Traffic Service Unit (ATSU).

Notes:

If a pilot is under radar control, he should maintain the last assigned speed and level, or minimum flight altitude, if higher, for a period of **7 minutes**.

If a pilot is being radar vectored by a Radar Controller, he must immediately revert to his filed flight plan.

N.B.: EAT is the time at which ATC expect an aircraft to leave the hold to commence an approach.

UNLAWFUL INTERFERENCE - (HI-JACK).

General.

Unlawful Interference is also known as Unlawful Seizure or, more commonly, hi-jack.

The transponder squawk for Unlawful Interference/Seizure is 7500 + Mode C.

The law states simply that an aircraft which is being subjected to unlawful interference shall:

- Endeavour to make a detailed report as to the circumstances of the interference to the appropriate ATSU as soon as possible.

- Inform the ATSU of any necessitated deviation from the current flight. A hi-jacked aircraft is given priority over all other aircraft.

The Procedure to be followed in the case of Unlawful Interference.

The most important considerations for the pilot are:

- To keep the atmosphere in the cockpit as calm as possible.

- To inform ATC by any means possible of the circumstances and – if this is not possible – any other aircraft.

- If he has filed a flight plan, to stick to the flight plan if possible until able to contact an ATSU.

- If he has a transponder, squawk 7500 and select Mode C.

If a pilot is forced to depart from track, he should:

- Attempt to broadcast warnings on the VHF Emergency frequency (121.5 MHz).

- Proceed in accordance with any special procedures for the airspace in which he is flying.

- If there are no such special procedures and he is flying in accordance with IFR, the pilot should proceed at a level that differs from the cruising level normally used for IFR traffic in the area by 300 m (1 000 feet), if above FL 290, or by 150 m (500 feet), if below FL 290.

Note:

1. ATC will not use the words "Hi-jack", "Unlawful Seizure" or "Unlawful Interference" unless these words have already been used by a member of the crew.

2. ATC will not expect replies from the aircraft and will continue to pass information/instructions and clearances to the aircraft.

INTERCEPTION.

General.

Every State has the right to intercept aircraft within its territorial airspace. Nevertheless interception will only be undertaken as a last resort.

The transponder squawk, if intercepted, is 7700 + Mode C, and contact should be made between aircraft on 121.50 MHz.

Procedure in the Event of Interception.

An aircraft which is intercepted must:

- Immediately obey the instructions given by the intercepting aircraft.

- Notify the appropriate ATSU giving as many details as possible.

- Attempt to establish radio communication with the interceptor by making a general call on 121.5 MHz and giving the identity of the intercepted aircraft and the nature of the flight.

- If equipped, select Code 7700 + Mode C on the aircraft transponder.

Signals Between Intercepted and Intercepting Aircraft.

Contracting States are to ensure that the signals shown in Annex A are adhered to by their aircraft.

Confliction of Signals from Interceptor and ATC.

Should there be a confliction between the signals shown by the intercepting aircraft and instructions received from ATC, the intercepted aircraft **must obey those received from the interceptor** and advise ATC of the circumstances.

Radio Communication During Interception.

If radio contact is established during interception but communication in a common language is not possible, attempts shall be made to convey instructions, acknowledgement of instructions, and essential information by using the phrases and pronunciations in the following tables and transmitting each phrase <u>twice</u>:

PHRASES FOR USE BY INTERCEPTING AIRCRAFT		
Phrase	**Pronunciation****	**Meaning**
CALL SIGN	<u>KOL</u> SA-IN	What is your call sign?
FOLLOW	<u>FOL</u>-LO	Follow me
DESCEND	DEE-<u>SEND</u>	Descend for landing
YOU LAND	<u>YOU-LAAND</u>	Land at this aerodrome
PROCEED	PRO-<u>SEED</u>	You may proceed

- The call sign required to be given is that used in radiotelephony communications with Air Traffic Service Units (ATSUs) and corresponding to the aircraft identification in the flight plan.

- Circumstances may not always permit, nor make desirable, the use of the phrase 'HI-JACK'

PHRASES FOR USE BY INTERCEPTED AIRCRAFT		
Phrase	**Pronunciation****	**Meaning**
CALL SIGN	<u>KOL</u>-SA-IN	My call sign is (call sign)
WILCO (Will comply)	<u>WILL</u>-KO	Understood & will comply
CAN NOT	<u>KANN</u> NOTT	Unable to comply
REPEAT	REE-<u>PEET</u>	Repeat your instruction
AM LOST	<u>AM LOSST</u>	Position unknown
MAYDAY	<u>MAYDAY</u>	I am in distress
HI-JACK #	<u>HI-JACK</u>	I have been hi-jacked
LAND (place name)	<u>LAAND</u> (place name)	I request to land at: (place name)
DESCEND	DEE-<u>SEND</u>	I require descent

**   In the second column of both tables, syllables to be emphasized are underlined.

\#   Circumstances may not always permit, nor make desirable, the use of the phrases "HI-JACK", "UNLAWFUL SEIZURE" and "UNLAWFUL INTERFERENCE".

VISUAL METEOROLOGICAL CONDITIONS (VMC).

Visual Meteorological Conditions are conditions expressed in terms of visibility, distance from cloud, and cloud ceiling, equal to or better than specified minima.

VFR flight must take place in VMC, but, in addition, the pilot must also be able to see the ground.

A basic JAR-FCL PPL holder will, on most occasions fly in accordance with the Visual Flight Rules (VFR). When flying **VFR**, the pilot must be able to manoeuvre and navigate his aircraft, and maintain separation from other aircraft, by reference to features outside the cockpit. Consequently, VFR flight is possible only when visibility cloud base and separation from cloud meet certain defined minima. These minima are defined as Visual Meteorological Conditions (VMC). VFR must take place in VMC, but, in addition, the pilot must be able to see the ground.

ICAO defines VMC as follows: *"meteorological conditions expressed in terms of visibility, distance from cloud, and cloud ceiling, equal to or better than specified minima."*

These VMC minima vary depending on the class of airspace in which a flight is being conducted, and on the aircraft's vertical position.

ICAO VMC Visibility and Distance from Cloud Minima.

Although VMC minima may be expressed slightly differently in your home state, you should note that the ICAO VMC minima are as follows:

Altitude Band	Airspace Class	Flight Visibility	Distance From Cloud
At and above 3 050 m (10 000 feet)* AMSL	B⁺CDEFG **ALL AIRSPACE**	8 km	1 500 m horizontally 300 m (1 000 feet) vertically ⁺(Class B = Clear of Cloud)
Below 3050 m (10 000 feet)* and above 900 m (3 000 feet) AMSL, or 300 m (1 000 feet) above terrain, whichever is the higher.	B⁺CDEFG **ALL AIRSPACE**	5 km	1 500 m horizontally 300 m (1 000 feet) vertically ⁺(Class B = Clear of Cloud)
At and below 900 m (3 000 feet) AMSL, or 300 m (1 000 feet) above terrain, whichever is the higher.	B⁺CDE **CONTROLLED AIRSPACE**	5 km	1 500 m horizontally 300 m (1 000 feet) vertically ⁺(Class B = Clear of Cloud)
	FG **UNCONTROLLED AIRSPACE**	5 km**	Clear of cloud and with the surface in sight

Notes:

*   When the height of the Transition Altitude is lower than 3 050 m (10 000 feet) AMSL, FL 100 should be used in lieu of 10 000 feet.

**   When so prescribed by the appropriate ATS authority, flight visibilites reduced to not less than 1 500 m may be permitted for flights operating:

a.   At speeds that, in the prevailing visibility, will give adequate opportunity to observe other traffic or any obstacles in time to avoid collisions.

b.   In circumstances in which the probability of encounters with other traffic would normally be low, e.g. in areas of low volume traffic or for aerial work at low levels.

(**NB.:** Helicopters may be permitted to operate in less than 1 500 m flight visibility, if manoeuvred at a speed that will give adequate opportunity to observe other traffic or any obstacles in time to avoid collision.)

Note especially that VFR flight is prohibited in Class A Airspace.

ICAO VMC minima are illustrated in *Figures 2.27* and *2.28* below.

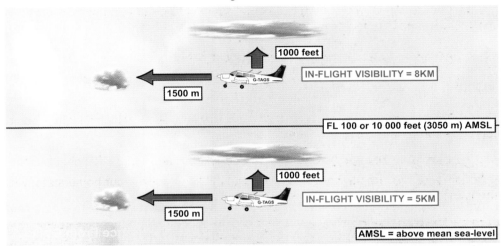

Figure 2.27 Controlled airspace classes: B, C, D & E - VMC minima.

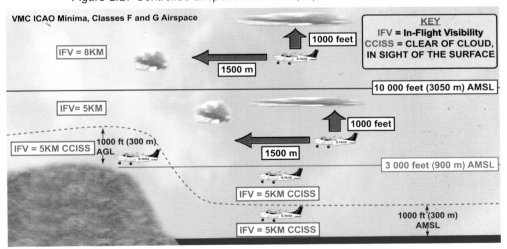

Figure 2.28 Uncontrolled airspace classes: F and G - VMC minima.

VMC minima and VFR flight in the various classes of controlled and uncontrolled airspace are also covered in Chapters 5 and 14 which deal with Airspace Division and Air Traffic Services.

VISUAL FLIGHT RULES (VFR).

General.
Except when operating as a Special VFR flight (SVFR), flights operating in accordance with the Visual Flight Rules (VFR) must be conducted in Visual Meteorological Conditions (VMC). However, the fact that VMC prevails is not, in itself, sufficient for VFR flight to be permitted. The pilot must also be able to see the ground. And that

means enough of the ground for him to be able to navigate his aircraft and maintain safe terrain separation by visual reference to the ground.

Minimum Conditions for Take-off, Landing and in the Traffic Pattern.

Except when a clearance is obtained from an Air Traffic Control Unit (ATCU), VFR flights shall not take off or land at an aerodrome within a Control Zone (CTR), or enter the Aerodrome Traffic Zone (ATZ) or traffic pattern:

All VFR flights must be conducted in VMC minima appropriate to the class of airspace which the aircraft is flying, and to its vertical position. In addition, the VFR pilot must be able to see the ground.

- when the ceiling is less than 450 m (1 500 feet),

or

- when the ground visibility is less than 5 km.

VFR at Night.

VFR flights between sunset and sunrise, or such other period between sunset and sunrise, may be permitted as prescribed by the appropriate national aviation authority.

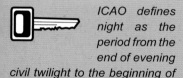

ICAO defines night as the period from the end of evening civil twilight to the beginning of morning civil twilight.

ICAO defines night as the period from the end of evening civil twilight to the beginning of morning civil twilight. The expression civil twilight is defined as being when the centre of the Sun's disk is 6 degrees below the horizon. In twilight conditions, illumination is sufficient, under good weather conditions, for terrestrial objects to be clearly distinguished.

The UK CAA also defines night differently from ICAO *(see Chapter 10)*. In the UK, VFR operations are not allowed at night.

Other Restrictions on VFR Flights.

Unless authorised by the appropriate Air Traffic Services authority, VFR flights shall not be operated:

- above FL 200,

or

- above FL 290 in RVSM (Reduced Vertical Separation Minima).

VFR Flights Above 3 000 Feet.

Except where otherwise indicated in Air Traffic Control clearances or specified by the appropriate Air Traffic Service (ATS) authority, VFR flights in level cruising flight when operated above 900 m (3 000 feet) from the ground or water, or a higher datum as specified by the appropriate ATS authority, must be conducted at a Flight Level appropriate to the magnetic track as specified in the Tables of Cruising Levels on Page 48.

Note: the United Kingdom Flight Level system differs from that of ICAO.

VFR Flights & Clearances.

VFR flights must comply with clearance requirements when:

- operated within Classes B, C and D airspace,

- forming part of aerodrome traffic at controlled aerodromes,

or

- operated as SVFR flights.

Controlled VFR Flights and Communications.

A VFR flight operating within or into areas, or along routes, that require the submission of a flight plan must:

- maintain continuous air-ground communication watch on the appropriate frequency,

and

- report its position as necessary to the ATSU providing The Flight Information Service (FIS).

General Speed Restriction.

Generally an aircraft must not fly faster than 250 kts IAS below 10 000 feet unless cleared by an Air Traffic Control Unit (ATCU).

Figure 2.29 The Rules: Generally an aircraft shall not fly faster than 250 kts IAS below 10 000 feet unless cleared by ATS.

Changing from VFR to IFR.

The pilot of an aircraft operated in accordance with the Visual Flight Rules who wishes to change to Instrument Flight Rules must:

- if a flight plan was submitted, communicate the necessary changes to his current flight plan,

or

- when required, submit a flight plan to the appropriate ATCU and obtain a clearance prior to proceeding in accordance with IFR when in controlled airspace.

Flight Level Cruising Rules.

An aircraft flying above the Transition Altitude must fly at Flight Levels based on a pressure altimeter setting of 1013.2 hPa dependent on the magnetic track of the aircraft, in accordance with the Semi-Circular Rule, as shown in the following table of cruising levels.

The cruising Flight Level is dependent on the aircraft's magnetic track and its flight rules.

TRACK							
From 000 to 179 degrees				From 180 to 359 degrees			
IFR Flights		VFR Flights		IFR Flights		VFR Flights	
FL	Feet	FL	Feet	FL	Feet	FL	Feet
10	1000	-	-	20	2000	-	-
30	3000	35	3500	40	4000	45	4500
50	5000	55	5500	60	6000	65	6500
70	7000	75	7500	80	8000	85	8500
90	9000	95	9500	100	10000	105	10500
110	11000	115	11500	120	12000	125	12500
130	13000	135	13500	140	14000	145	14500
150	15000	155	15500	160	16000	165	16500
170	17000	175	17500	180	18000	185	18500
190	19000	195		200	20000	205	
210	21000	215		220	22000	225	
230	23000	235		240	24000	245	
250	25000	255		260	26000	265	
270	27000	275		280	28000	285	
290	29000			300	30000		
310	31000			320	32000		
330	33000			340	34000		
350	35000			360	36000		
370	37000			380	38000		
390	39000			400	40000		
410	41000			430	43000		
450	45000			470	47000		
490	49000			510	51000		

Figure 2.30 Table of cruising levels - the Semi-Circular Rule.

Difference Between ICAO and UK Flight Level Cruising Rules.

One of the major differences between ICAO Flight Level Cruising Rules and the United Kingdom Flight Level Cruising Rules is that the ICAO Rules make a distinction as to whether a flight is operating under VFR or IFR in addition to the magnetic track of the aircraft. Therefore, the ICAO Semi-Circular Rule gives separate VFR and IFR cruising levels. (*See Figure 2.30.*) Over the UK, on the other hand, the Flight Level Cruising Rules depend only on the magnetic track of the aircraft. In other words, UK has no VFR Flight Levels, although this may change in the future.

A second major difference is that, in the United Kingdom, above the Transition Altitude and below Flight Level 195, outside controlled airspace, IFR flights follow a Quadrantal Rule, not the Semi-Circular Rule. Furthermore, in the UK, VFR flights are not obliged to follow any Flight Level Cruising Rule, outside controlled airspace. The United Kingdom Rules are covered in full in Chapter 11.

SPECIAL VFR (SVFR).

General.
A SVFR Flight is a VFR flight cleared by an Air Traffic Control Unit (ATCU) to operate within a Control Zone (CTR) in meteorological conditions below VMC.

SVFR is permitted only in a Control Zone (CTR).

The important points to remember about SVFR are:

*   A SVFR clearance is not a pilot's right and is granted by an ATCU only when traffic conditions allow, after a request has been made by the pilot.

*   A SVFR flight must obey all instructions from the ATCU.

*   A SVFR flight must remain clear of cloud and in sight of the ground at all times.

*   A SVFR flight is allowed only within a CTR.

*   Separation is provided between SVFR aircraft and all IFR traffic.

*   Two-way communications are mandatory. It should be noted that if a pilot has received a SVFR clearance to enter a CTR and experiences a communications failure prior to entry, the pilot must remain clear of the CTR.

*   A pilot may request SVFR in flight or prior to take-off from an aerodrome in the CTR.

MINIMUM CONDITIONS FOR SVFR.

A ground visibility of not less that 1 500 m is required before a SVFR flight can be authorised to:

     a.   enter a CTR.
     b.   take-off and depart from a CTR.
     c.   cross, or operate locally within a CTR.

In-flight requests for SVFR should be made at least 10 min before entering a CTR.

MINIMUM HEIGHTS AND LOW FLYING.

Congested Areas and Open-Air Assemblies.
Except as necessary for take-off or landing, or except by permission from the appropriate authority, a VFR flight must not be flown over the congested areas of cities, towns or settlements, or over an open-air assembly of persons, at a height less than 1 000 feet (300 m) above the highest obstacle within a radius of 600 m from the aircraft, or below a height which will permit the aircraft to land clear of persons or property on the ground, in the event of an engine failure, whichever is the higher.

An aircraft is not permitted to fly over a congested area below 1000 feet above the highest fixed obstacle within 600 metres of the aircraft, except as necessary for take-off or landing.

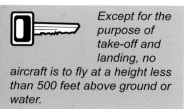

Except for the purpose of take-off and landing, no aircraft is to fly at a height less than 500 feet above ground or water.

Low Flying Absolute Minima.

Except for the purpose of landing and taking-off or with the permission of the appropriate authority, no aircraft is to fly at a height less than 500 feet (150 m) above the ground or water.

THE VISUAL CIRCUIT.

The Visual Circuit is a traffic pattern which imposes order on aerodrome traffic taking off, landing and flying in the immediate vicinity of an aerodrome. At a controlled aerodrome, the Visual Circuit is controlled by Aerodrome Control, usually from the Air Traffic Control Tower.

Figure 2.31 The Visual Circuit. Aircraft must conform to the traffic pattern being followed by other aircraft operating at an aerodrome.

All aircraft must either conform to the traffic pattern (circuit) being followed by other aircraft operating at an aerodrome, or else keep clear of the Visual Circuit.

The Standard Circuit.

The Standard Circuit is a left-hand circuit consisting of 4 "legs" as shown in the diagram below. In a left-hand circuit, all turns are made to the left.

A standard visual circuit is LEFT - hand. This means that all turns are to be made to the left.

Figure 2.32 A Left Hand Circuit.

If, for some operational reason, there is a right-hand circuit in force a pilot will normally be advised by the responsible Air Traffic Service Unit (ATSU) over the radio prior to joining the circuit. For aircraft with no radio there are designated signals in the signals square which inform pilots of the circuit direction in force *(see Annex A)*. If an aircraft is not fitted with a radio, the pilot should plan to carry out an overhead join to the aerodrome and make a careful check of the signals square.

If a pilot with a serviceable radio is in doubt about the circuit direction in force, he should confirm the direction with the ATSU.

Representative PPL - type questions to test your theoretical knowledge of ICAO Rules of the Air.

1.   When two aircraft are converging at approximately the same level the one that has the other on its right is required to give way. True or false?

      a.   True, provided they are in the same class
      b.   False. The one that has the other on its left is required to give way
      c.   True, unless the other aircraft has a glider on tow
      d.   The Rules of the High Seas apply

2.   An aircraft is not permitted to fly over a congested area below 1000 feet above the highest fixed obstacle within 600 metres of the aircraft, except in the following circumstances:

      a.   When carrying out a practice forced landing
      b.   When necessary to fix one's position on a cross-country flight
      c.   When landing or taking off
      d.   When carrying out a low flying exercise with a qualified flying instructor

3.   What is the definition of Visual Meteorological Conditions (VMC)?

      a.   Meteorological conditions in which all flights must take place in accordance with the Visual Flight Rules (VFR)
      b.   A set of rules which defines how aircraft are to be flown with reference to external, visual features
      c.   Meteorological conditions in which only VFR flights may take place
      d.   Meteorological conditions expressed in terms of visibility, distance from cloud, and cloud ceiling, equal to or better than specified minima

4.   What is the basic presumption about VFR flight?

      a.   That the pilot holds the correct rating to allow the aeroplane to be flown in VFR
      b.   That the flight will be flown in Visual Meteorological Conditions
      c.   That the flight will only take place in Class F or G airspace
      d.   That the flight will not take place above FL180

5.   In uncontrolled airspace, below FL 100, and above 3 000 feet AMSL or 1 000 feet above terrain, whichever is the higher, what are the VMC minima?

      a.   Clear of cloud and in sight of the surface with an in-flight visibility of 5 km
      b.   1 000 feet vertical and 1 500 m horizontal separation from cloud with an in-flight visibility of 5 km
      c.   1 000 feet vertical and 1 500 m horizontal separation from cloud with an in-flight visibility of 8 km
      d.   Clear of cloud with an in-flight visibility of 8 km

6.   An aircraft following a road, railway line, river, canal or other line feature should keep such a feature:

        a.   On its left
        b.   On its right
        c.   Directly underneath it
        d.   On its left during the day and on the right at night

7.   With certain exceptions, an aircraft must not fly closer than _____ feet to any person, vessel, vehicle or structure unless it is landing or taking off in accordance with normal aviation practice. Select the correct minimum separation distance from the following options:

        a.   1 000 feet
        b.   500 feet
        c.   1 500 feet
        d.   1 000 m

8.   When a pilot, for the purposes of practising instrument flight, is flying under simulated Instrument Meteorological Conditions such that his ability to see outside the cockpit is artificially restricted, which of the following regulations applies?

        a.   An observer must also be present in the cockpit
        b.   The exercise must be carried out at a licensed airfield
        c.   An appropriately qualified safety pilot must be present in one of the control seats. If necessary, an additional observer may need to be carried to ensure that an adequate lookout is being kept
        d.   The exercise must be carried out as part of a commercial or air transport pilot's licence flying training course at an approved Flying Training Organisation

9.   Which SSR Code should be selected to indicate radio failure?

        a.   7700 + Mode C
        b.   7500 + Mode C
        c.   7000
        d.   7600 + Mode C

10.   The definition "flying machine" may refer to:

        a.   Any aircraft of any category or classification
        b.   Fixed wing aircraft only
        c.   Gliders and power-driven aeroplanes or dirigibles
        d.   Any heavier-than-air, power-driven aircraft

11. You are about to overtake an aircraft at night from a position behind and almost immediately astern of the other aircraft. Which of its navigation lights will you see?

    a. A white and a red light
    b. A white light only
    c. It depends on which side you are overtaking the other aircraft
    d. A white and a green light

12. When flying in accordance with the Visual Flight Rules in uncontrolled airspace, responsibility for maintaining VMC and terrain clearance rests with:

    a. Any Air Traffic Control Unit with whom the pilot is in contact
    b. The Pilot-in-Command
    c. Any radar controller with whom the pilot is in contact
    d. Any Air Traffic Service Unit with whom the pilot is in contact

13. The definition of night, unless otherwise specified by a national aviation authority is:

    a. From the end of evening civil twilight to the beginning of morning civil twilight
    b. From the beginning to the end of civil twilight
    c. From the beginning of evening civil twilight to the end of morning civil twilight
    d. From the end of morning civil twilight to the beginning of evening civil twilight

14. If two aircraft are converging while taxiing on the apron, what is the priority rule?

    a. The aircraft which has the other aircraft on its right shall give way
    b. The aircraft which has the other aircraft on its left shall give way
    c. The aircraft which is farthest from a taxiway centre line shall give way
    d. The smaller of the two aircraft shall give way

15. The navigation lights of a flying machine or airship should cover the following arcs: green and red wingtip-lights _____ degrees each side from dead ahead and a white tail-light _____ degrees either side of dead astern.

    a. 220   140
    b. 110   70
    c. 100   90
    d. 90   90

16.   Which of a), b), c) and d) below, most correctly completes the following statement?

When two or more aircraft are on final approach:

    a.   The lower aircraft has the right of way unless ATC has already specified a landing order

    b.   The lower performance aircraft has right of way

    c.   The higher aircraft has the right of way

    d.   The aircraft which has the least horizontal distance to run to the runway threshold has the right of way

17.   Which of a), b), c) and d) below, provides the most correct conclusion to the following statement?

In order to minimise the risk of collision, the following rules apply when aircraft of different categories are converging:

    a.   Powered aeroplanes must give way to airships, gliders and balloons

    b.   Gliders must give way to powered aeroplanes and airships

    c.   Airships must give way to powered aeroplanes, gliders and balloons

    d.   Tug-aircraft with a glider on tow must give way to all other airspace users

18.   Complete the following sentence correctly. Except with permission of the Authority:

    a.   No aircraft shall fly within 500 feet of an open-air gathering of more than 500 people

    b.   No aircraft shall fly within 500 feet of an open-air gathering of more than 1 000 people

    c.   No aircraft shall fly within 1 000 feet of an open-air gathering of more than 500 people

    d.   No aircraft shall fly within 1 000 feet of an open-air gathering of more than 1 000 people

19.   While flying at night, as the pilot-in-command, you see an anti-collision light and a steady red light at the same altitude, which maintain a constant relative bearing from you of 050 degrees. Is there a risk of collision? And who has right of way?

    a.   Yes. You do

    b.   Yes. The other aircraft does

    c.   No. The other aircraft does

    d.   No. You do

20   As you are taxiing back to the apron you encounter a tractor towing an aircraft. Your correct course of action is to:

a.   Stop
b.   Continue because you have right of way
c.   Turn right
d.   Give way to the tractor/aircraft combine; it has the right of way

21.   You are IFR in VMC and experience a communication failure. Your correct actions are to:

a.   Adhere to your flight plan and continue to your destination
b.   Continue in VMC and land at the nearest suitable aerodrome and report your arrival to the appropriate ATSU
c.   Land immediately
d.   Adhere to your last ATC clearance for 20 minutes and then revert to your filed flight plan continuing to your planned destination

22.   You are intercepted by a fighter aircraft. On which frequency would you try and establish contact?

a.   The frequency with which you are in contact at the moment of interception
b.   121.5 MHz
c.   2182 MHz
d.   500 KHz

23.   Whilst maintaining a steady course, level and speed you see another aircraft in your 2 o'clock about 4 nautical miles away and at the same level as yourself. The danger of collision exists if the other aircraft:

a.   Appears to get bigger
b.   Remains in the same relative position
c.   Appears to be overtaking you, by moving towards your 12 o'clock
d.   Appears to be dropping behind you, moving towards your 4 o'clock

24.   When are navigation lights required to be shown?

a.   When moving on the manoeuvring area of an aerodrome
b.   From sunset to sunrise or when specified by the Authority
c.   Whenever the Pilot-In-Command thinks it is sensible to switch them on
d.   At night or when specified by the authority

25.   If two aircraft are approaching head on:

a.   Both aircraft must turn left
b.   A powered aircraft must give way to a glider by turning right
c.   Both aircraft should turn right regardless of aircraft type
d.   The larger aircraft should give way by turning right

26. If you were following a river which flows from east to west while maintaining a track of 270° True, which side of the river must you fly?

    a. To the North of the river, because you must fly to the right of the line feature
    b. To the South of the river, because you should fly to the left of the line feature
    c. Directly overhead the river
    d. Either side of the river as long as you keep a good look out for other aircraft

27. You see a red light of another aircraft on your right and it remains on a constant relative bearing. What must you do?

    a. Continue to maintain heading and speed, keeping a good watch on the other aircraft
    b. Take avoiding action; you are probably on a collision course
    c. Continue to maintain heading, altitude and speed, keeping a good watch on the other aircraft
    d. Immediately descend

28. You see a red and green light of another aircraft straight ahead of you. What must you do?

    a. Immediately turn left
    b. Immediately turn right
    c. Immediately descend
    d. Immediately climb

29. During the course of a night flight, you notice that a navigation light has failed; the correct action to be followed is:

    a. Make a "PAN" call on the frequency in use and proceed on planned route to destination
    b. Land as soon as practically possible unless permission to continue to your destination is given by the appropriate ATCU
    c. If the anti-collision light is working, switch off the navigation lights and continue to destination
    d. Land at the nearest suitable airfield

30. You see a red light of another aircraft on your left. What must you do?

    a. Continue to maintain heading and speed, keeping a good watch on the other aircraft; the aircraft is heading in an opposite direction to you
    b. Take avoiding action
    c. Continue to maintain heading, altitude and speed, keeping a good watch on the other aircraft
    d. Immediately descend

31.   In level flight at night, from your aircraft, you see an anti-collision beacon and a red navigation light. The lights are at the same altitude as yourself and are steady at 2 o' clock and closing. This indicates that there is:

   a.   An airship which should give way to you
   b.   A flying machine which should give way to you
   c.   A flying machine to which you should give way
   d.   No threat

32.   An aircraft is considered to be overtaking another when the faster aircraft is approaching from behind within:

   a.   10° of the extended centreline of the aircraft
   b.   20° of the extended centreline of the aircraft
   c.   70° of the extended centreline of the aircraft
   d.   80° of the extended centreline of the aircraft

33.   During a flight, by day, a pilot notices that an anti-collision light is inoperative. Which of the following actions is correct?

   a.   He should land as soon as safe to do so unless authorised by ATC to continue the flight
   b.   He may continue flight by day provided that the light is repaired at the earliest practical opportunity
   c.   He must land as soon as possible and get the light repaired
   d.   Provided the aircraft is flown VFR only, the problem may be ignored

Question	1	2	3	4	5	6	7	8	9	10	11	12
Answer												

Question	13	14	15	16	17	18	19	20	21	22	23	24
Answer												

Question	25	26	27	28	29	30	31	32	33
Answer									

The answers to these questions can be found at the end of this book.

CHAPTER 3
REGISTRATION (ICAO)

NATIONALITY, COMMON & REGISTRATION MARKS.

DEFINITIONS.

Nationality Mark.

The nationality mark consists of a character (letters and/or numbers) issued by the State of Registration of the aircraft which denote the nationality of the aircraft. For example, UK registered aircraft have the nationality mark of "G"; the nationality mark of the United States is "N" and that of Syria is "SY".

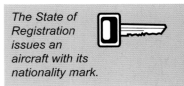

The State of Registration issues an aircraft with its nationality mark.

Figure 3.1 A UK registered aircraft showing the Nationality Mark and its registration.

Common Mark.

Should an aircraft belong to an international operator, registered in more than one state, it is issued with a Common Mark in place of a nationality mark by ICAO. For instance, the common mark 4YB has been issued by ICAO to Jordan and Iraq for registering aircraft operated by the company Arab Air Cargo.

Registration Mark.

The Registration Mark is issued to the aircraft by the State of Registry and follows the common or nationality mark. For example if an aircraft is designated G-ABCD, "G" is the nationality mark, and "ABCD" is the registration mark.

The Registration Mark is issued by the State of Registry.

Issuing Authorities.

*   A nationality mark is chosen by the State from the symbols allocated to it by the International Telecommunication Union. The State then notifies ICAO of which Nationality Mark has been selected.

*   The Common Mark is issued to the Common Mark Registering Authority by ICAO.

*   The Registration Mark is allocated to the aircraft by the State of Registry (or, in the case of an aircraft belonging to an international agency, by the Common Mark Registering Authority).

The Nationality Mark originates from The International Telecommunication Union.

Unusable Letter Combinations for Registration Marks.

Letter combinations are not to be used for the registration mark which might be confused with:

- The 5 letter combinations used in the International Code of Signals (for example flag signals used in Maritime operations).

- 3 letter combinations starting with the letter Q used in the Q Code (e.g. QNH, QFF, QDM etc.).

- The distress and urgency signals SOS, PAN, XXX.

- TTT, which is morse code for safety / sécurité.

Characteristics and Location of Markings.

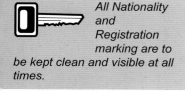

All Nationality and Registration marking are to be kept clean and visible at all times.

- All markings are to be painted, or affixed by any other means which ensure the same degree of permanence.

- They are to be kept clean and visible at all times.

- On heavier-than-air aircraft, the marking shall be on the:

  a. lower surface of the wings,

  and

  b. on each side of the fuselage or on the upper parts of the vertical tail surfaces.

Size of Markings.

On heavier-than-air aircraft, the markings shall be at least:

- 50 cms in height on the wings,

  and

- 30 cms in height on the fuselage and vertical tail surfaces.

Dispensation from Markings.

It is possible, with special permission, to dispense with markings on, for example, historic aircraft. However, this must be agreed on an individual basis with the Authority concerned.

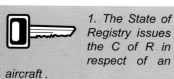

1. The State of Registry issues the C of R in respect of an aircraft.
2. It must be carried in the aircraft at all times.

The State of Registry will issue a Certificate of Registration (C of R) to the aircraft concerned, which must be carried in the aircraft at all times.

CONTENT OF THE CERTIFICATE OF REGISTRATION (C OF R).

The C of R certifies that the State of Registry has registered the aircraft. The C of R details comprise the following:

• The Nationality or Common Mark.

• The Registration Mark.

• The manufacturer's designation of the aircraft.

• The serial number of the aircraft.

• The name and the address of the owner.

• A certified statement that the aircraft has been entered on the registry of the State.

• The dated signature of the Registering Officer.

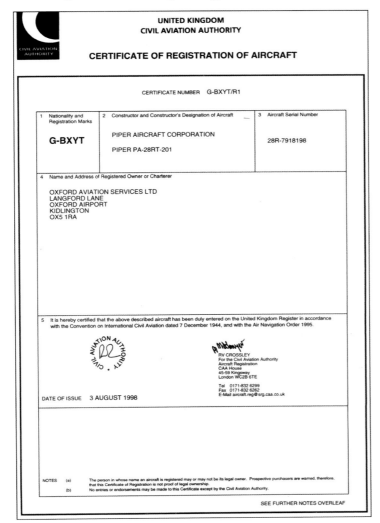

Figure 3.2 Certificate of Registration (C of R).

Application for Registration.

The application for registration must include the aircraft's correct classification. (*See Figure 3.3* below.)

IDENTIFICATION PLATE.

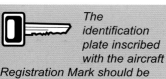

The identification plate inscribed with the aircraft Registration Mark should be made from fireproof metal or other fireproof material.

• All aircraft are to carry an identification plate which must be inscribed with, at least, its nationality/common mark and its registration mark.

• The identification plate must be made of fire-proof metal or other fire-proof material.

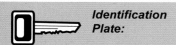

Identification Plate:

All aircraft are to carry an identification plate made of fire-proof material which must be secured to the aircraft in a prominent position near the main entrance.

• The identification plate must be secured to the aircraft in a prominent position near the main entrance.

Note: The identification plate is a requirement of ICAO Annex 7 but is not mandatory under the UK Air Navigation Order.

CLASSIFICATION OF AIRCRAFT – ICAO.

ICAO classifies aircraft as follows:

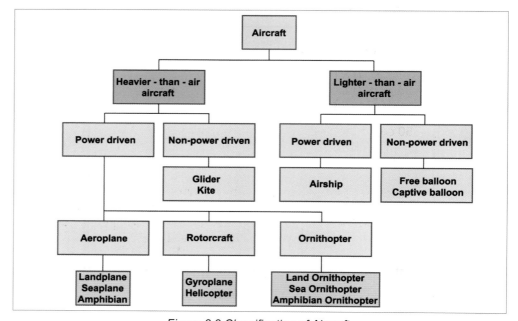

Figure 3.3 Classification of Aircraft.

Representative PPL - type questions to test your theoretical knowledge of ICAO Registration.

1.   What is a Common Mark?

     a.   The markings of an aircraft that has not received a C of A
     b.   The markings of an aircraft owned by an international agency
     c.   The markings of an aircraft owned by two or three different operators
     d.   The markings of an aircraft that is shared by two owners

2.   Which of the following would be an illegal registration marking?

     a.   MINE
     b.   PPP
     c.   TTT
     d.   YOU

3.   From which organisation does the Nationality Mark originate?

     a.   The Chicago Convention
     b.   The State of Manufacture
     c.   The International Telecommunication Union
     d.   The State of Design

4.   An aircraft's markings on its wings must be at least:

     a.   30 cms high
     b.   30 inches high
     c.   50 inches high
     d.   50 cms high

5.   Where must an aircraft's identification plate be located?

     a.   Inside the pilot's access door by the handle
     b.   In a prominent location close to the middle of the instrument panel
     c.   In a prominent location anywhere on the outside of the fuselage
     d.   In a prominent location near the main entrance

6.   Which State is responsible for issuing the registration mark of an aircraft?

     a.   The State of Manufacture
     b.   The State of Design
     c.   The State of Registration
     d.   The State of the Operator

7.   The identity plate must be made of:

     a.   Any metal
     b.   Any material
     c.   No particular material is specified
     d.   Fire-proof metal

Question	1	2	3	4	5	6	7
Answer							

The answers to these questions can be found at the end of this book.

CHAPTER 4
AIRWORTHINESS (ICAO)

CERTIFICATE OF AIRWORTHINESS

Civil Aviation Authority

Certificate Number:

041826/007

United Kingdom
Civil Aviation Authority

1. Nationality and Registration Marks	2. Manufacturer and designation of aircraft	3. Aircraft Serial Number
G-BTRY	**PIPER AIRCRAFT CORPORATION** **PIPER PA-28-161**	**28-8116190**

4. Categories

Normal and Utility Category Aeroplane

5. This Certificate of Airworthiness is issued pursuant to the Convention on International Civil Aviation dated 7 December 1944 and Regulation (EC) No 1592/2002, Article 5(2)(c) in respect of the above mentioned aircraft which is considered to be airworthy when maintained and operated in accordance with the foregoing and the pertinent operating limitations.

Date of Issue: **26 March 2008**   Signature:

Limitations/Remarks:

None

6. This Certificate of Airworthiness is valid unless revoked by the competent authority of the Member State of registry.

A current Airworthiness Review Certificate shall be attached to this Certificate.

EASA Form 25 20070816
This certificate shall be carried on board during all flights

AIRWORTHINESS OF AIRCRAFT - ICAO ANNEX 8.

General.
All Contracting States are responsible for ensuring that:

•   Aircraft registered with their own State are airworthy

and

•   that there are procedures to ensure the aircraft's continuing airworthiness.

All States are responsible for the continuing airworthiness of their aircraft.

To this end and to meet the appropriate standards, states are to issue their aircraft with a Certificate of Airworthiness. A Certificate of Airworthiness issued by a contracting state is to be recognised by other contracting states.

An aircraft is deemed to be airworthy when it complies with the operational and maintenance limitations specified in the:

•   Aircraft Flight Manual.

•   Aircraft placards.

•   ICAO Airworthiness Technical Manual.

Temporary Loss of Airworthiness.
Any failure to maintain an aircraft in an airworthy condition shall render the aircraft ineligible for operation until the aircraft is restored to an airworthy condition.

A Certificate of Airworthiness (C of A):

•   Shall be issued by the State of Registry.

•   Shall remain valid subject to the laws of the State of Registry.

•   Shall be recognised as valid by other Contracting States if it was issued in accordance with ICAO requirements and standards.

The State of Registry is not only responsible for issuing a C of A to an aircraft but is also responsible for the continuing airworthiness of that aircraft.

•   Shall consist of the following details (*See Figure 4.1.*)

   a.   Aircraft Nationality and Registration marks.

   b.   Name of aircraft manufacturer and manufacturer's designation of the aircraft (type and model).

   c.   Aircraft serial number.

   d.   Aircraft Category (Aircraft Classification).

   e.   A statement that the aircraft is airworthy.

   f.   Date of issue.

   g.   The dated signature of a qualified member of the Authority.

   h.   Date of expiry.

Certificate of Airworthiness.

CERTIFICATE OF AIRWORTHINESS

Civil Aviation Authority

Certificate Number: 041826/007	**United Kingdom Civil Aviation Authority**	
1. Nationality and Registration Marks **G-BTRY**	2. Manufacturer and designation of aircraft **PIPER AIRCRAFT CORPORATION** **PIPER PA-28-161**	3. Aircraft Serial Number **28-8116190**
4. Categories **Normal and Utility Category Aeroplane**		
5. This Certificate of Airworthiness is issued pursuant to the Convention on International Civil Aviation dated 7 December 1944 and Regulation (EC) No 1592/2002, Article 5(2)(c) in respect of the above mentioned aircraft which is considered to be airworthy when maintained and operated in accordance with the foregoing and the pertinent operating limitations. Date of Issue: **26 March 2008** Signature: CIVIL AVIATION AUTHORITY 141 Limitations/Remarks: **None**		
6. This Certificate of Airworthiness is valid unless revoked by the competent authority of the Member State of registry. A current Airworthiness Review Certificate shall be attached to this Certificate.		

EASA Form 25 20070816
This certificate shall be carried on board during all flights

Figure 4.1 Certificate of Airworthiness.

Validity of Certificate of Airworthiness.

In general, the period of validity of a Certificate of Airworthiness (C of A) is up to the date marked on the C of A itself.

However, for an aircraft regulated by the European Aviation Safety Agency (EASA), since 28 September 2007, EASA C of As have been issued in a non-expiring format, and are supported by a document called the Airworthiness Review Certificate which is renewable annually. Full compliance with EASA regulations by EASA member states has been required since September 2008.

CONTINUING AIRWORTHINESS.

The State of Registry is to ensure that procedures are followed to ensure the continued airworthiness of the aircraft.

- A Certification of Airworthiness (C of A) is considered to be invalid if the aircraft is modified, repaired or maintained in other than the manner approved by the Authority.

- Should a C of A be invalidated, the aircraft shall not participate in international navigation except with the permission and approval of the State whose territory is entered.

INSTRUMENTS AND EQUIPMENT.

The aircraft must be provided with approved instruments and equipment necessary for the safe operation of the aircraft in the anticipated operating conditions.

Safety & Survival Equipment.
The prescribed safety & survival equipment that the crew or passengers are expected to use in an emergency are to be:

- Reliable.

- Readily accessible.

- Easily identifiable.

- Plainly marked as to method of operation.

Never forget to check the survival equipment of your aircraft!

Figure 4.2 A Life Jacket.

Aircraft Lights.
Aircraft lights are to be installed in such a manner as to minimize the possibility that they may:

- Adversely affect the satisfactory performance of the flight crew.

- Subject an outside observer to harmful dazzle.

Figure 4.3 A Warrior at night.

AIRCRAFT OPERATING LIMITATIONS AND INFORMATION.

General.
The aircraft's operating limitations and other information necessary for the safe operation of the aircraft must be made available in the aircraft's:

Aircraft operating limitations are contained in the aircraft's Flight Manual.

- Flight Manual (and/or pilot's Operating Handbook).

- Markings and placards.

Aircraft Operating Limitations.

As a minimum, the following limitations must be made available:

- **Loading.** All limiting masses (weights), C of G positions, weight distribution and floor loadings.

- **Airspeed.** Limiting airspeeds.

- **Power Plant.** Engine limitations.

- **Equipment & Systems.** Limitations for all the various equipment and systems installed in the aircraft.

- **Aircrew.** Details of the minimum number of Flight Crew required to operate the aircraft.

Aircraft Operating Information.

At least the following information must be made available:

- **Loading.** Including empty weight, aircraft's empty weight configuration, C of G and datum.

- **Operating Procedures.** Normal and emergency procedures.

- **Handling information.** Significant or unusual handling characteristics of the aircraft together with stall speeds.

- **Performance.** Information as to the aircraft's performance at various aircraft configurations and power settings.

AIRCRAFT FLIGHT MANUAL.

The aircraft's Flight Manual must always be available to the pilot.

Note: Depending on the type of aircraft, the Flight Manual may be published in the form of a Pilot's Operating Handbook.

MARKINGS AND PLACARDS.

Aircraft markings and placards (*See Figure 4.5*) should convey limitations, information and instructions for the attention of:

- Flight crew

  and

- ground crew who may be involved in, for example, servicing, re-fuelling or towing the aircraft.

Figure 4.4 The Pilot's Operating Handbook.

Figure 4.5 Aircraft Placarding.

SERVICING AND MAINTENANCE OF AIRCRAFT.

The pilot should be aware that the servicing and maintenance of his aircraft must be carried out by a Part 145 approved organisation.

The pilot must be aware that the servicing and maintenance of his aircraft must be carried out by a Part 145 approved organisation.

Representative PPL - type questions to test your theoretical knowledge of ICAO Airworthiness.

1. Is the State of Registration responsible for the continuing airworthiness of the aircraft?

    a.   No
    b.   Yes at all times
    c.   Only in the case of aircraft over 5 700 kgs
    d.   Only when required to do so by ICAO

2. Where is the validity of a C of A specified?

    a.   In the national AIP
    b.   In the Aircraft Flight Manual
    c.   In the Certificate of Registration (C of R)
    d.   In the C of A itself

3. When an ICAO Contracting State issues an aircraft with a C of A, do other Contracting States have to recognise the C of A as valid?

    a.   Only if the aircraft is flying outside ICAO airspace
    b.   No
    c.   Yes
    d.   Only if it is flying within the airspace of the State of Registry

4. Information on aircraft placards is for:

    a.   Flight crew only
    b.   Ground crew only
    c.   Flight crew, ground crew and the general public
    d.   Both flight and ground crew

5. Safety and survival equipment must be:

    a.   Kept under the passenger seats
    b.   Inspected every week
    c.   Easily identifiable
    d.   Not be kept near aircraft emergency exits

6. In which document would you normally find the oil pressure limitations for your aircraft?

    a.   Operation Manual
    b.   Aircraft Placard
    c.   The Flight Manual or Pilot's Operating Handbook
    d.   The Technical Log

7. Which ICAO Annex concerns itself with Airworthiness?

    a. Annex 8
    b. Annex 9
    c. Annex 6
    d. Annex 7

8. What is the validity of the C of A?

    a. 1 year
    b. According to the Rules and Regulations of the State of Registry
    c. According to the Rules and Regulations of ICAO
    d. 6 months

9. Which of the following is included in the C of A?

    a. Empty weight C of G position
    b. Aircraft Category
    c. The Maximum Take-Off Mass
    d. The name and address of the owner

Question	1	2	3	4	5	6	7	8	9
Answer									

The answers to these questions can be found at the end of this book.

CHAPTER 5
AIRSPACE DIVISION AND AIR TRAFFIC SERVICES (ICAO)

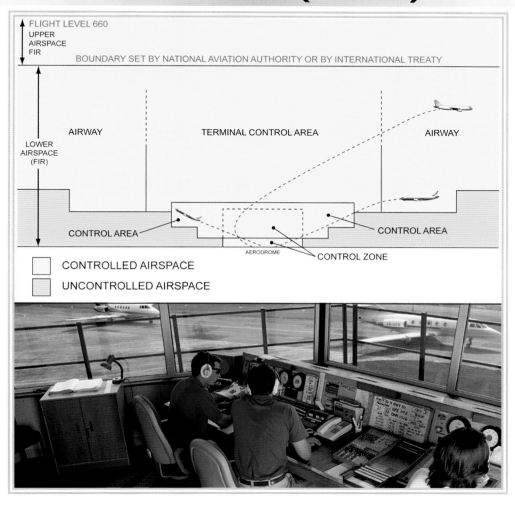

CLASSIFICATION OF AIRSPACE.

INTRODUCTION.

This Chapter deals with the Division of Airspace and Air Traffic Services as agreed internationally in the 'Convention on International Civil Aviation', and, most notably, in Annex 11 to that document.

Each ICAO contracting state, while undertaking to endeavour to apply the ICAO-agreed rules, may interpret the ICAO agreements in the context of its own particular requirements. When a contracting state's rules differ from the ICAO agreements, that state "files a difference" with ICAO. In the United Kingdom, these "differences" can be found in the UK Aeronautical Information Publication.

The Joint Aviation Authorities (JAA) and the European Aviation Safety Agency (EASA) are organisations which have undertaken to seek to normalise the aviation regulations of their member states by bringing them into line with ICAO standards. As this book is a text book for pilots studying for a JAR-FCL pilot's licence, the information on Airspace Division and Air Traffic Services contained in this Chapter deals exclusively with internationally agreed ICAO standards. For the most part, the information in this chapter will apply in all ICAO member states and in all JAA/EASA member states, but it is important that student pilots refer to their own country's aviation legislation to confirm which information is relevant to their country, and to identify where differences may exist.

Relevance of ICAO Standard Regulations to Pilots in the United Kingdom.

The United Kingdom (UK) has filed several differences with ICAO in respect of the Division of Airspace and Air Traffic Services. Those differences are covered in Chapter 14. The information contained in this Chapter will be relevant to UK-based pilots and student pilots, except in those cases where differences are noted in Chapter 14. Among the UK differences are important differences for Visual Meteorological Conditions (VMC) minima in respect of low-speed aircraft operating at lower levels in some classes of airspace, and in some aspects of aerodrome air traffic services.

THE NEED FOR AIRSPACE DIVISION.

Following the Second World War, civil aviation expanded rapidly throughout the world. With the advent of the jet engine, first used on military aircraft during the war years, the performance of airliners quickly surpassed that of wartime bombers and fighters, and so airliners began to fly ever faster and higher. At the same time, improvements in navigation and blind-flying instruments permitted commercial transport aircraft to operate in all weathers. As aircraft no longer depended solely on external references to manoeuvre and navigate, it was no longer safe for aircraft to fly on the principle of "see and be seen" in order to avoid conflict with other traffic.

Commercial passenger-carrying aircraft, especially, now required a radar-equipped air traffic service to ensure separation from other aircraft. Increasing traffic density, along with improving aircraft performance, meant that commercial aircraft, flying in accordance with Instrument Flight Rules (IFR), required protection and separation while taking off and landing at aerodromes, during climb to, or descent from, en-route cruising levels, and during the en-route section of the flight itself.

As a result of these developments, and because of the global scale of air travel, the International Civil Aviation Organisation (ICAO) recommended the adoption of a world-wide system of airspace division and classification.

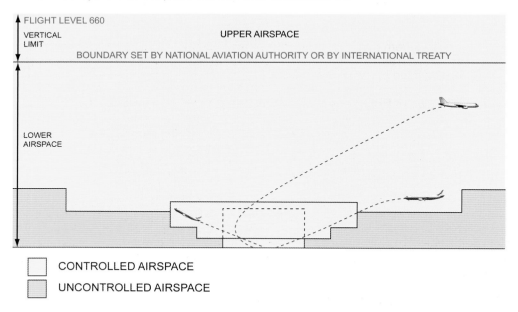

Figure 5.1 Airspace is divided into Controlled Airspace and Uncontrolled Airspace.

This system comprised two types of airspace: controlled and uncontrolled (*See Figure 5.1.*)

- Controlled airspace, entry into which required the aircraft to obtain a clearance from an Air Traffic Control Unit (ATCU). In controlled airspace, ATCUs regulated air traffic movements, and provided a separation service to aircraft flying IFR.

- Uncontrolled airspace, primarily for those aircraft flying in accordance with Visual Flight Rules (VFR) which could safely operate without ATC constraints being applied to their movements.

In the course of the years since World War II, the original ICAO system of airspace division has grown into the airspace classification system we have today, and which is enforced and administered around the world by the aviation authorities of all ICAO member states. This ICAO airspace classification system continues to evolve.

In the United Kingdom (UK), airspace classification is administered by the National Air Traffic Services. This chapter, however, deals with airspace classification as generally applied to all ICAO member states.

THE BASIC DIVISION OF AIRSPACE.

The division of airspace into controlled or uncontrolled airspace is made on the basis of criteria such as air traffic density, the type of air traffic activity (e.g. in airways, around aerodromes etc), and the level of air traffic service provided to pilots.

These criteria include:

- The requirement (or non-requirement) for an ATC clearance to aircraft to enter and operate in airspace under certain conditions contained within the clearance.

- The requirement (or non-requirement) for aircraft to operate under the control of an Air Traffic Control Unit (ATCU), and for separation between aircraft to be provided by an ATCU.

- The type of flight rules, VFR or IFR, permitted within the airspace.

- The requirement for a radio watch to be maintained by the pilot.

- The level of flight information given to an aircraft by an ATCU on the position and intentions of other aircraft sharing the same airspace.

In the ICAO system, the world's airspace is divided up into nine regions - the United Kingdom is part of the European and Mediterranean region - each of which is sub-divided into Flight Information Regions (FIRs) established from the surface up to flight levels set by national aviation authorities and applied by international treaty, and Upper Information Regions (UIR) above those levels. All airspace, controlled or uncontrolled, is contained within FIRs.

FLIGHT INFORMATION REGIONS.

A Flight Information Region (FIR) is airspace with specific dimensions, throughout which a Flight Information Service and Alerting Service are provided by Air Traffic Service Units (ATSUs), as a minimum level of air traffic service. All airspace, throughout the world, belongs to some specified FIR.

Oceanic airspace is divided into Oceanic Information Regions. The administration of Oceanic Information Regions (OIR) is undertaken, by international agreement with ICAO, by a national controlling authority bordering an OIR.

Figure 5.2 depicts FIRs in Europe and part of North Africa, as well as the Shanwick Oceanic Control Area.

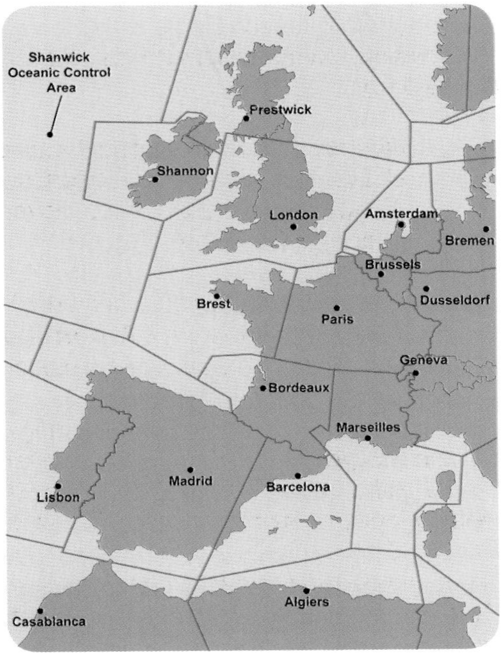

FIRs around the world are of varying dimensions as decided by the responsible national aviation authority. FIRs are divided into upper and lower regions above and below a given Flight Level. It is the lower region (Lower Airspace) which retains the designation FIR while the upper portion (Upper Airspace) is called an Upper Information Region (UIR).

Figure 5.2 All Airspace belongs to some specified Flight Information Region (FIR). Oceanic Airspace is divided into Oceanic Information Regions.

The subdivision of airspace throughout which a Flight Information Service and Alerting Service are provided is the Flight Information Region.

The boundary between the FIR and the UIR in a particular State is set by that State's national aviation authority.

The top of the FIR and base of the UIR is set by the national aviation authority. In the United Kingdom, the boundary between the FIR and the UIR is currently at Flight Level 245. In Germany, the boundary is Flight Level 245, but FL195 in most other European countries. European Union member states are currently discussing the creation of a "Single European Sky" with a European Upper Information Region which will presumably have a common lower boundary over all participating countries.

Currently, by international agreement, the upper limit of controlled airspace is at Flight Level 660.

Air Traffic Control Centres.

Each FIR/UIR is under the responsibility of an Air Traffic Control Centre (ATCC). The two UK FIRs, London and Scottish, are controlled and administered by National Air Traffic Services from the London Air Traffic Control Centre (LATCC - pronounced Lat-sea) and the Scottish Air Traffic Control Centre (SCATCC). Traffic in the London FIR which is not under the control of an aerodrome is controlled from LATCC, while similar traffic in the Scottish FIR is controlled from SCATCC. Area Control Centres (*See Page 101*) are often co-located with ATCCs.

Around the frontiers of the United Kingdom, there are other European FIRs controlled by ATCCs located in the cities shown in *Figure 5.2*. Within the context of plans for a Single European Sky, the European Union hopes that European airspace will eventually have fewer FIR boundaries and a reduced number of ATCCs.

The Upper Information Regions (UIR) above the Brussels, Amsterdam and Hamburg FIRs are combined to form the Maastricht UIR, under the control of Eurocontrol at the Maastricht ATCC.

As aircraft on international flights cross FIR boundaries, they transfer their communications at each FIR boundary from one ATCC to the next.

Air Traffic Services Provided Within the Flight Information Region.

As we have established, a Flight Information Region (FIR) is divided into controlled and uncontrolled airspace.

FIRs provide a Flight Information Service and Alerting Service to all aircraft flying in the FIR.

Within the FIR, the basic level of air traffic service provided is the Flight Information Service (FIS) and the Alerting Service. These two services, together, provide information pertinent to the safe and efficient conduct of flights, and alert the relevant authorities if an aircraft suffers an emergency. A Flight Information Service and an Alerting Service are available to <u>all</u> aircraft flying within an FIR.

Within controlled airspace, in addition to a Flight Information Service and an Alerting Service, higher levels of Air Traffic Advisory and Air Traffic Control (ATC) services are available to suitably equipped aircraft manned by appropriately qualified pilots, and in accordance with the ICAO classification of that portion of airspace.

ATCCs provide air traffic services to aircraft flying in controlled airspace which are not under the control of Air Traffic Service Units located at aerodromes.

THE MAIN DIVISIONS OF AIRSPACE WITHIN FIRS.

Airspace, then, is divided, basically, into either controlled or uncontrolled airspace.

Looking again at *Figure 5.1*, we can now add some basic labels to the principal sub-divisions of controlled and uncontrolled airspace to give us the airspace picture in *Figure 5.3*. It is important that you should realise that *Figure 5.3* is only a <u>representation</u> of the division of controlled airspace. For instance, Control Areas may stretch well beyond a Control Zone laterally, and may even extend up to the ceiling of the FIR, protecting IFR traffic departing from and arriving at several aerodromes. (This is the case, for instance, of the Daventry Control Area in the United Kingdom.)

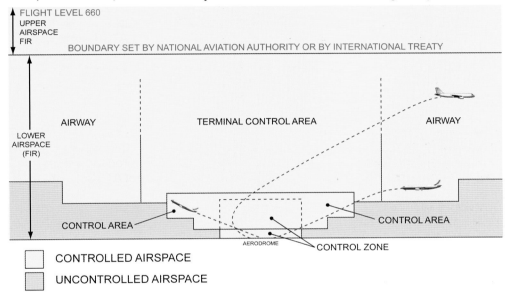

Figure 5.3 Basic Subdivisions of Controlled Airspace: Control Zone, Control Area, Terminal Control Area and Airway.

CONTROLLED AIRSPACE.

Access to controlled airspace is governed by ATC conditions which restrict entry to specified types of flight made by appropriately qualified pilots flying appropriately equipped aircraft, and (with certain exceptions) under the control of an Air Traffic Control Unit (ATCU).

All aircraft flying in controlled airspace must, with rare exceptions, have received an ATC clearance to do so.

Flight in controlled airspace in accordance with the Instrument Flight Rules (IFR) requires the pilot to submit a formal flight plan which includes the aircraft's call sign and type, estimated time of departure, desired altitude, route and destination. The acceptance of the flight plan by an ATCU constitutes permission for the pilot to carry out his planned flight.

Generally, provided they have clearance from an ATCU to do so, pilots flying in accordance with the Visual Flight Rules (VFR) are also permitted to fly in controlled airspace other than Class A airspace (see Pages 89 to 90 for details of airspace classification by letter).

When in controlled airspace, VFR pilots must normally maintain radio contact with the responsible ATCU, and obey ATC instructions. However, VFR flight may only take place in Visual Meteorological Conditions (VMC) and, because air traffic rules apply differently to different classifications of airspace, the conditions of visibility and distance from cloud which constitute VMC are defined differently depending on what type of controlled airspace the VFR flight is operating in. Sometimes, in uncontrolled airspace, the definition of VMC differs between countries. This topic is covered in more detail later in this chapter.

The main sub-divisions of controlled airspace are:

•   Control Zones.

•   Control Areas.

•   Airways.

Control Zones.

A CTR extends from ground or water level to either a published altitude or a published flight level.

Air traffic at major aerodromes can be dense and, so, it is important that all aircraft in the circuit of, and approaches to, major aerodromes should be known to the responsible Air Traffic Control Unit (ATCU), usually the ATCU at the aerodrome, itself. Consequently, around large aerodromes, Control Zones of specified lateral dimensions are established, extending from ground level to a published altitude or Flight Level. There is no standard size or height for a Control Zone, but typically, the Control Zone might have an upper boundary of 2 500 feet to 4 000 feet above aerodrome level.

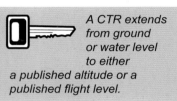

The lateral limits of a Control Zone must extend to at least 5 nm (9.3 km) from the centre of the aerodrome in the direction from which approaches are made.

The lateral limits of a Control Zone must extend to at least 5 nautical miles (9.3 kilometres) from the centre of the aerodrome in the direction from which approaches may be made. If a Control Zone is located beneath a Control Area, the upper limit of the Control Zone must be at least the lower limit of the Control Area; though often the Control Zone will extend up into the Control Area.

VFR traffic may be permitted to enter or transit Class A Control Zones, but only with a Special VFR clearance.

Within the Control Zone, the responsible ATCU provides protection and separation to aircraft taking off from and landing at the aerodrome. Both VFR and IFR traffic require a clearance to enter a Control Zone. Quite often, notably in Class A Control Zones, Instrument Flight Rules (IFR) are permanently enforced at large aerodromes, although non-IFR traffic may be allowed to enter, leave and transit Class A Control Zones with a Special VFR (SVFR) clearance.

Figure 5.4 Luxembourg CTR.

The abbreviation for Control Zone is **CTR**.

Figure 5.4 shows the Luxembourg CTR, as represented on an ICAO 1:500 000 scale aeronautical chart. The Luxembourg CTR extends upwards to 2 500 feet.

Control Areas.

Once in the climb, above, say, 2 500 feet, or while still descending through, say, 4 000 feet on an instrument approach, an aircraft does not need ATC protection down to ground level. So around and above and, often, well beyond the CTR, a Control Area is established specifically to protect aircraft in the climb and descent, and also aircraft which might be in a holding pattern awaiting clearance to begin the approach to land. It is important to realise that Control Areas are set up to encompass the airspace containing the flight paths of IFR flights requiring an Air Traffic Control service. Control Area dimensions will depend on local conditions and traffic density; but the lower vertical limit of a Control Area must not be less than 700 feet (200 metres) above the ground or water. The vertical limits of a Control Area are from a published altitude or flight level to a higher altitude or flight level.

The vertical limits of a Control Area are from a published altitude or Flight Level to a higher altitude or Flight Level.

The lower vertical limit of a Control Area must not be less than 700 feet (200 metres) above the ground or water.

The abbreviation for Control Area is CTA. *Figure 5.5* shows part of the Brussels CTA situated above the Oostende CTR.

Figure 5.5 Part of the Brussels CTA over the Oostende CTR.

If a CTA located in the vicinity of one or more major aerodromes is also the junction of several airways, it may be classified a Terminal Control Area (TCA). You should note that the abbreviation TMA is still used to designate a Terminal Control Area. This abbreviation is a relic of an earlier name, Terminal Manoeuvring Area. *Figure 5.6* depicts the Eelde TMA in the Netherlands.

A Control Area at the confluence of several airways or controlled routes, and in the vicinity of one or more major aerodromes, is called a Terminal Control Area, abbreviated to TCA or TMA.

Figure 5.6 The Eelde TMA.

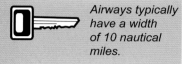

Airways typically have a width of 10 nautical miles.

The Airway.

An Airway is a corridor of controlled airspace which protects an air route linking major aerodromes, nationally and internationally. *Figure 5.7*, depicts five airways: N864, N862, L9, Y3 and N14. Airway L9, over the United Kingdom, extends from Flight Level 75 up to FL195. Notice that on the left hand part of the diagram, the lower boundary of Airway N864 steps up from FL75 to a higher base of FL95, and then Flight Level 125.

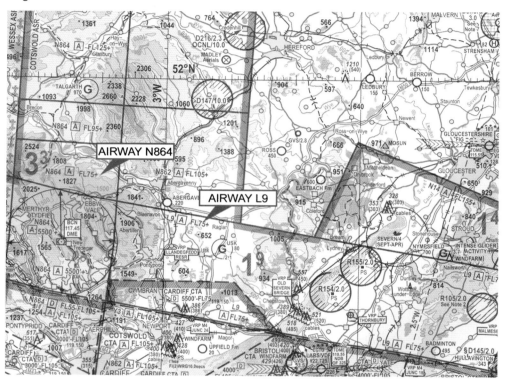

Figure 5.7 Airway L9, over the United Kingdom, extending upwards from Flight Level 75 (FL 75+)

Airways typically have a width of 10 nautical miles and may extend vertically from as low as a few thousand feet above the ground to the upper limit of the FIR bordering on the Upper Information Region (UIRs). In UIRs, airways are called Upper Air Routes.

Airways give protection to IFR traffic. In some parts of the world, including the United Kingdom, VFR flights are not permitted to fly in airways.

Airways are often established so that they route over land-based navigation aids such as VOR/DMEs and NDBs, though nowadays this is no longer so important because of the advent of Global Positioning Navigation Systems.

UNCONTROLLED AIRSPACE.

In uncontrolled airspace, outside CTRs, CTAs and Airways, aircraft may normally operate without any ATC clearance or permission, and without having to be in contact with any Air Traffic Service Unit. However, aircraft flying in uncontrolled airspace must at all times comply with the Rules of the Air laid down by their national aviation authority and which will have been established in accordance with ICAO regulations.

There is a general maximum speed limit of 250 knots imposed on all IFR and VFR traffic operating below Flight Level 100 in uncontrolled airspace.

Air Traffic Control Units (ATCUs) do, however, provide certain services to flights in uncontrolled airspace under both the Visual Flight Rules (VFR) and the Instrument Flight Rules (IFR). For example, ATCUs do notify the existence of Advisory Routes (*See Figure 5.8*) within uncontrolled airspace. These routes are not busy enough to warrant Airway status, but, if a pilot wishes to use them, he will be given an ATC service. In the UK, the Quadrantal Rule applies under IFR on Advisory Routes, which have designators ending in 'D'.

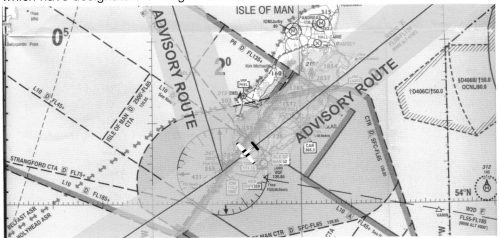

Figure 5.8 An Advisory Route in Uncontrolled Airspace.

AERODROME TRAFFIC ZONES.

Aerodrome Traffic Zones (ATZs) are zones immediately surrounding aerodromes and airfields to protect traffic flying in the aerodrome circuit. ATZs surround many aerodromes located in both controlled and uncontrolled airspace.

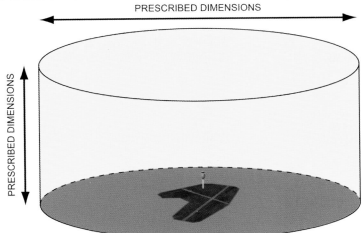

Figure 5.9 Aerodrome Traffic Zones of prescribed dimensions surround many aerodromes to protect traffic flying in the Aerodrome Circuit.

ATZs are usually of defined lateral and vertical dimensions; for instance, in the United Kingdom, they extend to 2 000 feet above aerodrome level, and have a radius of either 2 nautical miles or 2.5 nautical miles, depending on the length of the longest runway. But ICAO itself does not specify what ATZ dimensions should be. ICAO simply lays down that an ATZ is an airspace of dimensions decided and notified by the national aviation authority and established by that authority, around an aerodrome, for the protection of aerodrome traffic. ATZs are not given any particular airspace classification; they take on the classification of the airspace within which they are established. Within controlled airspace, ATZs are usually found within CTRs, but are often not depicted on charts.

Rules are established by national aviation authorities governing the operation of aircraft within an ATZ. The hours of watch, radio frequencies and other details of the ATZ are normally contained in the aeronautical information publications of the state concerned. In the United Kingdom, such details are contained in the ENR Section of the AIP.

If an ATZ exists around an aerodrome in uncontrolled airspace, permission is, nevertheless, required to operate within it. An aircraft must not take off, land or operate within the ATZ unless the Pilot-in-Command of the aircraft has obtained the permission of the responsible Air Traffic Service Unit (ATSU) to do so, irrespective of whether that ATSU provides full Air Traffic Control, or a lower level of service.

When entering an ATZ, a pilot must immediately report his height and position to the responsible ATSU.

Normally, regulations governing flight in an ATZ will, if you have a radio, require you to listen out on the appropriate frequency. More especially, when entering an ATZ a pilot must immediately report his height and position to the responsible ATSU. If your aircraft is not radio-equipped, you must normally consult the conditions prescribed by the aerodrome authority for the ATZ, before getting airborne, to obtain all the necessary permissions.

In *Figure 5.10*, below, you can see several ATZs surrounding London Heathrow CTR. Elstree and Wycombe Air Park ATZs lie just outside the CTR, while Denham is actually inside the CTR, and White Waltham ATZ is partially inside the CTR.

Figure 5.10 Elstree, Wycombe Air Park, White Waltham and Denham ATZs.

CLASSIFICATION OF AIRSPACE BY LETTER.

In 1990, ICAO adopted the current airspace classification scheme which identifies airspace, both controlled and uncontrolled, using the letters A to G.

The controlled airspace classes are: A, B, C, D and E.

The uncontrolled airspace classes are: F and G.

The letter allocated to each class of airspace determines the type of air traffic control service which IFR and VFR traffic receive in the airspace and the rules which apply to that airspace. The provisions which apply to each airspace class are given in the table, below.

CONTROLLED AIRSPACE
Class A All flights must be conducted under Instrument Flight Rules (IFR), unless flight under Special Visual Flight Rules (SVFR) is permitted. All flights are subject to ATC clearance, and all flights are separated from one another by ATC.
Class B Flights may be conducted under IFR, SVFR, or Visual Flight Rules (VFR). All aircraft are subject to ATC clearance. All flights are separated from one another by ATC.
Class C Operations may be conducted under IFR, SVFR, or VFR. All aircraft are subject to ATC clearance. Aircraft operating under IFR and SVFR are separated from one another and from flights operating under VFR. Flights operating under VFR are given traffic information in respect of other VFR flights.
Class D Operations may be conducted under IFR, SVFR, or VFR. All aircraft are subject to ATC clearance. Aircraft operating under IFR and SVFR are separated from one another, and are given traffic information in respect of VFR flights. Flights operating under VFR are given traffic information in respect of other VFR flights.
Class E Operations may be conducted under IFR, SVFR, or VFR. Aircraft operating under IFR and SVFR are separated from one another, and are subject to ATC clearance. Flights under VFR are not subject to ATC clearance. As far as is practical, traffic information is given to all flights in respect of VFR flights.
UNCONTROLLED AIRSPACE
Class F Operations may be conducted under IFR or VFR. ATC separation will be provided, so far as is practical, to aircraft operating under IFR. Traffic Information may be given as far as is practical in respect of other flights.
Class G Operations may be conducted under IFR or VFR. ATC separation is not provided. Traffic Information may be given, as far as is practical, in respect of other flights.

Each national aviation authority determines how it allocates the ICAO letter classifications to its Control Zones (CTR), Control Areas (CTA) and Airways. Furthermore, not all letter classifications are used in all countries. For instance, in the United Kingdom, there is currently no Class B airspace. In France, there is currently no Class B, C or F airspace. In Germany, there is no A and B airspace, and in the Netherlands there is no Class D airspace.

For the United Kingdom, the classifications of airspace are covered in detail in the UK AIP ENR 1-4, and in Chapter 14 of this book.

The Classification by Letter of Controlled Airspace.

Control Zones (CTRs) may be one of several classes of airspace. Heathrow CTR is Class A airspace. London City and Birmingham CTRs, like most UK CTRs, are designated Class D airspace.

In Germany, all CTRs are Class C.

In the Netherlands, most CTRs are Class C.

Amsterdam/Schiphol CTR is Class C, Dusseldorf CTR is Class D, Oostende CTR is Class C, Merville CTR is Class E. Brussels CTR, as depicted in *Figure 5.11*, is Class C.

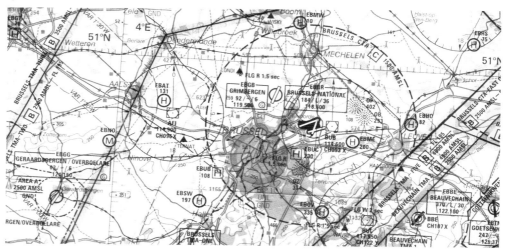

Figure 5.11 Brussels CTR is Class C Airspace.

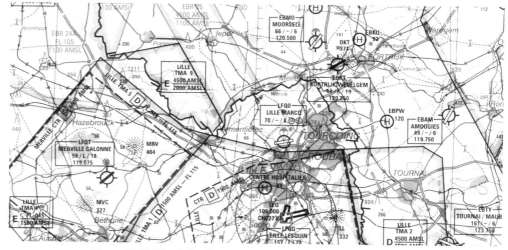

Figure 5.12 The Lille TMA is Class D. Merville CTR is Class E.

Control Areas (CTAs) and Terminal Control Areas (TCA or TMA) may be Class A, B, C, D or E airspace. Most UK CTAs are Class D.

The CTA above Heathrow, which is at the junction of several airways and bears the classification of Terminal Control Area (TMA), is Class A. The Lille TMA, above the Merville CTR is Class D (*See Figure 5.12, opposite.*)

Airways can also belong to several airspace classification categories. For instance, in the United Kingdom, all airways are Class A, whereas in Portugal, below Flight Level 245, airways are Class C. French airways can be Class E, up to Flight Level 115, and then Class D up to Flight Level 195. Irish airways can be Class C up to FL 245. (*See Figure 5.13.*)

Figure 5.13 Irish Airways can be Class C up to FL245.

Upper Information Regions (UIRs) are invariably controlled airspace. In the United Kingdom, UIRs are Class C airspace.

The Classification by Letter of Uncontrolled Airspace.
Uncontrolled airspace is classified as Class F or G. Class G covers the vast majority of uncontrolled airspace, being the Open FIR where aircraft may operate without ATC clearances or constraints.

Advisory Routes (*See Figure 5.8, Page 87*) within uncontrolled airspace are designated Class F. In Class F airspace, flights in accordance with IFR will receive an air traffic advisory service. VFR flights will receive a Flight Information Service, if they request one. Pilots flying VFR in Class F airspace should, however, consider staying clear of the advisory route itself, and, if they wish to cross the advisory route, make contact with the responsible Air Traffic Service Unit (ATSU), 10 minutes before crossing. On contacting the ATSU, pilots should be prepared to give position, level and the appropriate time information, as in a routine position report.

Airspace divisions and classifications are likely to continue to evolve, especially in the European Area, with the advent of the "Single European Sky."

FLIGHT RULES AND AIRSPACE CLASSIFICATION.

VFR flight may only take place in Visual Meteorological Conditions.

General.

Whenever they are airborne, aircraft must fly in accordance with either Instrument Flight Rules (IFR) or Visual Flight Rules (VFR). Flight in uncontrolled airspace is not subject to air traffic clearances or control, so VFR flight is permitted everywhere in uncontrolled airspace. However, as you can see from the table at *Figure 5.14*, aircraft flying VFR are also permitted to fly in controlled airspace other than Class A airspace, although, with the exception of Class E airspace, they need ATC clearance to do so and, so, have to maintain radio contact with ATC.

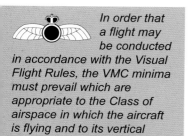

In order that a flight may be conducted in accordance with the Visual Flight Rules, the VMC minima must prevail which are appropriate to the Class of airspace in which the aircraft is flying and to its vertical position.

Most Private Pilot Licence holders will be VFR pilots. VFR flight is flight based on the principle that the pilot is able to manoeuvre and navigate his aircraft, and, most importantly, be able to avoid conflict and collision with other aircraft, by visual reference to external features. More especially, when flying VFR, the pilot must be able to navigate his aircraft by reference to ground features. Consequently, in order that the VFR principle may be adhered to at all times, VFR flight may only take place in Visual Meteorological Conditions (VMC) which allow the pilot to maintain appropriate visual contact with the world outside his cockpit. However, because air traffic rules apply differently to different classifications of airspace, VMC is also defined differently depending on the classification of airspace in which the VFR flight takes place, and on the aircraft's vertical position. VMC is defined, then, depending on airspace classification, by prescribed minimum visual conditions which are referred to as VMC minima.

VMC Minima in the Different Classes of Airspace.

The VMC minima for the various classifications of airspace are shown in the following tables. These VMC minima may sometimes be defined slightly differently in different countries of the world. For instance, in the United Kingdom, VMC definitions cater for speed differences in some classes of airspace, below 3 000 feet AMSL; (*See Chapter 13*).

To make the logic of the VMC minima clearer, we have included in the tables details of air traffic services and separation provided, as well as clearance requirements.

VMC Minima in the Different Classes of Airspace.

The ICAO VMC minima in the various classes of airspace tabulated below are illustrated pictorially in *Figures 2.27* and *2.28* in *Chapter 2.*

CLASS A - Controlled Airspace		
	IFR	VFR
Separation provided	All aircraft	**VFR FLIGHT NOT PERMITTED.**
Service provided	Air traffic control service	
VMC minima	Not applicable	
Speed limitation	Not applicable	
Radio communication	Continuous two-way	
ATC clearance	Required	

CLASS B - Controlled Airspace		
	IFR	**VFR**
Separation provided	All aircraft	All aircraft
Service provided	Air traffic control service	Air traffic control service
VMC minima	Not applicable	**At and above FL 100** 8 km visibility Clear of cloud **Below FL 100** 5km visibility clear of cloud
Speed limitation	Not applicable	Not applicable
Radio communication	Continuous two-way	Continuous two-way
ATC clearance	Required	Required

CLASS C - Controlled Airspace		
	IFR	**VFR**
Separation provided	IFR from IFR IFR from VFR	VFR from IFR
Service provided	Air traffic control service	Air traffic control service for separation from IFR. VFR traffic information (and traffic avoidance advice on request)
VMC minima	Not applicable	**At and above FL 100** 8 km visibility 1500 m horizontal and 1000 feet vertical distance from cloud **Below FL 100** 5 km visibility 1500 m horizontal and 1000 feet vertical distance from cloud
Speed limitation	Not applicable	250 kt IAS below FL 100
Radio communication	Continuous two-way	Continuous two-way
ATC clearance	Required	Required

In Class D airspace, both VFR and IFR traffic are controlled. IFR flights are separated from each other and receive information regarding VFR flights. VFR traffic receives information regarding all other traffic.

CLASS D - Controlled Airspace		
	IFR	VFR
Separation provided	IFR from IFR	Not provided
Service provided	Air traffic control service including traffic information about VFR flights (and traffic avoidance advice on request)	Traffic information between VFR and IFR flights (and traffic avoidance advice on request)
VMC minima	Not applicable	**At and above FL 100** 8 km visibility 1500 m horizontal and 1000 feet vertical distance from cloud **Below FL 100** 5 km visibility 1500 m horizontal and 1000 feet vertical distance from cloud
Speed limitation	250 kt IAS below FL 100	250 kt IAS below FL 100
Radio communication	Continuous two-way	Continuous two-way
ATC clearance	Required	Required

CLASS E - Controlled Airspace		
	IFR	VFR
Separation provided	IFR from IFR	Not provided
Service provided	Air traffic control service and traffic information about VFR flights as far as practical	Traffic information as far as practical
VMC minima	Not applicable	8 km visibility 1500 m horizontal and 1000 feet vertical distance from cloud
Speed limitation	250 kt IAS below FL 100	250 kt IAS below FL 100
Radio communication	Continuous two-way	Not required
ATC clearance	Required	Not required

CLASS F - Uncontrolled Airspace		
	IFR	**VFR**
Separation provided	IFR from IFR as far as practical	Not provided
Service provided	Air Traffic Advisory Service and Flight Information Service	Flight information service
VMC minima	Not applicable	**At and above FL 100** 8 km visibility 1500 m horizontal and 1000 feet vertical distance from cloud **Below FL 100** 5 km visibility 1500 m horizontal and 1000 feet vertical distance from cloud OR **At or below 900 m (3000 feet) AMSL or 300 m (1000 feet) above terrain, whichever is the higher** 5 km visibility Clear of cloud with surface in sight
Speed limitation	250 kt IAS below FL 100	250 kt IAS below FL 100
Radio communication	Continuous two-way	Not required
ATC clearance	Not required	Not required

CLASS G - Uncontrolled Airspace		
	IFR	**VFR**
Separation provided	Not provided	Not provided
Service provided	Flight information service	Flight information service
VMC minima	Not applicable	**At and above FL 100** 8 km visibility 1500 m horizontal and 1000 feet vertical distance from cloud **Below FL 100** 5 km visibility 1500 m horizontal and 1000 feet vertical distance from cloud OR **At or below 900 m (3000 feet) AMSL or 300 m (1000 feet) above terrain, whichever is the higher** 5 km visibility Clear of cloud with surface in sight
Speed limitation	250 kt IAS below FL 100	250 kt IAS below FL 100
Radio communication	Continuous two-way	Not required
ATC clearance	Not required	Not required

Figure 5.14 VMC Minima for VFR flight in controlled and uncontrolled airspace.

Observations on VMC Minima.

Except for Classes A and B airspace, there is a general speed limit of 250 knots imposed on traffic operating below Flight Level 100. Not surprisingly then, VMC minima, in terms of flight visibility, are least for aircraft operating below Flight Level 100. Below Flight Level 100, the forward visibility minimum is reduced from 8 km to 5 km outside controlled airspace.

Below 3000 feet above mean sea-level, or 1000 feet above the ground, whichever is the higher, there is no prescribed vertical distance from cloud. Aircraft are simply required to be clear of cloud and in sight of the surface.

You should note that in uncontrolled airspace, Classes F and G, the United Kingdom has registered differences from the ICAO standard so as to allow greater flexibility to VFR flights at and below 3000 feet above mean sea-level. United Kingdom based pilots should refer to Chapter 14 for VMC minima below 3000 feet when airspeeds are below 140 knots.

At higher altitudes, both in uncontrolled airspace and in controlled airspace, VFR pilots will be flying in airspace in which IFR flights flying at high speeds are being conducted. At these higher altitudes, VFR pilots must, naturally, continue to be able to see and avoid other aircraft. Therefore, because of the possibility that an IFR flight, under the control of an ATCU, might emerge from a cloud, a VFR flight must remain at a prescribed distance from clouds, both vertically and laterally, and must maintain a minimum designated visibility sufficient to give the two aircraft time to spot and avoid each other.

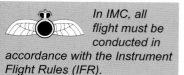

If the actual weather minima give visibility and cloud cover below the minima specified for VMC, then IMC exists. If the actual minima are equal to, or in excess of, specified minima VMC exists.

Consequently, above Flight Level 100 where the 250 knots speed limit is <u>not</u> in force, in-flight visibility is required to be 8 km. However, below Flight Level 100, in uncontrolled airspace, and in controlled airspace classified C, D and E, VMC minima reduce again to 5 kilometres in-flight visibility, 1000 feet clear of cloud vertically and 1500 metres clear of cloud horizontally. This is because the 250 knots speed limit applies in this lower airspace.

You should note that in controlled airspace of Class B, where separation is provided by ATC to <u>all</u> flights, VFR as well as IFR, VMC minima are reduced <u>at all flight levels</u>. In Class B airspace, there is no prescribed minimum distance from clouds.

Instrument Flight Rules and Instrument Meteorological Conditions.

In IMC, all flight must be conducted in accordance with the Instrument Flight Rules (IFR).

If VMC minima cannot be maintained, then Instrument Meteorological Conditions (IMC) prevail. In IMC, all flights must be conducted in accordance with Instrument Flight Rules (IFR). IFR flight is more tightly regulated than VFR flight. In order to fly IFR, aircraft generally have to carry appropriate specialised instrumentation and pilots require to be appropriately qualified.

AIR TRAFFIC SERVICES.

INTRODUCTION.

Before looking at air traffic services, themselves, we must give a definition of the two terms most commonly used when referring to the units and/or agencies which deliver the various levels of air traffic service. The two terms are: Air Traffic Control Unit and Air Traffic Services Unit.

Figure 5.15 An Air Traffic Control Unit.

Air Traffic Control Units.

Full air traffic control services are provided by Air Traffic Control Units (ATCUs). An ATCU is a unit from which instructions (the air traffic control service), advice and information are given by radio to aircraft in the interests of safety.

An Air Traffic Control Unit (ATCU) *refers to a unit providing a full air traffic control service.*

All ATCUs, in addition to an air traffic control service, provide a Flight Information Service and an Alerting Service to aircraft under their jurisdiction.

The provision of an Air Traffic Control Service normally takes precedence over the provision of a Flight Information Service.

Air Traffic Service Units.

The term Air Traffic Service Unit (ATSU) is the most general of the terms applied to units providing air traffic services. The term ATSU may refer to an ATCU providing full Air Traffic Control, or to a unit <u>not</u> providing full Air Traffic Control but providing a Flight Information Service, (*See Page 101*) or a basic aerodrome Air/Ground Communications Service, (*See Page 103*).

The term Air Traffic Service Unit (ATSU) *applies to a unit providing any level of air traffic services.*

AIR TRAFFIC SERVICES.

Air Traffic Services is a general expression applied to several categories of agency which, depending on the level of service, provide control, advice, information and assistance to aircraft.

The prime objective of Air Traffic Services as defined in ANNEX 11 to the Convention On International Civil Aviation is to prevent collisions between aircraft, whether taxiing on the manoeuvring area of an aerodrome, taking off, landing, flying en-route, or flying in the holding pattern at an aerodrome.

Air Traffic Services also have as their aim:

- the expediting and maintaining of an orderly flow of air traffic.
- the provision of advice and information for the safe and efficient conduct of flights.
- the provision of an alerting service for aircraft in distress.

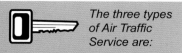

The three types of Air Traffic Service are:

• *Air Traffic Control Service.*

• *Flight Information Service.*

• *Alerting Service.*

Air Traffic Services are provided through one or more of the following:

• A full Air Traffic Control Service.

• A Flight Information Service.

• An Alerting Service.

FULL AIR TRAFFIC CONTROL SERVICE.

A full air traffic control service is provided by an Air Traffic Control Unit (ATCU). An ATCU provides instructions, advice and information to aircraft, by radio, for the purposes of:

• preventing collisions between aircraft in the air.

• assisting in preventing collisions between aircraft moving on the apron and the manoeuvring area of an aerodrome.

• assisting in preventing collisions between aircraft and obstructions on the manoeuvring area.

• expediting and maintaining an orderly flow of air traffic.

The exact nature of the full air traffic control service depends on the particular circumstances of the aircraft which is receiving the service and on the class of airspace in which the service is provided. A full air traffic control service may comprise one or more of the following:

• An Aerodrome Control Service.

• An Approach Control Service, with or without the aid of radar.

• An Area Control Service, with or without the aid of radar.

Aerodrome Control Service.

An Aerodrome Control Service provided by an ATCU consists of:

• The Aerodrome Control Service, itself.

• A Flight Information Service.

• An Alerting Service.

The Aerodrome Control Service provided by an ATCU is, principally, a service to:

• Aircraft flying with visual reference to the surface in, and in the vicinity of, the Aerodrome Traffic Zone (ATZ), whether or not the ATZ is situated within a Control Zone (CTR).

• Aircraft operating on the manoeuvring area.

Figure 5.16 Aerodrome Control Service.

A controller providing an Aerodrome Control Service is responsible for issuing information and instructions to aircraft under his control to achieve a safe, orderly and expeditious flow of air traffic and to assist pilots in preventing collisions between:

• aircraft flying in, and in the vicinity of, the ATZ.

• aircraft taking off and landing.

• aircraft moving on the apron.

• aircraft and vehicles, obstructions and other aircraft on the manoeuvring area.

Aerodrome Control may be divided into air control and ground movement control.

The Air Controller provides services for aircraft flying in, and in the vicinity of, the ATZ and for aircraft taking off and landing and has absolute authority over all movements on active runways and their access points.

The Ground Movement Controller provides services for aircraft moving on the apron and aircraft and vehicles, on the manoeuvring area, except on active runways and their access points.

Aerodrome Control is also responsible, among other matters, for

• Alerting the safety services.

• Disseminating pertinent information on IFR, Special VFR and VFR traffic including departures.

• Disseminating appropriate items of essential aerodrome information.

An ATCU providing an Aerodrome Control Service uses the call-sign "Tower" or "Ground" as appropriate.

Approach Control Service.

An Approach Control Unit provides:

• an Approach Control Service with or without the aid of radar.

• a Flight Information Service.

• an Alerting Service.

An Approach Control Unit may be combined with an Aerodrome Control Unit

Figure 5.17 Approach Control Unit.

Approach Control Services Within Controlled Airspace.

An ATCU at an aerodrome within controlled airspace (Class A to E airspace) provides approach control services to aircraft, according to the classification of the airspace within which the aerodrome is located, from the time and location at which:

• arriving aircraft are released by Area Control until control is transferred to Aerodrome Control.

• aircraft approaching from outside controlled airspace place themselves under the control of Approach Control until control is transferred to Aerodrome Control.

• departing aircraft are taken over from Aerodrome Control until:
    • they are transferred to Area Control, or
    • they are clear of controlled airspace.

• over-flying aircraft are within the relevant controlled airspace.

Approach Control provides standard separation between Special VFR and IFR flights.

Approach Control Services Outside Controlled Airspace.

An ATCU at an aerodrome outside controlled airspace (Class F and G airspace) provides approach control services to aircraft, as determined by the aerodrome operator and as approved by the national authority, from the time and location at which:

- arriving aircraft place themselves under the control of Approach Control until control is transferred to Aerodrome Control.

- departing aircraft are taken over from Aerodrome Control until they no longer wish to receive a service, or are 10 minutes flying time away from the aerodrome, whichever is the sooner.

- overflying aircraft place themselves under the control of Approach Control until they are clear of the approach pattern, and either no longer wish to receive a service or are 10 minutes flying time away from the aerodrome, whichever is the sooner.

Aircraft within an Aerodrome Traffic Zone (ATZ) are required to comply with instructions from the ATCU. Flight in uncontrolled airspace (Class F and G), outside the ATZ is permitted without an Air Traffic Control clearance. However, controllers may assume that pilots of aircraft flying in the vicinity of the aerodrome in radio contact with the ATCU are complying with instructions unless the ATCU states otherwise.

An ATCU providing an Approach Control Service uses the call-sign "Approach" or "Radar" as appropriate.

Area Control Service.

Area Control Centres (ACC) are established in Flight Information Regions to provide an Area Control Service in the airspace under its jurisdiction.

Figure 5.18 Area Control Centre.

An Area Control Service comprises radar and non-radar air traffic services in airspace which is not under the jurisdiction of an Approach or Aerodrome Control Unit.
An ACC providing an Area Control Service normally uses the call-sign "Control" or "Radar" as appropriate.

FLIGHT INFORMATION SERVICE.

A Flight Information Service is a basic form of air traffic service available to any aircraft within a Flight Information Region.

A Flight Information Service is provided to all aircraft flying in uncontrolled airspace, for the purpose of promoting the safe, orderly and efficient conduct of flights.

Please Note: *the UK FIS is fundamentally different.*

A Flight Information Service (FIS) is a non-radar service provided, either separately or in conjunction with other services, for the purposes of supplying information useful for the safe and efficient conduct of flights. In the UK this service is called the "Basic Service", and is one of four services which are collectively called the UK FIS. The FIS is probably the air traffic service most frequently used by VFR pilots flying in uncontrolled airspace (sometimes known as the Open FIR.)

An FIS includes information about:

- weather.

- changes of serviceability of facilities.

- conditions at aerodromes.

- any other information pertinent to flight safety.

An FIS is a very useful service for general aviation pilots flying VFR. Even if no particular information is desired by the pilot, it may be prudent for him to ask for an FIS when one is available. In that way, if a distress or urgency situation were to arise, the pilot is at least in contact with an ATSU which knows that he is airborne and what his route is.

There are numerous factors which limit the air traffic service given to a pilot receiving an FIS. For instance, because aerodromes and centres providing an FIS need only be equipped to a specified minimum level, accurate assessment of the possibility of collision hazard between aircraft in flight is very low.

Pilots should, therefore, recognise that no form of positive control or separation service can be provided to pilots receiving an FIS. It is of supreme importance that pilots understand that, while receiving an FIS, they are not under air traffic control and are, themselves, responsible for collision avoidance.

Receiving an FIS does not relieve the Pilot-in-Command of any responsibility as aircraft commander.

An ATSU providing a Flight Information Service uses the call-sign "Information" after the ground station identifier.

When you contact an ATSU to request a Flight Information Service, your transmission will take the form:

"Stephenville Approach, G-ABCD, Request Flight Information Service".

The Controller will reply "G-ABCD, Stephenville Approach, Go Ahead".

Your response, as a pilot, to the instruction "Go Ahead" will be to pass a standard report combining details of your aircraft type, route information, position, altitude, flight rules and intentions. A typical pilot response to the "Go Ahead" instruction would be:

"G-ABCD, PA-28, from Rissington Parva to Georgetown, 15 miles East of Stephenville, 2500 feet, QNH 987, VFR, estimate Wicken 46."

You will notice that details are passed to the FIS Controller in the following order:

1. Aircraft call-sign.
2. Aircraft Type.
3. Route or operation information.
4. Position.
5. Altitude.
6. Altimeter setting.
7. Flight rules (VFR or IFR).
8. Estimate of time at next waypoint.

Passing your details in this standard format will help the FIS controller to visualise your situation, and thus to give you a better service.

Note that, in the United Kingdom, when a pilot requests an FIS, the controller's response is **"Pass Your Message"** rather than the standard ICAO response of **"Go Ahead"**.

Flight Information Service at Aerodromes.

Where a full Air Traffic Control Service is not established at an aerodrome, the aerodrome may provide an Aerodrome Flight Information Service (AFIS) in order to give information useful for the safe and efficient conduct of flights in the Aerodrome Traffic Zone (ATZ).

When receiving an AFIS from an aerodrome, it is the responsibility of the Pilot-in-Command to decide the appropriate course of action to be taken to ensure the safe conduct of his flight and the safety of his aircraft when taking off, landing or flying in the ATZ.

An AFIS-provider will not issue instructions or clearances to pilots, but only information for aircraft operating in or around the ATZ. An aerodrome providing an AFIS will use the call sign "Information" after the aerodrome identifier.

Air/Ground Communication Service.

Where an aerodrome has neither a full Air Traffic Control Service, nor an Aerodrome Flight Information Service, for instance at airfields where only a flying club operates, an Air/Ground Communications Service may be available which will use the suffix "Radio" following the name of the airfield.

An Air/Ground Communications facility permits two way communication between an aircraft and a ground station in which the ground operator may pass only very basic information regarding the situation at the aerodrome.

AFIS and A/G providers cannot issue instructions or clearances.

Figure 5.19 An Air/Ground Radio Communications Service may pass only very basic information regarding the situation at the aerodrome.

ALERTING SERVICE.

An Alerting Service is provided by ATSUs to notify appropriate organisations regarding aircraft in need of search and rescue aid, and to assist such organisations as required.

Air traffic services provide an Alerting Service for all known aircraft operating within a Flight Information Region (FIR).

The responsibility for initiating action in respect of an aircraft which is experiencing an emergency is normally that of the ATSU which was last in communication with the aircraft.

Collation of information.

Flight Information Centres (FICs) and Area Control Centres (ACCs) are the organisations which are responsible for the collation of all information relevant to a state of emergency being experienced by an aircraft within the FIR. These centres then forward the information to the Rescue Coordination Centre (RCC).

Rescue Coordination Centre.

The RCC is responsible for all SAR operations

Each State is accountable for establishing a Rescue Coordination Centre (RCC) within its territory. The RCC is responsible for the coordination of all search and rescue (SAR) operations concerned with aircraft known, or believed, to be in need of help. It is the RCC which will coordinate any specialist effort such as mountain rescue teams or diving/helicopter organisations etc.

Aircraft Under the Control of Aerodrome or Approach Service.

If an aircraft is experiencing a state of emergency while under the control of Aerodrome or Approach Control Services, the ATCU Controller is responsible for:

- Passing a flow of information and updates to the FIC/ACC for forwarding to the RCC.

- Setting in motion all appropriate local rescue and emergency organisations which can give immediate assistance.

EMERGENCY PHASES.

The Phases of Emergency:

1. Uncertainty Phase.

2. Alert Phase

3. Distress Phase.

The Alerting Service comprises 3 phases. These are the:

- Uncertainty Phase.

- Alert Phase.

- Distress Phase.

Uncertainty Phase.

The Uncertainty Phase is declared when:

- There exists uncertainty as to the safety of an aircraft, for instance when no communication has been received from an aircraft within 30 minutes after the time a communication should have been received, or from the time an unsuccessful attempt to establish communications with an aircraft was first made, whichever is the earlier.

- An aircraft fails to arrive within 30 minutes of the Estimated Time of Arrival last notified to, or estimated by, an ATSU, whichever is the later.

Alert Phase.

The Alert Phase is declared when there exists apprehension about the safety of an aircraft and its occupants, and specifically when:

If an aircraft is subject to unlawful interference, the Alert Phase is declared.

- Following the Uncertainty Phase, subsequent attempts to establish communications with the aircraft, or inquiries to other sources, have failed to reveal any news of the aircraft.

- An aircraft has been cleared to land and fails to do so within 5 minutes of the estimated time of landing, and communications have not been re-established.

- Information has been received which indicates that the operational efficiency of the aircraft has been impaired, but not to the extent that a forced landing is likely, except when evidence exists as to the safety of the aircraft and its occupants.

- An aircraft is known, or believed, to be the subject of unlawful interference (hi-jack).

Distress Phase.

The Distress Phase is declared when there exists a reasonable certainty that an aircraft and its occupants are threatened by grave and imminent danger or require immediate assistance, and specifically when:

- Following the Alert Phase, further unsuccessful attempts to establish communications with the aircraft, and more widespread inquires, point to the probability that the aircraft is in distress.

- The fuel on board is considered to be exhausted, or to be insufficient to enable the aircraft to reach safety.

- Information is received which indicates that the operating efficiency has been impaired to the extent that a forced landing is likely.

- Information is received confirming that, or it is reasonably certain that, the aircraft is about to make, or has made, a forced landing.

Termination of an Emergency.

When the emergency situation no longer exists, the local ATSU, via the FIC or ACC, shall inform the RCC. The RCC has the responsibly for terminating all SAR operations.

Representative PPL - type questions to test your theoretical knowledge of ICAO Airspace Division and Air Traffic Services.

1.   You are a private pilot but hold neither an instrument rating nor an IMC rating. How would you enter a CTR which is Class A airspace?

   a.   Complete a flight plan prior to departure
   b.   Request a SVFR clearance to enter the Zone
   c.   Call 10 minutes prior to CTR penetration
   d.   You can enter the CTR as long as the conditions are VMC

2.   In which class of airspace are both IFR and VFR flights permitted, all flights are provided with ATC, IFR flights are separated from other IFR flights and receive traffic information concerning VFR flights while VFR flights receive traffic information in respect of all other flights?

   a.   Class B
   b.   Class C
   c.   Class D
   d.   Class E

3.   What is the Indicated Airspeed limit in Class C Airspace for VFR traffic?

   a.   120 kts TAS below 10 000 feet
   b.   There is no specified speed limit
   c.   250 kts IAS below FL 100
   d.   120 kts

4.   What airspace/s are considered "Controlled Airspace"?

   a.   A only
   b.   A, B, C and D only
   c.   A, B, C, D and E only
   d,   A, B, C, D, E and F only

5.   What are the 3 types of Air Traffic Services?

   a.   Air Traffic Control Service (ATCS), Flight Information Service (FIS) and the Alerting Service
   b.   ATCS, FIS and Radar
   c.   ATCS, Advisory Service and Alerting Service
   d.   Alerting Service, Advisory Service and Radar

6.   What is the definition of 'Alerting Service'?

   a.   A service provided by the air traffic services which provides search and rescue facilities

   b.   A service provided by the air traffic services in order to disseminate information about any aircraft in need of assistance

   c.   A service provided by the air traffic services in order to notify appropriate organizations about aircraft in need of search and rescue aid, and to assist such organizations, as required

   d.   A unit of the air traffic services established to coordinate search and rescue operations

7.   An aircraft is known or believed to be the subject of Unlawful Interference (hi-jack). What phase of the Alerting Service should be declared?

   a.   Emergency Phase
   b.   Uncertainty Phase
   c.   Alert Phase
   d.   Distress Phase

8.   An aircraft has been cleared to land and fails to do so within 5 minutes of the estimated time of landing, and communications have not been re-established. What phase of the Alerting Service should be declared?

   a.   Emergency Phase
   b.   Alert Phase
   c.   Uncertainty Phase
   d.   Distress Phase

9.   Which organisation is responsible for the coordination of Search and Rescue efforts within a State?

   a.   Flight Information Centre
   b.   Air Traffic Control Centre
   c.   Approach Control Centre
   d.   Rescue Coordination Centre

10.   To which of the following is the Alerting Service available?

   a.   All aircraft in Class F airspace
   b.   Any aircraft known to the air traffic services
   c.   All aircraft in Class G airspace
   d.   To all aircraft more than 15 minutes late at the destination airfield

11.   No communication has been received from an aircraft within 30 minutes after the time a communication should have been received. What phase of the Alerting Service must be declared?

   a.   Emergency Phase
   b.   Uncertainty Phase
   c.   Alert Phase
   d.   Distress Phase

12.   What is the standard width of an airway?

   a.   10 nautical miles
   b.   5 nautical miles
   c.   8 nautical miles
   d.   3 nautical miles

13.   What is the boundary separating the Flight Information Region from the Upper Information Region?

   a.   The national aviation authority of the State concerned sets the boundary
   b.   FL250
   c.   3000 feet
   d.   FL100

14.   What is the difference between a Control Zone (CTR) and a Control Area (CTA)?

   a.   A CTR extends from a Flight Level (FL) to a FL whereas a CTA extends from an altitude to an altitude
   b.   A CTA extends from a FL to a FL whereas a CTR extends from an altitude to an altitude
   c.   A CTR extends from a FL to a FL whereas a CTA extends from the ground or water to an altitude
   d.   A CTR extends from the ground or water to an altitude or FL whereas a CTA extends from an altitude or FL to a higher altitude or FL

15.   What meteorological conditions must prevail in order for a flight to take place in accordance with the Visual Flight Rules?

   a.   At least IMC
   b.   Clear of cloud and in sight of the surface
   c.   5 km in-flight visibility, with 1500 metres horizontal and 1000 feet vertical separation from cloud
   d.   VMC appropriate to the Class of Airspace in which the aircraft is flying and appropriate to its vertical position

16.   What minimum level of air traffic service is provided in a Flight Information Region?

   a.   A Flight Information Service and an Alerting Service
   b.   ATC and Flight Information Service
   c.   ATC and Advisory Service
   d.   Advisory and Alerting Services

17.   Where is a TMA most likely to be found?

    a.   At the confluence of airways or controlled routes and in the vicinity of one or more major airports
    b.   In the vicinity of an International Airport
    c.   When special routes are required for arrivals and departures
    d.   In the vicinity of Controlled Aerodromes

18.   Which class of airspace provides IFR flights with an Air Traffic Advisory Service and all flights with a Flight Information Service, if requested?

    a.   B
    b.   D
    c.   G
    d.   F

19.   What may be the lowest point of the CTA according to ICAO regulations?

    a.   From any specified height above the ground or water
    b.   From a specified height above ground or water being not less than 700 feet
    c.   At least 1000 feet amsl
    d.   There is no such regulation

20.   You are about to enter an Aerodrome Traffic Zone (ATZ) of an airfield at which you have received prior permission to land. Immediately upon entering the ATZ you must report your:

    a.   Height and magnetic heading
    b.   Height and position
    c.   Altitude and magnetic heading
    d.   Flight Rules and magnetic heading

21.   What is the lowest level of a CTA permitted by international agreement?

    a.   Not lower than 700 feet above the surface of the ground or water
    b.   Not lower than 1000 feet above the surface of the ground or water
    c.   Not lower than 1500 feet above the surface of the ground or water
    d.   Not lower than 500 feet above the surface of the ground or water

22.   What is the Class Airspace in which both VFR and IFR traffic is controlled and in which IFR and SVFR flights are separated from each other and receive information regarding VFR traffic, and in which VFR traffic receives information regarding all other traffic?

    a.   A
    b.   E
    c.   C
    d.   D

23. What action may a Pilot-in-Command elect to take if he judges that an ATC clearance does not suit his circumstances?

   a. He should say nothing to the air traffic controller and proceed in the manner he judges to be most suitable to his circumstances
   b. He may request an amended clearance
   c. He must accept the ATC clearance without question
   d. He must inform the air traffic controller of his intentions and then proceed as he judges to be most suitable to his circumstances

24. What are the lateral dimensions of a Control Zone?

   a. 10 nautical miles in the direction from which approaches are made, measured from the centre of the aerodrome or, where more than one aerodrome is covered, 10 nautical miles from the centre of the combined aerodromes in the direction from which approaches are made
   b. 5 nautical miles in the direction from which approaches are made, measured from the centre of the aerodrome or, where more than one aerodrome is covered, 10 nautical miles from the centre of the combined aerodromes in the direction from which approaches are made
   c. 5 kilometres in the direction from which approaches are made, measured from the centre of the aerodrome or, where more than one aerodrome is covered, 5 kilometres from the centre of the combined aerodromes in the direction from which approaches are made
   d. 5 nautical miles in the direction from which approaches are made, measured from the centre of the aerodrome or, where more than one aerodrome is covered, 5 nautical miles from the centre of the combined aerodromes in the direction from which approaches are made

25. A service provided by an Air Traffic Control Unit for all controlled flights arriving at or departing from an aerodrome is called:

   a. An Area Control Service
   b. An Approach Control Service
   c. A Flight Information Service
   d. An Alerting Service

26. If the actual or forecast conditions give the visibility and cloud base as less than specified minimum weather conditions and the distance from cloud is seen also to be less than specified minima, the prevailing weather conditions are referred to as:

   a. VMC
   b. IMC
   c. VFR
   d. IFR

Question	1	2	3	4	5	6	7	8	9	10	11	12
Answer												

Question	13	14	15	16	17	18	19	20	21	22	23	24
Answer												

Question	25	26
Answer		

The answers to these questions can be found at the end of this book.

CHAPTER 6
FLIGHT PLANS AND CLEARANCES (ICAO)

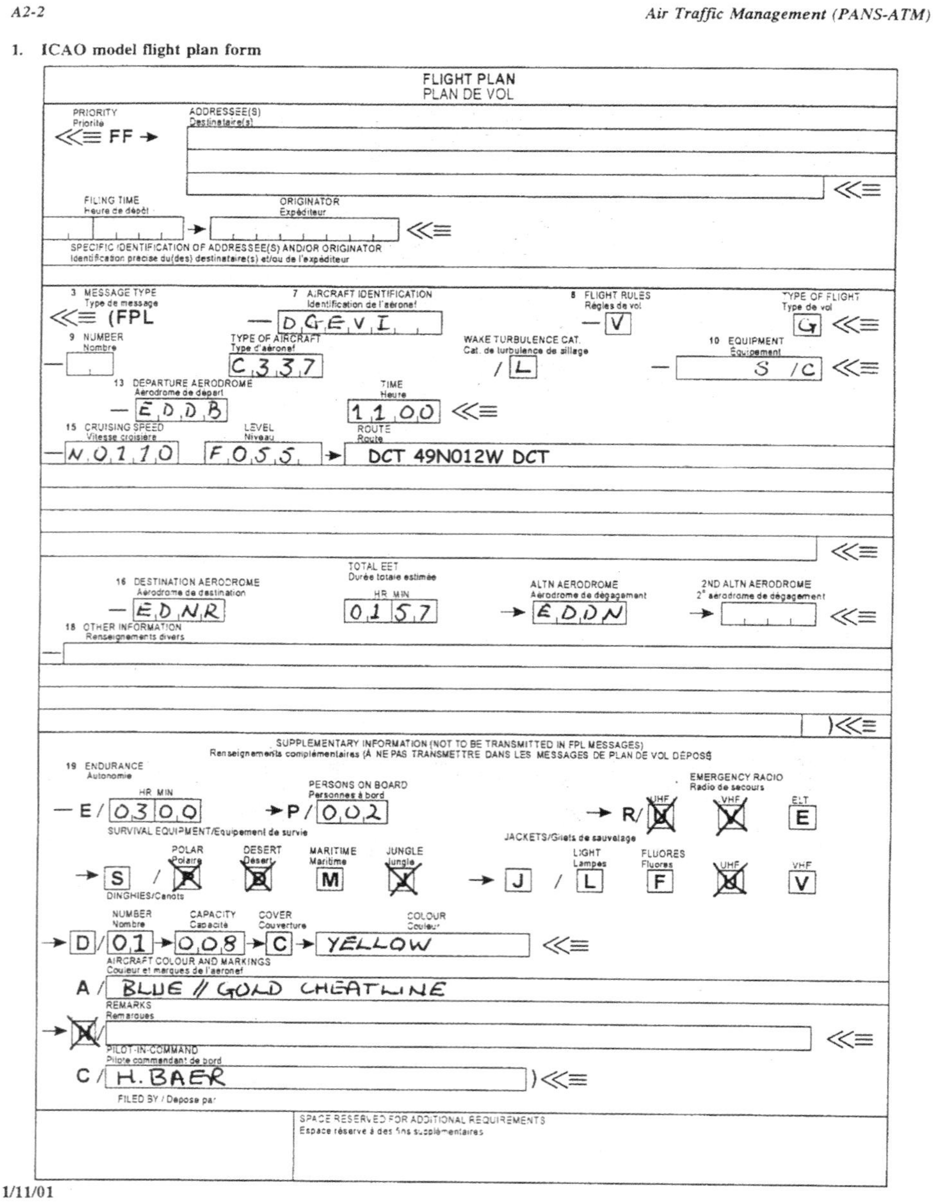

A2-2 *Air Traffic Management (PANS-ATM)*

1. **ICAO model flight plan form**

FLIGHT PLAN
PLAN DE VOL

PRIORITY / Priorité: <<≡ FF →
ADDRESSEE(S) / Destinataire(s): <<≡

FILING TIME / Heure de dépôt → ORIGINATOR / Expéditeur <<≡

SPECIFIC IDENTIFICATION OF ADDRESSEE(S) AND/OR ORIGINATOR / Identification précise du(des) destinataire(s) et/ou de l'expéditeur

3 MESSAGE TYPE / Type de message: <<≡ (FPL
7 AIRCRAFT IDENTIFICATION / Identification de l'aéronef: — DGEVI
8 FLIGHT RULES / Règles de vol: — V
TYPE OF FLIGHT / Type de vol: G <<≡

9 NUMBER / Nombre: —
TYPE OF AIRCRAFT / Type d'aéronef: C337
WAKE TURBULENCE CAT. / Cat. de turbulence de sillage: / L
10 EQUIPMENT / Équipement: — S / C <<≡

13 DEPARTURE AERODROME / Aérodrome de départ: — EDDB
TIME / Heure: 1100 <<≡

15 CRUISING SPEED / Vitesse croisière: — N0110
LEVEL / Niveau: F055
ROUTE / Route: → DCT 49N012W DCT
<<≡

16 DESTINATION AERODROME / Aérodrome de destination: — EDNR
TOTAL EET / Durée totale estimée HR MIN: 0157
ALTN AERODROME / Aérodrome de dégagement: → EDDN
2ND ALTN AERODROME / 2e aérodrome de dégagement: → <<≡

18 OTHER INFORMATION / Renseignements divers: —
)<<≡

SUPPLEMENTARY INFORMATION (NOT TO BE TRANSMITTED IN FPL MESSAGES)
Renseignements complémentaires (À NE PAS TRANSMETTRE DANS LES MESSAGES DE PLAN DE VOL DÉPOSÉS)

19 ENDURANCE / Autonomie HR MIN: — E / 0300
PERSONS ON BOARD / Personnes à bord: → P / 002
EMERGENCY RADIO / Radio de secours: → R / ~~UHF~~ ~~VHF~~ ELT E

SURVIVAL EQUIPMENT / Équipement de survie: → S / POLAR/Polaire ~~P~~ DESERT/Désert ~~D~~ MARITIME/Maritime M JUNGLE/Jungle ~~J~~
JACKETS / Gilets de sauvetage: → J / LIGHT/Lampes L FLUORES/Fluores F ~~UHF~~ VHF V

DINGHIES / Canots: → D / NUMBER/Nombre 01 → CAPACITY/Capacité 008 → COVER/Couverture C → COLOUR/Couleur YELLOW <<≡

AIRCRAFT COLOUR AND MARKINGS / Couleur et marques de l'aéronef
A / BLUE // GOLD CHEATLINE

REMARKS / Remarques
→ ~~N~~ / <<≡

PILOT-IN-COMMAND / Pilote commandant de bord
C / H. BAER)<<≡

FILED BY / Déposé par
SPACE RESERVED FOR ADDITIONAL REQUIREMENTS / Espace réservé à des fins supplémentaires

1/11/01

Fig 6.1 ICAO Flight Plan Form.

GENERAL.

Flight Plans are a method of informing Air Traffic Services (ATS) of the details of a pilot's aircraft and proposed route. When necessary, a flight plan is also submitted when an ATS clearance is required.

- Flight Plans can be written and filed on a standard ICAO Flight Plan Form. (*See Figure 6.1.*)

- The form should be completed using capital letters and should include an English text, in addition to the language(s) of the State concerned. A flight plan can be transmitted in an abbreviated form, by telephone, and, in flight, over the radio.

If the aerodrome of departure does not have a ATS reporting office, you must submit your flight plan by telephone or radio to the ATSU serving the departure aerodrome.

ICAO Definition of a Flight Plan.

The term "flight plan" is used to mean, variously, full information on all items comprised in the flight plan description, covering the whole route of a flight, or limited information required when the purpose of the flight plan is to obtain a clearance for a minor portion of a flight such as to cross an airway, to take off from, or to land at a controlled aerodrome. In other words there are 2 types of flight plan.

TYPES OF FLIGHT PLAN.

Full Flight Plan.

In this type of flight plan, the whole route of the flight and all details are completed following the format of the Flight Plan Form. (*See Figure 6.1.*)

Abbreviated Flight Plan.

This is normally passed by radio to Air Traffic Control, or by telephone, to obtain a clearance for part of a flight (e.g. to cross an airway or to enter controlled air space).

SUBMISSION OF A FLIGHT PLAN – ON WHAT OCCASIONS?

A flight plan is to be submitted, before departure of the flight, to an Air Traffic Services Reporting Office or, during flight, to the relevant Air Traffic Services Unit (ATSU).

A flight plan is to be submitted, prior to operating the following types of flight:

- Any flight or part of a flight which is to be provided with an Air Traffic Control Service.

- Any IFR flight within Advisory Airspace (Class F).

- Any flight within or into designated areas, when so required by the Air Traffic Services authority in order to facilitate the provision of:

  a.   A Flight Information Service.

  b.   An Alerting Service.

  c.   A Search and Rescue Service.

- Any flight within or into designated areas, when so required by the Air Traffic Services (ATS) authority, in order to facilitate co-ordination with military units or with ATSs in adjacent States in order to avoid the possible need for interception.

- Any flight across international borders.

SUBMISSION OF FLIGHT PLANS – TIME LIMITATIONS.

Unless otherwise prescribed by the ATS authority, a flight plan for a flight to be provided with an ATC service or an Air Advisory Service shall be submitted:

- On the ground to an ATS Reporting Office, at least 60 minutes before departure

or

- In flight, to the appropriate Air Traffic Services Unit (ATSU) at a time which will ensure its receipt by the ATSU and at least 10 minutes before the aircraft is estimated to reach:

    A.   The intended point of entry into a Control Area or Advisory Area

or

    B.   the point of crossing an airway or Advisory Route (ADR).

Note: Having submitted a flight plan, all aircraft must wait for a responding ATC Clearance before proceeding on course.

DELAY ON DEPARTURE.

In the event of a delay to an uncontrolled flight of 60 minutes in excess of EOBT, the flight plan should be amended or a new Flight Plan submitted and the old Flight Plan cancelled.

In the event of a delay, in excess of Estimated Off-Blocks Time (EOBT), of 30 minutes for a Controlled Flight, and 60 minutes for an Uncontrolled Flight, the flight plan should be amended or a new flight plan should be submitted and the old flight plan cancelled.

CONTENTS OF A FLIGHT PLAN.

A Flight Plan shall comprise the following information:

- Aircraft identification.

- Flight rules and type of flight.

- Number and type(s) of aircraft and wake turbulence category.

- Equipment.

- Departure aerodrome.

- Estimated Off-Block Time (in the case of an airborne flight plan this relates to the time over the first point of the route to which the flight plan refers).

- Cruising speed(s) (TAS).

- Cruising level(s).

- Route to be followed.

- Destination aerodrome and total estimated elapsed time to overhead.

- Alternate aerodrome(s).

- Fuel endurance.

- Total number of persons on board.

- Emergency and survival equipment.

- Other information.

CHANGES TO A FLIGHT PLAN.

All changes to a flight plan submitted for an IFR flight, or for a VFR flight operated as a controlled flight, shall be reported as soon as practicable to the appropriate Air Traffic Services Unit (ATSU).

Information submitted prior to departure regarding fuel endurance or total number of persons on board, if incorrect at time of departure, constitutes a significant change to the **flight plan** and, as such, must be reported.

ADHERENCE TO FLIGHT PLAN – CONTROLLED FLIGHTS.

Controlled flights must adhere to the current flight plan except in the event of an emergency situation, in which case the aircraft is to immediately inform the ATSU of the action being taken, or being authorised to divert from the flight plan by ATC.

Inadvertent Changes.
In the event that a flight inadvertently deviates from its current flight plan, the following action shall be taken:

- **Deviation from track:**
  Adjust the heading of the aircraft to regain track as soon as practicable.

- **Variation in true airspeed (TAS):**
  If the actual TAS at cruising level between reporting points varies, or is expected to vary, by ± 5% or more from the flight-planned TAS, the appropriate ATSU is to be informed.

You must inform The ATSU if your actual TAS differs by ± 5% from your flight planned TAS, or you are more than 3 minutes early or late for the next Reporting Point.

- **Change in time estimate:**
  If the ETA for the next reporting point, FIR boundary or destination, is found to be in error by more than 3 minutes from that notified to Air Traffic Services, a revised ETA shall be notified as soon as possible to the appropriate ATSU.

Intended Changes.

Intended changes of cruising level, route and destination are to be passed to the ATSU as soon as possible.

Weather Deterioration below Visual Meteorological Conditions (VMC).

When it becomes evident that flight in VMC will not be practicable due to weather deterioration, a controlled VFR flight shall:

- Request an amended clearance to continue in VMC to:

  a.   Destination,

  or

  b.   an alternative aerodrome,

  or

  c.   leave the airspace within which an ATC clearance is required.

- If no such clearance can be obtained, the aircraft is to:

  a.   Continue to operate in VMC,

  and

  b.   notify the appropriate Air Traffic Control Unit of the action being taken (either to leave the airspace concerned or to land at the nearest suitable aerodrome),

  or

  c.   if the flight is being conducted in a Control Zone, request authorisation to fly Special VFR (SVFR),

  or

  d.   request clearance to operate in accordance with IFR (if the pilot is qualified and the aircraft suitably equipped).

CLOSING A FLIGHT PLAN.

- A report of arrival must be made, in person, by radiotelephony or via data link, at the earliest possible moment after landing, to the appropriate Air Traffic Service Unit (ATSU) at the arrival aerodrome.

- When no ATSU exists at the arrival aerodrome, the arrival report shall be made as soon as practicable after landing, to the nearest ATSU.

- If neither of the above is possible (due to poor communications for example), the aircraft is to make the arrival report over the air, immediately *prior* to landing, to the ATSU serving the FIR in which the aircraft is operating.

CONTENTS OF AN ARRIVAL REPORT.

Arrival reports shall contain the following information:

- Aircraft identification.

- Departure aerodrome.

- Destination aerodrome (only in the case of a diversionary landing).

- Arrival aerodrome.

- Time of arrival.

On receipt of an Arrival Report, the flight plan is closed.

Note: Failure to comply with these provisions may cause serious disruption to air traffic services and incur great expense in carrying out unnecessary Search and Rescue (SAR) operations.

On receipt of an Arrival Report, the flight plan is closed.

AIR TRAFFIC CLEARANCES.

General.
An ATC clearance shall be obtained prior to operating a controlled flight, or a portion of a flight operated as a controlled flight. Such clearance shall be requested through the submission of a flight plan to an ATCU.

Note: An aircraft operated on a controlled aerodrome shall not taxi on the manoeuvring area without clearance from the aerodrome control tower.

Primary Functions of Air Traffic Clearances.
The primary functions of clearances are to:

- Expedite air traffic,

and

- ensure separation between aircraft.

Pilot Acceptance of a Clearance.
Many pilots, when they start to fly, are under the impression that an air traffic clearance is an instruction which must be obeyed, regardless of how inconvenient it may be. This is incorrect. If a clearance is not suitable to the pilot-in-command of an aircraft, he may request and, if practical, obtain an amended clearance. Normally ATC will always try and help as far as possible under these circumstances.

The receipt of an Air Traffic Clearance does not relieve the pilot from any responsibility to uphold all rules and regulations that may apply to the flight, especially from the responsibility of maintaining terrain clearance at all times.

Responsibility of the Pilot.

It is important to remember that an air traffic clearance does not constitute authority for the pilot to violate any rule or regulation. For example, even having received a clearance, the pilot is still responsible for maintaining the required terrain clearance.

Contents of a Clearance.

The format of Air Traffic Clearances is as follows:

- Aircraft identification.

- Clearance limit - normally a geographical limit (an aerodrome, Controlled Air Space boundary, or a specific point).

- Route of flight.

- Levels of flight.

- Any other information or instruction (e.g. SSR squawk, approach or departure manoeuvres, or time of expiry of the clearance).**

Note: ** The time of expiry of the clearance indicates the time after which the clearance will be automatically cancelled if the flight has not commenced.

Acceptance and Read-back of Clearances.

1. All Clearances must be read back to the Air Traffic Controller.

2. A Clearance, if unsuitable, may be changed or amended – if practical – at the request of the pilot .

The method of accepting a clearance by the pilot is for him to read back the clearance to the ATC Controller. The Controller listens to the read-back to ascertain that the clearance has been correctly acknowledged and will take immediate action to correct any discrepancies in the pilot read-back.

Once the pilot has read back the clearance correctly, the ATC Controller will normally acknowledge by using the phrase: **"Read-back correct".**

Representative PPL - type questions to test your theoretical knowledge of ICAO Flight Plans and Clearances.

1.   During a Controlled Flight, your actual TAS is 120 kts however your flight planned TAS is 115 kts. Must you inform ATSU?

   a.   Only if requested by ATC
   b.   Yes
   c.   No
   d.   Only if you are outside CAS

2.   Is the PIC of an aircraft obliged to accept an ATC clearance?

   a.   Yes
   b.   No
   c.   Only if it is an IFR clearance
   d.   Only is it is to be a controlled flight

3.   By when must you submit a Flight Plan prior to departure if you wish to be provided with an ATC service?

   a.   30 minutes
   b.   It depends whether you intend to fly VFR or IFR
   c.   It depends on whether you will be flying in Controlled Air Space (CAS) or outside CAS
   d.   60 minutes

4.   What event closes a flight plan?

   a.   Landing at the destination aerodrome
   b.   Arriving overhead the destination aerodrome
   c.   The receipt of an Arrival Report
   d.   Being on short finals

5.   You have flight planned to arrive over a Reporting Point at 1400Z. However, due to an unexpected tailwind, you realize that you will arrive at 1355Z. Do you have to inform the relevant ATCU?

   a.   Yes
   b.   No
   c.   Only if you are outside Controlled Air Space
   d.   Only if you are conducting the flight under Special VFR

6.   Do you have to submit a Flight Plan if you are crossing the London/Brest FIR boundary under VFR?

   a.   Yes
   b.   No

7.   You are entering an advisory route (ADR) under IFR. Do you have to submit a Flight Plan?

      a.   Yes
      b.   No
      c.   Only if that part of the ADR is Controlled Air Space
      d.   Only if that part of the ADR is an ATS route

8.   You have to cross an Airway. How soon prior to penetration must you file an in-flight Flight Plan?

      a.   At least 5 minutes
      b.   At least 10 minutes
      c.   At least 15 minutes
      d.   There is no set time limit

9.   Your take-off is delayed for an uncontrolled flight. At what point must you re-submit your Flight Plan?

      a.   30 minutes in excess of Estimated Off-Blocks Time (EOBT)
      b.   45 minutes in excess of EOBT
      c.   60 minutes in excess of EOBT
      d.   90 minutes in excess of EOBT

10.   Must you enter your wake turbulence category in a Flight Plan?

      a.   Only if the aircraft is in the Heavy category
      b.   No
      c.   Only if the aircraft is in the Medium or Heavy categories
      d.   Yes

11.   Do you have to send an in-flight Flight Plan to unexpectedly enter a CTR under SVFR?

      a.   Only if you are a Controlled Flight
      b.   Only if you are an Uncontrolled Flight
      c.   No
      d.   Yes

12. You are a Controlled VFR Flight landing at a private strip in a valley in Scotland. Your estimated landing time is exactly that which you entered in the Flight Plan prior to departure. As you descend you call ATC to inform them you are landing but receive no answer. What would be the correct course of action?

    a. No further action is necessary as your ETA is accurate
    b. Wait until your next take-off and, when airborne, inform ATC of the circumstances
    c. Assume your radio has failed and have it tested as soon as possible after landing
    d. Either climb and re-establish communications with ATC or telephone ATC as soon as possible (and within 30 minutes) after landing passing them your Arrival Report

13. What is one of the primary functions of an Air Traffic Clearance?

    a. To agree to allow a flight to proceed
    b. To ensure separation of aircraft
    c. To acknowledge that the information of the flight details have been logged by ATC
    d. To acknowledge that ATC is now responsible for the flight

14. How is an abbreviated Flight Plan normally submitted?

    a. By e-mail or fax
    b. Over the radio or by telephone
    c. By filling out only specific parts of the Flight Plan form
    d. In person

Question	1	2	3	4	5	6	7	8	9	10	11	12
Answer												

Question	13	14
Answer		

The answers to these questions can be found at the end of this book.

CHAPTER 7
AERONAUTICAL INFORMATION SERVICES (ICAO)

Aeronautical Information Service
CCN
Vooruitgangstraat, 80 Bus 2
B - 1030 Brussel

 **Belgocontrol**

Aeronautical Information Service
CCN
Rue du Progrès, 80 Boîte 2
B - 1030 Bruxelles

TEL : ++32 (0) 2 206 22 19 (Manager)
　　　++32 (0) 2 206 22 97 (Customer Service)
FAX : ++32 (0) 2 206 22 21
AFS : EBVAYOYX

AIC
05
26 MAR 1998

INFORMATION AT THE REQUEST OF THE CIVIL AVIATION AUTHORITY

VALIDATION OF LICENCES

1.　The holder of a valid pilot licence for aeroplanes, helicopters, gliders or free balloons issued by a Member State of the European Community in compliance with the specifications of Annex 1 to the Chicago Convention may exercise, without any further formality, the privileges granted by that licence in a Belgian registered aircraft certificated for single-pilot operation in order to make private flights by day and under VFR, provided that he meets the recent flight experience requirements imposed by the issuing State.

2.　In order to make other than private flights, licences issued by a Member State of the European Community must be rendered valid as previously.
　　Licences issued by non-Member States of the European Community must be rendered valid in all cases.

AIC NR 06/92 is hereby cancelled.

GENERAL.

The general aviation pilot does not need to know much about ICAO Aeronautical Information Services. Rather, he should study the Aeronautical Information Publications issued by the State in which he flies. The following brief outline of ICAO Aeronautical Information Services has been included for background purposes only. The private pilot flying in the United Kingdom is strongly advised to study Chapter 15 concerning Aeronautical Information issued by the United Kingdom Civil Aviation Authority.

RESPONSIBILITIES AND FUNCTIONS.

Each contracting state shall:

- Provide an aeronautical information service,

or

- agree with one or more other contracting state(s) for the provision of a joint information service,

or

- delegate the authority for the provision of the information service to a non-government organisation.

Provision.
A State's Aeronautical Information Service shall ensure that the information necessary for the safety and efficiency of air navigation is made available for the operational requirements of:

- Those involved in flight operations (including flight crews), flight planning and flight simulators

and

- the Air Traffic Services Units (ATSUs) responsible for providing a Flight Information Service, and services responsible for pre-flight information.

Integrated Aeronautical Information Package.
Aeronautical information shall be published by States as an Integrated Aeronautical Information Package which comprises:

- An Aeronautical Information Publication (AIP) including an amendment service.

- Supplements to the AIP.

- NOTAMs, (Notices to Airmen) including checklists and summaries of valid NOTAMs.

- Pre-flight Information Bulletins (PIB).

- Aeronautical Information Circulars (AIC).

THE AERONAUTICAL INFORMATION PUBLICATION.

General.
A State's Aeronautical Information Publication (AIP) constitutes the basic information source for information of a lasting character essential to air navigation.

The AIP is divided into 3 Parts :

Part 1 General (GEN).

Part 2 En-route (ENR).

Part 3 Aerodromes (AD).

Layout.
The AIP is divided into 3 Parts:

Part 1   General (GEN).

Part 2   En-route (ENR).

Part 3   Aerodromes (AD).

These parts are described in detail in Chapter 15, for the United Kingdom.

AIP Amendments and Supplements.
Permanent changes to the AIP are published as AIP Amendments. Temporary changes are published as AIP Supplements and must be kept in the AIP, as long as all or some of their contents remain valid.

Notices to Airmen (NOTAM).
NOTAMs are issued promptly for operationally significant aeronautical information which is composed of:

- Changes of a temporary and short-term nature (e.g. activation of a temporary Danger Area),

or

- permanent changes (e.g. introduction of a new Airway),

or

- temporary changes of long duration which are made at short notice (e.g. emergency and major repairs to a runway).

Checklists of valid **NOTAMS** are issued at intervals of not more than one month.

Pre-flight Information Bulletins.
Pre-Flight Information Bulletins are briefing Bulletins prepared at each aerodrome for aircrew. They contain the NOTAMs relevant to that particular aerodrome and other local operational information (e.g. the presence of temporary hazards at the aerodrome, and maintenance work on the movement area; failure of any of the aerodrome lighting system etc).

Aeronautical Information Circulars.

An Aeronautical Information Circular (AIC) is issued whenever it is necessary to promulgate aeronautical information which does not qualify for inclusion in the AIP or in a NOTAM; for example:

- Long-term forecasts of major changes in legislation, regulations, procedures or facilities.

- Information of a purely explanatory or advisory nature liable to affect flight safety.

- Information or notification of an explanatory or advisory nature concerning technical, legislative or purely administrative matters.

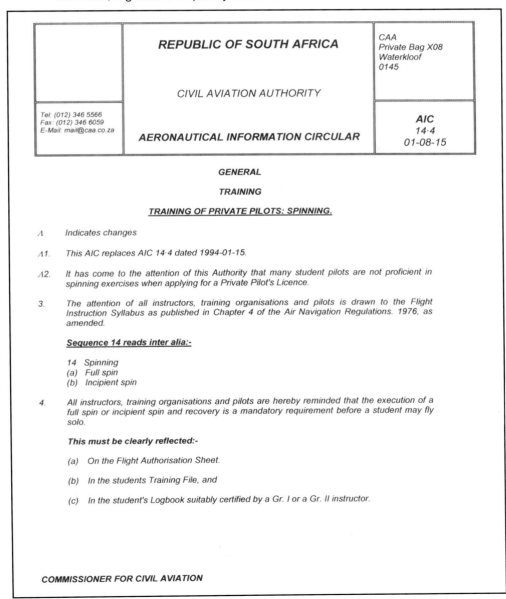

	REPUBLIC OF SOUTH AFRICA	CAA *Private Bag X08* *Waterkloof* *0145*
	CIVIL AVIATION AUTHORITY	
Tel: (012) 346 5566 Fax: (012) 346 6059 E-Mail: mail@caa.co.za	**AERONAUTICAL INFORMATION CIRCULAR**	**AIC** *14·4* *01-08-15*

GENERAL

TRAINING

TRAINING OF PRIVATE PILOTS: SPINNING.

Λ   *Indicates changes*

Λ1.   *This AIC replaces AIC 14·4 dated 1994-01-15.*

Λ2.   *It has come to the attention of this Authority that many student pilots are not proficient in spinning exercises when applying for a Private Pilot's Licence.*

3.   *The attention of all instructors, training organisations and pilots is drawn to the Flight Instruction Syllabus as published in Chapter 4 of the Air Navigation Regulations. 1976, as amended.*

Sequence 14 reads inter alia:-

14 Spinning
(a) Full spin
(b) Incipient spin

4.   *All instructors, training organisations and pilots are hereby reminded that the execution of a full spin or incipient spin and recovery is a mandatory requirement before a student may fly solo.*

This must be clearly reflected:-

(a) On the Flight Authorisation Sheet.

(b) In the students Training File, and

(c) In the student's Logbook suitably certified by a Gr. I or a Gr. II instructor.

COMMISSIONER FOR CIVIL AVIATION

Figure 7.1 AIC Issued by the Civil Aviation Authority of South Africa.

Representative PPL - type questions to test your theoretical knowledge of Aeronautical Information Services (ICAO).

1.   Contracting States are responsible for providing an Aeronautical Information Service for the operational requirements of:

    a.   Flight Crew only
    b.   Operational staff only
    c.   Those involved in Flight Operations (including flight crew), flight planning, flight simulators and the ATSU responsible for pre-flight information
    d.   All flight crew, ATC and Operations staff

2.   What are the names of the 3 parts of an AIP?

    a.   AGA, AD and GEN
    b.   ENR, AGA and GEN
    c.   ENR, AD and AGA
    d.   GEN, ENR and AD

3.   What kind of information is contained in a NOTAM?

    a.   Information of permanent changes only
    b.   Temporary and short-termed information only
    c.   Temporary changes of long duration which are made at short notice
    d.   Information of permanent changes, temporary and short-term information and temporary changes of long duration which are made at short notice

4.   What information is contained in a Pre-Flight Information Bulletin (PIB)?

    a.   NOTAMS and local operational information relevant to a particular aerodrome
    b.   Information of major changes (e.g. the introduction of a new airway)
    c.   Details of Danger, Restricted and Prohibited Areas within the UK
    d.   Information of general interest to pilots (e.g. information with regards to low level turbulence or altimeter errors)

5.   How is information of a purely explanatory or advisory nature published?

    a.   In a NOTAM
    b.   In an Aeronautical Information Circular
    c.   In an AIRAC
    d.   In an Pre-Flight Information Bulletin

Question	1	2	3	4	5
Answer					

The answers to these questions can be found at the end of this book.

CHAPTER 8
SEPARATION (ICAO)

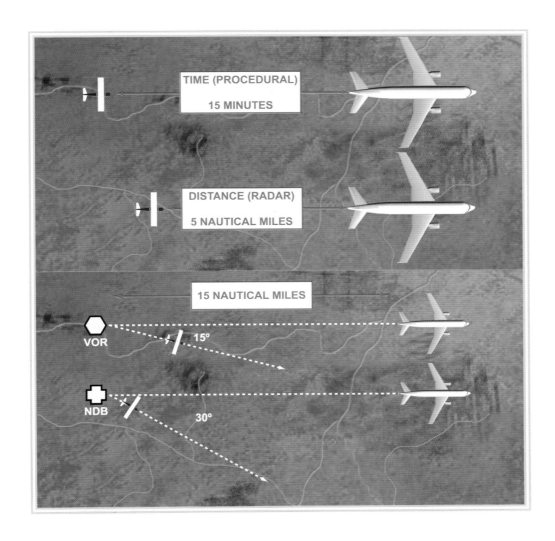

SEPARATION (ICAO).

General.
A broad definition of separation is the minimum distance or time between two aircraft that are either occupying the same altitude or Flight Level or climbing/descending through the same altitude or Flight Level.

However, there are times when it is possible that two aircraft may get so close to each other that one could be affected by the wake vortices of the other. This could happen on landing or taking-off, when both aircraft are using the same runway. In such a case, a mandatory minimum safety distance, or time, is laid down by the Authorities. This type of separation is called Wake Turbulence Separation. Wake Turbulence Separation is covered at the end of this Chapter.

TYPES OF SEPARATION.

There are three types of separation for IFR flights:

• Vertical Separation.

• Horizontal Separation which is subdivided into:

  a. Longitudinal Separation.

  b. Lateral Separation.

• Composite Separation.

SCOPE OF THIS CHAPTER.

Vertical Separation is covered in Chapter 2 ICAO Rules of the Air. Composite Separation is not included in the syllabus for the Private Pilot, so will not be dealt with here. This chapter limits itself to coverage of ICAO Horizontal Separation and ICAO Wake Turbulence Separation.

HORIZONTAL SEPARATION.

As stated above, Horizontal Separation is sub-divided into Longitudinal and Lateral Separation.

LONGITUDINAL SEPARATION.

General.
Longitudinal Separation can either be based on time (Procedural) or distance (when the aircraft is under the Radar Control).

Longitudinal Separation Based on Time (Procedural).

The normal minimum longitudinal separation between two aircraft following the same track is 15 minutes.

Longitudinal Separation Based on Distance (Radar).

The normal minimum longitudinal radar separation between two aircraft following the same track is 5 nautical miles.

Note: Separation can be reduced under certain circumstances.

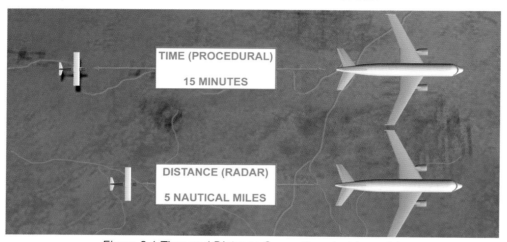

Figure 8.1 Time and Distance Separations (not to scale).

LATERAL SEPARATION.

Lateral Separation is based upon time only, and depends on the radio navigation aid that the two aircraft which are to be separated from each other are using.

Separation for aircraft using VOR and NDB is as follows:

VOR   15° at 15 nautical miles
NDB   30° at 15 nautical miles

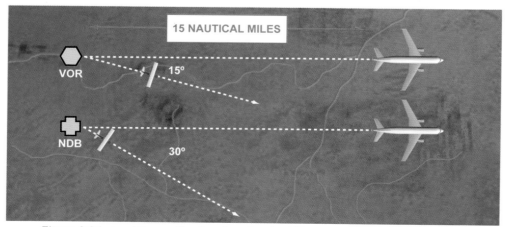

Figure 8.2 Lateral Separation for aircraft using VOR and NDB Navigational Aids.

If the aircraft are not using a navigational aid, but are navigating according to Dead Reckoning (DR) principles, lateral separation is increased to 45° at 15 nautical miles.

WAKE TURBULENCE SEPARATION.

When is Wake Turbulence Separation Applied?
Wake Turbulence Separation is applied under the following circumstances:

- When two aircraft are using the same runway, either for take-off or landing.

- Whenever the following aircraft is at the same height as, or less than 1 000 feet below, the leading aircraft.

Note: The pilot is always responsible for the safety of the aircraft and should add either further distance or time to the allocated separation factors if there is concern that the wake turbulence separation allowed by Air Traffic Control is not sufficient.

The pilot is always responsible for the safety of the aircraft and should add either distance or time if there is concern that, due to circumstances, the wake turbulence separation allowed for by Air Traffic is not sufficient.

Types of Wake Turbulence Separation.
Similarly to Longitudinal Separation, Wake Turbulence Separation can either be based on time (Procedural) or distance (when the aircraft is under the control of Radar).

Wake Turbulence Categories of Aircraft.
Since the severity of the wake turbulence is a factor of aircraft mass, the amount of separation time or distance is based upon the Wake Turbulence Category of the aircraft concerned. The categories are as follows:

Wake Turbulence Category of Aircraft	Minimum Take-Off Mass
Heavy	136 000 kgs and above
Medium	Below 136 000 kgs and above 7 000 kgs
Light	7 000 kgs and below

Wake Turbulence Categories:

Heavy
136 000 kgs and above.

Medium
Below 136 000 kgs and above 7 000 kgs.

Light
7 000 kgs and below.

Wake Turbulence Separation on Departure.
On departure, Wake Turbulence Separation is the minimum time from when the leading aircraft becomes airborne to the time when the following aircraft becomes airborne.

On departure, then, Wake Turbulence Separation is based only upon time (Procedural) and will depend on whether:

- Both aircraft are departing from the same point on the runway,

or

- the following aircraft is departing from an intermediate point of the runway.

A light aircraft taking off behind a heavy aircraft, and departing from the same point on the runway should allow a minimum of 2 minutes Wake Turbulence Separation.

If both aircraft are departing from the same runway, the Wake Turbulence Separation is as follows:

Leading Aircraft	Following Aircraft	Separation Minima
Heavy	Medium or Light	2 minutes
Medium	Light	2 minutes

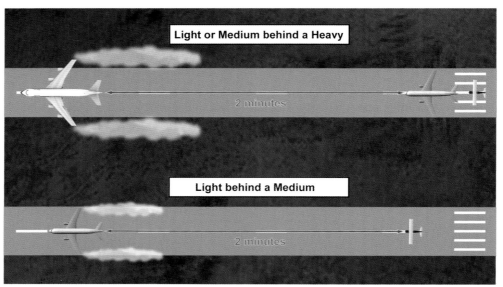

Figure 8.3 Both aircraft departing from the same point on a runway.

If the "following" aircraft is departing from an intermediate point on the runway, Wake Turbulence Separation is as follows:

Leading Aircraft	Following Aircraft	Separation Minima
Heavy	Medium or Light	3 minutes
Heavy or Medium	Light	3 minutes

A light aircraft taking off from an intermediate point on a runway behind a medium or heavy aircraft should allow at least 3 minutes separation.

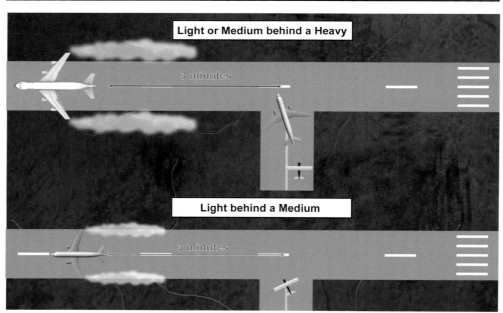

Figure 8.4 Following aircraft departing from an Intermediate point on the runway.

ARRIVING AIRCRAFT.

General.
Wake Turbulence Separation for arriving aircraft can be of two types:

- Procedural (non-radar): Wake Turbulence Separation which is measured in time.

- Radar: Wake Turbulence Separation which is measured in distance: provided to aircraft under radar control.

Procedural (non-radar) Wake Turbulence Separation.
The following times apply:

Leading Aircraft	Following Aircraft	Separation Minima
Heavy	Medium	2 minutes
Medium or Heavy	Light	3 minutes

Radar Wake Turbulence Separation.
Under **radar** separation, the following distances apply:

Leading Aircraft	Following Aircraft	Separation Minima
Heavy	Heavy	4 nautical miles
Heavy	Medium	5 nautical miles
Heavy	Light	6 nautical miles
Medium	Light	5 nautical miles

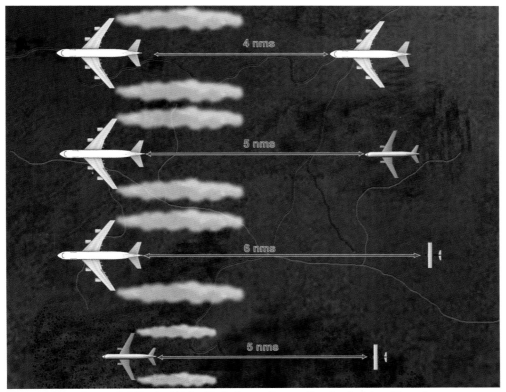

Figure 8.5 Radar Wake Turbulence Separation for Arriving Aircraft.

If the separation between yourself and a heavier aircraft is causing you concern, you must request clearance from Air Traffic Control to increase the separation minima.

REMEMBER !!

If the separation between yourself and a heavier aircraft is causing you concern, you must request clearance from Air Traffic Control to increase the separation minima.

Reduced Separation.

All the separation minima dealt with in this chapter may be reduced under certain circumstances.

Representative PPL - type questions to test your theoretical knowledge of Separation (ICAO).

1. A light aircraft is entering a runway from an intermediate point, following a heavy aircraft which is taking-off. What is the minimum wake turbulence separation which must be applied?

    a.   1 minute
    b.   2 minutes
    c.   3 minutes
    d.   4 minutes

2. ICAO divides separation into three types. These are:

    a.   Lateral, Longitudinal and Vertical
    b.   Vertical, Longitudinal and Composite
    c.   Vertical, Lateral and Composite
    d.   Vertical, Horizontal and Composite

3. What is the normal minimum longitudinal radar separation between two aircraft following the same track?

    a.   5 nautical miles
    b.   5 minutes
    c.   15 minutes
    d.   10 nautical miles

4. Which of the following statements is true?

    a.   Procedural (non-radar) wake turbulence separation is measured in distance
    b.   Radar wake turbulence separation is measured in time
    c.   Radar separation is normally closer than procedural separation
    d.   Procedural separation is normally closer than radar separation

5. What is the normal minimum longitudinal non-radar separation between two aircraft following the same track?

    a.   15 nautical miles
    b.   15 minutes
    c.   10 nautical miles
    d.   10 minutes

6. What is the minimum lateral separation between two aircraft using the same VOR?

    a.   15° at 15 nautical miles
    b.   30° at 15 nautical miles
    c.   45° at 15 nautical miles
    d.   30° at 20 nautical miles

7.   In which of the following circumstances is wake turbulence separation applied?

   a.   When operating below 700 feet, on finals
   b.   Whenever the following aircraft is at the same height as, or less than 1 000 feet above the leading aircraft
   c.   Whenever the following aircraft is at the same height as, or less than 1 000 feet below the leading aircraft
   d.   Whenever the following aircraft is at the same height as, or less than 500 feet below the leading aircraft

8.   What is the Maximum Take-Off Mass of a medium category aircraft in terms of its Wake Turbulence Category?

   a.   Between 136 000 kgs and 7 000 kgs inclusive
   b.   Below 136 000 kgs and above 7 000 kgs
   c.   Below 130 000 kgs and above 7 000 kgs
   d.   Below 136 000 kgs and above 8 000 kgs

9.   If the pilot of a following aircraft is concerned about the separation he has been given by ATC, what action should be taken?

   a.   None. ATC are solely responsible for separation between aircraft and have their own safety factors built in to separation minima
   b.   The pilot should inform ATC about his concern and receive clearance to increase the separation between the two aircraft
   c.   The pilot must increase the separation between the two aircraft. There is no need to inform ATC since the pilot ultimately is responsible for the safety of the aircraft
   d.   The pilot must decrease the separation between the two aircraft. There is no need to inform ATC since the pilot ultimately is responsible for the safety of the aircraft

10.   What is the minimum wake turbulence separation between a light aircraft taking off behind a heavy aircraft from the same point on the runway?

   a.   5 minutes
   b.   5 nautical miles
   c.   2 minutes
   d.   2 nautical miles

Question	1	2	3	4	5	6	7	8	9	10
Answer										

The answers to these questions can be found at the end of this book.

CHAPTER 9
AERODROMES

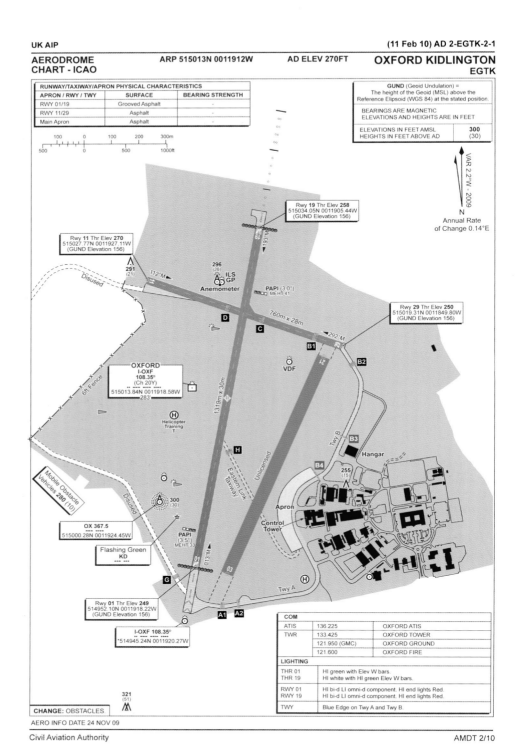

Figure 9.1 The aerodrome layout is, basically, divided into the Movement Area, the Apron, and the Manouevring Area.

INTRODUCTION.

The definition of "aerodrome" is given in Annex 14 to the Convention on International Civil Aviation (Chicago).

An aerodrome is a defined area on land or water (including any buildings, installations, and equipment) intended to be used either wholly or in part for the arrival, departure and surface movement of aircraft.

Aerodrome is also defined in Section 105 of the UK Civil Aviation Act 1982. That definition reads:

(The word aerodrome) "...means any area of land or water designed, equipped, set apart or commonly used for affording facilities for the landing and departure of aircraft and includes any area or space, whether on the ground, on the roof of a building or elsewhere, which is designed, equipped or set apart for affording facilities for the landing and departure of aircraft capable of descending or climbing vertically."

Those aerodromes where flights for the purpose of public transport operations and/ or flying training take place must be licensed, except for training operations by light aircraft and helicopters under the provision of the Air Navigation Order and JAR FCL 1.

In the United Kingdom, the CAA is responsible for ensuring that the holders of an aerodrome licence are competent and suitable persons to exercise the privileges of that licence.

Many **aerodromes** do not need a licence to carry out flying activities, although, in the United Kingdom, the CAA is still responsible for all matters affecting the safety of aircraft at **aerodromes** through its regulation of aircraft operations and maintenance.

The three basic divisions of an aerodrome are: the apron, the manoeuvring area, and the movement area.

Basic Definitions.
The basic division of an aerodrome layout is covered by three terms: the apron, the movement area and the manoeuvring area. *(See Figure 9.1, opposite.)*

The Apron.
The apron is a defined area on an aerodrome, intended to accommodate aircraft for purposes of loading or unloading passengers, mail, cargo, fuelling, parking or maintenance.

The Movement Area.
The **movement area** is part of an aerodrome which is used for the take-off, landing or taxiing of aircraft, consisting of the manoeuvring area and the apron(s).

The Manoeuvring Area.
The manoeuvring area is that part of an aerodrome which is used for the take-off, landing and taxiing of aircraft, excluding aprons.

CONDITIONS OF THE MOVEMENT AREA AND RELATED FACILITIES.

Information.

Up-to-date information on the conditions of the Movement Area and the operational status of related facilities is provided to Flight Information Service units so that this information can be passed to departing and arriving aircraft. Information on the movement area includes:

- Construction or maintenance work.

- Rough or broken surfaces on a runway, taxiway or apron.

- Snow, slush or ice on a runway, taxiway or apron.

- Water on a runway, taxiway or apron.

- Snow banks or drifting snow on a runway, taxiway or apron.

- Anti-icing or de-icing liquid chemicals on a runway or taxiway.

- Other temporary hazards including parked aircraft.

- Failure or irregular operation of part or all of the aerodrome visual aids.

- Failure of the normal or secondary power supply on a runway, taxiway or apron.

Water on a Runway.

Whenever water is present on a runway, a description of the runway surface conditions must be made available using the following terms:

- **DAMP** - the surface shows a change of colour due to moisture.

- **WET** - the surface is soaked but there is no standing water.

- **WATER PATCHES** - significant patches (25% of runway) of standing water are visible.

- **FLOODED** - extensive standing water is visible.

VISUAL AIDS FOR NAVIGATION.

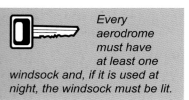
Every aerodrome must have at least one windsock and, if it is used at night, the windsock must be lit.

Wind Direction Indicators (Windsocks).

Every aerodrome must have at least one windsock and, if the aerodrome is to be used at night, the windsock must be lit.

Landing Direction Indicator (T).

The landing 'T' is used to indicate the direction in which an aircraft is to land.

- Where provided, a landing direction indicator should be located in a conspicuous place on the aerodrome.

- Landings must be made made along the vertical of the 'T' towards the crossbar.

- If it is to be used by night, the landing indicator must either be illuminated or outlined by white lights.

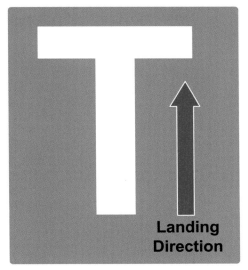

Figure 9.2 Landing Direction Indicator.

Signalling Lamp.

A signalling lamp must be provided at a controlled aerodrome in the aerodrome Control Tower. The signalling lamp is normally used for signalling messages to aircraft, in the event of loss of radio communications.

The lamp is hand-held and is capable of either shining a coloured steady light or emitting coloured flashes in red, white or green.

The signalling lamp must be capable of being aimed manually at any target required and must also be capable of transmitting a message, in any of the 3 colours, by Morse Code up to a speed of at least 4 words a minute.

Figure 9.3 A signalling lamp.

SIGNALS PANELS AND SIGNALS SQUARE.

Location.

The signals square should be located so as to be seen clearly from the air when viewed from a height of 300 m and should be surrounded by a white border. The signalling area must be on an even, horizontal surface.

The absence of a signal area at an aerodrome normally signifies that, except in an emergency, only radio-equipped aircraft are accepted. *(See Figure 9.4, overleaf.)*

Figure 9.4 Tower and Signals Square.

AERODROME MARKINGS.

Colours and Conspicuity.

- Runway markings are white. *(See Figure 9.5 et seq.)*

- Taxiway markings are yellow. *(See Figures 9.11.)*

- Apron safety lines are of any conspicuous colour which contrasts with that used for aircraft stand markings.

- At aerodromes where operations take place at night, all markings should be made with reflective materials.

The absence of a signals square at an aerodrome signifies that, except in an emergency, only radio equipped aircraft are accepted.

RUNWAY MARKINGS.

Runway Designation Markings.

Runway designation markings for single runways consist of a 2-digit number which indicates the direction of take-off and landing to the nearest 10° with reference to magnetic north. For example, a runway designated as Runway 23 would be aligned in the direction 230° Magnetic, to the nearest 10°. This means that an aircraft

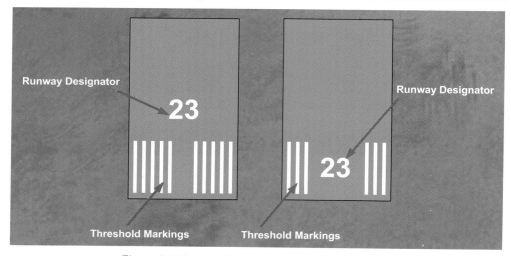

Figure 9.5 Runway Designators for single runways.

taking off from, or approaching to land on Runway 23 would have 230°, or nearly so, indicated on the magnetic compass, provided there was no crosswind component. If a runway designated Runway 23 were being used for take-offs and landings in the opposite direction, the runway would be designated Runway 05, that is, 180° from 230° Magnetic. Runway alignment is sometimes referred to as runway heading.

Runway designation markings are located at the threshold of a runway, either above or among the threshold markings, as shown in *Figure 9.5, previous page*.

Runway markings are coloured white.

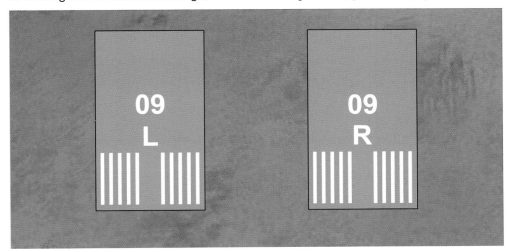

Figure 9.6 Runway designators for parallel runways, left and right.

Runway designation markings for parallel runways are supplemented by a letter. For a dual parallel runway, the letters would be: **L = Left R = Right**, as shown in *Figure 9.6*. If an aerodrome has three parallel runways, such as Los Angeles International, the centre runway would carry the letter C.

Runway Centre-Line Marking.
All paved runways are provided with centre-line markings, consisting of uniformly spaced white stripes and gaps.

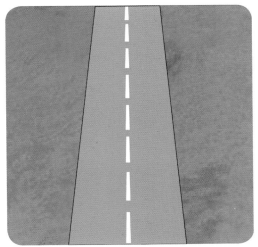

Figure 9.7 Runway centre-line markings.

Threshold Marking.

Threshold marking consists of a pattern of longitudinal stripes. The number of stripes varies with the runway width.

Transverse Stripe & Displaced Thresholds.

To indicate that the threshold is displaced from the end of the runway, a white transverse stripe is placed immediately in front of the threshold markings, thus creating a pre-threshold area.

A transverse white stripe marking on a runway signifies a displaced threshold.

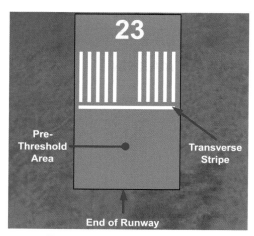

Figure 9.8 Displaced threshold.

Pre-threshold Area .

Various markings may be used on the pre-threshold area. The most important are as follows:

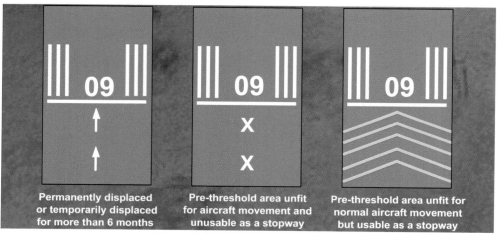

Figure 9.9 Pre-threshold markings.

Touchdown and Aiming Point.

The Touchdown Zone markings consist of one or more pairs of conspicuous white stripes on instrument runways, between 300 m and 400 m from the threshold (depending on the length of the runway). The Aiming Point markings, a pair of

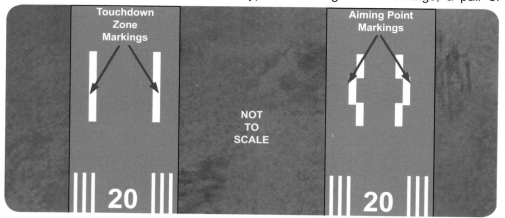

Figure 9.10 Touchdown zone and aiming point markings.

staggered white stripes, will usually be marked in conjunction with one or more pairs of Touchdown Zone markings, again depending on runway length.

TAXIWAY MARKINGS.

Figure 9.11 Taxiway centre-line and edge markings.

In general, taxiway markings are yellow in colour and consist, principally, of centre-line, runway holding position, and edge markings.

Taxiway Centre-Line Marking.
The taxiway centre-line marking is a continuous yellow line. A pilot should taxi his aircraft on the centre-line unless there is a good reason not to. With the aircraft on the centre-line, the aircraft's wing tips should be clear of any obstacles. It is the pilot's responsibility to avoid conflicting with other traffic.

Taxiway Edge Markings.
Taxiway edge markings should be used whenever it is necessary to separate a taxiway from a pavement that is not intended for aircraft use, or to mark the edge of a taxiway which is not otherwise clearly visible.

Runway Holding Position Markings.
To protect aircraft on take-off and landing, runway holding position markings are located on all taxiways that lead into a runway. Taxiing aircraft must not cross holding position markings without permission from ATC, nor until the pilot has checked that the approach is clear. There are two different runway position markings: Pattern A and Pattern B. *(See Figure 9.12.)*

Runway Holding Position Markings - Pattern A.
Pattern A markings consist of four yellow lines at right angles to the taxiway centre-line. The two lines nearer to the runway are broken. *(See Figure 9.12.)*

• Pattern A holding point markings are used if there is only one holding point.

A pair of parallel yellow lines together with a pair of parallel yellow broken lines across a taxiway marks a holding point just short of a runway entry point, beyond which an aircraft may not proceed without an ATC clearance.

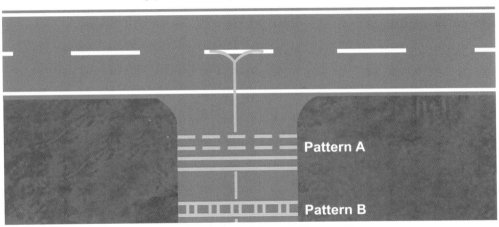

Figure 9.12 Runway holding position markings.

- When used in conjunction with Pattern B, Pattern A markings are always used to denote the holding point <u>closest</u> to the runway.

- The Pattern A marking is the holding point for all aircraft operating VFR.

- A pilot must always stop at a Pattern A holding point and proceed onto the runway only when cleared to do so by ATC, or if there is no ATC, when the pilot has ascertained that there is no conflicting traffic.

Runway Holding Point Markings - Pattern B.

Pattern B markings consist of 2 solid yellow lines at right angles to the taxiway centre-line, joined by cross lines to form a pattern which resembles a ladder. *(See Figure 9.12 previous page.)*

- Pattern B holding point markings are used if there is more than one holding position.

- The Pattern B holding point is the position further away from the runway, (normally for larger aircraft when low visibility operations are in progress).

Intermediate Holding Position Markings.

Intermediate holding position markings are used at the intersection of two paved taxiways in order to protect a priority taxiway. An intermediate holding position marking is a single broken yellow line. *(See Figure 9.13.)*

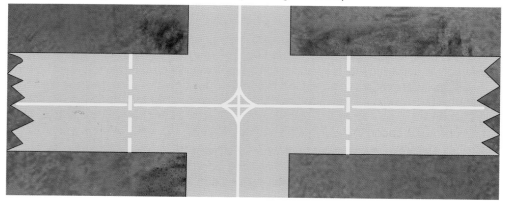

Figure 9.13 Intermediate holding position markings.

Apron Markings.

Apron markings, intended for the guidance of pilots are painted yellow.

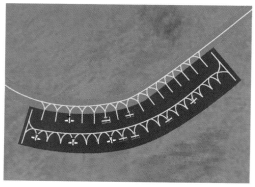

Figure 9.14 Apron markings.

AERODROME LIGHTING.

Light Signals are frequently used to pass information to pilots. Three colours are normally used: red, green and white.

Aerodrome Beacon.

An aerodrome beacon is provided for aerodromes intended for use at night in the following cases:

- Where information has to be passed to aircraft navigating predominantly by visual means.

- Where reduced visibilities are frequent.

- If it is difficult to locate the aerodrome due to surrounding lights or terrain.

Figure 9.15 Aerodrome beacons flashing either white, or green and white.

An aerodrome beacon indicates the location of an aerodrome but does not inform a pilot of its identity.

Aerodrome beacons flash either white or alternating green and white.

Identification Beacon.

An identification beacon identifies the aerodrome by flashing a two letter Morse Code identifier every 12 seconds.

An identification beacon is used at aerodromes which are intended to be used at night and cannot easily be identified by other means.

Beacon Flashing KD (Kidlington)

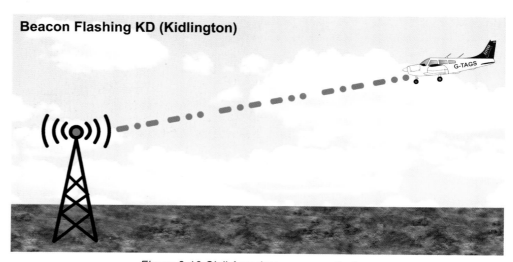

Figure 9.16 Civil Aerodrome - green flashes.

Military aerodrome identification beacons are red beacons flashing a 2-letter Morse Code identifier.

- Green flashes indicate a civil aerodrome.

Beacon flashing BZ (Brize Norton)

Figure 9.17 Military Aerodrome - red flashes.

- Red flashes indicate a military aerodrome.

Threshold Lighting.
Lights marking the runway threshold are fixed, unidirectional GREEN lights, showing in the direction of approach to the runway.

Runway End Lights.
The lights that indicate the end of the runway are fixed unidirectional RED lights.

Approach Slope Indicators.
Approach slope indicators help the pilot to establish his aircraft on a safe glideslope to land on the runway. The actual angle at which they are set is dependent on a number of

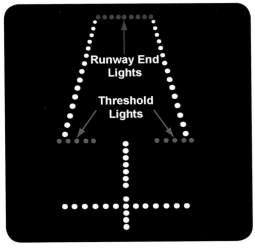

Figure 9.18 Threshold and End Lights.

Runway end lights are fixed unidirectional red lights, and threshold lights are fixed, unidirectional green lights, showing the direction of approach onto the runway.

factors (obstacles, topography, aerodrome layout etc.) but, normally, this angle is approximately 3° unless otherwise published. Approach slope indicators are permanent installations and tamper-free as far as it is possible. The three approach slope indicator systems that a Private Pilot may come across are:

- Visual Approach Slope Indictor (VASI). Very few aerodromes in the UK still use this system, but it can still be found.

- Precision Approach Path Indicator (PAPI).

- Abbreviated Precision Approach Path Indicator (APAPI).

Visual Approach Slope Indictor (VASI).
VASIs do not show an immediate change from white to red (or vice versa) but will show a transitional pink before turning fully red. A VASI system is shown in *Figure 9.19*.

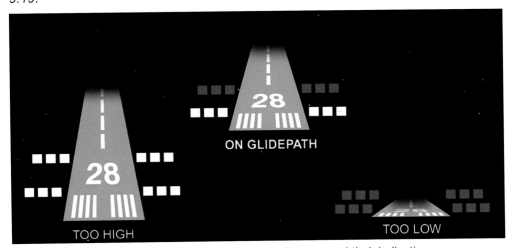

Figure 9.19 Visual Approach Slope Indicators, and their indications.

Precision Approach Path Indicator (PAPI).

- PAPI lights will turn almost immediately from red to white (and vice versa).

- When on the correct approach angle, the two lights closest to the runway will show red and the two furthest away will be white.

- The system of four lights will be located as a wing bar to the left of the runway threshold, but at large airports a PAPI set may be located either side of the runway.

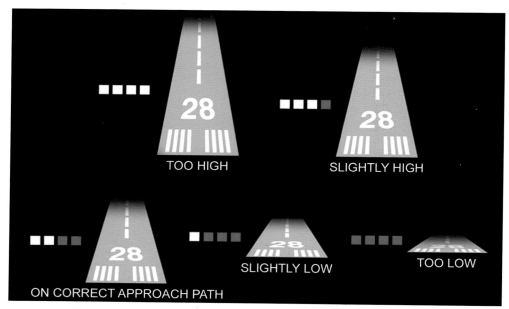

Figure 9.20 Precision Approach Path Indicators, and their indications.

Abbreviated Precision Approach Path Indicator (APAPI).

At smaller airfields, an abbreviated version of PAPIs may be found. With Abbreviated PAPI, instead of 4 lights, only 2 lights are used, as illustrated in *Figure 9.21*.

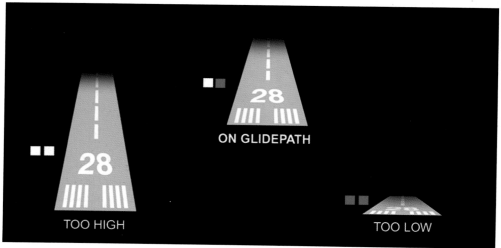

Figure 9.21 Abbreviated Precision Approach Path Indicators.

Runway Centre-Line and Edge Lights.

Runway centre-lights, which are installed at larger aerodromes, are colour coded to indicate runway distance remaining. Runway edge lights are white and are adjustable for brightness so that the pilot can ask ATC to increase or decrease the intensity.

Runway Approach Lights.

Runway approach lights are steady, unidirectional white lights, which can be adjusted for brightness, shining only in a narrow arc aligned with the approach. Runway approach lights normally consist of a centreline with a number of cross-bars. The centre-line extends from the threshold out to 500 metres, or 900 metres, and is designed to help the pilot line up with the runway centre-line. The cross-bars are designed to help the pilot orientate himself in the rolling plane, particularly as he regains visual contact with the runway, at the end of an instrument approach.

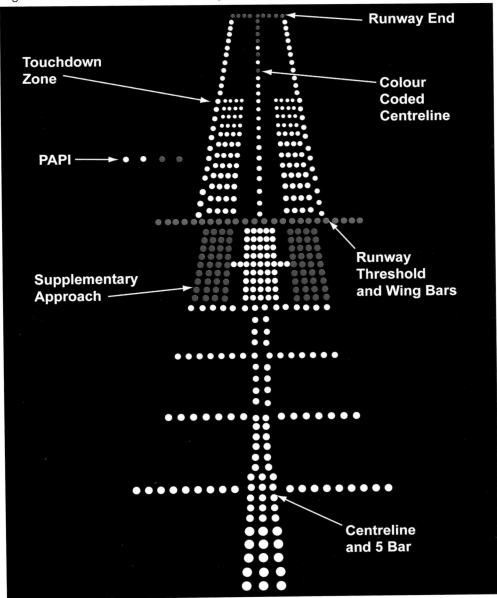

Figure 9.22 Lighting at a large aerodrome.

TAXIWAY LIGHTING.

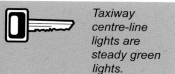

Taxiway centre-line lights are steady green lights.

Taxiway Centre-Line Lights.
Taxiway centre-line lights are steady green lights.

Runway/Taxiway Exit Centre Lights.
You should note that "exit taxiway" centre lights, leading from a runway, are initially green and yellow, changing to all green within the taxiway.

Taxiway Edge Lights.
Taxiway edge or side lights are coloured blue.

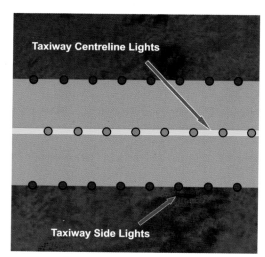

Figure 9.23 Taxiway Lights.

SIGNS.

General.

• All aerodrome signs are frangible. In other words, they are designed to break easily on impact.

• The only signs using the colour red are mandatory signs. Mandatory signs have a red background with the instruction superimposed in white lettering.

• All signs are retroflective or lit.

• The use of numbers alone on signs is reserved for runways.

• Location signs are depicted by yellow lettering on a black background, whereas destination signs have black lettering on a yellow background.

The following pages illustrate the most important aerodrome signs.

Mandatory Markings.
All mandatory markings consist of a white inscription on a red background. Mandatory markings normally mark lines which must not be passed without an ATC clearance. Examples of mandatory markings are:

• Runway holding position marking signs.

• Intermediate holding position signs.

• No entry signs.

Figure 9.24
No Entry Symbol (Top)
Holding Position.

Visual Runway Holding Position - denotes the visual Taxi-Holding Position and also the ILS CAT 1 Holding Position where the Visual and CAT 1 Holding Positions are co-located.

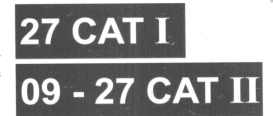

Mandatory aerodrome signs consist of white characters on a red background.

CAT 1/2 Runway Taxi-Holding Position Signs - denotes ILS CAT I/II Holding Position only where a visual Taxi-Holding Position is established closer to the runway in order to expedite traffic flow.

Intermediate Taxi-Holding Position Sign - marks a Holding Position established to protect a priority route.

No Entry Sign.

Note: You see above, figures referring to CAT I and CAT II. These signs refer to runways. Runways are categorised as CAT I, II or III according to the sophistication of the approach aids available.

Figure 9.25 Examples of Mandatory Airfield Signs.

Information, Location Signs and Destination Signs.

Location Signs.

Taxiway Location Sign identifying that the pilot is on taxiway A1.

Taxiway Ending Location Sign.

Runway Location Sign.

Figure 9.26a Examples of Airfield Location and Destination Signs.

Destination Signs.

Taxiway destination signs.

Runway destination sign.

Runway destination sign. Note the use of a hyphen to separate reciprocal designators.

Destination sign to different runways. Note the use of a dot to separate other designators.

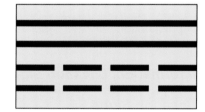

Runway vacated sign.

Figure 9.26b Airfield Information Signs.

MARKERS.

The most common markers on grass runways are boundary markers. Boundary markers are spaced at intervals along the boundary of the landing area.

Figure 9.27 Boundary Markers.

THE MARKING OF AERODROME OBSTACLES.

General.
An aerodrome obstacle is defined as any obstacle within 15 km of an aerodrome runway threshold.

- All obstacles on an aerodrome must either be marked (painted in a conspicuous colour/colours) or lit.

- Vehicles and other mobile objects are also considered to be obstacles and must be marked and lit.

- Aerodrome obstacles/obstructions are listed in the UK AIP (Aeronautical Information Publication), in the AD section.

- Instrument Approach and Landing charts also depict aerodrome obstacles.

Marking of Obstacles.

- All vehicles and moving objects must be coloured or must display flags.

- Normally, service vehicles are painted yellow. Emergency vehicles are most frequently coloured red, or, occasionally, yellowish green.

- Objects are painted either in a chequered pattern or in alternating bands of contrasting colours.

Lighting of Objects/Obstacles.

- Objects are usually lit as close to the top as possible.

- Obstacles may also be lit so as to indicate the edges of the obstacle.

- If an obstacle is over 45 m high, it may have a flashing red obstacle light at the highest points.

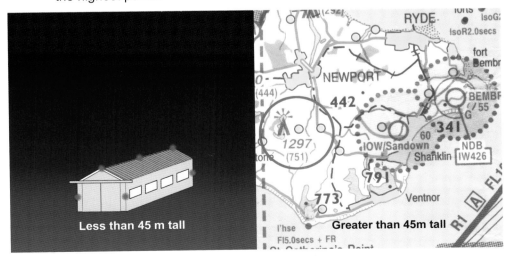

Figure 9.28 Obstacle Lights.

- In the UK, if obstacle lights fail on an obstacle with a height greater than 492 feet, the occurrence will be will be included in a NOTAM.

SIGNS FOR DENOTING AERODROME RESTRICTED USE AREAS.

Closed Runways.

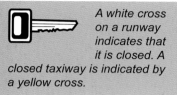

A white cross on a runway indicates that it is closed. A closed taxiway is indicated by a yellow cross.

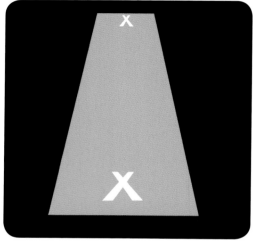

Figure 9.29 A Closed Runway.

Where a runway is permanently closed, a white X is placed at either end of the runway.

If only a section of the runway is closed, a white X is placed at the extremities of the closed section.

Closed Taxiways.

Where a taxiway is permanently closed, a yellow X is placed at either end of the taxiway. If only a section of the taxiway is closed, a yellow X is placed at the extremities of the closed section.

Figure 9.30 Closed Taxiway.

Temporarily Closed Runways or Taxiways.

If a runway or taxiway is closed temporarily, either breakable barriers are used or non-permanent surface markings to indicate this fact.

Other Markings.

When a runway or taxiway is permanently closed, all other normal runway and taxiway markings are obliterated.

Non-load Bearing Surfaces.

Where the surface is non-load bearing, yellow side stripes are used to delineate such an area, as depicted in *Figure 9.31*.

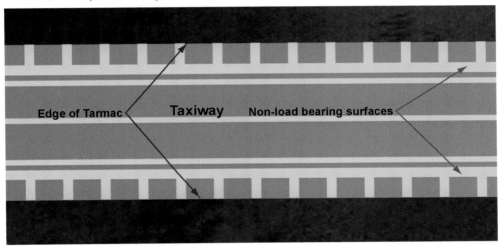

Figure 9.31 Non - Load Bearing Surfaces.

Other Unserviceable Areas.

Certain markers are used to indicate that an area is unserviceable, but that aircraft are still able to bypass it safely.

These can be:

- Markers (upstanding marker boards or cones), coloured red and white or orange and white vertical stripes. These markings will be in the form of vertical stripes, as shown in *Figure 9.32*.

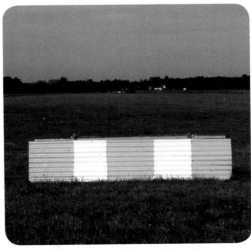

Figure 9.32 Marker Board.

- Marker lamps are normally low-intensity, steady red lights. These lamps are often called glim lamps.

Figure 9.33 Glim Lamp

- Cones marking unserviceable areas are normally coloured red, orange or yellow, or any one of these colours in combination with white.

Figure 9.34 Marker Cone

- Marker flags are normally coloured red, orange or yellow, or any one of these colours in combination with white.

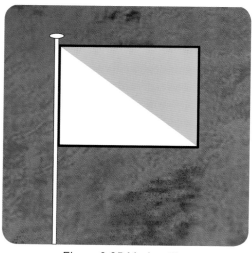

Figure 9.35 Marker Flag

AERODROME EMERGENCY & OTHER SERVICES.

FIRE & RESCUE SERVICES.

General.
Rescue and fire-fighting services are provided at all large aerodromes. All aerodromes have rescue and fire-fighting equipment.

Figure 9.36 Emergency Services.

Aerodrome Fire Stations.
Large aerodromes normally have their own fire station; however, an off-aerodrome station may provide fire cover if the prescribed response time can be met.

Figure 9.37 Fire Station at Kidlington, Oxon.

Response Time.
Emergency service response time is considered to be the time between the initial call-out and the time when the first responding vehicle is in position to apply foam anywhere on the movement area.

All rescue and fire fighting units should be able to achieve a response time of not exceeding 3 minutes.

Figure 9.38 Fire vehicles ready to respond.

Level of Protection.

The number of rescue and fire fighting vehicles held at an aerodrome is based upon the longest aeroplane using that aerodrome and its fuselage width.

Figure 9.39 Antonov An225.

Apron Management Service.

The apron management service is a service for controlling and regulating vehicle and aircraft movements, safely from, to, and within the apron areas.

Figure 9.40 A busy apron.

Normally, Aerodrome Control (the tower) is responsible for apron management service, but large aerodromes may have a separate apron organisation, with its own frequency and dedicated manpower and facilities.

The following two points are noteworthy:

•   An emergency vehicle responding to an emergency has priority over all other surface movements - including aircraft! Such a vehicle should be easily recognisable by its display of one or more flashing blue lights.

•   On the apron, vehicles will give way to emergency vehicles and aircraft which are taxiing, about to taxi or being pushed or towed.

Representative PPL - type questions to test your theoretical knowledge of Aerodromes (General).

1.   What colour are the markings on runways?

        a.   Yellow
        b.   Green
        c.   Yellow or white
        d.   White

2.   What is the colour of the markings on taxiways?

        a.   Yellow
        b.   Green
        c.   Yellow or white
        d.   White

3.   What is the definition of a "damp" runway?

        a.   The surface is soaked but there is no standing water
        b.   The runway has a shiny appearance due to the moisture
        c.   The surface shows a change of colour due to the moisture
        d.   The runway is affected by moisture but it is safe for landing
                operations

4.   A hand-held signalling lamp is to be held in Control Towers. What colours
        must it be capable of signalling?

        a.   White or red only
        b.   White, red or green
        c.   Green or red only
        d.   White, red, green or blue

5.   An aerodrome has no Signals Area. What does this imply?

        a.   It has no significance. Aerodromes may or may not have a Signals
                Area and the choice as to whether to have one or not is that of the
                owner of the Aerodrome
        b.   Except in an emergency no non-radio aircraft will be accepted
        c.   The aerodrome can only be used by day
        d.   Only IFR traffic is accepted

6.   What is the basic marking for a displaced threshold?

        a.   A yellow chevron marking at the end of the runway
        b.   Two white arrows at the end of the runway
        c.   A white transverse stripe
        d.   A single white arrow at the end of the runway

7. Which holding position is closest to the runway?

    a. Pattern 'A'
    b. Pattern 'B'
    c. Pattern 'C'
    d. Can be any of the above depending on the length of the runway

8. What colours indicate mandatory markings and signs?

    a. Yellow lettering on a black background
    b. Black lettering on a yellow background
    c. Red lettering on a white background
    d. White lettering on a red background

9. An Aerodrome Beacon flashes in what colour(s)?

    a. Green
    b. White
    c. Red
    d. White or green and white

10. What colour are threshold lights?

    a. Red
    b. Green
    c. Green threshold lights and red end lights
    d. Red and green

11. What colour are taxiway side lights?

    a. Red
    b. Green
    c. White
    d. Blue

12. What colour are taxiway centreline lights?

    a. Yellow
    b. Green
    c. Red
    d. Blue

13. How is a Location Sign depicted?

    a. Yellow lettering on a black background
    b. Black lettering on a yellow background
    c. Red lettering on a white background
    d. White lettering on a red background

14.   How is a closed runway indicated?

   a.   White cross
   b.   Yellow cross
   c.   With the use of barriers
   d.   The word "CLOSED" in white

15.   How is a non-load bearing surface to the side of a taxiway depicted?

   a.   A white side stripe
   b.   Yellow side stripes
   c.   A yellow or white side stripe
   d.   A yellow and white side stripe

16.   What is the Response Time for Fire and Rescue?

   a.   Not exceeding 1 minute
   b.   Not exceeding 2 minutes
   c.   Not exceeding 3 minutes
   d.   Not exceeding 5 minutes

17.   An emergency vehicle responding to an emergency will display what colour flashing light?

   a.   White
   b.   Green
   c.   Yellow
   d.   Blue

18.   An emergency vehicle responding to an emergency has priority over:

   a.   All vehicles
   b.   All aircraft only
   c.   All surface movements
   d.   It has no special priority

19.   All aerodromes must have:

   a.   At least 2 windsocks
   b.   At least 1 windsock
   c.   At least 1 windsock and a Landing 'T'
   d.   At least 2 windsocks and a Landing 'T'

20.   Runway approach lights are:

   a.   White and can be adjusted for brightness
   b.   White and cannot be adjusted for brightness
   c.   Red and can be adjusted
   d.   Red and cannot be adjusted

21.   Runway side lights are:

    a.   Green
    b.   White
    c.   Blue
    d.   Red

Question	1	2	3	4	5	6	7	8	9	10	11	12
Answer												

Question	13	14	15	16	17	18	19	20	21
Answer									

The answers to these questions can be found at the end of this book.

CHAPTER 10
UNITED KINGDOM AIR LAW
INTRODUCTION

SOURCES OF UK AVIATION LAW.

The primary sources of UK Air Law are the Civil Aviation Act of 1982 and the Airports Act of 1986 which have both been passed by Parliament.
From these two Acts stem:

The principal reference for UK Civil Aviation Law is CAP 393.

a.   The Air Navigation Order (ANO)
b.   Rules of the Air Regulations
c.   The Air Navigation (General) Regulations

For convenience these three documents, known as instruments, are published together by the CAA in the form of Civil Aviation Publication (CAP) 393.

The ANO is sub-divided into several Parts and Schedules, each dealing with a specific aspect of air navigation, such as: Registration and Markings of Aircraft, Aircraft Crew and Licensing, Air Traffic Services, Aerodrome Manual, Aircraft Equipment etc.

The Authority responsible for UK Civil Aviation is the United Kingdom Civil Aviation Authority.

THE AUTHORITY.

The Authority responsible for civil aviation in the United Kingdom (UK) is the Civil Aviation Authority (CAA) based at 45 - 49 Kingsway, London, WC2B 6TE.

THE AERONAUTICAL INFORMATION PUBLICATION (AIP).

The fine detail of air law, regulations and specific procedures within the UK are published in the Aeronautical Information Publication (AIP). The AIP is dealt with in detail in Chapter 15. The AIP should be the first source of information for any query the pilot may have.

CHAPTER 11
UNITED KINGDOM
RULES OF THE AIR

RULES OF THE AIR.

INTRODUCTION.

In Chapter 2, which deals with ICAO Rules of the Air, you learnt that the Rules of the Air which apply in any contracting ICAO state, of which the United Kingdom is one, follow, in general, the internationally agreed ICAO standards for Rules of the Air, as laid down in Annex 2 of the 'Convention on International Civil Aviation', known commonly as ICAO Annex 2. You learnt, too, that if there is a difference between the ICAO Rules of the Air and the Rules of the Air of the state in the airspace of which an aircraft is flying, the pilot must comply with that state's Rules of the Air.

This chapter deals with those Rules of the Air promulgated by the Parliament of the United Kingdom which may differ in some respect to the general ICAO-established Rules of the Air. You will inevitably, however, find material in this chapter which has already been dealt with in Chapter 2 because Rules of the Air cannot be dealt with in an entirely piecemeal fashion.

In general, if a Rules of the Air topic is not mentioned in this chapter, but is covered in Chapter 2, the ICAO Rule of the Air will apply in the United Kingdom, too.

A United Kingdom-based student should note that in the theoretical knowledge examination on Air Law for the JAR-FCL PPL, although he may reasonably expect all questions to be relevant to flying in the United Kingdom, questions will normally refer to ICAO Rules of the Air unless the wording of a question specifically refers that question to a United Kingdom Rule.

As far as the United Kingdom is concerned, at the present time, the UK Civil Aviation Authority's current policy (February 2007) is as expressed in the Preface to this book. That is: in the current UK Civil Aviation Authority JAR-FCL PPL theoretical knowledge examinations for Air Law & Operational Procedures, while the Air Law questions are, for the most part, based on ICAO Air Law, there are some questions on UK Air Law. Where UK Air Law differs from ICAO Air Law, these questions are annotated with 'UK Law' at the beginning of the relevant questions.

Students should make sure that they keep abreast of UK CAA policy on this issue.

Because individual states may have Rules of the Air which are different from ICAO standard Rules and UK Rules, before flying over the territory of a state, other than the United Kingdom, it is the responsibility of the pilot to familiarise himself with any of that state's Rules of the Air which are different from those with which he has been used to complying.

Applicability of United Kingdom Rules of the Air.
The Rules of the Air as promulgated in the **United Kingdom Air Navigation Order** apply to:

- All aircraft flying within the UK and in the neighbourhood of an offshore installation with regards to Low Flying (Rules of the Air 5),

and

• all aircraft registered in the UK, wherever they may be, provided that the UK Rules of the Air do not contradict the Rules which apply in a state in whose airspace the UK-registered aircraft is flying.

Departure from the Rules of the Air.

Figure 11.1 The Rules of the Air as promulgated in the UK ANO apply to all aircraft flying in UK airspace.

A pilot-in-command may depart from the Rules of the Air in order to:

• Avoid immediate danger

> or to

• comply with the law of a country, other than the UK, in which the aircraft is operating.

Should a pilot depart from the Rules of the Air, he must, within 10 days, in writing, inform the Authority of the country in whose territory he was at the time of the departure from the Rules.

If a pilot was over the High Seas at the time of departure from the Rules, he must inform the UK CAA, in writing, within 10 days.

VISUAL FLIGHT RULES.

Introduction.

In the United Kingdom, civil flights must be conducted in accordance with either Visual Flight Rules or Instrument Flight Rules.

Flight in accordance with the **Visual Flight Rules (VFR)** is based on the principle that the pilot is able to manoeuvre and navigate his aircraft, and be able to avoid collision with other aircraft by visual reference to features outside the cockpit. More especially, when flying VFR, the pilot must be able to navigate his aircraft by reference to ground features. Consequently, VFR flight is permissible only in conditions where certain minimum values of visibility prevail, and where minimum separation distances from cloud can be maintained. Such conditions are called Visual Meteorological Conditions (VMC). It is the responsibility of the Pilot-In-Command to determine whether or not the prevailing VMC minima permit a flight to be made in accordance with VFR.

The VMC minima, which must prevail in order for VFR flight to take place, are determined by class of airspace, vertical position and airspeed. As you learnt in Chapter 5, the ICAO Airspace Classification System comprises seven classes of airspace, each specifying the minimum Air Traffic Service provided, the ATC clearance requirements, and the obligations on pilots. The UK has adopted the ICAO Airspace Classification System except that, for the time being, there is no Class B airspace in the UK.

Airspace Classes A, C, D & E are Controlled Airspace, and Airspace Classes F & G are Uncontrolled Airspace. The division and organisation of UK Airspace is covered in detail in Chapter 14.

VMC Minima for Flights Outside Controlled Airspace.
The VMC minima outside controlled airspace are as follows.

VMC MINIMA FOR FLIGHT OUTSIDE CONTROLLED AIRSPACE			
	Distance From Cloud		**Flight Visibility**
	Horizontal	Vertical	
At and Above Flight Level 100	1500 metres	1000 feet	8 kilometres
Below Flight Level 100 but above 3000 feet	1500 metres	1000 feet	5 kilometres
At or Below 3000 feet			
Indicated Airspeed (IAS) > 140 knots	Clear of cloud and in sight of the surface		5 kilometres
Indicated Airspeed (IAS) < 140 knots (Other than helicopters)	Clear of cloud and in sight of the surface		1500 metres*

* **N.B.** Basic PPL holders without an Instrument Rating or IMC Rating are not allowed to fly as PIC of an aircraft when the in-flight visibility is less than 3 kilometres.

VFR Flight in Uncontrolled Airspace and the PPL Holder.
It is important for you to understand the difference between the meaning of the terms Visual Flight Rules (VFR) and Visual Meteorological Conditions (VMC). The VMC minima are actual weather minima which are defined by horizontal and vertical separation from cloud distances. However, the term VFR applies to <u>rules</u> laid down by ICAO and agreed internationally. For VFR flight to take place, VMC must prevail, and pilots must be able to see the ground. Sometimes, the restricted privileges of a basic licence such as the Private Pilot's Licence (PPL) may impose more restrictive flight conditions on the PPL holder than those imposed by the VMC minima, alone. For instance, at or below an altitude of 3000 feet, VMC outside controlled airspace is described as 1500 metres in-flight visibility, clear of cloud and in sight of the surface. These VMC minima allow flight to be conducted in accordance with VFR. However, PPL holders who do not also hold an Instrument Rating or Instrument Meteorological Conditions (IMC) Rating are subject to certain <u>extra</u> restrictions imposed by Schedule 8 of the Air Navigation Order.

Notable among these extra restrictions are that a PPL holder who does not hold an Instrument Rating or IMC Rating may not fly as Pilot-In-Command of an aircraft on a flight outside controlled airspace when the visibility is less than 3 km.

Therefore, a PPL holder with no additional ratings cannot fly in the absolute VMC minima applicable to airspace below 3 000ft. In other words, the basic PPL holder requires a minimum in-flight visibility of 3 km; he may not fly, therefore, in a visibility of 1 500 metres, even though VMC minima are technically met. Furthermore, Schedule 8 of the Air Navigation Order stipulates that a basic PPL holder without an Instrument or IMC Rating may not fly out of sight of the surface.

In the United Kingdom no aircraft may fly in accordance with the Visual Flight Rules at night.

VMC Minima for Flights Within Controlled Airspace.

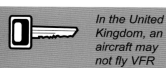

In the United Kingdom, an aircraft may not fly VFR at night.

When flying in controlled airspace (except Class E), unless otherwise authorised by the Air Traffic Control Unit (ATCU), the commander of aircraft flying in accordance with VFR must file a flight plan and obtain an ATC clearance. He must also maintain a listening watch on the appropriate frequency and comply with any instructions given by the ATCU. Under certain circumstances, the requirement to submit a flight plan may be satisfied by a pilot passing his flight details to the ATCU by radio, when airborne.

VFR is not permitted in Class A Airspace. However, if the Class A Airspace is a Control Zone (CTR), flights may be allowed with a Special VFR clearance.

VMC Minima within controlled airspace is shown below.

VMC MINIMA FOR FLIGHT WITHIN CONTROLLED AIRSPACE				
Class of Airspace	ATC Clearance Required	Distance From Cloud		Flight Visibility
		Horizontal	Vertical	
A	VFR FLIGHT NOT PERMITTED			
B (above FL 100)	Yes	Clear of cloud		8 kilometres
B (below FL 100)	Yes	Clear of cloud		5 kilometres
C (above FL 100)	Yes	1 500 metres	1 000 feet	8 kilometres
C (below FL 100)	Yes	1 500 metres	1 000 feet	5 kilometres
C (below 3000 feet) IAS < 140 knots	Yes	Clear of cloud and in sight of the surface		5 kilometres
D (above FL 100)	Yes	1 500 metres	1 000 feet	8 kilometres
D (below FL 100)	Yes	1 500 metres	1 000 feet	5 kilometres
D (below 3000 feet) IAS < 140 knots	Yes	Clear of cloud and in sight of the surface		5 kilometres
E (above FL 100)	No	1 500 metres	1 000 feet	8 kilometres
E (below FL 100)	No	1 500 metres	1 000 feet	5 kilometres
E (below 3000 feet) IAS < 140 knots	No	Clear of cloud and in sight of the surface		5 kilometres

You should be aware that the boundary between Lower Airspace (the FIR) and Upper Airspace (the UIR) in the United Kingdom and throughout Europe is under review and may soon be changed. Currently, this boundary is at Flight Level 245 in the United Kingdom.

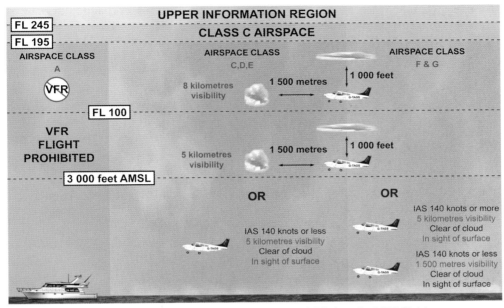

Figure 11.2 UK Airspace Classes and VMC Minima for VFR flight.

Note, however, that in the United Kingdom, all airspace above Flight Level 195 is Controlled Airspace, designated Class C, and VFR flight is not permitted unless specifically arranged as promulgated in the AIP ENR 1.1.4.

For all helicopters flying below 3 000 feet in Classes C, B and E Airspace, the VFR minima are "clear of cloud and in sight of surface".

Figure 11.2, above, is a pictorial summary of the VMC minima for VFR flights in all Classes of UK Airspace. Note that, currently, there is no Class B airspace in the UK.

N.B. Basic PPL holders without an Instrument Rating or IMC Rating are not allowed to fly in visibility lower than 3 kilometres.

Instrument Meteorological Conditions.
Weather minima which are below the VMC minima required for flight in accordance with VFR are defined as Instrument Meteorological Conditions (IMC).

INSTRUMENT FLIGHT RULES.

Introduction.
Flights not conducted in accordance with the Visual Flight Rules (VFR), must be conducted in accordance with the Instrument Flight Rules (IFR).

IFR Flight Outside Controlled Airspace.
You should note that a pilot does not have to hold an Instrument Rating in order to be able to fly according to IFR, outside controlled airspace. However, for UK JAR PPL holders JAR-FCL 1.175 prohibits flights under IFR, unless the pilot holds an Instrument Rating.

The UK CAA's Safety Sense Leaflet 8d; explains that "There is nothing mysterious about **IFR** within UK Airspace; they are there to ensure that you have adequate clearance from ground obstacles and that you are safely separated in the vertical plane, according to your magnetic track, from other aircraft in flight."

In the UK, regulations governing IFR flights outside controlled airspace are:

1. **Unless his aircraft is below an altitude of 3 000 feet clear of cloud and in sight of the surface, or as necessary for take-off and landing, a pilot flying in accordance with IFR must fly at least 1000 feet above the highest obstacle within 5 nautical miles of his aircraft.**

2. **If a pilot is in cruising level flight above 3 000 feet above mean sea level (AMSL), or Transition Altitude, whichever is the higher, he must fly at a Flight Level appropriate to his magnetic track, in accordance with the Quadrantal Rule.**

However, the holder of a JAA PPL may not fly in Instrument Meteorological Conditions (IMC) (i.e. in conditions which do not meet the VMC minima) unless he holds an Instrument Rating or an IMC Rating. Furthermore, a pilot may not fly in accordance with IFR in Controlled Airspace unless he holds an Instrument Rating.

The Quadrantal Rule.

Outside Controlled Airspace, (Class F and G), above an altitude of 3 000 feet, (Transition Altitude (TA) in the UK open FIR), an aircraft flying IFR, in level flight, must maintain adequate vertical separation from other IFR traffic by setting 1013 mb on his altimeter and flying at one of a series of Flight Levels determined by the aircraft's magnetic track, in accordance with the Quadrantal Rule.

The only exception to this requirement is when the aircraft is in a hold, following a published holding procedure, or is following instructions from an Air Traffic Control Unit. The Quadrantal Rule is illustrated in the table, and graphically, below, in *Figure 11.3*.

QUADRANTAL RULE	
Magnetic Track	**Flight Level (FL)**
360° but less than **090°**	**FL** 30, 50, 70, 90 etc, up to **FL 190**
090° but less than **180°**	**FL** 35, 55, 75, 95 etc, up to **FL 175**
180° but less than **270°**	**FL** 40, 60, 80, 100 etc, up to **FL 180**
270° but less than **360°**	**FL** 45, 65, 85, 105 etc, up to **FL 185**

Note:

• The Quadrantal Rule applies only below Flight Level 195 within United Kingdom Flight Information Regions outside Controlled Airspace. Flight Level 195 is not available as a cruising Flight Level. Below FL245, Quadrantal levels are only available for IFR traffic in active Temporary Restricted Airspace.

• It is not mandatory, in the UK, for VFR flights flying above 3 000 feet outside controlled airspace to comply with the Quadrantal Rule. However, VFR pilots are strongly advised to do so as the Quadrantal Rule may often be the only systematic way to ensure separation from other aircraft when flying above 3 000 feet.

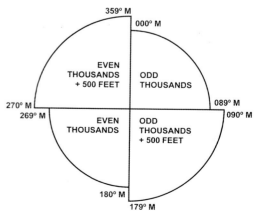

Figure 11.3 The Quadrantal Rule.

- Transition Level (TL), (which varies with ambient atmospheric pressure and will be physically between 0 and less than 500 feet above TA, but may, under high pressure conditions, be numerically less than altitude, eg FL25), is not available as a cruising level for reasons of vertical separation from traffic flying at TA. Minimum usable FL is TL + 500 feet. See Chapter 19.

IFR Flight Inside Controlled Airspace.

Within controlled airspace (Classes A to E), a pilot flying in accordance with the Instrument Flight Rules (IFR) must:

- Before proceeding with the flight, file a flight plan and obtain a clearance from the appropriate Air Traffic Control Unit (ATCU).

- Conduct the flight in accordance with clearances and instructions from the responsible ATCU.

- Maintain a listening watch on the appropriate radio frequencies.

- Report the position of the aircraft according to published procedures.

The Semi-Circular Rule.

Aircraft flying in controlled airspace in the United Kingdom in accordance with IFR, shall, unless instructed otherwise by an ATCU, fly at a cruising Flight Level determined by the aircraft's magnetic track, in accordance with the Semi-Circular Rule, as depicted in the table, and in *Figure 11.4*. **Please Note:**

1. FLs 10 and 20 are very unlikely to exist, being well below Transition Altitude; FL20 would require an atmospheric pressure in excess of 1050hPa/mb.

2. ICAO IFR semicircular levels are the same as UK levels, but differ for VFR above FL290, being 4 000 foot increments from FL300 for tracks 0 - 179deg, and from FL320 for tracks 180 - 359.

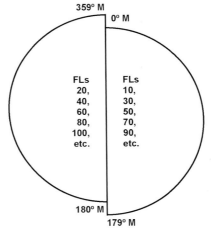

Figure 11.4 The Semi-Circular Rule.

SEMI-CIRCULAR RULE	
Magnetic Track 180° TO 359°	**Magnetic Track 000° TO 179°**
Flight Level (FL)	**Flight Level (FL)**
FL 20	FL 10
FL 40	FL 30
FL 60	FL 50
FL 80	FL 70
FL 100	FL 90
FL 120	FL 110
FL 140	FL 130
and so on, up to **FL 280**, then FL 310, and at 4 000ft intervals above.	and so on, up to **FL 290**, then at FL330, and at 4 000 foot intervals above.

FLIGHT IN CLASS A AIRSPACE.

No VFR flights are allowed in Class A Airspace. The only exceptions to this rule are:

- That gliders may cross certain notified sections of UK airways in Visual Meteorological Conditions (VMC). VMC in Class A is defined as: 8 kilometres flight visibility, 1 500 metres horizontally and 1 000 feet vertically clear of cloud.

- Under certain circumstances, aircraft may be cleared to enter Class A Control Zones (CTR) under Special VFR.

SPEED RESTRICTION.

In United Kingdom uncontrolled airspace there is a general speed restriction of 250 knots Indicated Airspeed applied to all aircraft flying VFR or IFR. This speed restriction also applies, in certain conditions, to traffic flying in some classes of controlled airspace. (See Chapter 14).

USE OF TRANSPONDERS.

Within the United Kingdom, no flight at or above Flight Level 100 may be conducted without a serviceable transponder, with both Modes A and C.

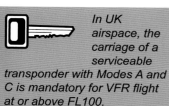

In UK airspace, the carriage of a serviceable transponder with Modes A and C is mandatory for VFR flight at or above FL100.

SPECIAL VFR (SVFR) IN THE UNITED KINGDOM.

General.

Generally speaking a Special VFR (SVFR) flight is a VFR flight cleared by an Air Traffic Control Unit (ATCU) to operate within a Control Zone (CTR) in meteorological conditions below VMC, or at night. An SVFR clearance may also be used by a private pilot with no instrument qualifications to enter and fly in a Class A CTR.

It is implicit in the clearance that a SVFR flight remains in sight of the surface and clear of cloud, at all times.

The rules concerning SVFR in the UK differ in substance from those stipulated by ICAO.

Rules and Conditions of SVFR.

An SVFR clearance may be requested without the submission of a filed flight plan and also whilst airborne. The pilot is required, however, to pass brief details of his flight to the appropriate ATCU. These details should include:

a. Aircraft call sign.

b. Aircraft type.

c. Pilot's intentions.

You should note, however, that a full Flight Plan must be submitted if the pilot wishes the destination aerodrome to be notified of the SVFR flight.

The following general rules and conditions apply to SVFR:

- SVFR is limited to a VFR flight within a CTR when unable to comply with IFR.

- If the departure aerodrome is in the vicinity of the CTR wishing to be entered, a request for a SVFR clearance may be made by telephone.

- All requests for SVFR flights into a CTR made over the radio or by telephone must specify the ETA for entering the CTR. A request by radio must be made between 5 and 10 minutes before entering the CTR.

- Pilots should assume that the ATCU may not be able to assure separation from all other aircraft and must, therefore, maintain a good lookout.

- An SVFR clearance will be granted only when traffic conditions permit the flight to take place without hindrance to normal IFR flights.

- Generally, a fixed wing aircraft will not be cleared to depart a CTR under SVFR when the visibility is 1 800 metres or less, and/or the cloud ceiling is less than 600 feet.

- Under an SVFR clearance a VFR pilot is not allowed to fly in a CTR when the visibility is less than 10 kilometres.

- The pilot is to remain at all times in conditions which will enable him to determine his flight path in order to avoid obstacles.

- When operating in accordance with SVFR the pilot must comply with ATC instructions.

- ATC may find it necessary to impose a height limitation on an SVFR flight.

- Pilots must not assume that an SVFR clearance into a CTR is a clearance into an ATZ within that CTR. Pilots will need to confirm with the appropriate ATC authority that they are, in fact, cleared into the ATZ concerned.

- An SVFR clearance absolves the pilot from the 1 000 feet Low Flying Rule but none of the other Low Flying Rules.

In-flight, in order to enter a CTR on an SVFR clearance, the visibility must be at least 10 kilometres.

LOW FLYING RULE (RULE 5).

General.
Where an aircraft is flying in circumstances such that more than one of the following prohibitions apply, it must fly at the greatest height required by any single prohibition.

Prohibitions.

Failure of a Power Unit.
An aircraft shall not be flown below such a height as would enable it, in the event of a power failure, to make an emergency landing without causing danger to persons or property on the surface.

The 500-feet Rule.
Except with the written permission of the CAA, an aircraft shall not be flown closer than 500 feet to any person, vessel, vehicle or structure.

The 1 000-feet Rule.

Where an aircraft is flying in circumstances such that more than one of the Low Flying prohibitions apply, the pilot must fly at the greatest height required by any of the prohibitions.

Except with the written permission of the CAA, an aircraft flying over a congested area of a city, town or settlement shall not fly below a height of **1 000 feet** above the highest fixed obstacle within a radius of **600 metres** of the aircraft. *(See Figure 11.5.)*

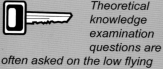

Theoretical knowledge examination questions are often asked on the low flying rules.

Figure 11.5 An aircraft shall not fly below 1000 feet above a congested area.

The Land Clear Rule.
An aircraft flying over a congested area of a city, town or settlement shall not fly below a height that will permit, in the event of a power failure, the aircraft to land clear of the congested area.

Flying Over Open Air Assemblies.
Except with the written permission of the CAA, an aircraft shall not fly over an organised open-air assembly of more than 1 000 persons below:

•   A height of 1 000 feet,

or

•   such height that will permit, in the event of a power failure, the aircraft to alight clear of the assembly, *whichever is the higher*.

Landing and Taking Off Near Open-Air Assemblies.
An aircraft shall not land or take off within 1 000 metres of an organised assembly of more than 1 000 persons except:

Figure 11.6 Flying over an organised open-air assembly is subject to the Low Flying Rule.

- At an aerodrome, in accordance with procedures notified by the CAA.

or

- At a landing site (other than an aerodrome), in accordance with procedures notified by the CAA and with written permission of the organiser of the assembly.

EXCEPTIONS TO LOW FLYING PROHIBITIONS.

Landing and Taking-off.

The following are exempt from all the above prohibitions, at a government or licensed aerodrome:

    a.   Aircraft landing and taking-off.

    b.   Aircraft practising approaches to land.

    c.   Aircraft checking navigational aids or procedures.

Special VFR (SVFR) and Notified Routes.

Aircraft flying in a Control Zone (CTR) at government or licensed aerodromes under SVFR or along notified routes, shall be exempt from the 1 000-feet Rule.

Note however that Aircraft are NOT exempt from the obligation to be able to land clear of a congested area in the event of a power failure.

When flying in a CTR on an SVFR clearance, an aircraft is exempt from the 1 000-feet Rule, but none of the other Low Flying Rules.

Balloons and Helicopters over Congested Areas.

- A balloon when landing but becalmed is exempt from the 1 000-feet Rule.

- Helicopters are exempt from the Land Clear Rule when over built up areas.

Flying Displays and Air Rules etc.

Aircraft taking part in a flying display, air race or contest are exempt from the 500-feet Rule when within 1 000 metres of the gathering or persons witnessing the event.

Figure 11.7 A fly-past at an air display.

Gliders Hill-Soaring.

Gliders, when hill-soaring, are exempt from the 500-feet Rule.

Picking Up and Dropping at an Aerodrome.

Any aircraft picking up or dropping tow-ropes, banners, or similar articles, at an aerodrome are exempt from the 500-feet Rule.

Manoeuvring Helicopters.

- Helicopters manoeuvring within the boundaries of a government or licensed aerodrome (or at other sites with the permission of the CAA) are exempt from the 500-feet Rule.

- Helicopters flying under the above exemption must not be operated closer than 60 metres to persons, vessels, vehicles or structures located outside the aerodrome or site.

Dropping Articles with CAA Permission.

- Any aircraft dropping articles as specified in the ANO (e.g. for the purposes of public health, such as measures against surface icing or oil pollution), and with the permission of the CAA, are exempt from the 500-feet Rule.

- Any aircraft dropping articles for agricultural, horticultural purposes (e.g. when crop spraying) must be issued with a Aerial Application Certificate by the CAA. These operations are also exempt from the 500-feet Rule.

Saving Life.

Nothing in the Low-Flying Rules shall prohibit an aircraft from flying in such a manner as is necessary for the purpose of saving life.

Figure 11.8 Crop Spraying.

SIMULATED INSTRUMENT FLIGHTS & PRACTICE INSTRUMENT APPROACHES.

Simulated Instrument Flights.

For simulated instrument flights, Instrument Meteorological Conditions (IMC) are simulated by placing screens in front of the handling pilot so that he cannot see through the windscreen or side windows. *(See Figure 11.9.)* Thus, the handling pilot has to fly solely with reference to the aircraft instruments.

An aircraft shall not be flown under simulated IMC in Visual Meteorological Conditions unless:

•   The aircraft is equipped with dual controls,

                        and

•   a qualified pilot occupies a second control seat to act as safety pilot. The safety pilot should have adequate vision forward, and to each side of the aircraft, in order to avoid collisions.

Figure 11.9 Simulated instrument flight.

Should the safety pilot have a restricted view, a competent observer in communication with the safety pilot shall occupy a position in the aircraft from which the observer's field of vision adequately supplements that of the safety pilot.

Practice Instrument Approaches.

A pilot wishing to carry out a practice instrument approach may only do so when:

- In VMC,

and

- carrying a competent observer with an adequate field of vision and in communication with the pilot flying the aircraft,

and

- having received clearance to do so by ATC.

DISPLAY OF LIGHTS BY AIRCRAFT.

In the event of a failure of any light required at night and which cannot be immediately repaired, an aircraft shall not depart from an aerodrome and shall land as soon as safe to do so, unless authorised by ATC to continue its flight.

The UK rules for lights displayed by aircraft are exactly the same as the ICAO rules, see Chapter 2, pages 33-38.

FAILURE OF NAVIGATION AND ANTI-COLLISION LIGHTS.

In the event of a failure of any light required to be shown at night, an aircraft:

- Must not depart from an aerodrome.

- Must land as soon as safe to do so, unless authorised by ATC to continue its flight.

If an anti-collision light fails, by day, an aircraft may continue its flight, provided that the light is repaired at the earliest practical opportunity.

If an anti-collision light fails by day, an aircraft may continue its flight, provided that the light is repaired at the earliest practical opportunity.

WEATHER REPORTS AND WEATHER MINIMA.

The Pilot-In-Command is responsible, prior to flight, for studying the current weather reports and forecasts of the en-route conditions, in order to determine whether Instrument Meteorological Conditions are likely to prevail during any part of the flight.

Furthermore any aircraft which is unable to communicate with the ATCU at the destination aerodrome shall not commence the VFR flight to a CTR if the weather at destination is forecasted to be, at the aircraft's ETA:

- Less than 10 kilometres visibility,

and

- less than 1 500 feet cloud ceiling, unless the permission of the ATCU at the destination is obtained.

RIGHTS OF WAY IN THE AIR AND ON TAKE-OFF AND LANDING.

The UK rules on collision avoidance and rights-of-way are, in general, the same as those of ICAO *(see Chapter 2)*. There are, however, some important differences and additions in the UK rules:

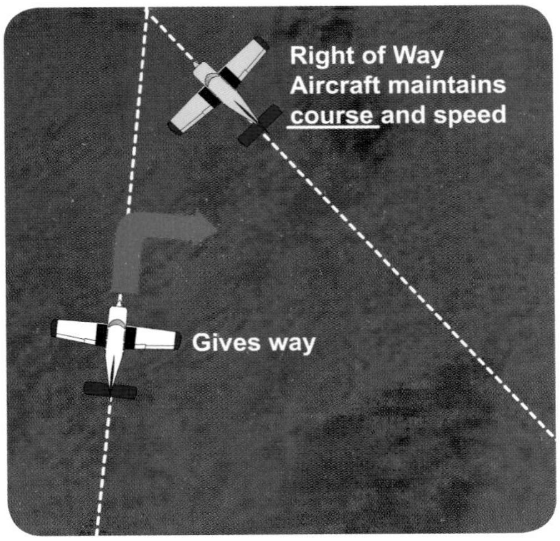

Differences.

When two aircraft, in the air, are on a converging course, the aircraft that has the right-of-way shall maintain its <u>course</u> and speed. The aircraft giving way in these circumstances with normally pass behind the priority aircraft, but must, in all cases, give way in a manner so as not to conflict or interfere with the aircraft having right-of-way.

Figure 11.10 The aircraft on the right has the Right of Way and maintains course and speed.

In the air, a **glider** may overtake another glider on either side.

Note: The ANO uses the word 'course'; this can be taken practically to mean heading, rather than the American meaning, equivalent to the UK term 'track'.

Additions.

The UK ANO states that when an Air Traffic Control Unit has communicated to any aircraft an order of priority for landing, the aircraft shall approach to land in that order.

When the pilot-in-command of a landing aircraft is aware that another aircraft is making an emergency landing, he will give way, notwithstanding that permission to land has been received. Having given way, the pilot is not to attempt to land until further permission has been received.

A flying machine, glider or airship must take-off and land in the direction indicated by ground signals or, in the absence of such signals, into wind, unless good aviation practice demands otherwise.

A flying machine or glider shall not land on a runway at an aerodrome if the runway is not clear of other aircraft, unless authorised by ATC.

Where take-offs and landings are not confined to a runway (e.g. on an area of grass):

   a.   When landing, a flying machine or glider is to leave clear on its LEFT any aircraft which has landed, is about to land, or about to take-off. When the landing is completed, the aircraft must make any turns to the LEFT.

   b.   A flying machine which is taking off must take up a position and manoeuvre in such a way as to leave clear on its LEFT any aircraft which has already taken off or is about to take-off.

c.   A flying machine towing a glider is considered to be one machine commanded by the Pilot-In-Command of the flying machine.

d.   A flying machine after landing must move clear of the landing area as soon as possible unless ATC authorises otherwise.

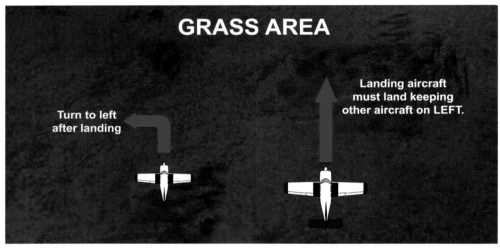

Figure 11.11 When landing, leave clear on the left an aircraft which has landed, is about to land or about to take off.

Right of Way on the Ground (Vehicles and Aircraft).

The following are the **rights of way** of aircraft and vehicles on the movement area of an aerodrome:

- Flying machines and vehicles shall give way to aircraft which are taking off or landing.

- Vehicles and taxiing flying machines shall give way to vehicles towing aircraft.

- Vehicles which are not towing aircraft shall give way to aircraft.

Figure 11.12 A tug towing an aircraft.

- In any case, an emergency vehicle going to the assistance of an accident or incident shall have priority over all other vehicles or aircraft on the ground.

Overtaking on the ground.

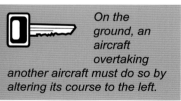
On the ground, an aircraft overtaking another aircraft must do so by altering its course to the left.

In the United Kingdom, an aircraft **overtaking** another aircraft, **on the ground**, must do so by altering course to the **LEFT**.

AEROBATICS.

An aircraft shall not carry out any aerobatic manoeuvre:

- Over the congested area of any city, town, or settlement,

or

- Within controlled airspace except with the consent of the appropriate Air Traffic Control Unit.

Figure 11.13 Aerobatics are not allowed over a congested area.

RIGHT-HAND RULE.

A pilot following a line feature (a railway, road, river or coastline etc.), must fly so that the line feature is on his LEFT, unless the aircraft is flying in controlled airspace and has been instructed otherwise by an Air Traffic Control Unit.

This rule ensures separation between two aircraft following the same line feature but flying in opposite directions.

Both aircraft will be flying to the right of the line feature.

Figure 11.14 When following a line feature, fly to the right of the feature.

> *A pilot following a line feature (a railway, road, river or coastline etc) in uncontrolled airspace must fly so that the line feature is on his LEFT.*

NOTIFICATION OF ARRIVAL AND DEPARTURE.

The **Pilot-In-Command (PIC)** is responsible for informing the destination aerodrome as quickly as possible of:

    a.   A change of intended destination,

        and

    b.   A delay of arrival of 45 minutes or more.

The PIC is also responsible for informing the appropriate Air Traffic Service Unit (ATSU), or the person in charge of an aerodrome, upon landing, and prior to departure from that aerodrome:

Landing and Departure Details.

For a flight for which the destination aerodrome is more than 40 kilometres from the departure aerodrome, and where the aircraft exceeds 5 700 kilograms Maximum Take-Off Mass, the Pilot-In-Command must ensure that the flight plan contains such details as may be necessary for Search and Rescue (SAR) and that these details are passed to the appropriate ATSU.

A flight plan need not be submitted for a flight crossing the Scottish FIR and the London FIR common boundary. However a Flight Plan is mandatory for flights entering or departing either of these two FIRs from or to a non-UK FIR.

BANNERS & TOWROPES ETC.

Tow ropes, banners, and similar objects towed by aircraft, shall not be picked up or dropped at an aerodrome unless:

- Permission has been obtained from the responsible Air Traffic Services Unit (ATSU). If there is no ATSU, permission must be sought from the person in charge.

- They are picked up or dropped in a designated area which is officially marked as such, and when the aircraft is flying in the direction appropriate for landing.

BRIEFING OF PASSENGERS.

Prior to departure, the PIC is responsible for briefing all passengers on the:

- Location of all aircraft exits,

  and

- the location and use of all safety equipment required to be carried on board the aircraft.

TWO-WAY RADIO COMMUNICATION FAILURE.

The general points to remember in the case of two-way radio communication failure in Visual Meteorological Conditions outside controlled airspace are:

In the event of communications failure in Visual Meteorological Conditions (VMC), the aircraft shall:

- Continue to fly in VMC.

- If equipped with a transponder, squawk 7600 and select Mode C.

- Land at the nearest suitable aerodrome.

- Look out for visual signals and instructions from the Control Tower or the Signals Square.

- Report arrival by the most expeditious means to the appropriate ATCU.

Figure 11.15 Radio Failure.

In case of radio failure, squawk 7600 and select Mode C.

Communications Failure While Under a Special VFR Clearance.

If an aircraft should suffer a communications failure while under SVFR, the procedure is as follows:

- If equipped, squawk 7600 and select Mode C.

- If just the radio receiver is suspect, transmit blind giving position reports and stating intentions.

- **Should the communications failure occur prior to entry into a CTR, the pilot must remain clear of the CTR, even if SVFR clearance to enter has previously been obtained.**

- If the aircraft is already inside the CTR when the failure occurs:

    a. If inbound - proceed in accordance with the SVFR clearance and land as soon as possible, watching out for visual signals from ATC.

    b. If transiting a CTR – continue the flight not above the cleared altitude and leave the CTR by the most direct route, conducive with obstacle clearance and areas of known dense traffic.

    c. In all cases the pilot must notify ATC as soon as possible after landing.

Representative PPL - type questions to test your theoretical knowledge of CAA Rules of the Air.

1. A power driven heavier-than-air aircraft is classified as:

    a.   An aeroplane
    b.   An aircraft
    c.   A flying machine
    d.   An airplane

2. In the UK, if a taxiing aircraft is overtaking another aircraft on the manoeuvring area it must do so by altering its course to the:

    a.   Right
    b.   Left
    c.   Left or right
    d.   It is prohibited to overtake another aircraft taxying

3. An aircraft's position with the altimeter set to 1013.2 hPa is reported as:

    a.   Altitude
    b.   Height
    c.   Elevation
    d.   Flight Level

4. You have a communications failure. What code must you squawk if your aircraft is fitted with a transponder?

    a.   7600 and select Mode C
    b.   0000 and select Mode C
    c.   7000 and select Mode C
    d.   7500 and select Mode C

5. Within the UK, in controlled airspace, is a SVFR flight absolved from complying with the 1 000 feet Rule when flying over a built-up area?

    a.   Yes
    b.   No
    c.   Yes, as long as the aircraft is able to glide clear of the area in the event of an engine failure
    d.   Yes, as long as visibility is 5 nautical miles or greater

6. An aircraft following a line feature such as a railway or motorway, unless following a Notified Route or when complying with an ATC instruction, must:

    a.   Fly with the feature on the left of the aircraft
    b.   Fly with the feature on the right of the aircraft
    c.   Fly directly over the feature
    d.   Not fly not below 1 000 feet AGL and ensure that the aircraft operates in uninterrupted VMC while following the line feature

7. You are flying outside controlled airspace above the Transition Altitude in the UK. Which of the following is a correct Flight Level to maintain if the aircraft has a magnetic heading of 092° and drift is 7° to port?

    a.   FL 50
    b.   FL 55
    c.   FL 60
    d.   FL 65

8. A PPL holder who is not in possession of any additional ratings and has received a SVFR clearance to enter a CTA must:

    a.   Maintain a visibility of at least 10 nautical miles, remain clear of cloud and in sight of the ground
    b.   Maintain a visibility of at least 8 km, remain clear of cloud and in sight of the ground
    c.   Maintain a visibility of at least 5 nautical miles, remain clear of cloud and in sight of the ground
    d.   Maintain a visibility of at least 10 kilometres, remain clear of cloud and in sight of the ground

9. At and above what Flight Level must an aircraft flying in the UK be equipped with a serviceable transponder?

    a.   FL 50
    b.   FL 90
    c.   FL 100
    d.   FL 245

10. Two aircraft are on finals for landing. Which has right of way ?

    a.   The lower aircraft
    b.   As dictated by the flight conditions
    c.   The higher aircraft
    d.   By mutual agreement

11. While flying in the United Kingdom, you see another aircraft to your right. Which of the following is correct?

    a.   You have right of way and must maintain heading speed and altitude
    b.   You have right of way and must maintain heading and speed
    c.   You have the right of way and must maintain course and speed
    d.   You must give way

12. You are flying in the UK in Controlled Air Space, tracking 180° magnetic. Which of the following would be a suitable flight level?

    a.   FL 50
    b.   FL 55
    c.   FL 60
    d.   FL 65

13.   Where an aircraft is flying in circumstances such that more than one of the low-flying prohibitions apply, it must fly:

a.   At the greatest height required by any of the prohibitions
b.   At the lowest height required by any of the prohibitions
c.   Not below 500 feet. unless landing, taking-off, authorised by ATC or in a state of emergency
d.   As prescribed by ATC

14.   You have received ATC clearance to enter a CTR under SVFR and suffer a complete communications failure 2 minutes prior to entry. Which of the following is the correct procedure to follow?

a.   Enter the CTR with caution squawking 7600 together with C and, avoiding areas of high intensity flying, land watching out for visual signals
b.   Enter the CTR reverting to your Flight Planned course
c.   Enter the CTR with caution squawking 7600 together with C, join overhead and await visual signals from the Aerodrome Control
d.   Remain clear of the CTR

15.   You are flying in the UK, outside controlled airspace, at 2 500 feet AMSL at 130 knots. What are the VMC minima?

a.   Visibility of 5 kilometres,1 500 metres horizontally clear of cloud and 1000 feet vertically clear of cloud
b.   Visibility of 8 kilometres,1 500 metres horizontally clear of cloud and 1 000 feet vertically clear of cloud
c.   Clear of cloud and in sight of the surface with 1 500 metres in-flight visibility
d.   Visibility of 5 kilometres1 500 metres horizontally clear of cloud and 1 000 feet vertically clear of cloud

16.   An aircraft flying under a Special VFR clearance is exempt from:

a.   both the 1 000 feet Rule and the "Land Clear Rule"
b.   the 1000 feet Rule but not the "Land Clear Rule"
c.   the 500 feet Rule but not the "Land Clear Rule"
d.   both the 500 feet Rule and the "Land Clear Rule"

17.   Except with the permission of the CAA in writing, an aircraft shall not fly over an organised open-air assembly of more than 1 000 persons below:

a.   Safety Altitude
b.   1 000 feet
c.   2 000 feet
d.   The higher of 1 000 feet or the height required to permit the aircraft to "land clear" of the assembly in the event of power failure

18.   If an aircraft is operating in accordance with the Instrument Flight Rules, which is the lowest altitude at which the pilot should fly, unless otherwise instructed by an ATCU?

    a.   The Minimum Elevation Figure for the relevant part of the course
    b.   1 000 feet above the highest obstacle within 5 nautical miles of his track
    c.   1 000 feet above terrain or water
    d.   500 feet above the highest obstacle within 5 nautical miles of his track

19.   In United Kingdom airspace, If you are converging with another aircraft and you have the right of way, you should maintain:

    a.   Heading and height
    b.   Course and speed
    c.   Altitude and speed
    d.   Heading and speed

20.   In the United Kingdom, VFR flight at night:

    a.   Is not permitted
    b.   Is permitted in VMC
    c.   Is permitted only when the pilot holds an Instrument Rating
    d.   May only be flown by a PPL holder with an IMC rating

21.   In the United Kingdom, a pilot overtaking another aircraft:

    a.   Must overtake to the left of the slower aircraft, when in the air, and on the ground when taxiing
    b.   Must overtake to the left of the slower aircraft, when in the air, but to the right of the slower aircraft when taxiing
    c.   Must overtake to the right of the slower aircraft, when in the air, but to the left of the slower aircraft on the ground when taxiing
    d.   May overtake either side of the slower aircraft, both in the air and on the ground

22.   According to the United Kingdom Air Navigation Order the lowest altitude for flight under IFR is:

    a.   above the transition level
    b.   1 500 feet above the ground
    c.   500 feet above the highest obstacle within 10 nm of track
    d.   1 000 feet above the highest obstacle within 5 nm of track

23.   Without a Night Qualification or an Instrument Rating it is illegal for the holder of a PPL to fly at night. How does the United Kingdom Air Navigation Order define "night"?

    a.   Dusk till dawn
    b.   30 minutes after sunset to 30 minutes before sunrise
    c.   Sunset to sunrise
    d.   From the end of evening civil twilight to the beginning of morning civil twilight

24.   To simulate Instrument Meteorological Conditions a pilot's vision may be artificially restricted by goggles or screens. In this situation:

    a.   An observer must be carried who has access to the aircraft controls
    b.   Quadrantal flight levels must be flown
    c.   A safety pilot with access to the aircraft controls must be carried and, if this safety pilot does not have the field of view to carry out an adequate look out, an additional observer to supplement the safety pilot's look out
    d.   A safety pilot with access to the aircraft controls must be carried

25.   Complete the following sentence. Except when taking off or landing:

    a.   No aircraft which is not a helicopter shall fly over a congested area below a height which would allow it to land clear of the area, in the case of an engine failure, or below a height of 2 000 feet above the highest fixed obstacle within 600 metres of the aircraft, whichever is the higher
    b.   No aircraft which is not a helicopter shall fly over a congested area below a height which would allow it to land clear of the area, in the case of an engine failure, or below a height of 1 000 feet above the highest fixed obstacle within 600 metres of the aircraft, whichever is the higher
    c.   No aircraft which is not a helicopter shall fly over a congested area below a height which would allow it to land clear of the area, in the case of an engine failure, or below a height of 2 000 feet above the highest fixed obstacle within 100 metres of the aircraft, whichever is the higher
    d.   No aircraft which is not a helicopter shall fly over a congested area below a height which would allow it to land clear of the area, in the case of an engine failure, or below a height of 1 500 feet above the highest fixed obstacle within 300 metres of the aircraft, whichever is the higher

26.   You are flying outside controlled airspace, above the Transition Level, on a heading which gives your aircraft a track over the ground of 355° True. If the Magnetic Variation is 5° West, which of the following Flight Levels (FL) would be the correct one at which to cruise?

        a.   FL 55
        b.   FL 45
        c.   FL 50
        d.   FL 75

27.   During a flight, by day, a pilot notices that an anti-collision light is inoperative.

        a.   He should land as soon as safe to do so unless authorised by ATC to continue the flight.
        b.   He may continue flight by day provided that the light is repaired at the earliest practical opportunity
        c.   He must land as soon as possible and get the light repaired
        d.   Provided the aircraft is flown VFR only, the problem may be ignored

Question	1	2	3	4	5	6	7	8	9	10	11	12
Answer												

Question	13	14	15	16	17	18	19	20	21	22	23	24
Answer												

Question	25	26	27
Answer			

The answers to these questions can be found at the end of this book.

CHAPTER 12
AIRCRAFT REGISTRATION
IN THE UNITED KINGDOM

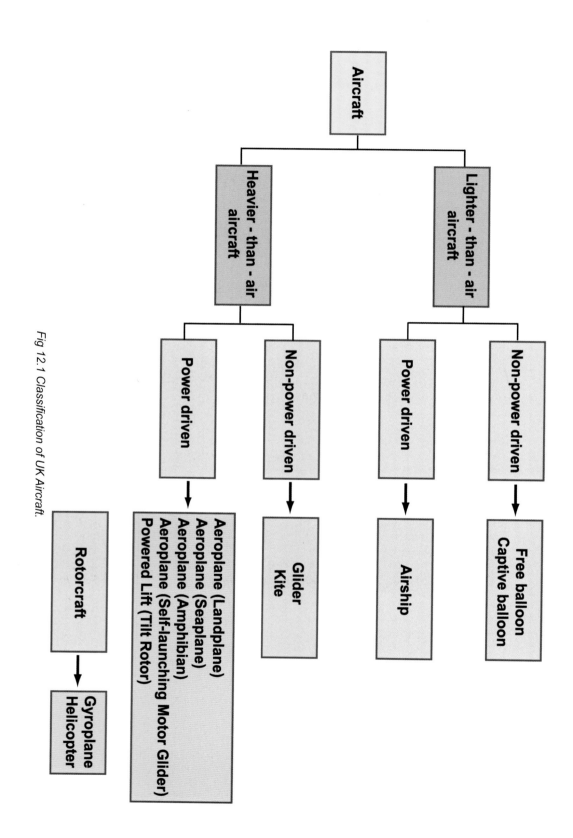

Fig 12.1 Classification of UK Aircraft.

UK AIRCRAFT MARKINGS & REGISTRATION.

REGISTRATION AUTHORITY.

The Civil Aviation Authority (CAA) is the Registration Authority for aircraft within the United Kingdom (UK). The UK CAA is responsible for maintaining a register recording the details of all UK registered aircraft.

APPLICATION FOR REGISTRATION.

Any application for aircraft registration must be made in writing to the CAA. Details of the aircraft, proof of ownership and, in particular, the classification of the aircraft must be submitted with this application.

CLASSIFICATION OF UK AIRCRAFT.

The general classification of aircraft in the UK is depicted in *Figure 12.1.*

CERTIFICATE OF REGISTRATION (C OF R).

If the application is successful, the CAA will issue a Certificate of Registration (C of R) to the person in whose name the aircraft is registered (normally the owner). The C of R contains the following information:

- Certificate number.

- Nationality and Registration Mark assigned to the aircraft by the CAA.

- Make and aircraft designation.

- Aircraft serial number.

- Name and address of the owner.

- A certified statement to the effect that the aircraft has been entered on the Registry.

- Date of Registration.

- Signature of Registering Officer.

UNITED KINGDOM
CIVIL AVIATION AUTHORITY

CERTIFICATE OF REGISTRATION OF AIRCRAFT

CERTIFICATE NUMBER G-BXYT/R1

1 Nationality and Registration Marks	2 Constructor and Constructor's Designation of Aircraft	3 Aircraft Serial Number
G-BXYT	PIPER AIRCRAFT CORPORATION PIPER PA-28RT-201	28R-7918198

4 Name and Address of Registered Owner or Charterer

OXFORD AVIATION SERVICES LTD
LANGFORD LANE
OXFORD AIRPORT
KIDLINGTON
OX5 1RA

5 It is hereby certified that the above described aircraft has been duly entered on the United Kingdom Register in accordance with the Convention on International Civil Aviation dated 7 December 1944, and with the Air Navigation Order 1995.

CIVIL AVIATION AUTHORITY

RV CROSSLEY
For the Civil Aviation Authority
Aircraft Registration
CAA House
45-59 Kingsway
London WC2B 6TE

Tel 0171-832 6299
Fax 0171-832 6262
E-Mail aircraft.reg@srg.caa.co.uk

DATE OF ISSUE 3 AUGUST 1998

NOTES (a) The person in whose name an aircraft is registered may or may not be its legal owner. Prospective purchasers are warned, therefore, that this Certificate of Registration is not proof of legal ownership.
(b) No entries or endorsements may be made to this Certificate except by the Civil Aviation Authority.

SEE FURTHER NOTES OVERLEAF

Fig 12.2 Certificate of Registration.

OWNER TO INFORM CAA IN WRITING OF CHANGE TO C OF R.

The owner must inform the CAA in writing immediately of:

- Any change in the aircraft's details as entered on the C of R (including change of ownership),

or

- The destruction of the aircraft or its permanent withdrawal from use.

CHANGE OF OWNERSHIP.

If an aircraft changes ownership, the previous owner must inform the CAA immediately. The new owner must inform the CAA within 28 days of ownership transfer.

If the CAA becomes aware that a change of ownership has taken place, without having been informed of the change by the previous, and subsequent owner, the Authority may cancel the registration within 2 months of receiving such information.

AIRCRAFT EXEMPTED FROM C OF R.

In the UK, certain powered aircraft need not be registered; for example, test or experimental aircraft, aircraft carrying out a demonstration flight, or aircraft undergoing certification test.

NATIONALITY & REGISTRATION MARKING.

General.
The Nationality Mark for all aircraft registered in the UK is the capital letter "G". The Registration Mark is a group of 4 letters. The two markings are separated by a hyphen. Nationality and Registration Marks are to be displayed to the best advantage.

If an aircraft changes ownership, the previous owner must inform the CAA immediately. The new owner must inform the CAA within 28 days of transfer.

Fig 12.3 A UK - registered aircraft showing the Nationality Mark and its Registration Mark.

All Nationality and Registration Marking are to be kept clean and visible at all times.

Visibility of markings.
The Nationality and Registration Markings are to be kept clean and visible at all times.

IDENTIFICATION PLATE.

The Nationality and Registration Markings are to be inscribed on a fire-proof metal plate which is to be fixed in a prominent position on the fuselage.

Identification Plate:

The Nationality and Registration Mark are to be inscribed on a fire-proof metal plate which is to be fixed in a prominent position on the fuselage.

Representative PPL - type questions to test your theoretical knowledge of CAA Registration.

1.   Which of the following types of aircraft may not need to be registered in the UK?

    a.   Aircraft concerned in crop-spraying operations
    b.   Experimental aircraft
    c.   Gliders
    d.   Private aircraft

2.   The Registration Mark for a UK registered aircraft consists of how many letters/numbers?

    a.   4 letters
    b.   5 letters
    c.   2 letters and 2 numbers
    d.   5 either letters or numbers

3.   Where must an aircraft's identification plate be located?

    a.   Inside the pilot's access door by the handle
    b.   In a prominent location close to the middle of the instrument panel
    c.   In a prominent location on the fuselage
    d.   In a prominent location near the main entrance

4.   You have bought a UK registered aircraft from a friend. When must you inform the CAA?

    a.   Within 7 days
    b.   Within 14 days
    c.   Within 21 days
    d.   Within 28 days

5.   You sell your aircraft to a friend. By when must you inform the CAA?

    a.   7 days
    b.   14 days
    c.   21 days
    d.   Immediately

6.   Must the name and address of the owner be included in the C of R?

    a.   Only the name
    b.   Yes
    c.   No
    d.   Only the address including the Post Code

7.   Are you breaking the law if you allow the Nationality and Registration
      Marking to be obscured by mud?

      a.   Yes
      b.   No, but it is poor airmanship
      c.   Only if the Registration Mark is obscured
      d.   Only if the Nationality mark is obscured

8.   If the CAA is not informed of a change of ownership but learns of it later,
      may the CAA cancel the Registration of the aircraft?

      a.   Yes, but only after a month of receiving the information
      b.   No
      c.   Yes, but only within 2 months of receiving the information
      d.   Yes, but only after 3 months of receiving the information

9.   When you register an aircraft with the CAA, what information, in particular,
      must be included in the application?

      a.   The serial number of the engines
      b.   The Registration mark
      c.   The Classification of the aircraft
      d.   The serial number of the fuselage

10.   The identity plate must be made of:

      a.   Any metal
      b.   Any material
      c.   No particular material is specified
      d.   Fire-proof metal

Question	1	2	3	4	5	6	7	8	9	10
Answer										

The answers to these questions can be found at the end of this book.

CHAPTER 13
AIRWORTHINESS IN THE
UNITED KINGDOM

CERTIFICATE OF AIRWORTHINESS

Certificate Number: **041826/007**	**United Kingdom** **Civil Aviation Authority**	
1. Nationality and Registration Marks **G-BTRY**	2. Manufacturer and designation of aircraft **PIPER AIRCRAFT CORPORATION** **PIPER PA-28-161**	3. Aircraft Serial Number **28-8116190**

4. Categories

Normal and Utility Category Aeroplane

5. This Certificate of Airworthiness is issued pursuant to the Convention on International Civil Aviation dated 7 December 1944 and Regulation (EC) No 1592/2002, Article 5(2)(c) in respect of the above mentioned aircraft which is considered to be airworthy when maintained and operated in accordance with the foregoing and the pertinent operating limitations.

Date of Issue: **26 March 2008**   Signature:

Limitations/Remarks:

None

6. This Certificate of Airworthiness is valid unless revoked by the competent authority of the Member State of registry.

  A current Airworthiness Review Certificate shall be attached to this Certificate.

EASA Form 25 20070816
This certificate shall be carried on board during all flights

AIRWORTHINESS OF AIRCRAFT AND RELEVANT DOCUMENTATION – UK.

Introduction.

When the United Kingdom Civil Aviation Authority (CAA) is satisfied that the design, construction, materials and workmanship of an aircraft conform to the laid down airworthiness requirements, a Certificate of Airworthiness (C of A) will be issued.

Fig 13.1 Certificate of Airworthiness.

CERTIFICATE OF AIRWORTHINESS.

The following are the most important points concerning the Certificate of Airworthiness according to the UK Air Navigation Order:

- The CAA may issue a C of A subject to any condition it feels fit.

- The C of A will be issued under the EASA regulations and under certain aircraft Categories which are linked to the design features of the individual aircraft.

- To keep a C of A valid you have to have a signed Airworthiness Review Certificate (ARC) issued by the CAA. A Continuing Airworthiness Manager can issue and extend the ARC twice, but thereafter it must be renewed. The ARC and C of A must be carried on board.

See Figure 13.2, overleaf, for an example of an EASA ARC.

Fig 13.2 Airworthiness Review Certificate

PERMIT TO FLY.

In the UK, generally, a private pilot may only fly an aircraft that has been issued with a valid C of A. However, in some limited and special circumstances, an aircraft that does not have a C of A can be issued by the CAA with an EASA Permit to Fly.

Aircraft undergoing tests, "positioning" aircraft with expired C of A, experimental or vintage military aircraft are often issued with a Permit to Fly.

TECHNICAL LOG.

Transport and Aerial Work Category aircraft must have a Technical Log into which the pilot-in-command (PIC) enters his signature to accept the aircraft prior to flight. On landing, the PIC must enter the details of the flight, and details of any defects, in the Technical Log

AIRCRAFT, ENGINE AND PROPELLER LOGBOOKS.

Owners of all aircraft are required to keep an up-to-date:

• Aircraft Logbook.

• Engine Logbook.

• Variable-Pitch Propeller Logbook.

The above logbooks are used to record the flying times for each flight, modifications, repairs and maintenance undertaken. The Private Pilot must enter aircraft defects in the Aircraft Logbook.

All of the above logbooks must be retained for at least 2 years after the particular aircraft, engine or variable-pitch propeller have been destroyed or permanently withdrawn from service.

CERTIFICATE OF RELEASE TO SERVICE AND MAINTENANCE STATEMENT.

The Certificate of Release to Service and Maintenance Statement is a certificate that states that defects entered in the Technical Log or the Aircraft Logbook have been rectified, or that the rectification has been deferred in accordance with procedures approved by the CAA.

The Certificate of Release to Service and Maintenence Statement is signed by the Continuing Airworthiness Manager.

If the aircraft is an aircraft of either the Special or Private Category, and of a maximum weight of less than 2 730 kgs, the licensed pilot is allowed to make minor repairs or replacements, such as:

• Replacement of the battery.

• The changing of landing gear tyres, oil or spark plugs.

• Setting of spark plug gaps.

• Replacement of the VHF radio (providing it has no input to the navigation equipment).

WEIGHT SCHEDULE.

Old weight schedules must be retained by the owner for a period of 6 months.

The Weight Schedule lays down the Centre of Gravity limitations of the aircraft and specifies its weight configuration.

The Weight Schedule enables the pilot to calculate the aircraft take-off mass and centre of gravity. Should there be a significant repair or modification to the aircraft, a new Weight Schedule must be prepared by the owner. The earlier Weight Schedule must be retained by the owner for a period of 6 months.

NOISE CERTIFICATE.

Except for certain types of Short Take-off and Landing (STOL) aeroplanes, all those registered after 1980 (unless they are flying overseas) require a Noise Certificate.

Civil Aviation Authority	1. State of registry **UNITED KINGDOM** 2. NOISE CERTIFICATE	3. Document Number: **019533**

4. Registration Marks: **G-GAFA**	5. Manufacturer and Manufacturer's Designation of Aircraft: **PIPER AIRCRAFT CORPORATION** **PIPER PA-34-200T**	6. Aircraft Serial Number: **34-7970218**

7. Engine: **CONTINENTAL MOTORS CORP TSIO-360-EB**	8. Propeller: **MCCAULEY 3AF34C502/80HA-4**

9. Maximum Take-Off Mass (kg) **1999**	10. Maximum Landing Mass (kg) **Not Applicable**	11. Noise Certification Standard: **Chapter 6**

12. Additional modifications incorporated for the purpose of compliance with the applicable noise certification standards:

None

13. Lateral/Full-Power Noise Level: **N/A**	14. Approach Noise Level: **N/A**	15. Flyover Noise Level: **N/A**	16. Overflight Noise Level: **76.4 dB(A)**	17. Take-Off Noise Level: **N/A**

Remarks:

None

18. This Noise Certificate is issued pursuant to Annex 16, Volume I to the Convention on International Civil Aviation dated 7 December 1944 and Regulation (EC) No. 216/2008, Article 6 in respect of the above-mentioned aircraft, which is considered to comply with the indicated noise standard when maintained and operated in accordance with the relevant requirements and operating limitations.

19. Date of Issue...... **10 December 2008** ....   20. Signature..............................

EASA Form 45 18042008

Fig 13.3 Noise Certificate.

FLIGHT MANUAL / PILOT'S OPERATING HANDBOOK.

Each aircraft has its own Flight Manual which contains the operational limitations and procedures of the machine.

For light aircraft, the Flight Manual often takes the form of a Pilot's Operating Handbook (POH).

It is most important to understand that the Flight Manual forms part of the C of A. Therefore, to operate outside limitations or procedures specified in the Flight Manual invalidates the C of A.

For example, should a glider be towed by an aircraft which is not specifically endorsed to do so in the Flight Manual, the C of A for the aircraft would be invalidated and the insurance coverage too.

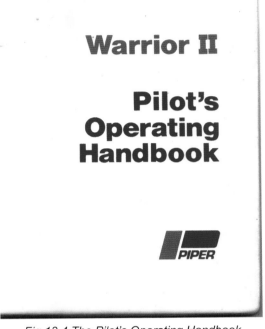

The Aircraft Flight Manual is considered to be part of the C of A.

Fig 13.4 The Pilot's Operating Handbook

INSURANCE.

As from 30th April 2005, the Civil Aviation Authority (Insurance) Regulations have come into force requiring all operators flying within, into, out of, or over, European Union member states to be insured. These Regulations set down the minimum insurance cover with respect to passengers, baggage, cargo and third parties. In certain cases there is a further requirement to insure against war and terrorism (generally known as War Risk.) *See Figure 13.5, Overleaf.*

Minimum Cover.
The minimum cover is dependent upon the number of passengers carried, and, in relation to third party cover, the MTOM (Maximum Take-off Mass). Insurance must be arranged on an individual basis, and some insurers lay down a minimum number of flying hours a pilot must have for the insurance to be valid.

All pilots, must carefully check that they have the legal amount of insurance cover for the aircraft to fly, and that the policies are up-to-date before flying.

The Willis Building, 51 Lime Street, London EC3M 7DQ
Telephone: 44 (0)20 3124 6000 Fax +44 (0)20 3124 8223 Website: www.willis.com

Willis

20 May 2009

To Whom It May Concern

Our reference: GCAT / 6003

Certificate of Insurance

THIS IS TO CERTIFY, in our capacity as Insurance Brokers, that Insurance has been effected in the name of Oxford Aviation Academy Luxembourg Sarl and associated and subsidiary and affiliated Companies and its Subsidiary OXFORD AVIATION TRAINING covering their operations in connection with aircraft owned or operated by or on behalf of the Insured whilst operating anywhere in the World, against the following risks and up to the limits stated:

AIRCRAFT THIRD PARTY and PASSENGER LEGAL LIABILITY, for a Combined Single Limit (Bodily Injury/Property Damage) of USD10,000,000 any one occurrence. The coverage provided in respect of War and Allied Risks is in accordance with the Extended Coverage Endorsement (Aviation Liabilities) AVN 52E and is subject to an annual aggregate, however this aggregate limit shall not apply to Passengers and Passenger Baggage.

It is further certified that coverage is extended to include:

a. flying training by the Insured of pilots employed by or on behalf of the CIVIL AVIATION AUTHORITY (CAA);

b. flying of the Insured's Aircraft by pilots employed by or on behalf of the CAA for the purpose of test flights, training flights or line flying.

It is further certified that the amounts of insurance stated above are in accordance with the minimum insurance cover requirements of Articles 6 and 7 of Regulation (EC) No. 785/2004 based on (a) the rates of exchange applicable to the Special Drawing Rights at inception of the insurances, (b) third party war, terrorism and allied perils being insured on an aggregate basis as above, and (c) it being understood that such aggregate limits may be reduced or exhausted during the policy period by virtue of claims made against aircraft or other operational interests covered by the insurances.

It is further certified that Insurers have applied the Date Recognition Exclusion Clause AVN 2000A and have agreed to provide limited writeback of coverage in respect thereof in accordance with the Date Recognition Limited Coverage Clause AVN 2001A (Amended), as applicable.

Willis Limited. A Lloyd's broker, authorised and regulated by the Financial Services Authority.
Registered office The Willis Building, 51 Lime Street, London EC3M 7DQ . Registered number 181116 England and Wales.

Fig 13.5 Insurance Certificate

Representative PPL - type questions to test your theoretical knowledge of Airworthiness (UK).

1. Is an aircraft allowed to fly in the UK without a valid C of A?

    a. No
    b. Yes, as long as the aircraft is a non-commercial category
    c. Yes, as long as the aircraft is below 2 730 kgs
    d. Yes, with a Permit to Fly issued by the CAA

2. If the aircraft is operated in the UK, must the aircraft be insured?

    a. Yes
    b. No
    c. Only if it carries passengers
    d. Only if the pilot at the controls is over 40 years old

3. Is a PPL Licence holder allowed to replace a VHF radio in a private aircraft ?

    a. Yes as long as the aircraft is less than 2 730 kgs
    b. No
    c. Yes, providing it has no input to the navigation equipment and the aircraft is less than 2 730 kgs
    d. Only if the pilot holds a relevant Engineering Licence

4. An aircraft is reweighed. How long must the owner retain the earlier Weight Schedule?

    a. 2 years
    b. 1 year
    c. 3 months
    d. 6 months

5. Where would a pilot find the operational limitations of the aircraft?

    a. The Technical Log Book
    b. The Aircraft Flight Manual (Pilot's Operating Handbook)
    c. The Aircraft Limitations Log Book
    d. The Aircraft Log Book

6. Is the Aircraft Flight Manual considered to be part of the C of A?

    a. No
    b. Yes

7.   The aircraft, engine and variable-pitch propeller logbooks must be retained for a particular time after the particular aircraft, engine or variable-pitch propeller have been destroyed or permanently withdrawn from service. How long is this time period?

a.   At least 6 months
b.   At least 1 year
c.   At least 2 years
d.   At least 5 years

8.   Which organisation issues the C of A in the UK?

a.   The Department of Transport
b.   ICAO
c,   NPLG
d.   CAA

9.   In which document would a Private Pilot enter details of aircraft defects?

a.   Aircraft Logbook
b.   Certificate of Maintenance Review
c.   Technical Log
d.   Certificate of Release to Service

10.   In the UK, how may categories of aircraft are stipulated?

a.   3
b.   4
c.   5
d.   6

Question	1	2	3	4	5	6	7	8	9	10
Answer										

The answers to these questions can be found at the end of this book.

CHAPTER 14
AIRSPACE DIVISION AND AIR TRAFFIC SERVICES IN THE UK

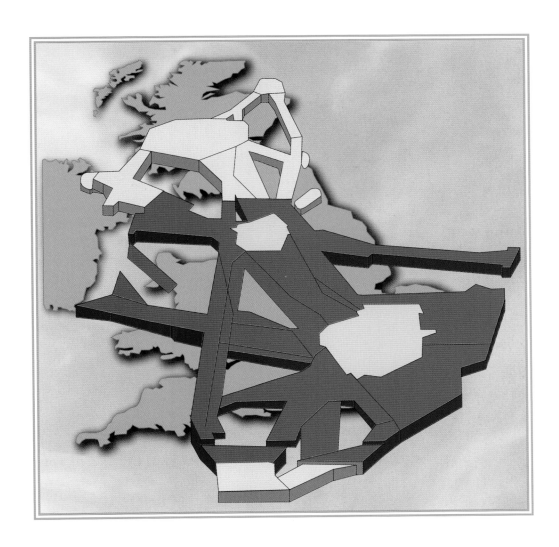

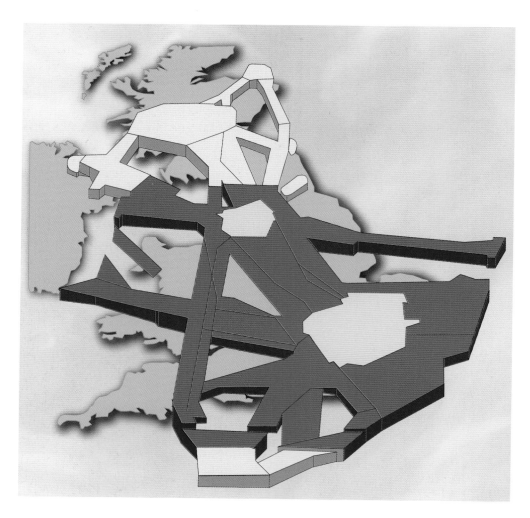

Figure 14.1 Representation of United Kingdom Airspace.

ORGANISATION AND DIVISION OF AIRSPACE IN THE UNITED KINGDOM.

INTRODUCTION.

The fundamental division and classification of United Kingdom Airspace is the same as the ICAO standard described in Chapter 5. You may wish to revise Chapter 5 at this point. This chapter concentrates solely on United Kingdom airspace, and highlights those aspects of United Kingdom airspace which differ from ICAO.

The airspace over the United Kingdom (UK) and adjacent sea areas is divided into four principal volumes. Between sea-level and Flight Level 245, in Lower Airspace, are the London and Scottish Flight Information Regions (FIRs) depicted in *Figure 14.2*. A Flight Information Service and an Alerting Service are provided in these FIRs. Above the two FIRs, in Upper Airspace, with the same lateral limits as the FIRs, are the London and Scottish Upper Information Regions (UIRs).

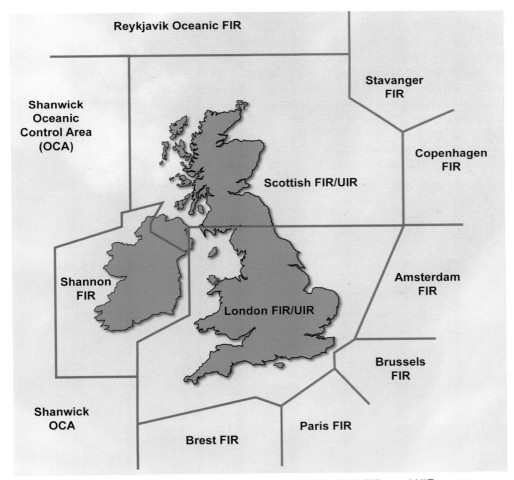

Fig 14.2 The lateral limits of the London and Scottish FIRs and UIRs.

The whole of Upper Airspace (the London and Scottish UIRs) is controlled airspace. The London and Scottish FIRs comprise both controlled and uncontrolled airspace.

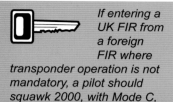

If entering a UK FIR from a foreign FIR where transponder operation is not mandatory, a pilot should squawk 2000, with Mode C, unless directed otherwise by an ATCU.

You should note that, unless directed otherwise by an Air Traffic Control Unit, the pilot of an aircraft entering one of the United Kingdom FIRs from a foreign FIR where transponder operation has not been mandatory should squawk 2000 with the transponder selected to Mode C.

Access to controlled airspace is governed by conditions promulgated in the Air Navigation Order which restricts entry into controlled airspace to specified types of flight made by appropriately qualified pilots flying appropriately equipped aircraft, and (with certain exceptions) under air traffic control.

Flights in uncontrolled airspace are not subjected to air traffic control, though all pilots must comply with the Rules of the Air as promulgated in the Air Navigation Order. Air Traffic Service Units do, however, provide certain services to flights in uncontrolled airspace under both the Visual Flight Rules (VFR) and the Instrument Flight Rules (IFR). These services are collectively called the UK Flight Information Service.

The diagrams at *Figures 14.1* and *14.3* give a very approximate representation of the division between controlled and uncontrolled airspace over the United Kingdom. You should note that while much of the country seems to be covered by extensive blocks of controlled airspace, Airways, Control Areas (CTAs) and Terminal Control Areas (TCAs/TMAs) have vertical limits, with uncontrolled airspace underneath them. Consequently, outside CTRs, and that portion of TCAs/TMAs in the immediate vicinity of aerodromes, much the greater part of UK airspace near ground level is uncontrolled airspace. Also, as depicted in *Figure 14.1*, there remain vast tracts of the country away from the major centres of population where uncontrolled airspace stretches from ground level up to the ceiling of the London and Scottish FIRs, currently at Flight Level 245 (i.e. 24 500 feet with an altimeter sub-scale setting of 1013.2 millibars), though this upper limit is under review.

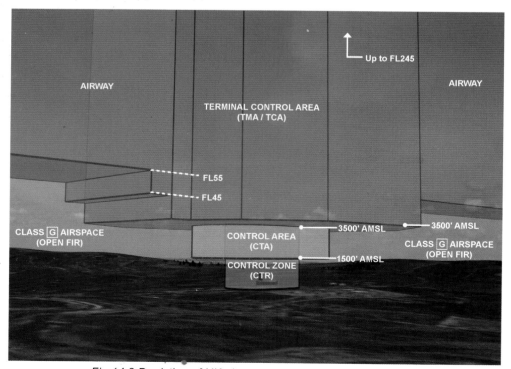

Fig 14.3 Depiction of UK airspace around a major aerodrome.

Familiarity with and understanding of the division of airspace and the system of airspace classification in the United Kingdom will come only after much study and a fair bit of flying experience. However, by concentrating on learning all about the airspace in the local area in which you fly, and by studying in detail the airspace along the route of any cross country flight that you make, and the rules with which you must comply within the different types of airspace, it should not be too long before you have a working command of this tricky subject.

CLASSIFICATION OF AIRSPACE IN THE UNITED KINGDOM.

In general, the United Kingdom has adopted ICAO-standard airspace classification covered in Chapter 5. The ICAO system divides airspace into seven classes identified by letters of the alphabet A to G, each class specifying whether or not ATC clearance is required, the air traffic services provided, the obligations on pilots, and the Visual Meteorological Conditions (VMC) minima, which prevail in that airspace, where relevant. However, the UK has registered differences with ICAO covering VMC minima in uncontrolled airspace (classes F and G), in order to offer greater flexibility to low speed VFR traffic.

All ICAO member countries tend to allocate letter classifications to CTRs, CTAs, TMAs or Airways which differ greatly from country to country. The letter classification of the various types of controlled airspace in the UK is fully covered in this chapter on pages 234-236.

Official details of UK airspace classifications are described in the UK AIP, ENR 1–4.

CONTROLLED AIRSPACE.

Airspace classes A, B, C, D and E are controlled airspace.

In general, in the United Kingdom, Aerodrome Control Zones (CTR) are either Class A or D airspace. Most CTRs in the UK are Class D.

Airways in the United Kingdom are Class A airspace.

Control Areas (CTA) in the United Kingdom can be Class A, D or E airspace, but are mostly Class A or D.

Terminal Control Areas (TCA or TMA) may be Class A airspace (London Heathrow), but may also be Class D (Edinburgh and Glasgow) or Class E (Belfast).

Currently, there is no Class B airspace in the United Kingdom.

The whole of Upper Airspace (the London and Scottish UIRs) and all FIR Airspace above FL195, is designated Class C Airspace.

N.B. VFR flight is not permitted in Class A airspace (with the exception of flight in CTRs with a Special VFR Clearance), but is permitted in the rest of controlled airspace, provided that certain conditions are met, such as:

- Stipulated VMC minima are complied with.

- Relevant air traffic control clearances are obtained.

- The aircraft has the required minimum radio-communication equipment.

Types of Controlled Airspace.

Various types of controlled airspace, such as CTR, CTA, Airway, TCA or TMA, are depicted schematically in *Figure 14.3*.

As we have mentioned, the classification letter of each type of airspace defines the requirements for entry, in terms of air traffic clearances, the service offered in terms of separation from other traffic, whether flight under Visual Flight Rules (VFR) rules is permitted and, if it is, the Visual Meteorological Conditions (VMC) minima requirements. These are summarised later in this chapter.

The type and classes of controlled airspace are marked on ICAO 1:500 000 and 1:250 000 Aeronautical Charts. These charts depict the lateral dimensions and give information on vertical dimensions of controlled airspace. *Figure 14.4* depicts a section of a 1:500 000 Aeronautical Chart of the United Kingdom, illustrating the lateral and vertical extent of three airways. These are Airways L9, N14A and N862 which are Class A airspace in which VFR flight is prohibited.

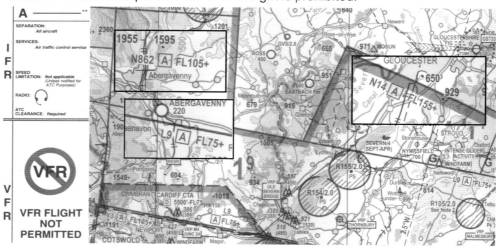

Fig 14.4 1:500 000 Aeronautical Chart showing Airways L9, N14A and N862 in the United Kingdom.

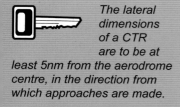

The lateral dimensions of a CTR are to be at least 5nm from the aerodrome centre, in the direction from which approaches are made.

At this point, let us revise the general structure of controlled airspace as depicted in *Figure 14.3*.

Around a large aerodrome, there would normally be a Control Zone (CTR), stretching from the surface to an altitude, typically, of 1 500 to 2 500 feet. The volume of the CTR must be sufficient to protect aircraft in the landing and taking-off phases of flight. The lateral dimensions of a CTR are to be at least 5 nautical miles radius, from the aerodrome centre, in the direction from which approaches are made. Most CTRs around UK airports are Class D, but London Heathrow, as a major international airport, has a Class A CTR.

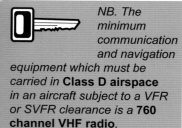

*NB. The minimum communication and navigation equipment which must be carried in **Class D airspace** in an aircraft subject to a VFR or SVFR clearance is a **760 channel VHF radio.***

Surrounding the CTR, and sometimes extending well above and well beyond the CTR may be a Control Area (CTA). The CTA protects aircraft in the climb-out from an aerodrome and on the approaches to the aerodrome. The CTA has defined vertical limits with its base as an altitude or flight level and its top as an altitude or flight level. The lowest point of a CTA must be not less than 700 feet above the Earth's surface or water. Most CTAs in the United Kingdom are Class D airspace. *Figure 14.5* shows the Bristol CTR and CTA, both of which are Class D.

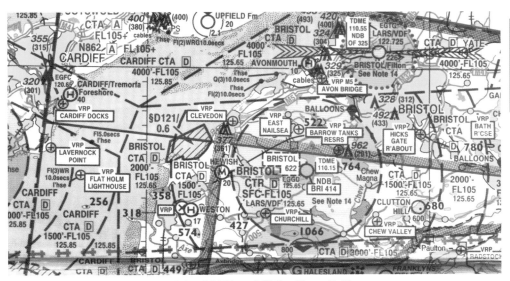

Fig 14.5 Bristol CTR and CTA - Class D Airspace.

In the case of aerodromes situated near a major international airport, such as London Heathrow, above the CTA there might be a Terminal Control Area. A Terminal Control Area is sometimes abbreviated as TCA and sometimes as TMA. The letters TMA actually stand for Terminal Manoeuvring Area, an earlier name for Terminal Control Area. A TMA might typically stretch from an altitude of 3500 feet or higher to Flight Level 245, the upper level of the Flight Information Region. The TMA is a sort of junction box, adjacent to one or more aerodromes, joining all the airways which are connected to it. The London Heathrow TMA is Class A *(See Figure 14.6)*, though Edinburgh and Glasgow TMAs are currently Class D and Belfast TMA is currently Class E.

> The lowest point of a CTA must be not less than 700 feet above the ground or water.

> A Terminal Control Area may be defined as a sort of junction box joining several airways and other routes, adjacent to one or more major airports.

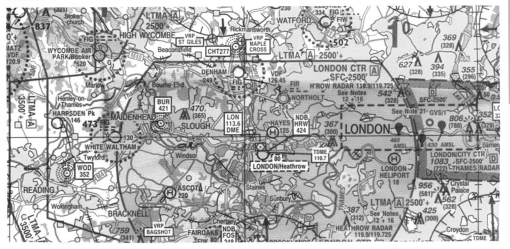

Fig 14.6 Heathrow CTR and the London Terminal Manoeuvring Area are Class A airspace.

Finally, there are the airways which, in the United Kingdom, are Class A airspace. *(See Figure 14.4.)* When airways transit TMAs the airway takes on the airspace class assigned to the TMA.

You should note that the minimum navigation and radio-communications fit required for VFR and SVFR flight in controlled airspace in the United Kingdom, below Flight Level 100, is a VHF 760 channel radio. (Section GEN 1.5.5 UK AIP.)

The minimum nav/radio fit required for VFR and SVFR flight in UK controlled airspace is a serviceable 760-channel VHF radio.

FLIGHTS IN CONTROLLED AIRSPACE IN ACCORDANCE WITH THE VISUAL FLIGHT RULES.

Flight in accordance with the Visual Flight Rules (VFR) is permitted in controlled airspace, except Class A airspace, under the conditions stipulated. One important condition is that the prescribed minima for Visual Meteorological Conditions (VMC) appropriate to the class of Airspace in which the flight is being conducted must be maintained. These VMC minima are given in the tables on pages 233-236, but VFR pilots may find the chart at *Figure 14.8* easier to interpret.

Additionally, when flying VFR in controlled airspace (other than Class E) a pilot must file a flight plan, obtain an ATC clearance, maintain a listening watch on the appropriate radio frequency, and comply with any instructions given by the responsible ATCU.

In certain circumstances, the requirement to submit a flight plan may be satisfied by a pilot passing his flight details to the ATCU by radio when airborne.

FLIGHTS IN CONTROLLED AIRSPACE IN ACCORDANCE WITH THE INSTRUMENT FLIGHT RULES.

All VFR flights in controlled airspace (except Class E) require a flight plan to be submitted. In certain circumstances, this may be done over the radio when airborne.

In order to fly in controlled airspace in accordance with the Instrument Flight Rules (IFR), four basic conditions must be fulfilled:

- the pilot-in-command of the aircraft must hold a valid Instrument Rating or IMC rating.

- the pilot must file a flight plan.

- the pilot must have obtained a clearance from an Air Traffic Control Unit (ATCU).

- the pilot must comply with ATCU instructions.

In controlled airspace, IFR flights are almost always under radar control from an ATCU. ATCUs ensure separation between IFR flights and other IFR flights, and sometimes, but not always, from VFR traffic, based on radar information and position reports, so that time, distance, and altitude separation may be applied to the controlled traffic.

In Classes B and C Airspace, ATCUs provide separation between IFR and VFR traffic.

In Classes D and E Airspace, separation is provided only between IFR traffic, but traffic information about VFR flights is provided to IFR flights.

An IMC Rating holder can fly in Class D and E Airspace in circumstances requiring flight under the Instrument Flight Rules.

MAJOR DIFFERENCES BETWEEN UK AND ICAO AIRSPACE RULES.

There are certain differences between the UK and ICAO rules governing flight in the various Classes of airspace. The major differences are summarised here.

- In certain notified portions of Class A airspace in the UK, notably for the purpose of crossing a notified airway, gliders are permitted to operate without reference to ATC. No separation or traffic information is provided with respect to these flights.

- In the UK, there is no mandatory requirement for continuous two-way radio communications in Classes F & G airspace when aircraft are flying in accordance with the Instrument Flight Rules.

- In the UK, there is no reference to "controlled aerodromes". The UK AIP does, however, list aerodromes in the UK at which a full aerodrome air traffic control service is provided.

SPECIAL VISUAL FLIGHT RULES.

As we have just discussed, aircraft flying in accordance with the Visual Flight Rules (VFR) are permitted to fly in controlled airspace only under prescribed minimum Visual Meteorological Conditions (VMC), appropriate to the Class of airspace in which the VFR flight takes place. We have also mentioned that VFR flights are prohibited altogether in Class A airspace.

Two basic questions that the VFR pilot might ask himself about this situation might be:

- Can I fly into or out of an airfield which lies within Class A airspace; for instance, into an airfield within the London (Heathrow) Control Zone (CTR), for surely that must be possible?

- Can I enter a CTR of, say, Class D if meteorological conditions are below the VMC minima for that airspace?

The answer to both these questions is "yes", but only under certain, prescribed conditions. Sometimes, a dispensation is granted to fly into an aerodrome near the edge of a CTR without a VFR flight needing individual permission. Otherwise, such flights may take place only in accordance with Special Visual Flight Rules (Special VFR) and provided that a Special VFR clearance has been obtained from the responsible Air Traffic Control Unit (ATCU).

A Special VFR flight is a flight made in a CTR, under circumstances which would normally require the flight to be made in accordance with the Instrument Flight Rules (IFR) but which, instead, is made with the permission of the responsible ATCU, and in accordance with stipulated conditions.

VFR flights must be conducted in accordance with Special VFR at all times within a Class A CTR and in any other CTR, at night, or when Instrument Flight Conditions (IMC) prevail.

The following conditions apply to all Special VFR flights:

- The pilot must always obtain an ATC clearance and comply with ATC instructions.

- The pilot must at all times remain clear of cloud and in sight of the surface.

- The pilot must at all times remain in flight conditions which will enable him to determine his flight path and to remain clear of obstacles.

When flying in a CTR in accordance with a Special VFR Clearance, a PPL holder without any higher ratings must remain clear of cloud, in sight of the surface, and have a flight visibility of at least 10 kilometres.

A pilot may request a Special VFR clearance from the responsible ATCU to enter a CTR when airborne. The pilot must pass his flight details, to include an estimated time when he expects to be at a specified entry point to the CTR, usually a Visual Reference Point (VRP) marked on his aeronautical chart. An airborne request for a Special VFR clearance should be made between 5 and 10 minutes before reaching the VRP.

A Special VFR clearance will normally be granted by the ATCU only when traffic conditions are such as to enable the Special VFR flight to take place without hindering IFR traffic.

No SVFR clearance will be issued to a fixed-wing aircraft to depart from a CTR when visibility is less than 1800 metres, or cloud ceiling lower than 600 feet.

Weather limitations for Special VFR flights arriving at or departing from a CTR are detailed in the UK AIP. A PPL holder without an IMC Rating must at all times remain clear of cloud and in sight of the surface; forward in-flight visibility must be at least 10 kilometres.

No Special VFR clearance will be issued to a fixed-wing aircraft intending to depart from a CTR when visibility is less than 1800 metres or cloud ceiling lower than 600 feet.

If a pilot flying on a Special VFR clearance experiences radio failure, he must squawk 7600, with Mode C, if his aircraft is suitably equipped.

A Special VFR clearance does not absolve the pilot-in-command from complying with the prevailing CTR or ATZ rules.

Although a Special VFR clearance may stipulate an operating height below the Rule 5 Low Flying Rule minimum, the Special VFR Clearance does <u>not</u> absolve the pilot from the requirement of that Rule in respect of flying over a congested area or from operating his aircraft at such a height as would enable him to put his aircraft down, in the event of an emergency, without danger to persons and property on the ground.

The ATCU will provide standard separation between all Special VFR flights and between Special VFR flights and IFR flights.

A Special VFR clearance does not absolve the pilot from avoiding an active ATZ situated within a CTR, or, if the ATZ is to entered, from obtaining the necessary permission from the ATZ authority.

Radio Failure Procedure for Special VFR Flights.
If a pilot should experience radio failure when flying in accordance with a Special VFR clearance, he should adopt the following procedure:

- Squawk 7600 with Mode C, if the aircraft is suitably equipped.

- If he believes that the radio transmitter is functioning, transmit blind position reports and intentions.

- If the aircraft is not yet within the CTR, do not enter the CTR even if the Special VFR clearance to do so has already been obtained.

- If within the CTR and inbound to the aerodrome, continue in accordance with the Special VFR clearance to the aerodrome and land as soon as possible. Watch for visual signals when in the aerodrome traffic circuit.

- If transiting the CTR, continue the flight, not above the cleared level, and leave the CTR by the most direct route taking into account the weather conditions, obstacles and known areas of dense traffic.

- Notify the Air Traffic Control Unit concerned as soon as practicable.

> *If a pilot experiences radio failure when flying in accordance with an SVFR clearance and has not yet entered the CTR, he must remain outside the CTR.*

UNCONTROLLED AIRSPACE.

Uncontrolled airspace is classified as either Class F or Class G.

Class F Airspace.

Class F airspace is advisory airspace. *(See Figure 14.7).* Pilots wishing to use the advisory service from a participating Air Traffic Service Unit (ATSU), must file a flight plan and the flight will then take place under the Instrument Flight Rules (IFR).

Fig 14.7 Class F Uncontrolled Airspace - Advisory Routes.

Flights in Class F Airspace which are conducted in accordance with the Visual Flight Rules (VFR) may receive a Flight Information Service if pilots request one.

Additional features of Class F Airspace are as follows:

- No aircraft need submit a flight plan unless the pilot wishes to receive the Advisory Service.

- Neither an IFR flight nor a VFR flight has to maintain continuous two-way communications, if not using the Advisory Service.

- Advisory Routes are deemed to be 10 nm wide (5 nm either side of the centreline) although only the centreline is shown on charts.

- Advisory Routes should be crossed at right angles at the correct Flight Level, according to the Quadrantal Rule.

Class G Airspace.

Class G Airspace is open airspace within the Flight Information Region (FIR), often called the "Open FIR". Class G Airspace is basically all the airspace on your chart which is not labelled. The only services that the London and Scottish Air Traffic Control Centres are required to provide to aircraft flying in Class G Airspace are the Basic Service of the UK Flight Information Service (FIS) and an Alerting Service. As well as the Basic Service, the full suite of the UK FIS and the Alerting Service may also be available from participating ATSUs based at certain aerodromes.

However, at and below Flight Level 95, in uncontrolled airspace, a Lower Airspace Radar Service (LARS), which does offer the full suite of the UK FIS may be available from participating ATSUs *(See Page 250).*

London Flight Information Service.

If a pilot is receiving a Basic Service from London Information he will be required to squawk 7401. This is in order to enable any radar - equipped ATSUs whose airspace looks likely to be infringed by the aircraft, to ask London Information to transfer the aircraft to its frequency until the situation is resolved.

VFR Flight in Uncontrolled Airspace.

As long as the Rules of the Air are complied with, VFR flights may take place in Class G Airspace, in the Visual Meteorological Conditions (VMC) minima which apply to an aircraft's vertical position, without the pilot being in contact with, and without any reference to, an ATSU. The pilot-in-command is responsible for determining whether or not the VMC minima permit flight in accordance with VFR.

No flight plan needs to be filed for a VFR flight in uncontrolled airspace, though, if the pilot wishes, he <u>may</u> file a flight plan for any flight.

Obviously, as a matter of routine, a VFR pilot must be especially vigilant in his observation of the rules which apply to Air Traffic Zones (ATZ), as well as Prohibited, Restricted and Danger Areas that are likely to lie on the route along which he is flying.

In the UK, VFR flights at and above FL100 must carry a serviceable transponder with Modes A and C.

When cruising above the transition altitude (See Chapter 19), which is 3000 feet across most of the United Kingdom, VFR pilots are strongly recommended to fly at the Flight Level appropriate to their magnetic track, in accordance with the Quadrantal Rule.

If a VFR flight is made at Flight Level 100 or above, in the United Kingdom, the carriage of a serviceable transponder with both Modes A and C is mandatory. However, Mode S will become mandatory after March 2012, and is already so for flight in Class A to C controlled airspace for powered aircraft.

VFR Flight in Uncontrolled Airspace and the PPL holder.

A great many holders of a Private Pilots Licence do not possess any higher rating than a basic class rating covering the class of aircraft they fly. PPL holders who do <u>not</u> also hold an Instrument Rating or Instrument Meteorological Conditions (IMC) Rating are subject to certain restrictions, even when flying in uncontrolled airspace, imposed by virtue of the basic privileges of the PPL (See Schedule 8 of the Air Navigation Order), which are more stringent than the Visual Flight Rules, themselves. Notable among these extra restrictions are that a PPL holder who does not hold an Instrument Rating or IMC Rating may <u>not</u> fly as pilot-in-command of an aircraft:

- On a flight outside controlled airspace when the visibility is less than 3 km.

- Out of sight of the surface.

IFR Flight in Uncontrolled Airspace.

Flights in uncontrolled airspace may take place in accordance with the Instrument Flight Rules (IFR) provided the IFR Minimum Height Rule and the Quadrantal Rule are complied with.

The IFR Minimum Height Rule states that an aircraft may not fly at a height less than 1 000 feet above the highest obstacle within 5 nm unless below 3 000 feet, clear of cloud, and in sight of the surface, or unless taking off or landing.

As far as the majority of PPL holders are concerned, the Minimum Height Rule and the Quadrantal Rule may be summed up as follows:

Minimum Height Rule.

In order to comply with IFR, an aircraft may not fly at a height of less than 1000 feet above the highest obstacle within a distance of 5 nautical miles, unless:

- It is necessary to do so in order to take-off and land.

- The aircraft is flying at an altitude not exceeding 3000 feet above mean sea-level, and remains clear of cloud and in sight of the surface.

The Quadrantal Rule.

In order to comply with IFR, an aircraft in level flight above an altitude of 3000 feet (or the transition altitude, whichever is the higher) and below Flight Level 195, must fly at a Flight Level (i.e. with the altimeter sub-scale set to 1013.2 mb) appropriate to its magnetic track, in accordance with the Quadrantal Rule, (See Chapters 10 and 19).

All flights at night in the United Kingdom must be conducted in accordance with the Instrument Flight Rules.

Pilots who do not hold an Instrument Rating or IMC Rating may not fly in accordance with the Instrument Flight Rules unless Visual Meteorological Conditions prevail.

All flights at night, in the United Kingdom, must be conducted in accordance with IFR.

DETAILS OF UNITED KINGDOM AIRSPACE, BY CLASS OF AIRSPACE, WITH VMC MINIMA.

The following tables summarise the details of airspace in the UK by letter classification.

For each class of airspace, the following details are included:

- Air traffic services provided.

- Separation criteria.

- VMC minima.

- Speed limitation.

- Radio communication requirements.

- ATC clearance requirements.

CLASS A - Controlled Airspace		
	IFR	VFR
Separation provided	All aircraft	**VFR FLIGHT NOT PERMITTED.**
Service provided	Air traffic control service	
VMC minima	Not applicable	
Speed limitation	Not applicable	
Radio communication	Continuous two-way	
ATC clearance	Required	

CLASS B - Controlled Airspace		
	IFR	VFR
Separation provided	All aircraft	All aircraft
Service provided	Air traffic control service	Air traffic control service
VMC minima	Not applicable	**At or above FL100** 8 km visibility. Clear of cloud. **Below FL100** 5 km visibility. Clear of cloud.
Speed limitation	Not applicable	Not applicable
Radio communication	Continuous two-way	Continuous two-way
ATC clearance	Required	Required

CLASS C - Controlled Airspace		
	IFR	VFR
Separation provided	All aircraft	VFR from IFR
Service provided	Air traffic control service	Air traffic control service providing: • Separation from IFR traffic • VFR traffic information (and traffic avoidance advice on request)
VMC minima	Not applicable	**At or above FL100** 8 km visibility, 1 500 m horizontal and 1 000 feet vertical distance from cloud **Below FL100** 5 km visibility, 1 500 m horizontal and 1 000 feet vertical distance from cloud **Below 3 000 feet** **Aeroplanes**: Airspeed less than 140 knots, 5 km flight visibility, Clear of cloud, In sight of the surface **Helicopters**: Clear of cloud, In sight of the surface, Forward visibility compatible with speed
Speed limitation	Not applicable	250 kts IAS below FL 100
Radio communication	Continuous two-way	Continuous two-way
ATC clearance	Required	Required

CLASS D - Controlled Airspace		
	IFR	**VFR**
Separation provided	IFR from IFR	Not provided
Service provided	Air traffic control service including traffic information about VFR flights (and traffic avoidance advice on request)	Air traffic control service providing traffic information on all other flights
VMC minima	Not applicable	**At or above FL100** 8 km visibility, 1 500 m horizontal and 1 000 feet vertical distance from cloud **Below FL100** 5 km visibility, 1 500 m horizontal and 1 000 feet vertical distance from cloud **Below 3 000 feet** **Aeroplanes**: Airspeed less than 140 knots, 5 km flight visibility, Clear of cloud, In sight of the surface **Helicopters:** Clear of cloud, In sight of the surface, Forward visibility compatible with speed
Speed limitation	250 kt IAS below FL 100	250 kts IAS below FL 100
Radio communication	Continuous two-way	Continuous two-way
ATC clearance	Required	Required

CLASS E - Controlled Airspace		
	IFR	**VFR**
Separation provided	IFR from IFR	Not provided
Service provided	Air traffic control service and traffic information about VFR flights as far as practical	Air traffic control service providing traffic information as far as practical.
VMC minima	Not applicable	**At or above FL100** 8 km visibility 1 500 m horizontal and 1 000 feet vertical distance from cloud **Below FL100** 5 km visibility 1 500 m horizontal and 1 000 feet vertical distance from cloud **Below 3 000 feet** **Aeroplanes**: Airspeed less than 140 knots. 5 km flight visibility. Clear of cloud, in sight of the surface **Helicopters:** Clear of cloud, in sight of the surface. Forward visibility compatible with speed.
Speed limitation	250 kt IAS below FL 100	250 kt IAS below FL 100
Radio communication	Continuous two-way	Not Required
ATC Clearance	Required	Not Required

CLASS F - Uncontrolled Airspace		
	IFR	**VFR**
Separation provided	IFR from IFR (participating IFR traffic)	Not provided. Traffic and Deconfliction Service may be available.
Service provided	Procedural Service or Deconfliction Service (A Traffic Service may be provided in addition to a Procedural Service)	Basic Service (A Traffic Deconfliction or Procedural Service may be available.)
VMC minima	Not applicable	**At or above FL100** 8 km visibility, 1 500 m horizontal and 1 000 feet vertical distance from cloud **Below FL100** 5 km visibility, 1 500 m horizontal and 1 000 feet vertical distance from cloud **At or below 3000 AMSL Aeroplanes: Airspeed 140 knots or more.** 5 km visibility, Clear of cloud, In sight of surface **Airspeed below 140 knots.** 1500 metres visibility,* Clear of cloud, In sight of surface
Speed limitation	250 kt IAS below FL 100	250 kt IAS below FL 100
Radio communication	Not required	Not required
ATC clearance	Not required	Not required

CLASS G - Uncontrolled Airspace		
	IFR	**VFR**
Separation provided	Not provided	Not provided. Traffic and Deconfliction Service may be available.
Service provided	Basic Service (Traffic, Deconfliction and Procedural Service may be available).	Basic Service (Traffic, Deconfliction and Procedural Service may be available).
VMC minima	Not applicable	**At or below 3000 AMSL Aeroplanes: Airspeed 140 knots or more.** 5 km visibility, Clear of cloud, In sight of surface **Airspeed below 140 knots.** 1500 metres visibility,* Clear of cloud, In sight of surface
Speed limitation	250 kt IAS below FL 100	250 kt IAS below FL 100
Radio communication	Not required	Not required
ATC clearance	Not required	Not required

* N.B. Although this is the VMC minimum visibility you should note that PPL holders who do not possess either an Instrument Rating or IMC Rating are not allowed to fly as PIC of an aircraft when the in-flight visibility is less than 3 kilometres.

Note: The 250kt speed limitation does not apply to military aircraft.

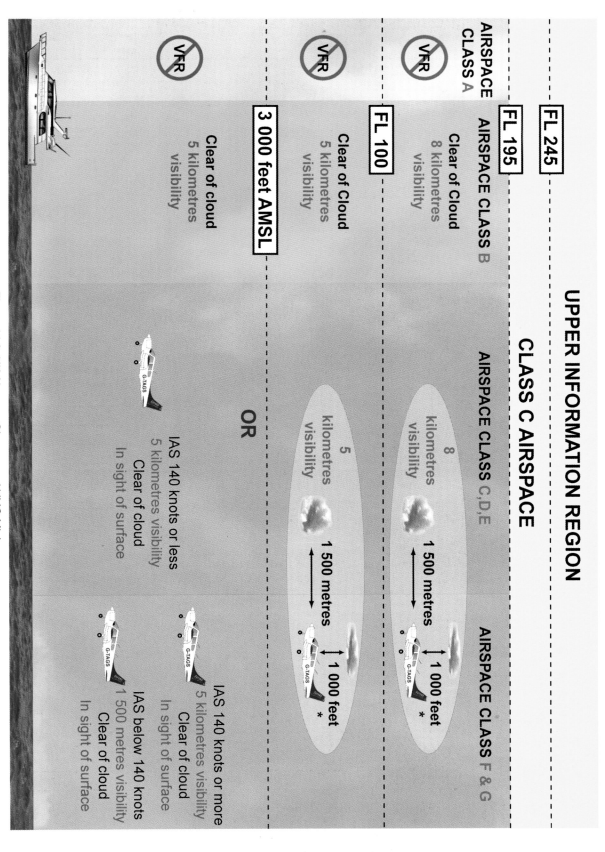

Figure 14.8 UK Airspace Classes and VMC Minima.

*NB Pilots without an Instrument Rating or IMC Rating must maintain sight of the surface at all times.

CROSSING AN AIRWAY.

VFR Flight is not permitted in UK Airways, all of which are Class A airspace.

Gliders.

There are certain exemptions for gliders if the airway is notified for the purpose of Air Navigation Order Rule 21(2). However, specific conditions apply to the exercise of the exemption. Glider pilots must arrange to be briefed on these conditions, and on the airways to which the conditions apply, by a recognised authority, before taking advantage of the exemptions.

Pilots without an Instrument Rating.

PPL holders without an Instrument Rating may cross the base of the en-route section of an airway, at right-angles, in VMC only, and only where the lower vertical limit of the airway is defined as a Flight Level. But VFR traffic must never enter the airway.

Pilots with an Instrument Rating.

Pilots who hold an Instrument Rating, while piloting an aircraft not equipped for IFR Flight, may cross an airway only:

a.   In VMC.

b.   By day.

c.   By the shortest possible route (usually at right angles to the airway).

d.   Having filed a flight plan – either before departure or in the air.

e.   Having received crossing clearance from the Air Traffic Control Unit, at least 10 minutes prior to penetration of the airway.

AERODROME TRAFFIC ZONES.

Aerodrome Traffic Zones are not included in the Airspace Classification System. They have the same classification as the airspace within which they are situated. So an Aerodrome Traffic Zone may have any classification from A to G. Many aerodromes in the United Kingdom which are located outside controlled airspace have an Aerodrome Traffic Zone (ATZ) established around the aerodrome in order that aircraft operating in the ATZ, and especially the circuit pattern, should be protected from aircraft flying in the vicinity of the ATZ.

ATZs are established around the following types of aerodromes within the United Kingdom:

*   Licensed aerodrome having two-way communications with aircraft.

*   Any aerodrome providing Air Traffic Control Service or an Airfield Flight Information Service.

*   Government aerodromes.

Air Traffic Zone Dimensions.

The dimensions of **ATZs** in the United Kingdom are as follows: *(See Figure 14.9)*

Vertical: Surface to 2 000 feet above aerodrome level (AAL)

Horizontal: A circle centred on the mid-point of the longest runway being a radius of:

* 2 nm if the longest runway is 1 850 m or shorter,

or

* 2.5 nm if the longest runway is over 1 850 m.

NB: If there is less than 1.5 nm clearance from the end of all runways, the radius of the **ATZ** is expanded from 2 nm to 2.5 nm.

Dimensions of an ATZ.

Vertical:
Surface to 2 000 feet AAL.

Horizontal: *2 nms radius if the longest runway is 1 850 m or shorter, and 2.5 nms if the runway is over 1 850 m*

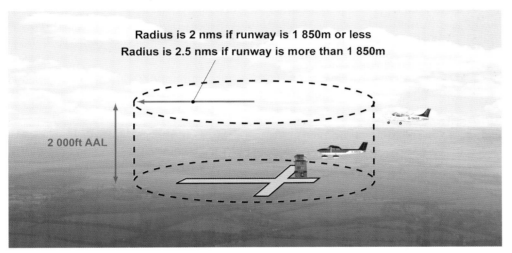

Radius is 2 nms if runway is 1 850m or less
Radius is 2.5 nms if runway is more than 1 850m

2 000ft AAL

Fig 14.9 The Dimensions of an Aerodrome Traffic Zone in the United Kingdom.

An off-shore installation (e.g. an oil-rig) normally has an **ATZ** of 2 000 feet Above Mean Sea Level (AMSL) and a radius of 1.5 nm. *(See Figure 14.10).*

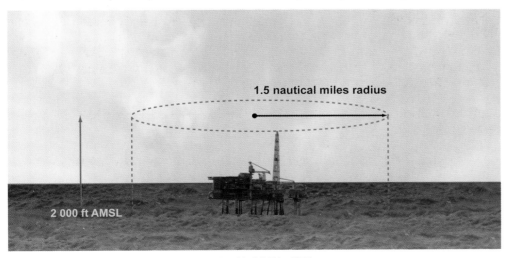

1.5 nautical miles radius

2 000 ft AMSL

Fig 14.10 Oil Rig ATZ.

Rules Governing Flight Within Aerodrome Traffic Zones in the United Kingdom.

Where a full Air Traffic Control (ATC) service is available, an aircraft shall not fly, take off, transit, or land, within the ATZ unless the commander of the aircraft has obtained the permission of the responsible Air Traffic Control Unit (ATCU).

Where there is no ATCU, the pilot-in-command shall not fly, take-off, transit or land, within the ATZ unless he has obtained from the Aerodrome Flight Information Service Unit or Air/Ground Radio Unit, at that aerodrome, sufficient information to enable the flight within the ATZ to be conducted with safety.

If equipped with a radio, the pilot-in-command of an aircraft flying within an ATZ must ensure that a continuous radio watch is maintained on the appropriate radio frequency.

When an aircraft is not equipped with radio, the pilot-in-command must keep a watch out for visual instructions from the Air Traffic Service Unit (ATSU) or comply with the indications of the signals square.

On entering an ATZ and immediately prior to leaving it, a pilot must communicate his position and height to the responsible ATSU.

When the aircraft is fitted with a radio, the pilot-in-command must communicate his position and height to the responsible ATSU, on entering the zone and immediately prior to leaving it.

Hours of Operation.

Hours of operation of aerodromes are to be found in the AD section (Aerodrome & Heliport Index - Specific) of the UK Aeronautical Information Publication (AIP). However, permanent changes (or temporary extensions) to these hours may be published in NOTAMS.

Failure to establish 2-way communications with the ATSU during the notified hours of operation must <u>not</u> be taken as an indication that the ATZ is inactive. If no communication is established with the ATZ aircraft must remain clear of the ATZ – unless the aircraft is in a state of emergency.

MILITARY AERODROME TRAFFIC ZONES.

Most military aerodromes in the United Kingdom which conduct regular flying operations have a Military Aerodrome Traffic Zone (MATZ) established around them, as well as a normal ATZ. The MATZ is of greater dimensions than the normal ATZ.

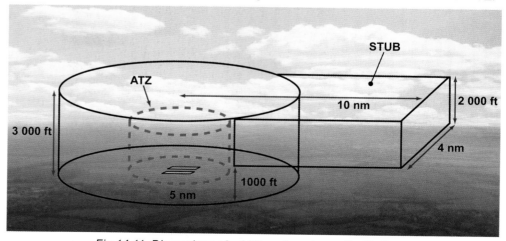

Fig 14.11 Dimensions of a Military Aerodrome Traffic Zone.

The Dimensions of Military Aerodrome Traffic Zones.

Most MATZs extend from the surface up to 3 000 feet above airfield level at a radius of 5 nm from the mid-point of the longest runway. *(See Figure 14.11)*.

The MATZ may have either one or two stubs projecting from it to 10 nm from the mid-point of the runway and having a width of 4 nm. The height of the stub(s) is 1 000 feet AAL to 3000 feet AAL. A stub is an extension of the MATZ in the direction from which instrument approaches are made. Some MATZ may differ from the above general dimensions.

Sometimes, one or two neighbouring MATZs are amalgamated to form a Combined MATZ (CMATZ), with one of the aerodromes being designated as the controlling authority of the CMATZ.

The Locations of Military Aerodrome Traffic Zones.

The locations of MATZs are depicted in *Figure 14.12*.

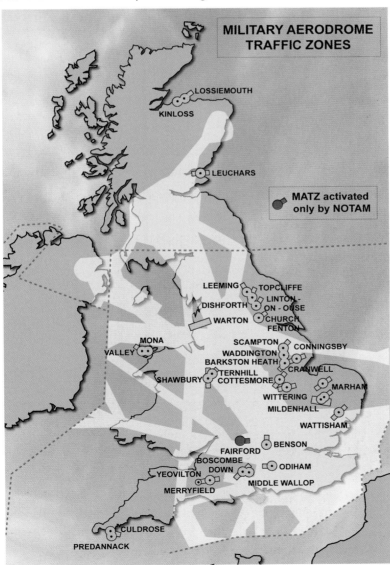

Fig 14.12 U.K. Military Air Traffic Zones.

Operating hours.

Operating hours for MATZs can be found in the ENR section of the AIP (unlike for the ATZ where the operating hours are found in the AD section of the AIP). However, the nature of military operations is such that a MATZ may be required to be operational outside the notified hours.

Operating in and Penetration of a MATZ.

Although permission is not required from the MATZ controller to penetrate the wider MATZ (permission _is_ required to enter the ATZ), a pilot would be foolish to enter a MATZ without contacting the MATZ controller.

When intending to enter or penetrate a MATZ, the pilot should make contact with the MATZ controller, either at a range of 15 nautical miles from the MATZ boundary, or at 5 minutes flying time from the MATZ boundary, whichever is the earlier.

Fig 14.13 The Benson MATZ as depicted on a 1:500 000 Aeronautical Chart, showing the ATZ at the centre of the MATZ.

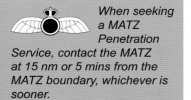

When seeking a MATZ Penetration Service, contact the MATZ at 15 nm or 5 mins from the MATZ boundary, whichever is sooner.

The following general observations apply to flight of civil aircraft within a MATZ:

- Pilots must comply with any instructions issued by the MATZ controller and maintain a continuous listening watch on the MATZ frequency.

- Pilots should advise the MATZ controller when clear of the MATZ.

- QFE is the usual altimeter subscale setting used within a MATZ.

- Within a Combined MATZ, a "Clutch QFE" will be passed to aircraft. Clutch QFE is the QFE of the aerodrome within the MATZ whose elevation is highest.

- Maintaining terrain clearance is the responsibility of the pilot.

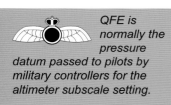

QFE is normally the pressure datum passed to pilots by military controllers for the altimeter subscale setting.

AIR TRAFFIC SERVICES WITHIN THE UNITED KINGDOM.

Air Traffic Services in the United Kingdom comply, in general, with ICAO-standard air traffic services already described in Chapter 5. Within United Kingdom Airspace, as within ICAO standard airspace, air traffic services consist of a full air traffic control service, a flight information service and an alerting service. However, it is important to understand that in the UK, unlike in ICAO, the Flight Information Service is a suite of four services. One of these, the Basic Service, is comparable to ICAO's Flight Information Service.

If you feel it necessary, you should revise the section of Chapter 5 dealing with air traffic services, before continuing.

In addition to the **ICAO air traffic services** detailed in Chapter 5, the United Kingdom provides the following additional services:

- Traffic Service.

- Deconfliction Service. } These services, together with the Basic Service make up the UK Flight Information Service

- Procedural Service

- Off-shore Service.

- Military Air Traffic Zone (MATZ) Penetration Service.

- Danger Area Crossing Service (DACS).

- Danger Area Activity Information Service (DAAIS).

The MATZ Penetration Service has already been dealt with in this chapter. The Danger Area Crossing Service (DACS) and the Danger Area Activity Information Service (DAAIS) will be covered in Chapter 18.

The offshore service is not relevant to your present level of study.

Therefore, the principal topics that we have to deal with in this chapter are the four services of the UK Flight Information Service. However, to begin with, we will look again at United Kingdom air traffic services in the context of traffic approaching and departing from aerodromes.

UNITED KINGDOM AIR TRAFFIC CONTROL IN RESPECT OF AERODROME TRAFFIC.

In a similar way to the ICAO-standard, full Air Traffic Control in the United Kingdom, in respect of aerodrome traffic, is divided into:

- Approach Control.

- Aerodrome Control.

Note: Although, in the UK, the division of responsibilities for Approach Control and Aerodrome Control may differ from aerodrome to aerodrome, it may generally be said that, on departure, the pilot will contact Aerodrome Control, first, for instructions and will, initially, on approaching a destination aerodrome, contact Approach Control for joining and landing instructions.

APPROACH CONTROL.

General.
Approach Control is either a radar or non-radar service and is the link between Area Control and Aerodrome Control. Approach Control is the service provided to arriving and departing aircraft. Approach Control is provided at all aerodromes which are within controlled airspace and at some which are not.

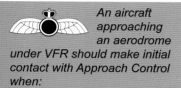

An aircraft approaching an aerodrome under VFR should make initial contact with Approach Control when:

- 15 nms
  or
- 5 minutes flying time from the CTR or ATZ boundary whichever is the sooner.

Arriving VFR Aircraft.

An aircraft approaching an aerodrome, flying in accordance with the Visual Flight Rules (VFR), should make initial contact with Approach Control when:

- 15 nm,

  or

- 5 minutes flying time from the Control Zone or ATZ boundary, whichever is the sooner.

Approach Control will then, generally, pass to the pilot landing information which will consist of:

- The runway in use.

- Current meteorological information which will include:

  a. Surface wind direction (in degrees magnetic) and speed.

  b. Visibility.

  c. Present weather.

  d. Significant cloud amount and height of cloud base.

  e. QFE or QNH.

  f. Any other information (gusts, icing etc).

- Runway surface conditions where appropriate.

- Any changes to the operational status of visual aids, where appropriate

In addition to the above landing information, Approach Control will pass to the arriving aircraft details of known traffic to assist the VFR pilot to maintain separation from both IFR and other VFR flights.

Departing Aircraft.

Within Controlled Airspace, aircraft are taken over from Aerodrome Control by Approach Control until they are handed over to the Area Control or Zone Control.

Outside controlled airspace, departing aircraft are taken over from Aerodrome Control by Approach Control until they:

- state that they no longer wish to be controlled,

  or

- are more than 10 minutes flying time away from the aerodrome, whichever is the sooner.

An Air Traffic Control Unit (ATCU) providing an Approach Control Service uses the call-sign "Approach" or "Radar", as appropriate, after the airfield designator.

AERODROME CONTROL.

The Aerodrome Control is a service provided by Aerodrome Control Towers. Aerodrome Control distributes information and issues clearances, in order to achieve a safe, orderly and expeditious flow of air traffic on and in the vicinity of an aerodrome, to:

• Aircraft, in the air, in the aerodrome circuit and in the vicinity of an aerodrome.

• Aircraft landing and taking off.

• Aircraft and vehicles on the manoeuvring area.

Departing Traffic.

The communications between Aerodrome Control and the pilot-in-command of an aircraft departing from the aerodrome in accordance with VFR will be of the following nature.

• There will be an initial call from the departing aircraft stating the intentions of the pilot, the number of persons on board and asking for taxi instructions. If there is an Automatic Terminal Information Service (ATIS), the pilot will pass to Aerodrome Control the letter identifying the ATIS broadcast to confirm that he has received the information; otherwise ATIS information will be passed to the pilot by Aerodrome Control

• Aerodrome Control will issue a clearance to the aircraft to taxi to a clearance limit on the aerodrome, normally the holding point of the runway in use. If there is no ATIS at the aerodrome, the runway in use will be specified by Aerodrome Control, along with the relevant QNH and the surface wind direction and strength.

• When the pilot announces that he is ready for departure, Aerodrome Control will pass a clearance to line up, and then to take-off. A take-off clearance may be issued directly. Surface wind direction and strength may be repeated at this point. Any condition to the clearance will precede the clearance, e.g. 'After the landing aircraft, line up', and must be read back in the given sequence.

Fig 14.14 Aerodrome Control Service.

Arriving Traffic.

The communications between Aerodrome Control and the pilot-in-command of a VFR flight arriving at the aerodrome will be of the following nature.

- There will be an initial call from the arriving aircraft stating the pilot's intention to enter the ATZ or CTR and to land. If there is an Automatic Terminal Information Service (ATIS), the pilot will pass to Aerodrome Control the letter identifying the ATIS broadcast to confirm that he has received the information; otherwise ATIS information will be passed to the pilot by Aerodrome Control along with any necessary clearance to enter the Zone and to join the aerodrome circuit for a designated runway-in-use. This information will include the runway-in-use, circuit direction and QNH.

- If Zone entry and approach to land are acceptable to Aerodrome Control, Aerodrome Control will normally issue a succession of clearances to proceed in the circuit and to land.

- The clearance to land itself will be accompanied by Aerodrome Control's passing, once again, the surface wind direction and strength.

- After landing, Aerodrome Control will issue instructions to the pilot as to where to vacate the runway, and a clearance to proceed to a specified parking area. The pilot will normally announce to Aerodrome Control that he has vacated the runway.

- Aerodrome Control will issue parking instructions, if necessary.

- The callsign of Aerodrome Control is the aerodrome identifier (for example, Oxford or Brize) followed by the word "Tower".

AUTOMATIC TERMINAL INFORMATION SERVICE (ATIS).

General.

At some busy aerodromes an Automatic Terminal Information Service (ATIS) broadcasts routine arrival and departure information to aircraft. The presence of an ATIS reduces the number of radio transmissions that need to be made and, thereby, the work load of controllers. ATIS is transmitted on a discrete frequency. Beware! Some aerodromes may only give departure information. Be careful not to use this information if on an arrival.

Code Letter (Designator).

ATIS broadcasts will normally commence and end with an identifying code letter (designator), expressed in the phonetic alphabet. As significant changes take place in the aerodrome conditions, ATIS information will be updated, and the broadcasts identified by different code letters, working sequentially through the alphabet.

Pilot Confirmation.

Departing aircraft must, and arriving aircraft should, confirm receipt of the latest ATIS broadcast. For departing aircraft, this is done when taxi clearance is requested:

For arriving aircraft, the confirmation of receipt of ATIS information is made on initial contact with either Approach or Aerodrome Control.

Contents of an ATIS Broadcast.

A basic ATIS broadcasts should contain all or part of the following information:

- Name of aerodrome.

- Identifying code letter of the broadcast.

- Time of observation.

- Runway in use.

- Significant runway conditions and - if appropriate - braking action.

- Surface Wind.

- Visibility.

- Present weather.

- Cloud below 5 000 feet or below the highest sector altitude, whichever is the greater; the presence of any cumulonimbus; if the sky is obscured, vertical visibility when available.

- Air temperature.

- Dew point.

- Altimeter settings.

- Any significant weather in the approach, take-off and climb-out areas.

- Any specific ATC instructions.

AERODROME TRAFFIC SERVICES AT NON-CONTROLLED AIRFIELDS.

In the United Kingdom, where aerodromes are located outside controlled airspace, and do not have a full air traffic control service, a more basic aerodrome traffic service may be provided. This more basic service can be one of two types:

- The Aerodrome Flight Information Service.

- The Air-Ground Radio Service.

The units providing these two basic services are included under the description Air Traffic Service Unit (ATSU).

Aerodrome Flight Information Service.

An Aerodrome Flight Information Service (AFIS) does not provide an air traffic control service. An AFIS provides information to air traffic arriving at, departing, or operating on the manoeuvring area of an aerodrome around which an Aerodrome Traffic Zone (ATZ) is established. When receiving an AFIS, the responsibility for maintaining separation from other traffic remains that of the pilot-in-command. An AFIS is provided by a Flight Information Service Officer (FISO) who is regulated by the CAA but will not have been trained to the level of an Air Traffic Control Officer.

When receiving an AFIS, the responsibility for maintaining separation from other traffic remains that of the Pilot-in-Command.

A FISO is responsible for issuing information to aircraft concerning:

- Other aircraft within the ATZ, in order to assist pilots in preventing collisions.

- Other aircraft, vehicles and obstacles on the Manoeuvring Area, again to assist pilots in preventing collisions. (Note that a FISO is authorised to give instructions to vehicles and aircraft on the Manoeuvring Area).

- The state of the aerodrome and its facilities.

The callsign of an AFIS is the aerodrome designator, with the suffix "Information".

The FISO is also responsible for alerting the safety services as necessary and for initiating overdue action. The callsign of an AFIS is the aerodrome identifier, followed by the word "Information".

Air-Ground Radio Service.

Air - Ground Radio Operators may pass only basic information to aircraft, concerning runway-in-use, and other traffic using the aerodrome.

This is the most basic type of aerodrome air traffic service. The Aerodrome Air-Ground Service is provided by Radio Operators who are not licensed but have obtained a certificate of competency from the CAA. Air-Ground Radio Operators may pass only basic information to aircraft concerning runway-in-use and other traffic on the aerodrome and in the aerodrome circuit.

Fig 14.15 Air/Ground Radio Communications.

An Air - Ground Radio Service is identified by the suffix "Radio", after the aerodrome designator.

An Air-Ground Radio Service is identified by the name of the aerodrome, followed by the word "Radio".

VFR FLIGHT IN THE AERODROME CIRCUIT PATTERN.

General.

It is essential that pilots should be familiar with the standard aerodrome circuit pattern. Because of the diverse nature of local conditions and of differing aircraft performance characteristics, it is not possible to define a common circuit procedure applicable to all aerodromes. However, the following guidelines for joining the aerodrome circuit and making position reports within the circuit should be applicable in most cases, especially in the case of uncontrolled airfields.

Standard Overhead Join.

A pilot who has been instructed or advised by an Air Traffic Service Unit (ATSU) to complete a standard overhead join, should:

- Overfly the aerodrome at 1 000 feet above published circuit height.

- Descend on the dead side to circuit height making all turns in the circuit direction.

- Join the circuit by crossing the upwind end of the runway at circuit height.

- Position the aircraft downwind.

The standard overhead join procedure is shown in *Figure 14.16*.

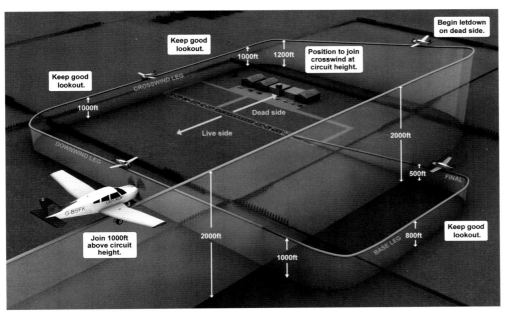

Fig 14.16 Standard Overhead Join.

Position Reports.

Position reports should be made as follows:

"Downwind"

When abeam the upwind end of the runway.

"Late Downwind"

When on the downwind leg of the circuit and unable to report "Downwind" at the correct position, having passed abeam the downwind end of the runway.

"Base Leg"

If requested by ATC, immediately on completion of the turn onto base leg.

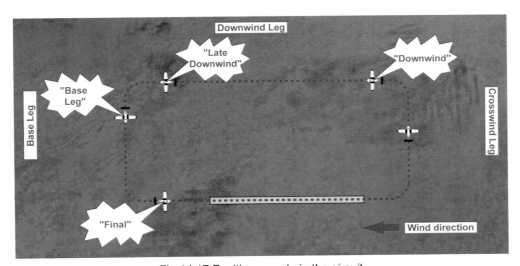

Fig 14.17 Position reports in the circuit.

For a straight-in approach, "Long Final" is called at 8 nms from the end of the runway.

If wishing to carry out a straight-in approach, all pilots should make absolutely certain that they are cleared to do so by ATC and that they keep an extra good look out for other aircraft.

"Final"

After completion of the turn onto the final approach and when at a range of not more than 4 nm from the approach end of the runway. The call should include the pilot's intention, e.g. land.

"Long Final"

•   When on final approach at a greater distance than 4 nm, (Call "Final" when a range of 4 nm is reached).

•   **When flying a straight-in approach at 8 nm from the approach end of the runway. (Call "Final" when a range of 4 nm is reached**.*)*

Notes:

•   At grass aerodromes, the area to be used for landing should be regarded as the runway for the purposes of position reporting.

•   It should be remembered that it is the pilot's responsibility to conform to the traffic pattern. In many cases, a straight-in approach may not be approved. If wishing to carry out a straight-in approach at a controlled airfield, all pilots should make absolutely certain that they are cleared to do so by the Air Traffic Control Unit.

UK FLIGHT INFORMATION SERVICE.

In the UK, Air Traffic Services Outside Controlled Airspace (ATSOCAS) are provided by a variety of air traffic units and used by a wide variety of users from General Aviation to commercial flights and military aircraft.

The suite of services is collectively known as the "UK Flight Information Service". They are detailed in CAP 774 and summarised here.

Outside controlled airspace, it is not mandatory for a pilot to be in receipt of an air traffic service. This principle generates a traffic environment over which air traffic controllers have no oversight. Consequently, outside controlled airspace, it is the pilot who bears responsibility for collision avoidance and terrain/obstacle clearance.

There are 4 distinct services to the new "UK Flight Information Service":

1. Basic Service; 2.Traffic Service; 3.Deconfliction Service; 4 Procedural Service

The various services are designed to cater for a wide variety of airspace users and tasks. It is essential that controllers and pilots all have a detailed knowledge of the services.   Within an FIR, the only service that is required to be offered, as mandated by ICAO, is the Basic Service. The other three services may be provided by ATSU's if they are suitably equipped and have the capacity to do so. However, the UK Lower Airspace Radar Service (LARS) will, within their operating hours, offer the more comprehensive Traffic and Deconfliction Service which require radar surveillance equipment.

Pilot compliance is relied upon in order to promote a safer operating environment, but it is not mandatory.

Pilots should determine the most appropriate service for the phase and conditions of the flight and request that service from the controller. You should note that a FISO will provide a Basic Service only.

Basic Service.

A Basic Service is intended to offer the pilot maximum autonomy. Avoidance of other traffic and terrain is solely the pilot's responsibility.

The controller/FISO will pass information pertinent to the safe and efficient conduct of flight. This can include weather, changes of serviceability of facilities, conditions at aerodromes and general activity information within an air traffic service unit's (ATSU) area of responsibility. Pilots should not expect traffic information when outside an ATZ.

It is not necessary to have an ATS surveillance system to offer a Basic Service. It is important that pilots should be aware of this fact. The Basic Service is, therefore, not an appropriate service for flight in IMC.

Within a Basic Service, "Agreements" between pilots and controllers (and FISOs) can be established to restrict an aircraft to a specific flight level or altitude, level band, heading, route, or operating area.

Please note that the Flight Information Service referred to by ICAO, is the same as the Basic Service as provided in the UK.

Traffic Service.

A Traffic Service provides the pilot with surveillance-derived traffic information on conflicting aircraft. No deconfliction advice is passed and the pilot is responsible for collision avoidance.

A Traffic Service contains the information available in a Basic Service, and additionally, controllers will endeavour to provide surveillance-derived traffic information on relevant traffic which is anticipated to pass within 3 nm and 3000 ft.

Deconfliction advice is not offered.

A Traffic Service is available under any flight rules or meteorological conditions. However, it is not an appropriate service for flight in IMC if another more suitable service can be offered.

Agreements can be established to restrict an aircraft to a specific level, level band, heading, route, or operating area.

A pilot may operate under his own navigation or a controller may provide headings or levels for positioning, sequencing or navigational assistance.

A pilot must not change general route, manoeuvring area, heading or levels or a controller-allocated heading without first advising and obtaining a response from the controller.

Allocated levels will be terrain safe.

Deconfliction Service.

A Deconfliction Service provides the pilot with traffic information and deconfliction advice on conflicting aircraft. However, the avoidance of other aircraft is ultimately the pilot's responsibility.

A Deconfliction Service contains the information available in a Basic Service, and, additionally, controllers will aim to assist the pilot with his responsibility for the safety of the aircraft by passing traffic information and deconfliction advice.

Headings and/or levels will also be issued for positioning, sequencing and/or deconfliction advice.

The pilot may decide not to act on the advice, in which case he must inform the controller and then accept responsibility for deconfliction.

A Deconfliction Service is available under any flight rules or meteorological conditions.

Controllers will expect the pilot to accept headings and/or levels that may require flight in IMC.

A Deconfliction Service is to be provided only to aircraft operating at or above the ATC unit's terrain safe level unless the aircraft is on departure from an aerodrome or on an instrument approach.

A pilot must not change heading or level without first advising and obtaining a response from the controller. If a heading or level allocation is unacceptable, the controller must be immediately informed.

Procedural Service.

A Procedural Service is a non surveillance service during which instructions are provided which, if complied with, will achieve deconfliction minima with respect to other aircraft in receipt of a Procedural Service from the same controller.

The avoidance of other aircraft is the pilot's responsibility.

A Procedural Service contains the information available in a Basic Service, and, additionally, controllers will aim to assist the pilot with his responsibility for the safety of the aircraft by providing vertical, lateral, longitudinal, and time instruction, aimed at achieving deconfliction minima with respect to other aircraft to which the controller is also providing a Procedural Service.

A Procedural Service is available under any flight rules or meteorological conditions.

Controllers will expect the pilot to accept radial, track, level and time allocations that may require flight in IMC.

Pilots who do not require deconfliction advice should not request a Procedural Service.

Under a Procedural Service, high reliance is placed on the pilot's ability to follow radial, track and time allocations; therefore in high controller workload and/or where airspace availability is limited, controllers may not be able to provide a Procedural Service to a pilot who is flying purely by visual references.

Controllers will provide deconfliction instructions by allocating levels, radials, tracks and time restrictions, or use pilot position reports, aimed at achieving planned deconfliction minima with respect to other aircraft receiving a Procedural Service.

If a radial, track, time or level allocation is unacceptable to the pilot, the controller must immediately be informed, and pilots must not change radial, track, or time allocation without first advising and obtaining a response from the controller

In a Procedural Service, controllers may specify required altitudes or flight levels.

LOWER AIRSPACE RADAR SERVICE (LARS).

The Lower Airspace Radar service (LARS) was introduced in 1979 as a funding scheme to reimburse Air Navigation Service Providers for the provision of the radar service element of Air Traffic Services Outside Controlled Airspace (ATSOCAS).

A LARS is provided outside Controlled airspace up to and including FL95, within approximately 30 nm of the participating aerodrome.

All traffic flying IFR in controlled airspace will generally be in receipt of a radar service. In the United Kingdom, aircraft flying VFR in uncontrolled airspace may also be able to receive a surveillance radar service when in receipt of a Traffic or Deconfliction Service as part of the UK FIS. LARS forms an integral part in offering ATSOCAS.

A LARS is available from a number of participating ATSUs, mostly at military aerodromes.

Participating aerodromes are depicted in *Figure 14.18*. Aerodromes offering a LARS are listed in the En-Route Section of the AIP.

The following points about LARS are worth remembering.

- LARS is available outside controlled airspace up to and including FL 95, within the limits of radar/radio cover.

- LARS is provided within approximately 30 nm of each participating aerodrome.

- LARS is normally available Mondays to Fridays between 0800 & 1700 hrs in summer, and 0700 & 1600 hrs in winter, although sometimes the service will be available outside these hours.

- While receiving a LARS, the Pilot-In-Command remains responsible for maintaining terrain clearance.

- The controller providing a LARS will not be aware of all the aircraft operating in the airspace in which the aircraft receiving is operating. Therefore, a sharp lookout should be maintained at all times by pilots receiving a LARS.

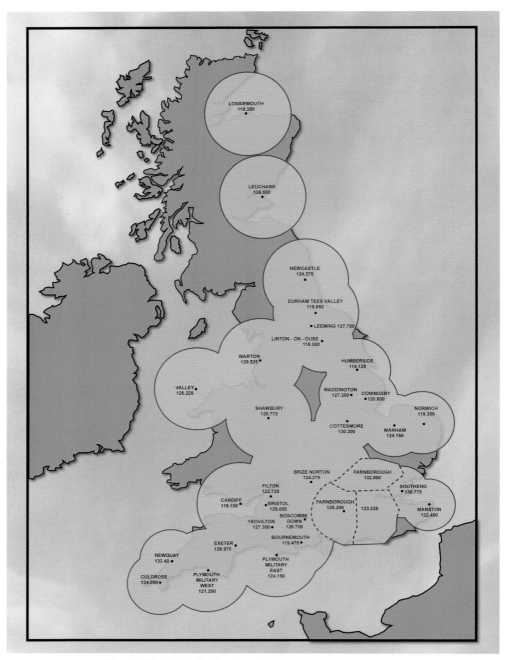

Fig 14.18 Air Traffic Service Units participating in LARS.

When the LARS controller and the pilot requesting a LARS have established contact, and the LARS has been confirmed, the pilot should:

- Maintain a listening watch on the allocated frequency.

- Follow advice issued by the controller or, if unable to do so, inform the controller.

- Advise the controller when the service is no longer required.

DANGER AREA CROSSING SERVICE (DACS) & DANGER AREA ACTIVITY INFORMATION SERVICE (DAAIS).

Details of these 2 services can be found in Chapter 18.

Representative PPL - type questions to test your theoretical knowledge of Airspace Division and Air Traffic Services in the United Kingdom.

1.   An arriving VFR aircraft intending to enter an ATZ should make contact with the Approach Controller when:

   a.   25 nm or 10 minutes flying time from the ATZ boundary whichever is the greater
   b.   25 nm or 10 minutes flying time from the ATZ boundary whichever is the lesser
   c.   15 nm or 5 minutes flying time from the ATZ boundary whichever is the sooner
   d.   15 nm or 5 minutes flying time from the ATZ boundary whichever is the lesser

2.   You wish to make a standard join overhead at an aerodrome. At what height would you overfly the aerodrome to initiate the join?

   a.   1 500 feet AAL
   b.   2 000 feet AAL
   c.   1 000 feet AGL
   d.   1 000 feet above circuit height.

3.   On what side of the aerodrome should an aircraft let down to circuit height during a standard join overhead?

   a.   The active side
   b.   The up-wind side
   c.   The dead side
   d.   The downwind side

4.   On a straight-in approach to land, at what distance from the threshold should the pilot report "Long Final" ?

   a.   10 nm
   b.   8 nm
   c.   5 nm
   d.   3 nm

5.   Who is responsible for terrain clearance when an aircraft is receiving a Deconfliction Service?

   a.   The Radar Controller
   b.   The pilot-in-command
   c.   Approach Control
   d.   The ATCU concerned

6.   In what airspace in the UK would a LARS be available?

   a.   Outside controlled airspace at FL 95 and below
   b.   Inside controlled airspace at FL 95 and below
   c.   Outside controlled airspace at FL 100 and below
   d.   Outside controlled airspace at FL 95 and above

7. At approximately what distance from a participating unit should a pilot contact the ATCU with a view to receiving a Lower Airspace Radar Service?

   a. 30 nm
   b. 10 nm
   c. 15 minutes
   d. 40 nm

8. What class of airspace are the two UIRs over the UK?

   a. A
   b. B
   c. C
   d. F

9. Up to what height do the FIRs extend over the UK?

   a. FL 95
   b. FL 100
   c. FL 245
   d. FL 250

10. A Lower Airspace Radar Service is available in the United Kingdom from participating ATSUs:

    a. At and below FL 245 within approximately 50 km of the participating ATSU
    b. At and below FL 100 within approximately 50 nautical miles of the participating ATSU
    c. At and below FL 95 within approximately 30 nautical miles of the participating ATSU
    d. At and below FL 195 within approximately 30 km of the participating ATSU

11. After the name of the airfield, a basic air-ground radio communications service at an uncontrolled airfield bears the name:

    a. Information
    b. Tower
    c. Approach
    d. Radio

12. For VFR flights in the United Kingdom, the carriage of a serviceable transponder is mandatory for flights:

    a. At and above 2 500 feet
    b. At and above FL 050
    c. At and above the transition level
    d. At and above FL 100

13. When flying in a Control Zone in accordance with a Special VFR Clearance, what flight visibility must be maintained by the holder of a PPL without any additional ratings?

    a. 5 km remaining clear of cloud and insight of the surface
    b. 10 km remaining clear of cloud and insight of the surface
    c. 8 km remaining clear of cloud and insight of the surface
    d. 3 km remaining 1000 feet vertically and 1 500 metres horizontally from cloud

14. While receiving a Radar Advisory Service as a PPL holder without any additional ratings, you are instructed by the LARS controller to alter course onto a heading which will take you into Instrument Meteorological Conditions. You should:

    a. Not respond to the instruction because you are not qualified to fly in IMC
    b. Acknowledge the controller's instructions and comply with them
    c. Advise the controller that you are unable to comply with the instruction as you have no IMC or Instrument Rating
    d. Comply with the controller's instructions but advise him that you have no IMC or Instrument Rating

15. The aerodrome traffic service provided by an Aerodrome Flight Information Service:

    a. Provides information in plain language for the safe and efficient conduct of flights in an Aerodrome Traffic Zone, but cannot control, give instructions or advise
    b. Provides a full air traffic control service
    c. Provides local weather information only
    d. Bears the suffix "Radio" after the name of the aerodrome

16. Which classes of airspace are considered Controlled Airspace?

    a. A & B only
    b. A, B & C only
    c. A, B, C, D & E only
    d. A only

17. What is Class F Airspace otherwise known as?

    a. Controlled Airspace
    b. Advisory Airspace
    c. Restricted Airspace
    d. Partially Controlled Airspace (PCA)

18. Would the radar controller give you headings and, if necessary, height changes to avoid conflicting traffic with a Traffic Service?

    a. Yes-always
    b. Yes but only if you are flying under IFR
    c. Yes but only if you are flying in a MATZ
    d. No

19. When would you normally call "Downwind" in a visual circuit?

    a. Once established on the downwind leg of the circuit
    b. Abeam the downwind end of the runway
    c. Abeam the upwind end of the runway
    d. Just prior to turn onto the base leg

20. Could an aerodrome with the callsign "Dopford Information" give an aircraft permission to land?

    a. Yes
    b. Yes but only to an aircraft flying VFR
    c. No
    d. Yes but only to training aircraft in the visual circuit

21. Unless otherwise instructed by an ATCU, what squawk is required from the pilot-in-command of an aircraft entering a United Kingdom FIR from a foreign FIR where no transponder operation was mandatory?

    a. 7000 Mode Alpha and, at the same time, Mode Charlie
    b. 7000 Mode Alpha
    c. 2000 Mode Alpha and, at the same time, Mode Charlie
    d. 7600 Mode Alpha

22. What are the obligations on a pilot-in-command flying in a Control Zone on a Special VFR Clearance with regards to the Low Flying Rule:

    a. The pilot is absolved from both the 1 000 feet Rule and the 500 feet Rule
    b. The pilot is absolved only from the rule that he shall not fly over a congested area or settlement below such height as will permit the aircraft to land clear of the congested area in the event of a power unit failure
    c. The pilot is absolved from the 500 feet Rule only
    d. The pilot is absolved from the 1 000 feet Rule but not the rule that he shall not fly over a congested area or settlement below such height as will permit the aircraft to land clear of the congested area in the event of a power unit failure

23. You are about to enter an Aerodrome Traffic Zone (ATZ) of an airfield at which you have PPR permission to land. Immediately upon entering the ATZ you must report your:

    a Height and magnetic heading
    b Height and position
    c Altitude and magnetic heading
    d Flight Rules and magnetic heading

24. You have obtained an ATC clearance to enter a Control Zone Special VFR, but then suffer a radio failure before you have entered the Control Zone. You must

    a Proceed as cleared and land as soon as possible
    b Proceed as cleared and land when you have received the appropriate light signal
    c Proceed into the Control Zone and make a straight-in approach
    d. Remain clear of the Control Zone

25. When flying in a Control Zone in accordance with a Special VFR Clearance, what VMC minima must be maintained by a PPL holder without any additional ratings in his licence?

   a   Clear of cloud, in sight of the surface, and 5 km visibility
   b   Clear of cloud, in sight of the surface, and 10 km visibility
   c   Clear of cloud, in sight of the surface, and 1 500 metres visibility
   d   1 000 feet vertically from cloud, 1 500 metres horizontally from cloud and 8 km visibility

26. What is the minimum communication and navigation equipment which must be carried within Class D Airspace by a pilot of a light aircraft under VFR or SVFR?

   a.   VHF Radio, Transponder with Modes A and C
   b.   VHF Radio, Transponder with Modes A, VOR
   c.   VHF Radio, VOR, ADF, Transponder with Modes A and C
   d.   VHF Radio

27. In United Kingdom airspace, the carriage of serviceable SSR transponder with Modes A and C is mandatory for VFR flight:

   a.   At and above FL 80
   b.   At and above FL 100
   c.   At and above 3 000 feet
   d.   at all altitudes and levels

28. What is the lowest permissible vertical level of a Control Area?

   a.   1 000 feet above ground or water
   b.   1 800 feet above ground or water
   c.   500 feet above ground or water
   d.   700 feet above ground or water

Question	1	2	3	4	5	6	7	8	9	10	11	12
Answer												

Question	13	14	15	16	17	18	19	20	21	22	23	24
Answer												

Question	25	26	27	28
Answer				

The answers to these questions can be found at the end of this book.

CHAPTER 15
FLIGHT PLANS AND CLEARANCES IN THE UK

OXFORD AVIATION TRAINING	FLIGHT PLAN

PRIORITY
<<≡FF–

ADDRESSEE(S)

AD. <<≡

FILING TIME – ORIGINATOR EGTKZGZX <<≡

SPECIFIC IDENTIFICATION OF ADDRESSEE(S) AND/OR ORIGINATOR

3 MESSAGE TYPE <<≡(FPL
7 AIRCRAFT IDENTIFICATION – G.A.B.C.D.
8 FLIGHT RULES – V
TYPE OF FLIGHT G <<≡

9 NUMBER –
TYPE OF AIRCRAFT P28A
WAKE TURBULENCE CAT. / L
10 EQUIPMENT – S /C <<≡

13 DEPARTURE AERODROME – E.G.T.K
TIME 1.2.4.5 <<≡

15 CRUISING SPEED – N0103
LEVEL A020
ROUTE – DCT 5220N00240W DCT

<<≡

16 DESTINATION AERODROME – E.G.N.R
TOTAL EET HR. MIN 0059
ALTN AERODROME – E.G.G.P
2ND. ALTN AERODROME – <<≡

18. OTHER – RMK/ PPL QUALIFYING CROSS COUNTRY NAVEX

)<<≡

SUPPLEMENTARY INFORMATION (NOT TO BE TRANSMITTED IN FPL MESSAGES)

19 ENDURANCE HR MIN –E/ 0630
PERSONS ON BOARD –P/ 00.1
EMERGENCY RADIO UHF ☒ VHF ☐ ELBA ☒ –R/

SURVIVAL EQUIPMENT –S/ ☒ POLAR ☒ DESERT ☒ MARITIME ☒ JUNGLE ☒
JACKETS –J/ ☒ LIGHT ☒ FLUORES ☐ UHF ☐ VHF ☐

DINGHIES –D/ ☒ / NUMBER – CAPACITY – COVER ☒ / COLOUR <<≡

AIRCRAFT COLOUR AND MARKINGS A/ WHITE WITH BLUE STRIPES

REMARKS –☒ / <<≡

PILOT IN COMMAND C/ STUART PATTERSON)<<≡

Received by

FILED BY OXFORD AIR TRAINING
SPACE RESERVED FOR ADDITIONAL REQUIREMENTS 01865 123456

WHITE COPY - AIS, YELLOW COPY - AIR TRAFFIC, PINK COPY - PILOT

261

OXFORD AVIATION TRAINING   FLIGHT PLAN

PRIORITY	**ADDRESSEE(S)**	
<<≡FF-		
	AD.	<<≡

FILING TIME	ORIGINATOR	
–	EGTKZGZX	<<≡

SPECIFIC IDENTIFICATION OF ADDRESSEE(S) AND/OR ORIGINATOR

3 MESSAGE TYPE	7 AIRCRAFT IDENTIFICATION	8 FLIGHT RULES	TYPE OF FLIGHT
<<≡(FPL	– G A B C D	– V	G <<≡

9 NUMBER	TYPE OF AIRCRAFT	WAKE TURBULENCE CAT.	10 EQUIPMENT
–	P 2 8 A	/ L	– S / C <<≡

13 DEPARTURE AERODROME	TIME	
– E G T K	1 2 4 5	<<≡

15 CRUISING SPEED	LEVEL	ROUTE
– N 0 1 0 3	A 0 2 0	– DCT 5220N00240W DCT

<<≡

16 DESTINATION AERODROME	TOTAL EET HR. MIN	ALTN AERODROME	2ND. ALTN AERODROME
– E G N R	0 0 5 9	– E G G P	– <<≡

18. OTHER

– RMK/ PPL QUALIFYING CROSS COUNTRY NAVEX

)<<≡

SUPPLEMENTARY INFORMATION (NOT TO BE TRANSMITED IN FPL MESSAGES)

19 ENDURANCE HR MIN	PERSONS ON BOARD	EMERGENCY RADIO UHF VHF ELBA
–E/ 0 6 3 0	–P/ 0 0 1	–R/ ☒ ☒ ☒

SURVIVAL EQUIPMENT ☒ / POLAR ☒ DESERT ☒ MARITIME ☒ JUNGLE ☒   JACKETS –☒ LIGHT / ☒ FLUORES ☒ UHF ☒ VHF ☒

DINGHIES
–☒ / NUMBER CAPACITY –☒ / COVER COLOUR <<≡

AIRCRAFT COLOUR AND MARKINGS

A/ WHITE WITH BLUE STRIPES

REMARKS
–☒ / <<≡

PILOT IN COMMAND

C/ STUART PATTERSON)<<≡

FILED BY   Received by

OXFORD AIR TRAINING

SPACE RESERVED FOR ADDITIONAL REQUIREMENTS
01865 123456

WHITE COPY - AIS, YELLOW COPY - AIR TRAFFIC, PINK COPY - PILOT

Figure 15.1 UK CA 48 Flight Planning Form.

FLIGHT PLANS.

INTRODUCTION.

This chapter deals specifically with the filing of flight plans in the United Kingdom, and primarily with flight plans pertaining to flights made in accordance with the Visual Flight Rules (VFR) within United Kingdom Airspace.

CAA guidance on the completion of flight plans is currently published in Civil Air Publication 694, 'The UK Flight Planning Guide'.

ATCU = Air Traffic Control Unit.

ATSU = Air Traffic Services Unit.

A flight plan is a message concerning a planned flight, submitted by the Pilot-in Command to Air Traffic Services, of specific content and format, agreed by ICAO member countries. In the United Kingdom, flight plans are submitted on Flight Plan form CA48.

A pilot may file a VFR or IFR Flight Plan for any flight but must do so in specified cases. He <u>must</u> file a flight plan if he intends to fly in some classes of airspace. When considering whether or not to file a flight plan, the pilot should be especially mindful of any mandatory requirements of the classes of airspace he will be operating in, or transiting, during the flight.

There are three categories of flight plan:

The Full Flight Plan.
In the full flight plan, information on the whole route of the flight is entered on Flight Plan Form CA48, an example of which is shown in *Figure 15.1*, and then filed with the Parent Air Traffic Services Unit (ATSU).

The Abbreviated Flight Plan.
Limited information is passed by the pilot to the appropriate Air Traffic Control Unit (ATCU) in order to obtain a clearance for a limited portion of a flight (e.g. entering a Control Zone (CTR) or crossing an airway). This kind of flight plan can be submitted either by telephone, or over the aircraft radio whilst airborne.

Repetitive Flight Plan.
Used by commercial companies for regular flights.

It is important to note that the destination aerodrome will be advised of the flight only if the flight plan information covers the whole route of the flight.

FILING A VFR FLIGHT PLAN.

For flights made in accordance with VFR in the United Kingdom, flight plans <u>must</u> be submitted on the following occasions:

- For a flight from, or back to, the United Kingdom which will cross the United Kingdom FIR boundary. (NB: A flight plan need not be filed for a flight which crosses the London/Scottish FIR Boundary.)

- For all flights in controlled airspace of Classes B, C and D.

Notes on Classes A, B, C, and D controlled airspace:

1. VFR flight is not permitted in Class A airspace.
2. There is currently no Class B airspace in the UK.
3. All airspace at and above Flight Level 195 in Class C airspace.
4. The class of controlled airspace which will mostly concern VFR pilots is Class D airspace. Most Control Zones and Control Areas in the UK are Class D airspace. The requirement to submit a flight plan for flights within or across Class D airspace may be satisfied by passing flight details by radio to the responsible ATCU, in order to obtain a clearance to enter the airspace.

- any flight from an aerodrome in the United Kingdom, being a flight whose destination is more than 40 km from the aerodrome of departure, and where the aircraft Maximum Total Weight Authorised exceeds 5700 kg.

- any flight in Class F Airspace wishing to participate in the Air Traffic Advisory Service.

It is <u>advisable</u> to file a VFR flight plan when:

- intending to fly out to sea more than 10 nautical miles from the UK coastline.

- Intending to fly over sparsely populated areas where Search and Rescue operations might be difficult.

Remember, however, that a VFR flight plan <u>may be filed</u> for any flight, if the Pilot-In-Command so wishes.

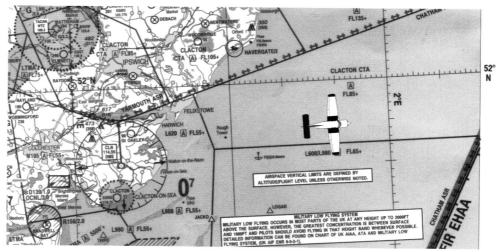

Figure 15.2 It is advisable to file a flight plan if you are intending to fly out to sea more than 10 nm from the shoreline.

FILING AN IFR FLIGHT PLAN.

An IFR Flight Plan must be filed in the following circumstances.

- For all flights within or across Class A, C or D airspace, i.e. controlled airspace.

- Any flight wishing to participate in the Advisory Service offered in Class F airspace.

- All flights to or from the UK which cross the UK FIR boundaries.

- All flights from a UK aerodrome where the destination is more than 40 km from the aerodrome of departure and the Maximum Take-off Mass exceeds 5700 Kgs.

COMPLETING A VFR FLIGHT PLAN.

A full flight plan is submitted by completing Flight Plan Form, CA48, an example of which is shown in *Figure 15.1*. There follow brief notes on how to complete the form for a VFR flight made by a light aircraft, assumed to be a PA28. Full details of how to complete the Flight Plan Form are given in CAP 694, the AIP and various Flight Information Supplements. Note that CA48 must be completed in block capitals. The same form can be used to file an IFR Flight Plan.

Leave the top part of the Form CA48 blank, and begin completing the form at Item 7, on the form.

Item 7 - Aircraft Identification.

Insert aircraft registration. When the radiotelephony call sign is the aircraft registration, the hyphen should be omitted.

| GABCD |

Item 8 - Flight Rules.

Insert **V** to denote that the category of flight rules in accordance with which the flight is being made is VFR (NB: Other letters apply if the flight is to be made under IFR, IFR then VFR, or VFR then IFR.)

| V |

Type of Flight.

Insert **G** for general aviation.

| G |

Item 9 - Number.

Insert number of aircraft, only if more than one aircraft is covered by the flight plan.

Type of Aircraft.

Insert aircraft type designator, For example:

Piper PA28 : P28A ; de Havilland Tiger Moth: DH82; de Havilland Chipmunk: DHC1; Cessna 152: C152; Grob 109: G109.

> P28A

Wake Turbulence Category.

Insert **L** for a light aircraft of 17 000 kg or less.

> L

Item 10 - Equipment.

In front of the oblique stroke, insert one letter as appropriate to the equipment carried:

N – If the aircraft is equipped with no communications, navigation or approach aids, or if the equipment is unserviceable.

S – If the aircraft is equipped with the standard communications, navigation or approach aids required for the route to be flown.

After the oblique stroke, insert one of the following letters to describe the serviceable SSR equipment carried:

N – nil.
A – Transponder Mode Alpha 4096 Codes.
C – Transponder Mode Alpha 4096 Codes and Mode Charlie.
S – Mode S with both a/c identification and pressure altitude transmission.

> S/C

Item 13 - Departure Aerodrome.

Insert the location indicator of the departure aerodrome or ZZZZ if no ICAO location indicator is assigned.

> EGTK

Time.

Insert Estimated Off - Block Time in Universal Co-ordinated Time (UTC).

| 1245 |

Item 15 - Cruising Speed.

Insert cruising True Air Speed for initial or whole cruise as follows:

> **N** = knots followed by 4 digits (e.g. **N0090**).
> (**K** = kilometres per hour).

| 0103 |

Level.

Insert cruising level for initial or whole cruise as follows:

> **A** – Altitude in hundreds of feet (use 3 digits e.g. A025).
> **F** – Flight Level (use 3 digits e.g. F055).

| A020 |

Route.

Insert the route to be flown as follows:

For flights off designated routes, list points normally not more than 30 minutes flying time apart, and enter DCT (DIRECT) between successive points. Points may be navigation aids, or bearings and distances from navigation aids, or co-ordinates.

| **DCT 5220N00240W DCT** |

Item 16 - Destination Aerodrome.

Insert location indicator(s) of the designation aerodrome, or **ZZZZ** if there is no assigned indicator(s).

| EGNR |

Total EET.

Insert total ESTIMATED ELAPSED TIME (EET), en-route, as a four figure group, expressed in hours and minutes.

| 0059 |

Alternate Aerodrome(s).

Insert location indicator(s) of no more than two alternate aerodromes, or **ZZZZ** if there are no assigned indicator(s).

EGGP

ZZZZ

Item 18 - Other Information.

Insert **0**, if there is no other information to give, or any other necessary information of the type shown below, in the form of an appropriate indicator followed by an oblique stroke and the information to be recorded. For example,

> **DEP/** – Name of departure aerodrome if **ZZZZ** is inserted above.
> **DEST/** – Name of destination aerodrome, if **ZZZZ** is inserted above.
> **ALTN/** – Name of alternate aerodrome(s) if **ZZZZ** is inserted above.
> **RMK/** – any additional information.
> **REG/** – the registration of the aircraft if the pilot is using a callsign over the radio which differs from that of the aircraft registration.

Item 19 - Supplementary Information (Not to be transmitted in flight plan messages).

Endurance.

Use a four-figure group to express fuel endurance.

If there is no ATSU at the aerodrome of departure of a flight for which a flight plan must be submitted, the flight plan must be submitted by telephone, fax, or radio to the ATSU serving the departure aerodrome.

0430

Persons On Board.

Includes passengers and crew; use **TBN** if number not known at time of filing.

1

Emergency Radio.

Cross out equipment not available.

The flight plan must be closed within 30 minutes of the pilot arriving at his destination airfield, by informing the parent ATSU.

Survival Equipment, Jackets, Dinghies etc.

Cross out equipment not available.

Aircraft Colour and Markings.

WHITE WITH BLUE STRIPES

Remarks.

Enter other remarks regarding survival equipment or cross out N if no remarks.

Filed By.

Insert name of the unit, agency or person filing the flight plan.

SUBMITTING A VFR FLIGHT PLAN.

The written flight plan, on Form CA48/RAF F2919, is normally filed through the ATSU at the departure aerodrome. The flight plan is then forwarded to what is known as the "parent ATSU", located at London Heathrow, Manchester or at Scottish ACC.

NATS recommend that pilots should use the FIS frequency (e.g. London Information) to file an Airborne Flight Plan.

The pilot is responsible for submitting the flight plan to the Air Traffic Service Unit (ATSU) at the departure aerodrome, at least 60 minutes before clearance to start up or taxi is requested. If there is no ATSU at the departure aerodrome, or if the departure aerodrome is not connected to the Aeronautical Fixed Telecommunications Network (AFTN), the pilot is responsible, himself, for arranging for the flight plan to be filed with the appropriate Parent ATSU Unit for onward transmission.

If pilots submit their flight plans by fax, or make use of a computer based flight plan system, they must ensure that the flight plan has been accepted and has been transmitted by AFTN on their behalf. A telephone call to the ATSU receiving the flight plan, or contact with the ATSU at the aerodrome of departure, will enable pilots to confirm that their flight plan has been received, accepted and transmitted.

ACTIVATING AND CLOSING A VFR FLIGHT PLAN.

If the aerodrome at which a pilot files a full flight plan has an ATSU, the aerodrome ATSU will inform the Parent ATSU of the pilot's time of departure. The flight plan is activated at the time of departure, and, from time of departure, the Parent ATSU obtains an estimated arrival time (ETA) at the pilot's destination aerodrome or airfield. If the departure aerodrome does not have an ATSU, the flight plan can be activated by the pilot's informing the FIR controller, once airborne, or by nominating a responsible person to contact the Parent ATSU by telephone to pass on his departure time.

The parent ATSU must be contacted within 30 minutes of the pilot arriving at his destination, in order that the flight plan may be closed. It is the pilot's responsibility for ensuring that this action is taken. If the parent ATSU were not to be informed of the arrival of the flight at its destination, within the prescribed 30 minutes, the ATSU would initiate alerting action.

TIME PARAMETERS.

Prior to take-off, submission of a VFR flight plan to the ATSU at the departure aerodrome should be made at least 60 minutes before the request for start or taxi clearance. Exceptionally, when 60 minutes notice is not possible, pilots should give as much notice as they can but never <u>less than 30 minutes.</u>

A VFR flight plan should be submitted at least 60 minutes before start-up or taxi, and never less than 30 minutes.

<u>If airborne, the abbreviated flight plan must be submitted at least 10 minutes prior to penetration of any Controlled airspace.</u>

REMEMBER! Before flying VFR in Classes C or D airspace, a flight plan is required and a clearance must be received.

DELAYS TO FLIGHT PLANS.

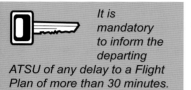

It is mandatory to inform the departing ATSU of any delay to a Flight Plan of more than 30 minutes.

In the UK, it is mandatory to inform the departure ATSU of any delay to a flight plan, of more than 30 minutes.

CHANGES TO FLIGHT PLAN.

In the UK, the parent ATSU must be informed as quickly as possible in the following circumstances:

•   a change of destination.

•   any delay to the aircraft's ETA of 45 minutes or more.

ACTION IN THE EVENT OF DIVERSION.

If a pilot on a flight for which a flight plan has been filed lands at a diversion airfield, he must notify the ATSU at the planned destination within 30 minutes of the ETA in the flight plan.

If a pilot lands at an aerodrome in the UK other than the destination specified in the **flight plan**, he must ensure that the ATSU at the original destination is informed of the diversion, <u>within 30 minutes</u> of his original ETA.

CANCELLING AN IFR FLIGHT PLAN IN FLIGHT.

If a pilot has begun a flight in Controlled Airspace (CAS) under an IFR flight plan, he may decide, on entering VMC, to cancel the IFR flight plan. If so, he must inform the ATSU with which he is in contact.

If the pilot merely reports that he is flying in VMC, this does **not** constitute a cancellation of an IFR flight plan and the flight will continue to be regulated as an IFR flight.

SPECIAL VFR.

An SVFR clearance may be requested without the submission of a filed flight plan and also whilst the aircraft is airborne. Brief details of the flight should be passed to the appropriate ATCU. These details should include:

•   Aircraft call sign.

•   Aircraft type.

•   Pilot's intentions including the phrase "request Special VFR".

GENERAL NOTES ON SUBMITTING FLIGHT PLANS.

If you transmit your flight plan to an ATSU by telephone, in order to make the process as smooth as possible ensure that you have a copy of your **flight plan** already filled in, so that you can pass the information quickly, and in the correct order.

If you file your flight plan by fax, it is recommended that you include a contact telephone number in the remarks section. It is also recommended that you telephone the ATSU, yourself, to confirm that the flight plan has been received.

It is essential that the appropriate ATSU be advised as soon as possible of cancellations of flight plans, of delays of over 30 minutes, and of any other changes to flight plan details.

When taking off on a flight from a minor airfield, do not assume that the Air/Ground Operator or Flight Information Service Officer will transmit your departure time to the Parent ATSU. If you cannot activate the flight plan yourself, always check with the Air/Ground Operator that the necessary information has been passed, or nominate a responsible person to do this for you.

CLEARANCES.

General.

•   An ATC Clearance authorises an aircraft to proceed under conditions specified by an ATCU.

•   Clearances are based solely on known traffic.

•   Clearances are required in the UK for any flight, or portion of a flight, which is provided with ATC or an Advisory Service.

If an ATC clearance is judged unsuitable by a Pilot-in-Command, he may request an amended clearance.

•   Submission of a flight plan is one method of requesting a clearance.

•   Clearances do not constitute authority for a flight to violate any rule or regulation laid down by the CAA or any associated organisations.

•   All clearances must be read back precisely to the ATCU controller.

•   An ATC clearance is deemed to have been accepted by the pilot on correct read-back of the clearance to the ATCU controller.

Unsuitable Clearances.
If the pilot receives an ATC **clearance** which he considers to be unsuitable, he has the right to ask for a revised **clearance**. In such a case, ATC will endeavour, if practical, to supply a more suitable clearance.

Contents of a UK Clearance.
An ATC clearance shall include the following items:

•   Aircraft identification.

•   Clearance limit (an aerodrome, reporting point or a controlled airspace boundary).

•   Route.

Flight levels, changes of levels, and the following items may be added as necessary:

- Time restrictions.

- Communications instructions.

- Special instructions (e.g. approach and departure manoeuvres).

BOOKING OUT.

In the case of a flight in the UK, for which a flight plan is not required or filed, the Pilot-in-Command is still responsible for informing the aerodrome of departure of his flight details. This action is known as "Booking Out"; but unlike the normal flight plan procedure, the information will not be transmitted to any other ATSU by the departure aerodrome.

At many airfields, the pilot books out over the radio. The Pilot-in-Command should verify, before embarking, whether or not this is the procedure at the airfield from which he is departing.

Representative PPL - type questions to test your theoretical knowledge of CAA Flight Plans and Clearance Questions.

1.   You are flying in Class G airspace in VMC, can you file a flight plan?

   a.   No. It is not necessary
   b.   Yes. You can submit a flight plan for any flight

2.   You are flying an aircraft with an MTOW exceeding 5 700 kgs and intend to fly more than 40 nms from the aerodrome of departure. Must you submit a flight plan?

   a.   Yes
   b.   No
   c.   No but you are advised to do so
   d.   Only if you are intending to enter Controlled Airspace

3.   You intend to fly under VFR on an Advisory Route within the UK and wish to take advantage of the Advisory Service. Which of the following answers is correct?

   a.   You may file a flight plan
   b.   You must file a flight plan
   c.   You need only file a Flight Plan if the ADR crosses the London/Scottish FIR boundary
   d.   You must not file a flight plan

4.   At what time interval prior to take-off, are you required to file a flight plan?

   a.   At least 60 minutes prior to departure
   b.   At least 60 minutes in excess of EOBT
   c.   At least 30 minutes prior to departure
   d.   At least 30 minutes in excess of EOBT

5.   You wish to penetrate controlled airspace within the UK. When must a flight plan be filed?

   a.   At least 5 minutes prior to penetration of CAS
   b.   At least 15 minutes prior to penetration of CAS
   c.   At least 20 minutes prior to penetration of CAS
   d.   At least 10 minutes prior to penetration of CAS

6.   You are about to undertake a VFR flight in the UK and a Flight Plan is not required. Do you have to inform anyone of your flight details?

   a.   Yes - the aerodrome of departure
   b.   Yes - the destination aerodrome and an ETA must be included in the flight details
   c.   No - because a Flight Plan is not required
   d.   Yes – any UK aerodrome

7.   If you "book out" a VFR flight at your departure aerodrome without having filed a flight plan, will your flight details be passed to the ATSU of the destination aerodrome?

   a.   Yes - always
   b.   Yes - but only if your route cruising level is to be over FL50
   c.   No
   d.   Only if you are a SVFR flight

8.   After what delay to ETA must a VFR flight inform the destination aerodrome?

   a.   30 minutes or more
   b.   More than 30 minutes
   c.   More than 45 minutes
   d.   45 minutes or more

9.   If the departure aerodrome is not connected to the Aeronautical Fixed Telecommunications Network (AFTN), the pilot is responsible for arranging that the flight details are passed to:

   a.   The destination Aerodrome
   b.   Area Control
   c.   Any ATCU
   d.   The Parent Unit

10.   You are diverted because of bad weather during a VFR flight in the UK for which you have filed a flight plan. What must you do on arrival at your alternate aerodrome?

   a.   Ensure that the ATSU of your original destination is informed within 15 minutes of the flight planned ETA
   b.   Ensure that the ATSU of the departure aerodrome is informed within 15 minutes of the flight planned ETA
   c.   Ensure that the ATSU of the departure aerodrome is informed within 30 minutes of the flight planned ETA
   d.   Ensure that the ATSU of your original destination is informed within 30 minutes of the flight planned ETA

11.   Can a pilot request to enter a CTR, under special VFR, in the UK without submitting a filed flight plan?

   a.   No
   b.   Yes
   c.   Yes - but by day only
   d.   Yes - but only if the aircraft is not equipped with a radio

12. Does a pilot have to accept an ATC Clearance?

    a.   Yes - always
    b.   No - but only if the flight is to be conducted under VFR
    c.   No
    d.   Yes - but only if the flight is to be conducted under IFR

13. A pilot who has submitted a flight plan to a Parent ATSU is obliged to contact the Parent ATSU with landing details within what time period?

    a.   Within 10 minutes of landing
    b.   Within 15 minutes of landing
    c.   Within 20 minutes of landing
    d.   Within 30 minutes of landing

Question	1	2	3	4	5	6	7	8	9	10	11	12
Answer												

Question	13
Answer	

The answers to these questions can be found at the end of this book.

CHAPTER 16
AERONAUTICAL INFORMATION SERVICES IN THE UK

UNITED KINGDOM	AIC 67/2005
AERONAUTICAL INFORMATION CIRCULAR	(Pink 84)
	21 July

National Air Traffic Services Ltd
Aeronautical Information Service
Control Tower Building, London Heathrow Airport
Hounslow, Middlesex TW6 1JJ
Editorial: 020-8745 3457
Distribution: 0870-8871410 (Documedia Solutions Ltd)
Content: 020-7453 6535 (DAP/S & SM)
Website: www.ais.org.uk

NOTIFICATION OF GPS JAMMING TRIALS

1 Introduction

1.1 The purpose of this Circular is to give notification of trials to be performed by QinetiQ on behalf of the Ministry of Defence (MoD), in which Global Positioning System (GPS) signals will be intentionally jammed. This Circular contains details of the times and locations of the trials, a description of the predicted effects and a point of contact.

2 Dates, Times and Areas Affected

Date: **30 August - 16 September 2005** inclusive.

Time: Between 0800 and 1600 UTC daily.

2.1 Location: Land based jammers within 3 nm radius of 520110N 0033641W, within MoD Sennybridge Training Area, Powys, Wales.

2.2 Predictions show that the areas affected will be as follows:

2.2.1 Omni (5W EIRP) – 30 August to 3 September, 5 to 10 and 12 to 16 September 2005 (all inclusive)

    (a) At 10 m agl – Areas with clear line of sight to the transmitter positions.

    (b) At 10000 ft amsl – 38 nm from the transmitter site in all directions.

    (c) At 30000 ft amsl – 38 nm from the transmitter site in all directions.

2.2.2 Directional (100W ERP) – 5, 6, 7, 8 and 15 September 2005 (two hours per day)

    (a) At 10 m agl – Areas with clear line of sight to the transmitter positions.

    (b) At 10000 ft amsl to a predicted maximum of 122 nm from the transmitter in all directions.

    (c) At 30000 ft amsl to a predicted maximum of 189 nm from the transmitter in all directions.

    The trials should not cause interference to other land based or airborne navigation or communication systems.

AERONAUTICAL INFORMATION SERVICES IN THE UNITED KINGDOM.

UNITED KINGDOM AERONAUTICAL INFORMATION SERVICES.

The United Kingdom Aeronautical Information Service (AIS) is responsible for the collection and dissemination of information and data necessary for the safety and efficiency of air navigation throughout the United Kingdom, including the airspace over the High Seas which is under the jurisdiction of UK Air Traffic Control Services.

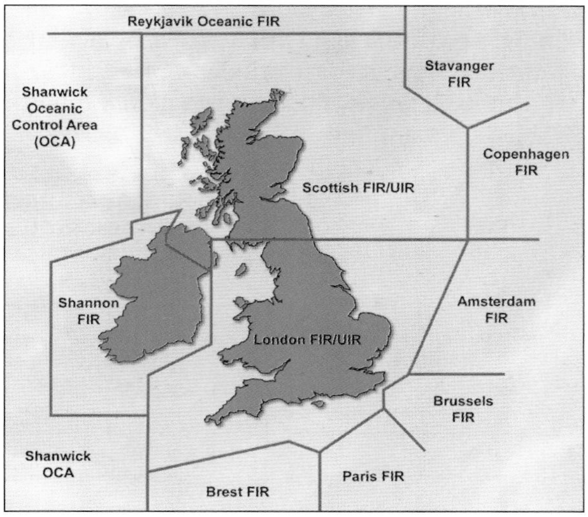

Figure 16.1 The UK AIS disseminates information throughout the UK, pertinent to air navigation.

ORGANISATION OF THE UK AERONAUTICAL INFORMATION SERVICE.

The UK AIS is organised and administered by the National Air Traffic Services (NATS) on behalf of the CAA.

The address and contact details of the UK AIS are contained in the GEN Part of the UK Aeronautical Information Publication. UK AIS also have an Internet site at http://www.ais.org.uk. A simple registration process is all that needs to be followed in order to gain access to the whole of AIS. Using the AIS site, it is possible to input a flight profile and obtain all relevant aeronautical information tailored to that particular flight.

THE INTEGRATED AERONAUTICAL INFORMATION PACKAGE.

The UK AIS is organised and administered in accordance with ICAO Annex 15, and publishes aeronautical information as an integrated package which comprises:

- An Aeronautical Information Publication (AIP), including an amendment service.

- AIP Supplements (SUP).

- Aeronautical Information Circulars (AIC).

- NOTAMs.

- Pre-flight Information Bulletins (PIB).

- Check lists.

THE UK AERONAUTICAL INFORMATION PUBLICATION.

General.

The UK Aeronautical Information Publication (UK AIP) not only constitutes the basic information source for information of a lasting character essential to air navigation, but also includes notifications required by the UK Air Navigation Order (ANO). The UK AIP is often referred to as the "UK Air Pilot". *(See Figure 16.2.)*

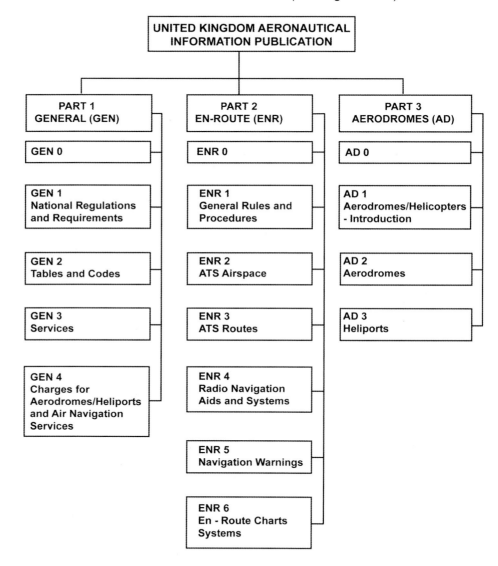

Figure 16.2 The UK AIP.

Layout and Contents of the UK AIP.

The AIP is divided into three Parts:

- Part 1   General (GEN).

- Part 2   En-route (ENR).

- Part 3   Aerodromes (AD).

The most important areas covered in Parts 1, 2 and 3 are:

Part 1 (GEN).

National Regulations & requirements; Customs & immigration procedures; Differences between UK rules and regulations and those of ICAO Standards and Recommended Practices (SARPS); Aeronautical Information Services; Tables & codes, Air Traffic services; Meteorological services; Search & Rescue organisation and procedures; Charges for aerodrome/heliports and air navigation services.

The AIP is divided into 3 Parts:

Part 1   General (GEN).

Part 2   En-route (ENR).

Part 3   Aerodromes (AD).

Part 2 (ENR).

General rules and procedures; Position reporting; Communication failures; Airspace classifications, Visual Flight and Special Visual Flight Rules; Instrument Flight Rules; Airspace restrictions; Prohibited, Danger & Restricted Areas; Hazards to flights; Radar services, Flight planning, Air traffic incidents (AIRPROX), Interception procedures.

Part 3 (AD).

Aerodrome operating minima; Index to Aerodromes and Heliports; Rescue and fire-fighting facilities; Handling and passenger facilities; Aerodrome contact details & radio frequencies; Aerodrome lighting and obstacles; Noise abatement procedures; Aerodrome Operating hours.

Availability.

The **UK AIP** is available on the internet (http://www.ais.org.uk). It is also distributed in CD-ROM form and in hard copy.

Amendments and Supplements to the UK AIP.

Amendments (permanent changes) and Supplements (temporary changes) are distributed by NATS. Supplements should be kept with the AIP until no longer valid.

AERONAUTICAL INFORMATION REGULATION AND CONTROL (AIRAC).

Permanent changes to the AIP (amendments) and changes of operational significance (e.g. a change in the dimensions of a CTR) must be collected, collated, printed, and distributed to operators well before the effective date of the changes. This aim is achieved under the Aeronautical Information Regulation and Control (AIRAC) system which ensures that operators receive this information, ideally 28 days, but at least 14 days in advance of the effective date. This allows time for the documents to be amended and personnel briefed. Information distributed under this system is annotated with the acronym AIRAC.

AERONAUTICAL INFORMATION CIRCULARS.

General.

As a general rule, Aeronautical Information Circulars (AICs) refer to subjects of an administrative rather than an operational nature. AICs are, however, used to publish advance warnings of impending operational changes. They are also used to add explanations - or emphasis - to matters of safety. *(See Figure 16.3.)*

	UNITED KINGDOM	AIC 67/2005
Civil Aviation Authority	**AERONAUTICAL INFORMATION CIRCULAR**	(Pink 84) 21 July

National Air Traffic Services Ltd
Aeronautical Information Service
Control Tower Building, London Heathrow Airport
Hounslow, Middlesex TW6 1JJ
Editorial: 020-8745 3457
Distribution: 0870-8871410 (Documedia Solutions Ltd)
Content: 020-7453 6535 (DAP/S & SM)
Website: www.ais.org.uk

NOTIFICATION OF GPS JAMMING TRIALS

1   **Introduction**

1.1   The purpose of this Circular is to give notification of trials to be performed by QinetiQ on behalf of the Ministry of Defence (MoD), in which Global Positioning System (GPS) signals will be intentionally jammed. This Circular contains details of the times and locations of the trials, a description of the predicted effects and a point of contact.

2   **Dates, Times and Areas Affected**

Date: **30 August - 16 September 2005** inclusive.

Time: Between 0800 and 1600 UTC daily.

2.1   Location: Land based jammers within 3 nm radius of 520110N 0033641W, within MoD Sennybridge Training Area, Powys, Wales.

2.2   Predictions show that the areas affected will be as follows:

2.2.1 Omni (5W EIRP) – 30 August to 3 September, 5 to 10 and 12 to 16 September 2005 (all inclusive)

(a) At 10 m agl – Areas with clear line of sight to the transmitter positions.

(b) At 10000 ft amsl – 38 nm from the transmitter site in all directions.

(c) At 30000 ft amsl – 38 nm from the transmitter site in all directions.

2.2.2 Directional (100W ERP) – 5, 6, 7, 8 and 15 September 2005 (two hours per day)

(a) At 10 m agl – Areas with clear line of sight to the transmitter positions.

(b) At 10000 ft amsl to a predicted maximum of 122 nm from the transmitter in all directions.

(c) At 30000 ft amsl to a predicted maximum of 189 nm from the transmitter in all directions.

The trials should not cause interference to other land based or airborne navigation or communication systems.

3   **Use of GPS**

3.1   The policy for the use of GPS for UK air navigation services is given in AIC 93/2002 (Pink 41).

3.2   Although GPS equipment is an accepted means of compliance with B-RNAV requirements, one of the conditions of its use is that the aircraft must carry serviceable radio navigation equipment in order to allow reversionary means of navigation. Operators of aircraft should not rely on GPS for B-RNAV operations in the areas predicted to be affected by the jamming trials, and should be prepared to revert to the alternative means of navigation.

3.3   The use of GPS to support Oceanic or remote operations, and helicopters in off-shore en-route operations, is accepted subject to it having received the appropriate operational approval.

3.4   For IFR en-route and terminal area operations, only radio navigation equipment required by the rules for IFR operations should be used.

Figure 16.3 A Pink AIC.

Normally an AIC is valid for 5 years but there are a number of AICs which are amended and repeated. In general, there are AICs covering such subjects as Low Level Turbulence, Wake Turbulence, Thunderstorms, Icing, Effects of Alcohol, Malaria, etc.

All pilots should keep up-to-date with the latest AICs.

Availability of AICs.

AICs are available on the internet, currently at http://www.ais.org.uk. They are also distributed in CD-ROM form and in hard copy. AICs are normally issued every 28 days.

Colour Coding.

In the UK, **AICs** are colour - coded according to their subject matter as follows:

White — Administrative matters (e.g. licence examination dates, services and publications).

Yellow — Operational matters (including ATS facilities and requirements).

Pink — Safety related matters.

Mauve (Purple) — UK airspace restrictions imposed under the Restriction of Flying Regulations ** (See note).

Green — Maps and Charts.

** Note: Under Article 85 of the ANO, The Secretary of State may, in the public interest, restrict or prohibit flying because of:

- A gathering or movement of a large number of persons.

- An aircraft race, contest or flying display.

- National defence or any other reason affecting the public interest.

An example of such a restriction was a Mauve AIC issued prior to the meeting of the G8 countries at Gleneagles in 2005, restricting flying within the area.

UK AICs are colour coded according to their subject matter as follows:

White — Administrative matters (e.g. licence examination dates, services and publications).

Yellow — Operational matters (including ATS facilities and requirements).

Pink — Safety related matters.

Mauve — UK airspace restrictions imposed under the Restriction of Flying Regulations**

Green — Maps and Charts.

NOTAMS.

General.

Operationally significant information concerning temporary or permanent changes to information in the AIP is distributed by NOTAMs. The expression NOTAM stands for the words "Notices to Airmen".

NOTAMs are distributed, as required, to ATSUs, flying schools and flying clubs.

NOTAMs are kept as precise and concise as possible, using plain language and ICAO abbreviations. It is essential that pilots checks all current NOTAMs before every flight.

"Trigger" NOTAM.

If there is an operationally significant amendment to the UK AIP, or if a Supplement to the UK AIP is to be issued, this information is also distributed by NOTAM. In these circumstances, the NOTAM is known as a "Trigger" NOTAM.

The "Trigger" NOTAM will give:

- A brief summary of the change to the AIP.

- The effective date of the change (indicated by a 10 figure group – Year/Month/Day/Time).

- The Amendment or SUP reference number.

A **"Trigger" NOTAM** will remain valid for:

- 14 days after the effective date of a permanent change,

   or

- For the complete duration of any temporary change.

Types of NOTAM.

3 types of NOTAM are published:

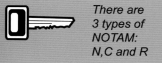
There are 3 types of NOTAM: N,C and R

A **NOTAMN** contains new information.

```
ZCZC  ZKA360   270941
GG  EGTKZGZX
270941  EGGNYNYX
(L3194/05 NOTAMN
Q) EGTT/QLPXX/IV/BO/A/000/999/5345N00253W005
A)  EGNO B)0510270940 C)  05102710600

E)RUNWAY 26 NORTHSIDE PAPI UNSERVICEABLE)
```

Figure 16.4a A NOTAMN.

A **NOTAMC** cancels a previous NOTAM.

```
ZCZC  ZKA390   271028
GG  EGTKZGZX
271028  EGGNYNYX
(L3195/05 NOTAMC L3194/05
Q)  EGTT/QLPAK/IV/M/A/000/999/
A)  EGNO B) 0510271028

E) PAPI RESUMED NORMAL OPERATION)
```

Figure 16.4b A NOTAMC.

A **NOTAMR** replaces a previous NOTAM.

```
ZCZC  ZKA240   161011
GG  EGTKZGZX
161011  EGGNYNYX
(L0133/06 NOTAMR L3955/05
Q)  EGTT/QMDCH/IV/NBO/A/000/999/5006N0054W005
A)  EGHC B) 061161011 C)  0601300800

E) THR 16 TEMPORARILY DISPLACED 220M, THR 34 TEMPORARILY DISPLACED
138M, DUE TO SOFT GROUND. RWY DECLARED DISTANCES TEMPORARILY REDUCED:
```

Figure 16.4c A NOTAMR.

Requests for NOTAMs.

NOTAMs are currently available on the Internet site http://www.ais.org.uk.
They can also be requested by fax. Details of the NOTAM service are contained in
Part 1 (GEN) of the UK AIP.

PRE-FLIGHT INFORMATION BULLETINS.

General.

Most aerodromes in the UK have available "self-briefing" documents known as
Pre-Flight Information Bulletins (PIB) which form a part of the Aeronautical Information
Service (AIS). From PIBs, pilots may obtain the latest information pertaining to a
proposed flight. PIBs are also available on the AIS website at http://www.ais.org.uk.

For information on the full range of PIBs available, see the above website using the
Help pages and Frequently Asked Questions (FAQs).

Responsibility for PIBs.

Aerodrome Operators are responsible for providing briefing facilities which make available to pilots the UK AIP, AIP SUPs, AICs, NOTAM. Aerodrome operators may create pre-selected PIBs but must make all documents available for reference and "self-briefing". An example of a PIB is given at *Figure 16.5*.

```
                    UK Pre-Flight Information Bulletin
_____

PRE-FLIGHT              AREA                 U N I T E D   K I N G D O M
INFORMATION             ROUTE           AERONAUTICAL INFORMATION SERVICE (NATS LTD)
BULLETIN                R2400963                04/05/24 13:49 UTC
UK AIS Telephone: +44 (0) 20 8745 3464.         WEB SITE: WWW.AIS.ORG.UK


PERIOD: 04/05/24 14:00 UTC TO 04/05/24 18:00 UTC


PIB INCLUDES  NOTAM/BIRDTAM


FLIGHT NUMBER: CSE24                   ADEP: EGTK(10NM)   ADES: EGHH(10NM)
TRAFFIC: IFR                        PURPOSE: GENERAL AND MISCELLANEOUS
LOWER: 030    UPPER: 080               SUBJECT:


ALTN: EGHI
FIR : EGTT
--------------------------------------------------------------------------------
--------------------------------------------------------------------------------
EXCLUDING NOTAM THAT HAVE BEEN ACTIVE FOR MORE THAN 5 DAYS
        THE FOLLOWING PERMANENT NOTAM ARE NOT INCLUDED :  EGGN C0512/04
     EGGN L0906/04     EGGN L0906/04     EGGN B2141/03     EGGN B0532/04    EGGN
     B0491/04    EGGN B0741/04    EGGN B0805/04    EGGN B0841/04    EGGN
     B0488/04


A E R O D R O M E - I N F O R M A T I O N :

AERODROME (DEPARTURE) - EGTK (OXFORD KIDLINGTON) :

NO INFO RECEIVED OR MATCHING THE QUERY.

AERODROME (DESTINATION) - EGHH (BOURNEMOUTH HURN) :

AGA : FROM 04/05/24 07:00 TO 04/06/18 17:00              C1687/04
      E) TWY GOLF FM THE EAST AND WEST APRONS CLSD TO HOLDS D1 AND G3.
         ACCESS TO PROFESSIONAL AIR TRAINING AND LONG TERM PARKING WILL BE
         AVBL AS ADVISED BY ATC


AGA : FROM 04/05/24 06:00 TO 04/06/18 16:30              C1697/04
      E) RESTRICTIONS TO ACFT OPR INTO OR OUT OF BOURNEMOUTH MAY
         APPLY DUE WIP ON TWY G


COM : FROM 04/05/24 10:56 TO 04/05/25 17:00              C1709/04
      E) ILS RWY 08 U/S



AERODROME (ALTERNATE) - EGHI (SOUTHAMPTON) :

NO INFO RECEIVED OR MATCHING THE QUERY.

E N - R O U T E - I N F O R M A T I O N :

EGTT (LONDON) :

NAVW: FROM 04/05/19 15:30 TO 04/06/11 17:00             H3346/04
      D) MON-FRI 1530-1700
      E) DANGER AREA EG D402A (EXCLUDING THAT PART OF THE DANGER AREA WI
         ATS ROUTE P600) ADDIONALLY ACTIVE ABOVE NORMAL LEVEL
      F) SFC G) 23000FT AMSL


NAVW: FROM 04/05/24 07:45 TO 04/05/24 21:00             H3408/04
      D) 0745-1030, 1330-1530, 1700-2100
      E) SOUTHERN MDA EG D323B ACTIVATED
      F) 5000FT AMSL G) 35000FT AMSL
```

Figure 16.5 A Pre-Flight Information Bulletin.

POST FLIGHT REPORTING.

It is important for all pilots to be aware of their responsibilities with regards to post-flight reporting.

If, during a flight, the pilot experiences anything that may generally affect other aircraft (e.g. the unserviceablity of a navigation aid or the presence of birds) he must complete a Post Flight Report and present it to the ATSU on landing.

OTHER SOURCES OF AERONAUTICAL INFORMATION.

Three common publications from which pilots obtain UK aeronautical information are:

- **LASORS** (Licensing, Administration and Standardisation, Operating Requirements & Safety) is published by The Stationery Office on behalf of the CAA. Latest updates to this book can be found on http://www.caa.co.uk./srg.

  The ISBN for LASORS is 1874783 527.

  LASORS can be ordered by e-mail (book.orders@tso.co.uk), or by mail from:

  TSO
  P.O. Box 29
  Norwich
  NR3 1GN

- **The UK Aeronautical Information Manual** (UKAIM) published by Camber Publishing Limited.

- **ATSIN**, the Air Traffic Services Information Notice.

Note: The **ATSIN** dated 29th January 2007 included the following information of interest to general aviation pilots:

From 15 March 2007, within the vicinity of an aerodrome, transponder-equipped aircraft will normally operate with the transponder remaining on, either squawking the VFR Conspicuity Code, 7000, with Modes A and C selected (where fitted), or squawking a discrete code as instructed by the Air Traffic Services Unit. At aerodromes with a high concentration of visual circuit traffic, a specific VFR Aerodrome Traffic Pattern Conspicuity Code of 7010 will normally be the code used. The reason for this change is to facilitate greater availability of the collision avoidance 'safety net' provided by Airborne Collision Avoidance Systems, which are increasingly available to light aircraft. These systems depend on recognising SSR transmissions.

Representative PPL - type questions to test your theoretical knowledge of Aeronautical Information (CAA).

1.   In which part of the UK AIP would you find information on meteorology?

      a.   GEN
      b.   AGA
      c.   ENR
      d.   AD

2.   After how long does an AIC normally lapse?

      a.   1 year
      b.   2 years
      c.   3 years
      d.   5 years

3.   What colour are UK AICs which are concerned with safety related matters?

      a.   White
      b.   Mauve
      c.   Pink
      d.   Yellow

4.   What is the purpose of a NOTAM which is designated "NOTAMN"?

      a.   It replaces a previous NOTAM
      b.   It is a NOTAM containing new information
      c.   It cancels a previous NOTAM
      d.   It amends a previous NOTAM

5.   What publication constitutes the basic information source for information of a lasting character essential to Air Navigation in the UK?

      a.   LASORS
      b.   AIC
      c.   UKAIM
      d.   AIP

6.   Which of the following is not a Part of the UK AIP?

      a.   GEN
      b.   ADR
      c.   AD
      d.   ENR

7.   In which part of the UK AIP would you find information on Prohibited, Danger and Restricted areas?

     a.   GEN
     b.   AGA
     c.   ENR
     d.   AD

8.   You are due to fly to a small licensed aerodrome and wish to find out whether the fire-fighting cover will be available at your planned ETA. To which Part of the AIP would you turn?

     a.   GEN
     b.   AGA
     c.   ENR
     d.   AD

9.   How would information concerning the dangers of microbursts and advice on how to avoid them be published?

     a.   AIC
     b.   NOTAM
     c.   Special NOTAM
     d.   PIB

10.   How are permanent changes to the UK AIP published?

     a.   SUP
     b.   Amendment
     c.   Class 2 NOTAM
     d.   Special update

11.   A major flying display is about to take place and aerial activity in the immediate area is to be restricted. What colour AIC might be distributed?

     a.   White
     b.   Mauve
     c.   Pink
     d.   Yellow

12.   In which part of the UK AIP would you find information concerning Visual Flight Rules?

     a.   GEN
     b.   AGA
     c.   ENR
     d.   AD

13. If there is an operationally significant amendment to the UK AIP, or a Supplement to the UK AIP is issued, how is this information additionally distributed?

   a.   AIC
   b.   NOTAMC
   c.   "Trigger" NOTAM
   d.   NOTAMR

14. How long does a "Trigger" NOTAM remain valid when the information is concerning a permanent change to the UK AIP?

   a.   28 days after the effective date of a permanent change
   b.   14 days after the effective date of a permanent change
   c.   7 days after the effective date of a permanent change
   d.   1 month after the effective date of a permanent change

15. Effective dates contained in a NOTAM appear as:

   a.   12 figure groups (Year/Month/Day/Time)
   b.   10 figure groups (Year/Month/Day/Time)
   c.   12 figure groups (Time/Day/Month/Year)
   d.   10 figure groups (Time/Day/Month/Year)

16. Who is responsible for ensuring that PIBs and/or self-briefing material is available for pilots?

   a.   The CAA
   b.   NATS Limited
   c.   The FIS Authority
   d.   Aerodrome Operators

17. During a flight you experience an intermittent signal from a VOR. All other VORs that you have used throughout the trip have operated normally. What should you do?

   a.   Nothing. All navigation aids are automatically monitored by the Authority
   b.   Report the fact to an aircraft avionics engineer on arrival
   c.   Complete a post-flight report and present it to the ATSU on landing
   d.   Contact another aircraft using the same VOR and, if it is experiencing the same problem, report the fact to ATC

18. How long prior to the effective date does the AIRAC system endeavour to ensure that operators receive operational significant changes?

    a.   14 days prior to the effective date
    b.   28 days prior to the effective date
    c.   1 month prior to the effective date
    d.   3 months prior to the effective date

19. What makes up the Integrated Aeronautical Information Package?

    a.   Aeronautical Information Publication (AIP) including an amendment service, AIP Supplements (SUP), Aeronautical Information Circulars (AIC), NOTAM, Pre-flight Information Bulletins (PIB) and Check lists
    b.   AIP Supplements (SUP), Aeronautical Information Circulars (AIC), NOTAM, Pre-flight Information Bulletins (PIB) and Check lists only
    c.   Aeronautical Information Publication (AIP) including an amendment service only
    d.   NOTAM and AICs only

Question	1	2	3	4	5	6	7	8	9	10	11	12
Answer												

Question	13	14	15	16	17	18	19
Answer							

The answers to these questions can be found at the end of this book.

CHAPTER 17
SEPARATION (UK)

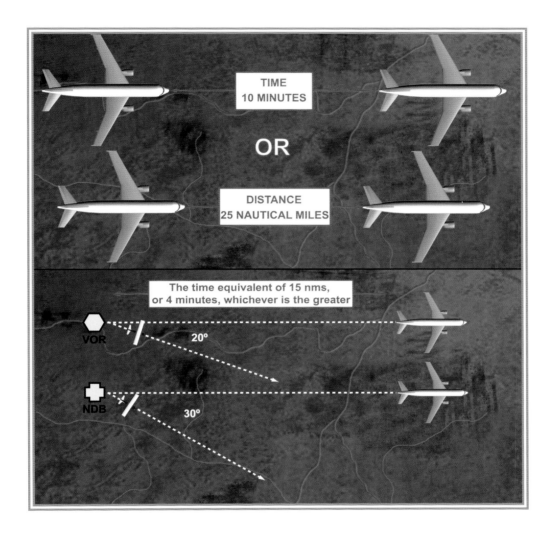

SEPARATION.

GENERAL.

A broad definition of separation is as follows:

minimum distance or time between two aircraft that are either:

- occupying the same altitude or Flight Level,

or

- climbing/descending through the same altitude or Flight Level.

However, there are also times when it is possible that two aircraft may get so close to each other that one could be affected by the wake vortices of the other. This could happen on landing or taking off when using the same runway. In such a case, a mandatory minimum safety distance or time is laid down by the CAA. This safety factor is called Wake Turbulence Separation. Wake Turbulence Separation is covered at the end of this Chapter.

TYPES OF SEPARATION.

There are two types of Separation in the United Kingdom for IFR traffic:

Vertical Separation.
Within controlled airspace in the two UK FIRs, the minimum **vertical separation** is 1 000 feet. Outside controlled airspace, when flying IFR above the transition level, pilots must select a cruising Flight Level in accordance with the Quadrantal Rule. Vertical Separation is covered in more detail in Chapter 11.

There are two types of separation in the UK for IFR traffic:

Vertical.

Horizontal which is subdivided into:

- *Longitudinal.*
- *Lateral.*
- *Radar.*

Horizontal Separation.
Horizontal Separation is subdivided into:

- Longitudinal.

- Lateral.

- Radar.

Scope of this Chapter.
This Chapter concerns itself with UK Horizontal Separation and UK Wake Turbulence Separation.

Longitudinal Separation.

General.
Longitudinal Separation may either be based upon time or distance.

Based upon Time.

The normal longitudinal separation between two aircraft following the same track is 10 minutes. *(See Figure 17.1.)*

Based upon distance.

The normal minimum longitudinal radar separation between two aircraft following the same track is 25 nms. *(See Figure 17.1.)*

Note: both of the above separation criteria can be reduced under certain circumstances.

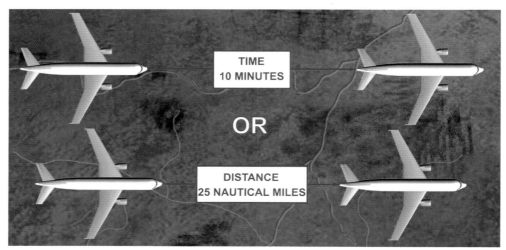

Figure 17.1 Time and Distance Separations.

Lateral Separation.

Lateral Separation is based upon time and depends on what type of radio navigation aid the two aircraft are using. The aircraft are deemed to be separated if the track divergence and distance from the aid is as follows:

VOR   20°, at the time equivalent of 15 nms, or 4 minutes, whichever is the greater.
NDB   30°, at the time equivalent of 15 nms, or 4 minutes, whichever is the greater.
(See Figure 17.2.)

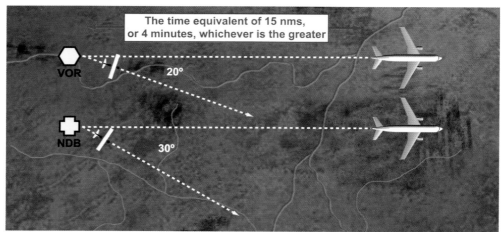

Figure 17.2 Lateral Separation.

WAKE TURBULENCE SEPARATION.

General.

When flying in proximity to large aircraft, the effects of wake turbulence must always be considered. The severity of the wake turbulence generated by an aircraft is directly proportional to the aircraft's mass, and inversely proportional to its speed. Consequently, the separation time or distance between aircraft is based upon the Wake Turbulence Category of the aircraft concerned.

The UK categories are as follows:

United Kingdom Wake Turbulence Categories of Aircraft.

Category	Maximum Take-Off Mass
Heavy (H)	136 000 kgs and above
Medium (M)	40 000 - 136 000 kgs
Small (S) **(See Note)	17 000 - 40 000 kgs
Light (L)	17 000 kgs and below

Note: The UK Wake Turbulence Categories are similar to those of ICAO; however, they differ in one aspect. The UK has an additional category: **SMALL**.

The Wake Turbulence Category should be entered in flight plans in accordance with the ICAO weight definitions - i.e. Heavy (H), Medium (M) or Light (L). In the UK, "Small" category aircraft is to be entered in the Flight Plan as "Medium" (M).

UK Wake Turbulence Categories of Aircraft:

Heavy (H)
136 000 kgs and above.

Medium (M)
40 000 - 136 000 kgs.

*Small (S) ***
17 000 – 40 000 kgs.

Light (L)
17 000 kgs and below.

WAKE TURBULENCE SEPARATION ON DEPARTURE.

General.

Wake Turbulence Separation, on departure, is the minimum time from when the leading aircraft becomes airborne to the time when the following aircraft becomes airborne.

Wake Turbulence Separation, on departure, is applied by measuring the airborne time between successive aircraft. On departure Wake Turbulence Separation is based upon time only (Procedural) and will depend on whether:

• Both aircraft are departing from the same point on the runway,

or

• the following aircraft is departing from an intermediate point of the runway.

When both aircraft are departing from the same point on the runway, Wake Turbulence Separation is as shown in the table below:

Leading Aircraft	Following Aircraft	Separation minima
Heavy	Medium, Small or Light	2 minutes
Medium or Small	Light	2 minutes

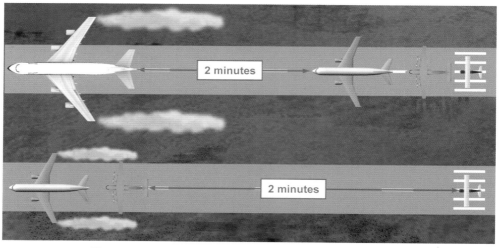

Figure 17.3 Departures from the same point on the Runway.

Where a heavier aircraft has started the take-off run from the threshold, and the lighter aircraft has entered the runway for take-off from an intermediate point on the runway, the Wake Turbulence Separation is as follows:

Leading Aircraft	Following Aircraft	Separation minima
Heavy	Medium, Small or Light	3 minutes
Medium or Small	Light	3 minutes

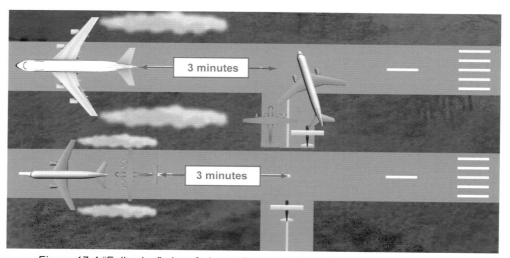

Figure 17.4 "Following" aircraft depart from an Intermediate point on the Runway.

WAKE TURBULENCE SEPARATION ON ARRIVAL.

Wake Turbulence Separation in the UK, on arrival, is as follows:

Leading Aircraft	Following Aircraft	Separation Minima
Heavy	Heavy	4 nms
Heavy	Medium	5 nms
Heavy	Small	6 nms
Heavy	Light	8 nms
Medium	Medium	3 nms **
Medium	Small	4 nms
Medium	Light	6 nms
Small	Medium	3 nms
Small	Small	3 nms
Small	Light	4 nms

Note ** For certain aircraft types (B757, B707, IL62 or VC10) this distance is increased to 4 nms.

NB: It is important to appreciate that the separation stated below cannot entirely obviate the possibility of a following aircraft encountering wake turbulence. The objective of **separation** is to reduce the probability to an acceptably low level and to minimise the effect when an encounter occurs.

If the distance between yourself and a heavier aircraft is causing you concern, you must increase that distance and at the same time inform the responsible ATSU as soon as possible.

If the distance between yourself and a heavier aircraft is causing you concern, you must increase that distance and at the same time inform the responsible ATSU as soon as possible.

WAKE TURBULENCE SEPARATION IN FLIGHT.

In flight, the Wake Turbulence Separation minima for arriving traffic also apply when:

- an aircraft is directly behind another at the same height or less than 1 000 feet below,

or

- an aircraft is crossing behind at the same altitude or less than 1 000 feet below the leading aircraft.

IMPORTANT CONSIDERATIONS WITH REGARDS TO WAKE TURBULENCE.

- The heavier the aircraft, the greater the wake turbulence. Wake turbulence is further exacerbated if the aircraft is flying slowly.

- The majority of serious incidents, close to the ground, occur when winds are light.

- A light quartering wind, in particular on take-off, will increase and lengthen the effects of wake turbulence vortices along the runway.

- Always observe the wake turbulence minima and, if you are concerned, increase the separation, informing ATC of your intentions.

- If you are affected by wake turbulence, you are advised to fill in a report and pass it to ATC.

- Avoid flying below and within 1 000 feet of a heavier aircraft.

- Helicopters generate a disproportionately greater amount of wake turbulence than aeroplanes for the same mass. Of particular danger is a large helicopter hover-taxiing. Always make sure you give such helicopters a wide berth.

Figure 17.5 Vortex movement along the ground in still air.

Figure 17.6 In a cross-wind, vortices will be displaced by the cross-wind component.

- Remember that vortex generation begins when the nosewheel lifts off the runway.

- In a cross-wind, vortices will be displaced by the cross-wind component. *(See Figure 17.6.)*

- A clean aircraft (wheels up and flaps retracted) produces greater wake turbulence than an aircraft in any other configuration.

- **Wake turbulence is invisible. You disregard it at your peril.**

Representative PPL - type questions to test your theoretical knowledge of Separation (CAA).

1.   What is the normal longitudinal separation (based upon distance) between 2 aircraft in the UK?

        a.   10 nms
        b.   15 nms
        c.   20 nms
        d.   25 nms

2.   Which of the following statements is true concerning wake turbulence?

        a.   It is directly proportional to the size and weight of the aircraft and inversely proportion to its speed
        b.   It is inversely proportional to the size and weight of the aircraft and directly proportion to its speed
        c.   No wake turbulence will be experienced if the laid down separation minima between aircraft are observed
        d.   Generally, a helicopter in the hover-taxi produces less wake turbulence than a taxying aeroplane

3.   What is the normal lateral separation between 2 aircraft in the UK which have passed over the same VOR?

        a.   30° at the time equivalent of 15 nms or 4 minutes whichever is the greater
        b.   30° at the time equivalent of 15 nms or 5 minutes whichever is the greater
        c.   30° at the time equivalent of 20 nms or 4 minutes whichever is the greater
        d.   20° at the time equivalent of 15 nms or 4 minutes whichever is the greater

4.   An aeroplane with a Maximum Take-Off Mass of 20 000 kgs has a UK Wake Turbulence Category of:

        a.   Heavy
        b.   Medium
        c.   Small
        d.   Light

5.   What Wake Turbulence Category is entered in the Flight Plan with regards to the aeroplane in Question 4, in the UK?

        a.   Heavy
        b.   Medium
        c.   Small
        d.   Light

6.   A Light category aircraft in the UK has a Maximum Take-Off Mass of:

      a.   7 000 kgs
      b.   17 000 kgs
      c.   5 700 kgs
      d.   4 000 kgs

7.   Wake turbulence is normally exacerbated by:

      a.   A strong cross-wind
      b.   A strong head wind component
      c.   Light winds
      d.   Nil wind conditions

8.   What is the UK wake turbulence separation time between a light aircraft taking off from the same point on a runway behind a heavy category aircraft?

      a.   2 minutes
      b.   3 minutes
      c.   5 minutes
      d.   8 nms

9.   If the above light aircraft were taking off from an intermediate point on the runway behind the heavy aircraft, what is the wake turbulence separation increased to?

      a.   10 nms
      b.   3 minutes
      c.   5 minutes
      d.   6 minutes

10.   Wake turbulence must be taken in consideration if the following aircraft is:

      a.   Within 500 feet above or below the preceding aircraft
      b.   Within 1 000 feet above or below the preceding aircraft
      c.   Within 1 000 feet below the preceding aircraft
      d.   Within 1 000 feet above the preceding aircraft

11.   On final approach-to-land, in the UK, a light aircraft is following a heavy aircraft. What wake turbulence separation must be applied?

      a.   3 minutes
      b.   4 nms
      c.   6 nms
      d.   8 nms

12.   On final approach to land in the UK, a light aircraft is following a small aircraft. What wake turbulence separation must be applied?

    a.   2 nms
    b.   4 nms
    c.   6 nms
    d.   8 nms

13.   Should you experience wake turbulence, the CAA advises you to:

    a.   Inform ATC as soon as possible
    b.   Inform ATC as soon as practicable
    c.   Inform ATC prior to landing or take-off
    d.   Complete a report and pass it to ATC

14.   On take-off, wake turbulence begins:

    a.   On application of take-off power
    b.   As soon as the aircraft starts to roll down the runway
    c.   When the nosewheel lifts off the runway
    d.   On rotation

15.   Which configuration would generally produce most wake turbulence?

    a.   Flaps selected and wheels retracted
    b.   Flaps selected and wheels down
    c.   Clean
    d.   Flaps and spoilers selected

Question	1	2	3	4	5	6	7	8	9	10	11	12
Answer												

Question	13	14	15
Answer			

The answers to these questions can be found at the end of this book.

CHAPTER 18
OBSTACLES (UK)

UK OBSTACLES TO AIR NAVIGATION, PROHIBITED, RESTRICTED & DANGER AREAS.

LAND-BASED, OFFSHORE, AERODROME & EN-ROUTE OBSTACLES.

Land-based Air Navigation Obstacles.

Land-based Obstacles are any building or work, including waste heaps, which exceed a height of 300 feet. These are listed in the ENR section of the UK AIP.

Offshore Obstacles.

Offshore obstacles are associated with offshore oil & gas exploitation. The fixed installations can vary in height up to 541 feet, AMSL and display warning navigation lights. Most of the rigs are equipped with helicopter pads which are classed as aerodromes. Most rigs burn off high pressure gas and the flame, which may not be visible in bright sunlight, can extend up to 300 feet.

> *Pilots flying close to oil rigs must always assume there is a danger of high pressure venting of gas.*

Aerodrome Obstacles.

Aerodrome obstacles are defined as those located up to 15 kms from runway thresholds. Aerodrome obstacles as listed in the AD section of the UK AIP and are also shown on Instrument Approach and Landing Charts.

En-route Obstacles.

Strictly speaking the definition of an en-route obstacle is an obstacle which is over 15 kms from an aerodrome threshold.

All en-route obstacles within the UK (buildings, chimneys, towers, masts etc) are detailed in the ENR section of the UK AIP.

It is recommended that en-route obstacles should be lit if they are:

Figure 18.1 Lit and Unlit Obstacles.

- 150 metres (492 feet) or more in height, AGL.

- Less than 150 metres (492 feet) in height, AGL, but, nevertheless, are considered a significant hazard to aviation.

En-route obstacles are also depicted on aeronautical charts, marked with both their height AGL and altitude in feet.

- Should en-route obstacles be lit, the obstacle will be printed in aeronautical charts and instrument approach charts with a series of dashes around the top of the depicted obstacle. *(See Figure 18.1.)*

Details of Unserviceability.
Details of the unserviceability of **en-route** obstacle lighting are always promulgated by NOTAM, if the obstacle is 150 metres (492 feet) AGL, or more, in height.

Should the obstacle be less than 150 metres AGL in height, unserviceabilities of associated obstacle lighting are not normally promulgated, in the UK.

Lighting of En-route Obstacles.

All obstacles over 492 feet (150 metres) must be lit by a red, steady light, but in exceptional circumstances may also be lit by high intensity white flashing warning lights. Whichever types of lights are used, they will be as close to the top of the obstacle as possible, and at regular intervals below top light and ground, no more than 52 metres apart, visible from all directions.

All obstacles over 492 feet (150 m) must be lit by steady red lights, as close to the top as possible.

However, many lower obstacles can be of equal danger to pilots who may be flying at low level.

Aerials and Tall Communication Masts.
Pilots must take particular care to avoid aerials and tall communication masts.

Many of them have surrounding support wires that spread out for a considerable distance from the mast itself. In certain light conditions these become invisible. So avoid all such obstacles by a very wide margin.

High-Tension Masts and Cables.
Although the cables are normally marked with coloured spherical markers, many are not. In certain light conditions, these cables, may be difficult to see. (See *Figure 18.3.*)

Mountains and Hills.
Conspicuous mountains and hills which are regarded as hazards to aviation are marked by red obstacle-lights and are listed in the ENR section of the UK AIP.

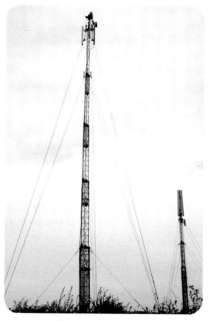

Figure 18.2 Masts.

Figure 18.3 Cables may be invisible!

PROHIBITED, DANGER & RESTRICTED AREAS.

Prohibited, Danger and Restricted Areas are detailed in the En-route (ENR) Section of the UK AIP and normally they all start at ground level.

Prohibited, Danger and Restricted Areas.

Prohibited, Danger and Restricted Areas are depicted on aeronautical charts showing the designated number of the area together with its upper limit. For example *Figure 18.4* depicts a Prohibited Area which reaches to an altitude of 2 500 feet. Prohibited, Danger and Restricted Areas are identified on charts by a 3-digit code number preceded by an identifying letter, as follows:

P   **Prohibited area.**
R   **Restricted area.**
D   **Danger area.**

Figure 18.4 Prohibited Area P106, with an upper altitude of 2 500 feet, ,and Danger Area D129, upper limit FL120.

The prefix letter for a Prohibited area is P, Restricted area is R, and D for Danger area.

Code numbers indicate approximate location: first digit gives latitude, e.g. 1 indicates north of 51N, 2 north of 52N, etc., and the second two digits longitude, generally increasing from west to east. For example **P106/2.5 = Prohibited Area** number 106 with an upper altitude of 2 500 feet AMSL. *(As Figure 18.4.)*

D129/FL120 = Danger Area 129, upper level FL120 (note that most Danger Areas have an upper limit given as an altitude or unlimited (UNL). D129 is unusual in that it is partly in controlled airspace)

PROHIBITED AREAS.

All flights are prohibited within Prohibited Areas. Prohibited Areas may be permanent or temporary. No aircraft may enter a Prohibited Area at any time.

RESTRICTED AREAS.

A Restricted Area is an area in which flights are restricted in accordance with certain specified conditions. Restricted Areas may be either permanent or temporary *(See Figure 18.5.)*, but if annotated on the map 'see Note 2', apply only to helicopters.

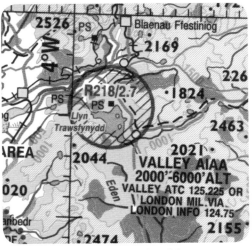

Figure 18.5 Restricted Area.

Note: Within the UK, the Authority may at any time enforce a temporary Restricted or Danger Area in the vicinity of an emergency incident or an SAR operation. In this case, an Emergency Controlling Authority (ECA) is set up. Any aircraft wishing to penetrate the area may only do so with permission of the ECA.

DANGER AREAS.

Danger Areas are areas within which activities are taking place which pose a danger to aircraft at such times as may be notified. Such activities might be:

Figure 18.6 Danger Areas.

- Weapon ranges.

- Aerial combat training areas.

- Parachute training areas.

- Demolition areas.

Several of the above activities may be taking place at the same time.

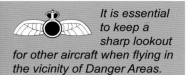

It is essential to keep a sharp lookout for other aircraft when flying in the vicinity of Danger Areas.

Marking of Danger Areas.
Danger areas are marked on aeronautical charts in the UK with:

- A solid red outline. These are scheduled Danger Areas which are active within the published times (these times may be found in the ENR section of the UK AIP).

- A pecked red outline. These are Danger Areas which are inactive unless notified by NOTAM. The number and the upper limit of the Danger Area are clearly shown on aeronautical charts.

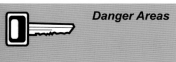

Danger Areas

Solid red outline: active within the published times.

Pecked red outline: inactive unless notified by NOTAM.

Marking of Danger Areas.
The number and the height (AMSL) of Danger Areas are marked in a similar way to those identifying Prohibited Areas. *(See Figure 18.6.)* For example:

D208/2.5 = **Danger Area 208** extending to **2 500 feet AMSL.**

Note: The annotation OCNL means OCCASIONALLY, for example:

D208/2.5 OCNL/7.5 means: **Danger Area 208** extending to **2 500 feet** and **occasionally 7 500 feet AMSL**.

Beware! Danger Areas in which upper limits do not exceed 500 feet, are not necessarily shown on aeronautical charts but are found in the ENR section of the UK AIP. Rifle ranges are found in this category of Danger Areas.

Note: Temporary Danger Areas may be established at short notice around the scene of emergency incidents. ATC should warn you of these - but it is essential to check NOTAMS prior to take-off.

Crossing Danger Areas.

Within the UK, two services are available to help you to obtain information about Danger Areas to confirm whether they are active or not. There are:

Danger Area Activity Information Service (DAAIS).

Details of the frequencies to contact this service are found in the ENR section of the UK AIP and are also printed on the UK 1:500 000 UK ICAO Aeronautical Charts legends.

It must be stressed that the **Danger Area Activity Information Service (DAAIS)** is purely an information service that will inform you whether or not a particular Danger Area is active. A DAAIS cannot give you clearance to enter or cross a Danger Area.

Details of the format of radio calls to be made when contacting a DAAIS are contained in the ENR section of the UK AIP.

Danger Area Crossing Service (DACS).

A **Danger Area Crossing Service (DACS)** is available for approximately a quarter of the UK Danger Areas. Details of the DACS frequencies are found in the ENR section of the UK AIP and are also printed on the UK 1:500 000 UK ICAO Aeronautical Chart legend.

AREAS OF INTENSE AERIAL ACTIVITY (AIAA).

Areas of Intense Aerial Activity (AIAA) are areas within which there is a high intensity of civil or military flying, or aircraft regularly participating in unusual manoeuvres. AIAAs are depicted in aeronautical charts by blue diamond markings, and detailed in the ENR section of the UK AIP.

D206/6.0 is a Danger Area, number 206, (between 52 and 53N), extending to 6 000 feet AMSL.

It is good airmanship to assume that danger areas are active and to avoid them by a good margin.

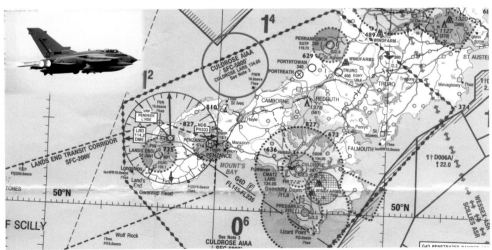

Figure 18.7 Culdrose Area of Intense Aerial Activity.

If it is absolutely necessary to enter, or fly in close proximity to an AIAA, the pilot is strongly advised to contact the controller on the listed frequency. Normally there is a radar service associated with AIAAs which will be able to give the pilot precise and safe instructions.

AERIAL TACTICS AREAS.

Air combat training regularly takes place in **Aerial Tactics Areas**. A radar service is associated with Aerial Tactics Areas, in the same way as for AIAAs.

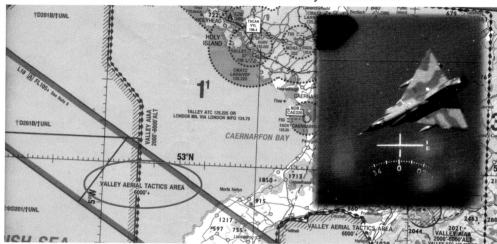

Figure 18.8 Aerial Tactics Area (ATA).

Aerial Tactics Areas are depicted on aeronautical charts by blue diamond markings, and detailed in the ENR section of the UK AIP.

UK MILITARY LOW FLYING SYSTEM.

Military low flying occurs in most parts of the UK at any height up to 2 000 feet AGL. However, the greatest concentration is between 250 feet and 500 feet AGL and you are advised to avoid flying within this height band whenever possible.

Figure 18.9 Low Flying Tornado - Image courtesy of Brian Proctor.

Plan your cross-country and local flights to take place above 2 000 feet.

AIR-TO-AIR REFUELLING AREAS (AARA)

AARAs are areas, usually long and approximately rectangular and located either over the sea or sparsely populated area, that are designated for practice and operational aerial refuelling. Most have base levels of FL70 or higher, except Area 9 (just off the coast near Gt Yarmouth) from 2 000 ft to FL50, and so will be of little concern to most PPL pilots. Full details are in the UK AIP ENR 5.2; if a transit is planned, however, it is recommended that a flight plan is filed. Any tanker/receiver formations should be avoided by a wide margin, as they have limited manoeuvrability.

HIGH INTENSITY RADIO TRANSMISSION AREAS.

Within **High Intensity Radio Transmission Areas**, airspace there is radio energy of an intensity which may cause interference with radio transmissions and, on rare occasions, damage to navigation equipment such as radio altimeters, VOR and ILS receivers. There is also the danger that 'pacemakers' can be affected.

Figure 18.10 The Oakhanger High Intensity Radio Transmission Area.

High Intensity Radio Transmission Areas are marked on aeronautical charts *(see Figure 8.10)* and should be avoided by as wide a margin as practicable.

RADIOSONDE BALLOON ASCENTS.

The Met Office have a number of locations (listed in ENR section of the UK AIP) from which Radiosonde Balloons are launched. The balloons are approximately 1.5 m in diameter and the instruments hang beneath by up to a length of 33 m.

They can attain altitudes of over 80 000 feet. They can also be dropped from the air. This activity is promulgated by NOTAM.

Figure 18.11 Radiosonde balloon launch.

313

GAS AND OIL OPERATIONS.

Gas and Oil operations can take place both on and off-shore. Gas and Oil rigs can reach 250 - 300 feet AGL and, if they are burning off, "the flarestack" can reach a further 600 feet in height. Flames from flarestacks may be difficult to see, and, in the vicinity of "flarestacks" turbulence may be experienced.

Figure 18.12 Oil Rig and Flarestack

Gas and oil installations should, therefore, be given a wide birth. There are also **Gas Venting Stations (GVS)** *(see Figure 8.13)* which present similar hazards to aircraft. Both **"Flarestacks"** and GVS's are listed in the ENR section of the UK AIP. A minimum altitude for over-flight is annotated in the case of GVSs.

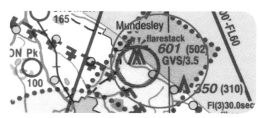

Figure 18.13 Map showing Gas Venting Station.

AERIAL SPORTING AND RECREATIONAL ACTIVITIES.

There has been a huge expansion in aerial recreational activities in recent years and this trend is continuing. Of note are:

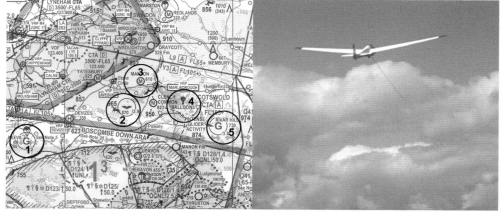

Figure 18.14 Left: Chart showing 1) Keevil - Parachuting and Gliders 2) White Horse - Hang Gliders 3) Manton - Microlights 4) Clench Common - Balloons and 5) Rivar Hill - Gliders. Right: glider winch launch.

Glider Sites.

Glider launching takes place from designated glider sites which are regarded as aerodromes and are listed in the ENR Section of the UK AIP. Although winch or towing operations using cables are normally up to 2 000 feet AGL, this height may be exceeded. Should a number be printed on the chart within the glider site, this indicates the altitude up to which cables may be used. In Figure 18.14, the KEEVIL site is shown to have cable operations up to 3 200 ft AMSL.

Hang Gliding, Paragliding and Parascending Sites.

Because of the low speed characteristics of hang gliders and paragliders, these craft may be difficult to spot.

Winch and cable operations may exceed 2 000 feet AGL at some sites. Note that the actual launch of paragliders may be anywhere within 1.5 nms of the notified position of the site.

Figure 18.15 Paragliding.

If no information is available, it should be assumed that all Danger, Prohibited, Restricted, or Parachute Drop Zones are active.

Free-fall Parachuting Drop Zones.

Intensive free-fall parachuting operations may be conducted up to FL150 at any of the Drop Zones listed in the ENR section of the UK AIP. However, parachuting may also take place during daylight hours at any government or licensed aerodrome. Air Traffic Service Units (ATSUs) should be able to inform the private pilot of these activities.

Parachuting may also take place at temporary sites which are notified by NOTAM.

A parachutist in free-fall is virtually impossible to spot. Pilots are strongly advised to give a wide berth to Parachute Drop Zones.

Microlight Flying Sites.

Microlight Flying sites are also listed in the ENR section of the UK AIP. Such sites are regarded as aerodromes, and are marked on aeronautical charts. *(See Figure 18.14 for chart symbol.)*

Captive and Free Flight Manned Balloon Sites & Kite Flying.

Balloon flights and kite flying also take place both, notified and otherwise. High flying kites may be hazardous because of the possibility of collision with the kite-line. Some kites are flown at heights above 200 feet (60 m). *(See Figure 18.14 for chart symbol.)*

Representative PPL - type questions to test your theoretical knowledge of Obstacles.

1.   In which section of the UK AIP are details found concerning obstacles and Danger Areas?

      a.   GEN
      b.   ENR
      c.   AD
      d.   AGA

2.   An en-route obstacle is one that is:

      a.   Over 15 kms from an aerodrome threshold
      b.   Over 15 kms from an aerodrome threshold and over 150 m in height
      c.   Over 15 nms from an aerodrome threshold
      d.   Over 15 nms from an aerodrome threshold

3.   A land-based obstacle is that which exceeds a height of:

      a.   100 feet
      b.   200 feet
      c.   300 feet
      d.   150 m

4.   In which section of the AIP would you find details of an aerodrome obstacle?

      a.   GEN
      b.   ENR
      c.   AD
      d.   AGA

5.   An en-route obstacle must be lit should it exceed:

      a.   150 feet
      b.   150 m
      c.   200 feet
      d.   200 m

6.   Are unserviceabilities of en-route obstacles above 150 m in height always promulgated by NOTAM?

      a.   Yes but they are promulgated by AIRREP
      b.   Yes
      c.   Yes but only if they are not lit by night
      d.   No

7.   Where in the UK AIP would you find details of Prohibited and Restricted Areas?

   a.   GEN
   b.   ENR
   c.   AD
   d.   AGA

8.   How are high tension cables marked?

   a.   Red or yellow flags
   b.   Low intensity steady red lights
   c.   Coloured spherical markers
   d.   High intensity flashing white lights

9.   How are conspicuous mountains and hills lit if they are regarded as hazards to aviation?

   a.   Red obstacle lights
   b.   They are not lit
   c.   Flashing white obstacle lights
   d.   Flashing yellow obstacle lights

10.   Decode: R311/2.5
                                   OCNL/7.5

   a.   Random route number 25 on a track of 311° but occasionally can be changed
   b.   Restricted area number 311 extending to a height of 2 500 feet AGL and occasionally to a height of 7 500 feet AGL
   c.   Restricted area number 311 extending to a height of 2 500 feet AMSL and occasionally to a height of 7 500 feet AGL
   d.   Restricted area number 311 extending to an altitude of 2 500 feet AMSL and occasionally to an altitude of 7 500 feet AMSL

11.   If a temporary Danger Area is enforced during, for example, extensive SAR operations, which organisation may give permission for an aircraft to enter the area?

   a.   The Rescue Co-ordination Centre (RCC)
   b.   ATC
   c.   Emergency Controlling Authority (ECA)
   d.   The Civil Aviation Authority (CAA)

12.   A Danger Area is marked on an aeronautical chart with a red pecked outline. What does this signify?

   a.   The Area is permanently active
   b.   The Area is always inactive unless notified by NOTAM
   c.   The Area is active only by day
   d.   The Area is active only by night

13.   Where would you find information on Danger Areas not extending to a height of 500 feet?

   a.   The ENR section of the UK AIP
   b.   Aeronautical charts
   c.   The GEN section of the UK AIP
   d.   Aeronautical maps

14.   In what part of the UK AIP would you find details concerning Glider Launching Sites?

   a.   GEN
   b.   ENR
   c.   AD
   d.   AGA

15.   Should you have no information as to a Danger Area or Restricted area you should:

   a.   Assume it is not active
   b.   Should not take-off until you have obtained the necessary information
   c.   Contact FIS to try and find out the necessary information prior to entry
   d.   Assume it is active

16.   Whom would you contact prior to entering an AIAA?

   a.   FIS
   b.   The radar Controller
   c.   ATC
   d.   The Alerting Service

17.   Between what heights is the greatest concentration of low flying military aircraft in the UK?

   a.   1 000 - 2 000 feet AGL
   b.   1 500 - 3 000 feet AGL
   c.   2 000 - 5 000 feet AGL
   d.   250 - 500 feet AGL

18.   How should a pilot treat a High Intensity Radio Transmission Area?

   a.   You can enter these areas as long as ATC is informed
   b.   They are of temporary nature only and are notified by NOTAM
   c.   They are to avoided by a wide margin
   d.   You can enter these areas as long as the MATZ Controller is informed

19.   What is a Danger Area Activity Information Service?

   a.   This service may clear you into Danger Areas or Restricted areas
   b.   This service may clear you into a Restricted areas only
   c.   This service is purely an information service and is only capable of telling you whether a Danger or a Restricted area is active
   d.   This serviceable may only clear you to cross a Danger or Restricted area

20.   Where would you find details as to the radio calls to be made to the DAAIS?

   a.   The UK ANO
   b.   The ENR section of the UK AIP
   c.   The GEN section of the UK AIP
   d.   The AGA section of the UK AIP

Question	1	2	3	4	5	6	7	8	9	10	11	12
Answer												

Question	13	14	15	16	17	18	19	20
Answer								

The answers to these questions can be found at the end of this book.

CHAPTER 19
ALTIMETER SETTINGS (UK)

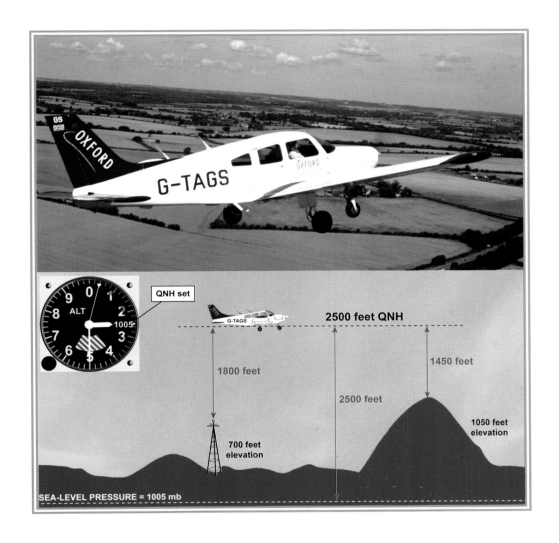

INTRODUCTION.

The altimeter is one of the most essential of the pilot's instruments. The subject of altimeters and altimetry is covered in detail in the 'Aeroplanes' and 'Meteorology' volumes of this series. In this chapter, we confine ourselves to the topic of pressure settings on the altimeter.

The altimeter indicates the vertical separation of the instrument from a defined pressure datum level.

Basically, the aircraft's altimeter is an instrument which measures atmospheric pressure and, in doing so, is so calibrated as to indicate the vertical separation of the aircraft from a <u>defined pressure datum level</u>.

In the regions of the atmosphere in which most aircraft fly (certainly all light aircraft), atmospheric pressure decreases with increasing distance from the Earth's surface at a linear rate*, so it is fairly straightforward to calibrate the altimeter to indicate to the pilot his vertical distance in feet - the standard unit of altitude in aviation in most parts of the world - from a selected pressure datum. This pressure datum is set in the altimeter when the pilot selects what is known as an altimeter subscale setting. In analogue altimeters, the altimeter subscale setting is usually displayed in a small rectangular window on the face of the instrument. The figures displayed in this window usually express the pressure datum in millibars or hectopascals. Some altimeters may have instead a vernier scale in millibars at the 3 o'clock position and possibly a second scale at the 9 o'clock position in inches of mercury.

The rate of pressure decrease is 1 millibar in just over 27 feet, but for ease of calculations, 1 mb in 30 feet is generally used.

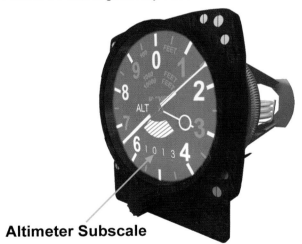

Altimeter Subscale

Figure 19.1 The altimeter subscale set to the Standard Pressure Setting of 1013 mb.

In the ICAO Standard Atmosphere (ISA), the sea-level pressure is 1013.2 millibars (hectopascal). This pressure setting is known as the Standard Pressure Setting (SPS) which pilots select on their altimeters when flying above the transition altitude by reference to Flight Level. You should note that in Europe, outside the United Kingdom, the unit of pressure used in aviation is the hectopascal. Fortunately, 1 hectopascal (hPa) = 1 millibar (mb), so the figures representing pressure in these two units are identical. In the United States of America, altimeter subscale pressures are give in inches (in) of Mercury (Hg), the SPS being 29.92 in Hg.

From day to day, of course, pressure at sea-level in the real atmosphere varies, so if a pilot wished to read his vertical separation above sea-level (defined as altitude) on any given day, he would have to set the sea-level pressure in his altimeter subscale. Sea-level pressure has been known to vary from about 975 millibars to 1065 millibars,

Atmospheric pressure changes rapidly. Therefore, in order to have accurate information on terrain clearance, pilots must obtain frequent updates of sea-level pressure, known in the UK as the Regional Pressure Setting.

in the United Kingdom. In fact, atmospheric pressure changes rapidly, and we cannot even assume that it will remain constant from one hour to the next. Consequently, pilots who are flying near to the Earth's surface, and for whom a primary concern is to maintain terrain clearance, will regularly need to obtain sea-level pressure values (either QNH or Regional Pressure Setting (RPS), which are not necessarily the same - see below) from appropriately equipped Air Traffic Service Units. This is, of course, of particular importance when flying over hilly or mountainous terrain. If the subscale setting is not reset periodically during a flight of more than short duration, the altimeter may give a false indication of the vertical separation between an aircraft and the terrain.

In the context of Air Law, our examination of altimetry will concentrate primarily on altimeter subscale settings. As we have discussed, one primary purpose of altimeter subscale settings is to enable pilots to ensure proper and adequate clearance from the ground. Another important function of the altimeter is to ensure that an aircraft maintains safe vertical separation from other traffic.

In order to achieve the above-mentioned aims, pressure settings are disseminated by Air Traffic Service Units to aircraft flying below what is known as the Transition Altitude (TA) (explained later in this chapter).

When flying above the transition altitude, by reference to Flight Levels, pilots set the Standard Pressure Setting (SPS) of 1013.2 mb (hPa) on their altimeters.

For the United Kingdom, altimeter setting procedures are defined in the UK AIP Enroute Section (ENR) Chapter 1-7.

CHANGING ATMOSPHERIC PRESSURES.

As we have established, pressure at sea-level and throughout the atmosphere will vary with time and with changing weather systems. Consequently, any flight of more than very short duration, especially a cross-country flight, will inevitably require the altimeter subscale to be reset periodically.

If the sub scale is not reset periodically, the altimeter is likely to give false indications of the vertical distance of the aircraft above the ground or water.

The three altimeter subscale settings which vary with location and time and which need to be frequently updated by the pilot are known as QFE, QNH and RPS. The first two codes are part of what is known as the "Q" code which dates back to the days when the Morse Code was the main method of communicating between aircraft and ground stations.

QFE AND QNH.

The QFE is the pressure setting at the aerodrome reference point.

QFE.
QFE is defined as the pressure setting for aerodrome elevation. This will normally be the pressure setting at the aerodrome reference point, usually the highest point on the landing area,. Aerodrome elevation is defined as the vertical distance of the aerodrome above sea-level. So, if an aircraft is on the ground at the highest point on the landing area of an aerodrome with the aerodrome QFE set on the altimeter subscale, the altimeter will indicate zero feet.

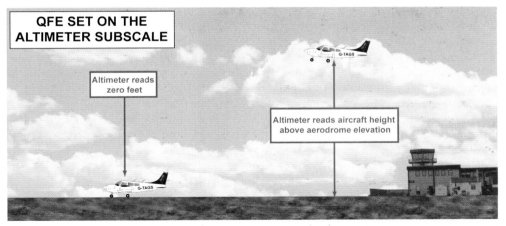

Figure 19.2 QFE set on the altimeter subscale.

In general, with aerodrome QFE set on the altimeter, the altimeter will read zero when the aircraft is on the ground at the aerodrome.

You should note that at many aerodromes the aprons are higher or lower than the aerodrome elevation. Thus, if a pilot asks ATC for the QFE while on the apron, the altimeter may not read precisely zero feet. For example, the apron at Oxford/ Kidlington is 240 feet above mean sea-level (amsl), whereas the general aerodrome elevation is 270 feet amsl. Therefore, if a pilot sets the QFE given to him by the Tower, while on the apron, his altimeter would read minus 30 feet.

When an aircraft with QFE set on the altimeter subscale is in the air, its altimeter will read height above aerodrome elevation. You should note that the word height is, by definition, the vertical distance of an aircraft, in flight, above the pressure datum level defined by the QFE set on the altimeter subscale.

With QFE set on the altimeter subscale, the altimeter of an aircraft in flight will read height above the aerodrome.

QNH.

QNH is the pressure measured at any point, corrected for temperature error and then reduced to mean sea-level under standard ISA conditions.

So, if an aircraft is at the ground at an aerodrome with the QNH set on its altimeter subscale, the altimeter will read the elevation of the ground on which it is standing.

When we speak of the elevation of ground, we are referring to its vertical distance from sea-level.

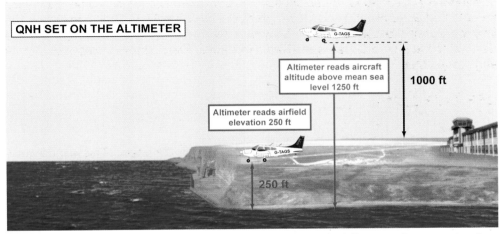

Figure 19.3 QNH set on the altimeter subscale gives vertical distance above sea-level.

With QNH set on the altimeter subscale, the altimeter of an aircraft in flight will read altitude - that is, the vertical distance of the aircraft above mean sea-level.

When airborne, the altimeter, with QNH set, will read the altitude of the aircraft; that is, its vertical distance above mean sea-level.

RT Phraseology.

In order to confirm that the pilot has correctly understood the QFE or QNH passed to him by a ground station, he is required to "read back" the QFE or QNH. Note that, in the UK, when the QFE or QNH is 1000 millibars or below, the word "millibars" is included in the radio transmission, whereas for pressure settings above 1000 mb, spoken as "one thousand millibars", it is customary to omit the word "millibars".

Aircraft request: **"Oxford Tower, G-ABCD, request QFE"**

ATC reply: **"G-CD, QFE 996 millibars"**

Aircraft read-back: **"QFE 996 millibars, G-CD"**

or

Aircraft request: **"Oxford Tower, G-ABCD, request QNH"**

ATC reply: **"G-CD, QNH 1003"**

Aircraft read-back: **"QNH 1003, G-CD"**

Should I set QFE or QNH?

If a pilot remains in the circuit at the aerodrome, it is appropriate to use QFE so that the pilot has the height information he needs to fly the circuit pattern correctly. Be aware, though, that some aerodromes may give circuit information in QNH.

When flying locally, outside the circuit, QNH should generally be used so that a pilot has the altitude information he needs in order to compute the vertical separation between his aircraft at the terrain beneath him.

CROSS-COUNTRY FLYING AND ALTIMETER SUBSCALE SETTINGS.

General.

When flying cross-country, it is essential that the pilot should remain aware of the vertical separation between his aircraft and the terrain and obstacles over which he is flying. When flying in the vicinity of an aerodrome (generally accepted to be within 25 nm), it is useful to have that aerodrome's **QNH** set on the altimeter subscale. However, in the United Kingdom, when on an extended cross-country flight, it is more usual for the pilot to request the **Regional Pressure Setting** for the region of the country he is flying over. Regional Pressure Settings are the lowest forecast mean sea-level pressure for a given altimeter setting region and for a given period of 1 hour. RPSs are covered in detail later in this chapter.

On charts, the top of all obstacles (high ground, tall buildings, radio masts etc) is referenced to mean sea-level, so, with QNH set, obstacle clearance can be assured with the help of simple arithmetic.

By subtracting the elevation of an obstacle from the altimeter reading, the pilot will know his approximate height above the obstacle.

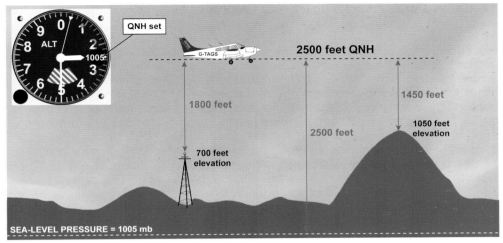

Figure 19.4 Flying cross-country at 2500 feet with QNH set.

However, although flying on a cross-country route with QNH set will enable a pilot to compute his vertical separation from terrain and obstacles, this is not the whole story in terms of maintaining a safe altitude.

Remember, the altimeter is indicating an aircraft's vertical separation from a pressure level; that is, the level at which the pressure prevails which is set on the altimeter subscale. With QNH set, the pressure datum level is mean sea-level. If the pressure at sea-level changes while the aeroplane maintains level flight, the altimeter reading will change. But if the pressure changes and the aircraft flies in such a manner as to maintain a constant altimeter reading, the aircraft will either climb or descend. Let us look at an example of this latter situation.

Figure 19.5 When flying into a region of falling atmospheric pressure while maintaining a constant altimeter subscale setting, the aircraft descends.

The aircraft in *Figure 19.5* is leaving its departure aerodrome on a cross-country flight that the pilot intends to carry out at an altitude of 2 500 feet. The pilot has set the departure aerodrome QNH of 1020 millibars on his altimeter and elects, unwisely, to remain on that QNH for the duration of the flight. Let us assume that, unbeknown to the pilot, as he flies towards his destination aerodrome he is flying into an area of falling pressure. As we have established, because the pilot elects not to update the altimeter setting and maintains 2 500 feet as indicated by the altimeter, the changing pressure situation means that he will either climb or descend. But why should this be?

For the departure aerodrome, we know that the calculated sea-level pressure is 1020 millibars, and the pilot has set this on his altimeter subscale as the QNH. As he leaves the aerodrome at his cruising altitude of 2 500 feet indicated, the aircraft is actually flying along an invisible pressure datum line of about 935 millibars. We can calculate the pressure at 2 500 feet fairly easily, as pressure falls at an approximate rate of 1 millibar for every 30 feet gain of height.

If we assume that the pressure reduced to sea-level at the destination airfield is 1 000 mb (this will be the destination aerodrome's QNH), you can see from *Figure 19.5* that the pressure datum lines are sloping downwards. The aircraft that we are considering, then, as it is following the 935 millibar pressure datum line, will be descending along its route, even though the pilot is unaware of this because of his poor flight planning and because he is maintaining a constant altimeter reading of 2 500 feet. It is not difficult to work out that, if the destination QNH is 1000 millibars, by following the 935 millibar pressure datum line, the aircraft will be only 1950 feet above sea-level when it arrives at its destination, even though the altimeter still indicates 2 500 feet. Of course, had the pilot reset the QNH to 1000 mb, the indicated 2 500 feet altitude would have reflected his true altitude. So, in the situation we have described, the aircraft's true altitude is reducing while its indicated altitude remains the same. This is a potentially hazardous situation, especially in poor visibility. However, the situation is hazardous in good visibility, too, because an ATZ, Control Zone, or Danger Area could be penetrated when a pilot thinks he is passing above the Zone or Area.

Therefore, a pilot must exercise particular caution when flying into an area of falling atmospheric pressure.

In the opposite situation, flying towards a high pressure area, an aircraft which maintained a constant indicated altitude, without the pilot updating the QNH, would actually be climbing. Though this situation is not hazardous from the terrain clearance point of view, a pilot may unwittingly enter an airway and cause danger to itself and others as a result.

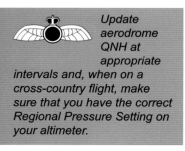

Update aerodrome QNH at appropriate intervals and, when on a cross-country flight, make sure that you have the correct Regional Pressure Setting on your altimeter.

Consequently, it is of the utmost importance that the pilot should update the QNH regularly. This updating of QNH along a cross-country route may be effected by requesting QNH from aerodromes along the route, or, if in the United Kingdom, by requesting the Regional Pressure Setting.

Regional Pressure Setting.

The United Kingdom is divided into a number of Altimeter Setting Regions (ASRs) (*See Figure 19.6*) for each of which the Met Office calculates the lowest forecast pressure, for the next two hours. These pressure settings are known as Regional Pressure Settings. RPSs are updated every hour and are valid for one hour ahead, (e.g. RPS issued at 1300 is valid for 1400-1500); they are not, strictly speaking, QNHs, as they are forecast and not observed values.

The Regional Pressure Setting (RPS) may be obtained from all aerodromes providing an Air Traffic Service, or on the London, Manchester or Scottish Flight Information Service frequencies. The purpose of RPS is to enable pilots to maintain safe terrain clearance when a local aerodrome QNH is not available. Because of the nature of the RPS, and its purpose, an altimeter with RPS set on it will always indicate lower than the actual altitude, which errs on the safe side. RPS must not be used as the vertical reference in the vicinity of controlled airspace.

When approaching the destination airfield, the pilot will be given the QNH of the aerodrome, and possibly, also, its QFE.

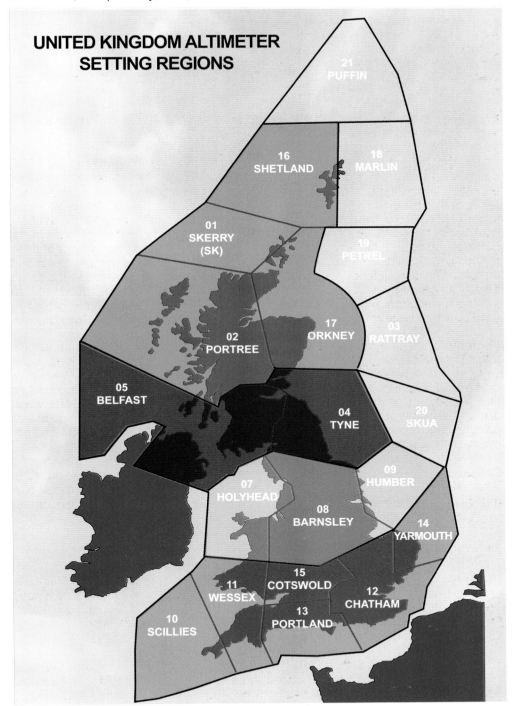

Figure 19.6 United Kingdom Altimeter Setting Regions.

Remaining Clear of the Base of Controlled Airspace.

Control Zones (CTRs) and Control Areas (CTAs), with certain exceptions, are not part of the Altimeter Setting Region network. Therefore, when flying near to the base of a

CTA (or TMA), pilots should obtain a QNH from a nearby aerodrome in order that they may avoid, unwittingly, entering the CTA/TMA from beneath. When flying beneath an airway whose base is expressed as an altitude, pilots are likewise recommended to obtain a QNH from an adjacent aerodrome, in order to avoid entering the base of the airway.

THE STANDARD PRESSURE SETTING OF 1013.2 MILLIBARS.

During flights well above terrain, changes in atmospheric pressure along a route, and over time, are not so critical to terrain clearance considerations. At these higher altitudes, the fact that a pilot may fly over long distances without updating the altimeter subscale pressure setting will not endanger the aircraft. In fact, having all aircraft use the same altimeter subscale setting, above a defined altitude, will actually help an Air Traffic Control Unit (ATCU) maintain vertical separation between the aircraft that the ATCU is controlling or in communication with.

So, by international agreement, above a certain defined altitude, called the transition altitude, which varies from country to country and even, in some cases, from aerodrome to aerodrome, the **Standard Pressure Setting (SPS)** of **1013.2 mb** (or **hPa**) is used. The use of the SPS is obligatory in controlled airspace above the transition altitude, and strongly recommended for VFR flights conducted above the transition altitude, outside controlled airspace. For IFR flights, the use of the SPS is obligatory above the transition altitude, both inside and outside controlled airspace.

THE TRANSITION ALTITUDE.

Transition Altitudes (TA) are established by national aviation authorities to meet the air traffic and flight safety requirements of local conditions. Obviously, over countries with lots of mountainous areas, the TA will be higher than over lowlands. The TA in the United Kingdom is 3 000 feet over most of the country and at all aerodromes, unless otherwise notified. There are exceptions, however. Aberdeen, Belfast, Bristol, Cardiff, Durham/Tees, Edinburgh, Glasgow, Newcastle, the Solent CTA, Sumburgh, and the London and Scottish TMAs have a TA of 6 000 feet; Doncaster, Leeds/Bradford and Manchester have TAs of 5 000 feet and Birmingham and East Midlands 4 000 feet.

Wherever possible, there is a common transition altitude for all aerodromes within a Control Zone.

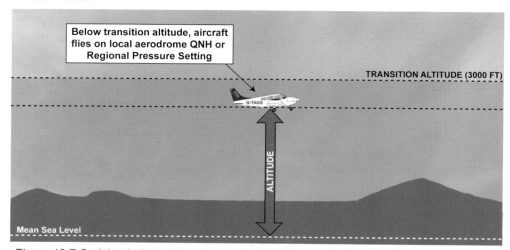

Figure 19.7 Cruising below a transition level of 3000 feet with Regional Pressure Setting, or local Aerodrome QNH set on the altimeter subscale.

In the United States and Canada, the TA over both countries is 18 000 feet. In New Zealand, the transition altitude is, generally, 13 000 feet.

When flying below the transition altitude, pilots set an aerodrome QNH or the Regional Pressure Setting (RPS) on the altimeter in order that they can maintain separation with terrain and obstacles. (*See Figure 19.7.*)

Typically, on a cross-country flight, a VFR pilot will have studied the ICAO 1:500 000 topographical chart closely. The elevation of all high ground and obstacles will be given on the chart so the pilot will know the vertical distance of hill tops and obstacle summits from mean sea-level. By subtracting known elevations from his altimeter reading, with QNH or RPS set, he will know how high he is above the terrain.

1:500 000 charts also show Maximum Elevation Figures (MEF) in quadrants marked on the chart. The MEFs, as the name suggests, show the elevation of the highest known features in each quadrant, expressed in thousands and hundreds of feet amsl rounded up to the nearest hundred. *Figure 19.8* highlights an MEF of 1 300 feet for the Isle of Wight which indicates a tower whose actual elevation is 1 297 feet above mean sea level. Where an obstacle is not man-made, i.e. high ground/hill, the MEF will be raised by 300 ft to allow for any undeclared structures, e.g. a small mast or pylons. An example is the hill 10 nm north-east of Cheltenham at 1 001 ft, making the MEF 1 400 ft. Note that an MEF is not a Safety Altitude.

Maximum Elevation Figures are not Safety Altitudes.

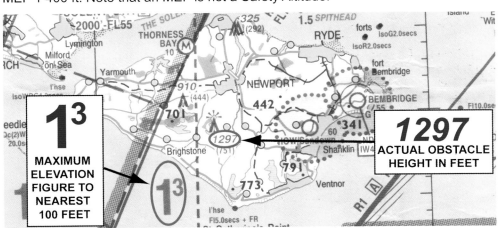

Figure 19.8 Maximum Elevation Figures on the Isle of Wight. With the altimeter set to QNH or RPS, the pilot can compute the vertical separation between his aircraft and terrain or obstacles.

Above the transition altitude the SPS of 1013 mb is set. When an aircraft is equipped with two or more altimeters, it is usual, when flying above the transition altitude, that one altimeter should remain set to QNH so that the pilot may still know his clearance from terrain.

Above the transition altitude, with the SPS of 1013 mb set on the altimeter, altimeter indications are referred to as Flight Levels.

Above the transition altitude, with 1013.2 mb (hPa) set on the altimeter subscale (the pilot can only dial up the digits 1013, of course), the indications on the altimeter are referred to as Flight Levels.

When air traffic controllers and pilots transmit Flight Levels over the radio, or when Flight Levels are written down, the last two zeros of the altimeter reading are omitted. So, when flying by reference to Flight Levels above the transition altitude, with 1013 mb (hPa) on the altimeter, an altimeter indication of 5 000 feet would be referred to as

Flight Level 50; an indicated 6 500 feet would be referred to as Flight Level 65, and an altimeter reading of 15 000 feet would be referred to as Flight Level 150.

Flight Levels are not established for every altimeter reading with the SPS set on the subscale. Flight Levels (FL) are given for intervals of 500 feet between transition altitude and FL 250 and at intervals of 1000 feet above FL 250; e.g. FL 35, FL 40, FL 45 and so on up to FL 245; then FL 250, FL 260, FL 270 and so on.

Flight Levels are used principally so that Air Traffic Controllers can maintain adequate separation between aircraft flying in accordance with Instrument Flight Rules (IFR), but aircraft flying in accordance with the Visual Flight Rules (VFR) in controlled airspace must also use SPS and fly by reference to Flight Levels when instructed to do so by the ATCU.

With all aircraft flying at Flight Levels, invariably during the en-route phase of flight, Air Traffic Controllers know that all aircraft are flying at vertical distances from the same pressure datum level of 1013.2 mb (hPa). In these circumstances, with altimeter indications referenced to the same standard pressure datum level, Air Traffic Controllers can safely allocate Flight Levels to the aircraft under their control and be confident that vertical separation will be maintained, if pilots keep to their assigned levels.

At this point, it is pertinent to give a formal definition of the transition altitude.

The 'transition altitude' is the altitude at or below which the vertical position of an aircraft is normally monitored by reference to altitude.

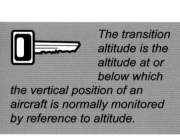

The transition altitude is the altitude at or below which the vertical position of an aircraft is normally monitored by reference to altitude.

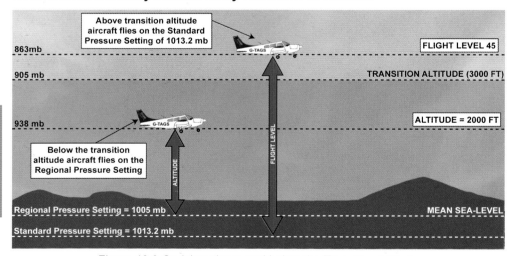

Figure 19.9 Cruising above and below the Transition Altitude.

The transition level is always above the transition altitude.

Below the transition altitude, an aircraft flying cross-country, in the United Kingdom, will normally have the Regional Pressure Setting (RPS) on the subscale of its altimeter (though it <u>may</u> have a local aerodrome QNH set), and will refer to its vertical position as altitude. Above the transition altitude, the aircraft may have, and under IFR normally will have, the SPS of 1013.2 mb set on the altimeter, and will refer to its vertical position as a Flight Level.

For example, in *Figure 19.9*, the RPS is 1005 mb, and the transition altitude is 3 000 feet, as is standard outside controlled airspace in the United Kingdom. For an RPS of 1005 mb, 3 000 feet represents a pressure surface of about 905 mb.

(Remember, atmospheric pressure falls by 1 mb for every 30 feet gain of height. So, 3000 feet represents approximately 1005 mb − (3000/30) mb = 1005 mb − 100 mb = 905 mb.)

The lower aircraft, cruising below the transition altitude, is at an altitude of 2 000 feet. In other words, the aircraft is flying at 2 000 feet above mean sea-level, along the 938 mb pressure surface.

The higher aircraft, flying above the transition altitude, and so has 1013 mb set on its altimeter subscale. The pilot has elected to fly at 4 500 feet indicated, and will report his vertical position as Flight Level 45. The aircraft is, of course, flying at 4 500 feet above the pressure datum of 1013.2 mb, and so, as you should now be able to calculate, will be flying along the 863 mb pressure surface (at an actual altitude of 4 260 ft.) *Note: You do not need to know the pressure at cruising level, only the relevant datum values of SPS, QNH or RPS and, if required, QFE.*

THE TRANSITION LEVEL.

The lowest Flight Level above the transition altitude which is available for use is called the Transition Level (TL) and is the next whole- or half-thousand level above TA. The airspace between theTL and the TA is called the transition layer. *(See Figure 19.10.)* The transition layer will never be more than 500 feet deep, and will be only a few feet in the case of a QNH close to SPS.

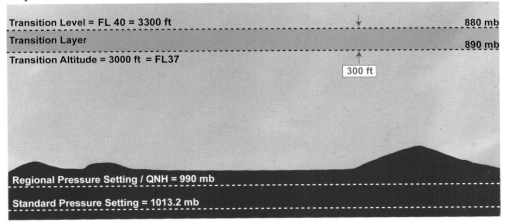

Figure 19.10 The Transition Level is the lowest available Flight Level above the Transition Altitude. Here, the Transition Level is FL 40, and the Transition Layer is 300 feet deep.

The transition altitude is, as you have learnt, an altimeter indication established by the national aviation authority. Above the United Kingdom it is 3000 feet, unless otherwise notified. The transition altitude, like any other altitude, is measured against a constantly changing value of mean sea level pressure which is passed to the pilot as an aerodrome QNH or Regional Pressure Setting (RPS).

The transition level, however, is not set at a level identified by a given altimeter indication, but is measured against the constant pressure datum for Flight Levels of 1013 mb (hPa). So, because the transition level is always above the transition altitude, the Flight Level which identifies the transition level (i.e. the lowest useable Flight Level above the transition altitude) will change with changing QNH or RPS.

The transition level always lies above the transition altitude.

This is not an easy concept to grasp, so let us examine the issue using an actual example.

Take a look again at *Figure 19.10*. In the diagram, the QNH (or RPS) is 990 millibars. The transition altitude is shown as being 3 000 feet above that pressure datum. The Standard Pressure Setting (SPS), of 1013.2 mb will, in this situation, lie <u>below</u> the Regional Pressure Setting (RPS) datum.

A Flight Level is, as you have learnt, measured as a vertical position measured with reference to the SPS. Furthermore, the transition level, which is the lowest useable Flight Level on any given day, must lie above the transition altitude.

So what Flight Level represents the transition level in the circumstances depicted in *Figure 19.10*?

We know that the transition altitude of 3 000 feet is 3 000 feet above the RPS datum of 990 mb, so it will, necessarily, be at a greater vertical distance above the 1013.2 mb datum. This SPS datum is, in fact, 23.2 mb "lower" than the RPS datum. At 30 feet per millibar, that makes the SPS datum almost 700 feet lower (696 feet, to be exact), and puts the transition altitude of 3 000 feet at 3 700 feet above the SPS datum. Consequently, the lowest available Flight Level above the transition altitude is Flight Level 40; i.e., 4 000 feet above the SPS datum of 1013.2 mb at a pressure level of 880 mb. In these conditions, the transition layer will be 300 feet in depth. Note, too, that at Flight Level 40, in the prevailing conditions illustrated in *Figure 19.10*, an aircraft will be only 3 300 feet above sea-level, not the 4 000 feet indicated on the altimeter.

By a similar calculation process, if the **QNH/RPS** were **950 mb**, the lowest available Flight Level the transition level would be Flight Level 50. *(See Figure 19.11.)*

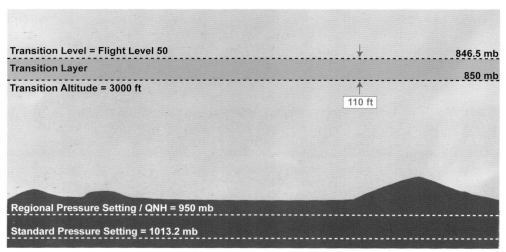

Fig 19.11 In the atmospheric pressure conditions depicted here, the Transition Level is FL 50, and the Transition Layer is 110 feet deep.

The SPS datum level would be 63 mb or approximately 1 890 feet (63 x 30) lower than the RPS datum, making the transition altitude of 3 000 feet, 4 890 feet above the SPS datum, and giving a lowest available Flight Level of Flight Level 50. An aircraft would, of course, have to climb 110 feet to get from the transition altitude to the transition level of Flight Level 50. The transition layer would be, in this case, therefore, about 110 feet deep, and at FL 50, the aircraft is only 3 110 feet above sea level.

Looking at this situation from a slightly different perspective, let us imagine that, with a QNH of 950 mb set, a pilot has just approached the transition altitude of 3 000 feet. He now resets 1013 mb on his altimeter subscale, winding on 63 mb to change the subscale setting from 950 to 1013. At 30 feet per millibar, the pilot sees his altimeter indication rise from 3 000 feet to 4 890 feet. The pilot knows, therefore, that he must climb a further 110 feet to give an altimeter reading of 5 000 feet. As he now has the SPS in his altimeter subscale, that puts him at Flight level 50. But the aircraft remains only 3 110 feet above sea-level. Hence the importance of flying with QNH or RPS in the altimeter subscale when descending <u>below</u> the transition level.

Care should be taken in conditions of abnormally low atmospheric pressure when an altimeter set to SPS may indicate an apparently safe altitude while the actual altitude is much lower.

FLIGHT AT OR ABOVE THE TRANSITION LEVEL.

In cases of high pressure, for example 1033mb, the TL can be numerically (but not physically) lower than the TA. The 20mb difference from SPS, worth approximately 600 ft, makes TA 3 000 = FL24, therefore the TL will be FL25 (at an actual altitude of 3 100 ft), Transition Layer thus being 100 ft deep.

Inside Controlled Airspace.
If a pilot is flying inside controlled airspace, above the transition altitude, he must set the Standard Pressure Setting (SPS), 1013 mb (hPa), on his altimeter, and report his level to the responsible Air Traffic Control Unit (ATCU) as a Flight Level. If a second altimeter if fitted to the aircraft, the pilot should set the Regional Pressure Setting (RPS) or appropriate aerodrome QNH on that altimeter in order that he may compute his vertical distance from terrain and obstacles. When a pilot is cleared to descend below the transition level in controlled airspace, the ATCU will pass the appropriate QNH to the pilot.

Note: The RPS system does not apply within CTRs, and in and below TMAs and CTAs except airways and the Daventry and Worthing CTAs. See UK AIP ENR 1.7.

Outside Controlled Airspace.
Outside controlled airspace, when above the transition altitude, in level flight, an aircraft flying in accordance with the Instrument Flight Rules (IFR) must set the SPS on his altimeter (1013 mb) and, if below Flight Level 195, fly at a Flight Level determined by the aircraft's magnetic track, as stipulated by the Quadrantal Rule. The Quadrantal Rule is based on magnetic track, and effectively, divides all possible magnetic tracks into four sectors, confining aircraft to specific Flight Levels within each sector. Magnetic tracks are used as the reference instead of magnetic heading because slow moving aircraft are affected much more by drift than high-speed aircraft. Consequently, aircraft may well be on converging tracks even when steering the same compass heading. The Quadrantal Rule is summarised in *Figure 19.12*.

Outside controlled airspace, when flying above the transition level, IFR traffic must, and VFR traffic should, follow the Quadrantal Rule.

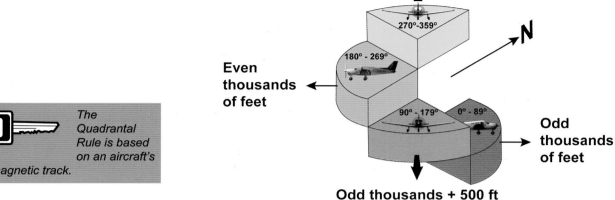

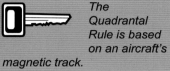

The Quadrantal Rule is based on an aircraft's magnetic track.

Fig 19.12 The Quadrantal Rule - to be followed when flying IFR or VFR outside controlled airspace, above the transition altitude but below FL 195.

The simple procedure for flying in accordance with the Quadrantal Rule is:

1. The pilot determines the magnetic track he needs. This is normally done on the ground during the flight planning stage.

2. The pilot chooses a cruising level appropriate to his magnetic track in compliance with the Quadrantal Rule.

Pilots flying in accordance with the Visual Flight Rules (VFR), while not obliged to fly Flight Levels, are <u>strongly advised</u> to set their altimeters to the SPS and to fly at a Flight Level compliant with the Quadrantal Rule, although it is sensible to avoid flight at TL if possible, owing to the reduced vertical separation from traffic flying at TA.

Following the Quadrantal Rule may often be the only systematic way to ensure separation from other aircraft when flying VFR in marginal visual conditions above the transition level.

ALTIMETER SETTING PROCEDURES.

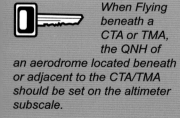

When Flying beneath a CTA or TMA, the QNH of an aerodrome located beneath or adjacent to the CTA/TMA should be set on the altimeter subscale.

The following general altimeter setting procedures should be used by VFR flights.

Take-off, Climb and Cruise.
Outside controlled airspace, there is no stipulated altimeter subscale setting. However, the following considerations should be borne in mind:

• If departing on a cross-country flight, aerodrome QNH may be an appropriate altimeter setting for the take-off and climb out. At the selected cruising level, if below the transition altitude, obtain the Regional Pressure Setting (RPS) through a Flight Information Service or Lower Airspace Radar Service.

• If passing below a Control Area (CTA) or Terminal Control Area (TMA), the QNH of an aerodrome situated beneath or adjacent to the CTA/TMA should be used.

• Above the transition altitude, VFR pilots are strongly advised to set the Standard Pressure Setting (SPS) of 1013 mb on their altimeter and to fly at a Flight Level appropriate to their magnetic track in accordance with the Quadrantal Rule.

At a controlled airfield, a VFR pilot will normally be given the aerodrome QNH from the Air Traffic Control Unit (ATCU), before take-off. Within a Military Aerodrome Traffic Zone (MATZ), pilots will normally be given the airfield QFE.

- On leaving the CTR, Aerodrome Traffic Zone (ATZ) or MATZ, the ATCU controller will normally pass the Regional Pressure Setting to the pilot. If the pilot remains underneath a CTA or TMA on leaving the CTR, ATZ or MATZ, he should remain on aerodrome QNH.

- At and above the transition altitude, if the pilot remains in controlled airspace, he should set the SPS of 1013 mb on his altimeter and report all levels as a Flight Level.

- If, in controlled airspace, the aircraft is below the transition altitude, the pilot will be passed the appropriate QNH or RPS by the responsible ATCU.

Approach and Landing.
Approaching an aerodrome with a **CTR** or **ATZ**.

- When descending from above the transition level, where the aircraft will have been flying at a Flight Level, the aerodrome QNH will be passed by the CTR controller or Aerodrome Flight information Service Officer (AFISO). On vacating his Flight Level to commence the descent, the pilot will replace the SPS on his altimeter by the aerodrome QNH, unless a CTR controller wishes him to continue reporting Flight Levels in the descent.

- When descending from below the transition altitude with the RPS set, the CTR controller or AFISO will pass the aerodrome QNH to the pilot, who should select it immediately, in place of the RPS. If the aircraft has been cruising below a TMA or CTA immediately prior to the descent, it will have the aerodrome QNH set on the altimeter already.

- A clearance will be required to enter a CTR around a destination aerodrome.

- Normally the aerodrome QNH will be kept on the altimeter for the circuit and approach to land. If so, a pilot must always be sure to add the aerodrome elevation to all altimeter readings in the circuit in order to maintain the correct height above airfield level, at all times. However, the pilot may be passed the QFE. He may also, of course, request the QFE.

Approaching an aerodrome with only an Air-Ground Radio Service.

- When descending from a Flight Level above the transition altitude, obtain the RPS from an Air Traffic Service Unit providing a Flight Information Service or Lower Airspace Radar Service. On making contact with the air-ground radar service, an advisory QNH or QFE may be given. If not, the pilot will have to retain the RPS on his altimeter for the circuit and approach to land, making sure to subtract the airfield elevation from all altimeter readings in the circuit in order to maintain the correct height above airfield level at all times.

- When descending from below the transition altitude the RPS or an aerodrome QNH from a nearby ATSU will normally already be set. On making contact with the air-ground radar service, the pilot may have to retain the RPS or QNH on his altimeter for the circuit and approach to land

- If so, the pilot must be sure to subtract the airfield elevation from all altimeter readings in the circuit in order to maintain the correct height above airfield level at all times.

The air-ground radio operator may be able to pass an advisory QFE to the pilot. Pilots should, however, exercise caution when setting advisory QFE. The instruments from which air-ground radio operators obtain the QFE are often not regularly calibrated or otherwise checked. Of course, the VFR pilot should always be able to assess visually his separation from the ground.

ALTIMETER SETTING SUMMARY.

The table, below, is a summary of the altimeter subscale settings covered in this chapter, as they may apply to a VFR flight in a light aeroplane. The table contains details of the type of pressure datum set in the altimeter subscale, the term used to refer to the vertical distance associated with subscale setting, and when each setting is used.

ALTIMETER SUBSCALE SETTING (PRESSURE DATUM)	VERTICAL DISTANCE FROM PRESSURE DATUM REFERRED TO AS	WHEN USED
Standard Pressure Setting, 1013.2 mb (hPa)	Flight Level	• Above the **Transition Altitude**, the lowest useable **Flight Level** being known as the **Transition Level**.
Aerodrome QNH	Altitude	• At or below the **Transition Altitude**. • When descending from a **Flight Level** unless **ATC** require further level reports. • At the pilot's discretion, on final approach.
QFE	Height	• Normally, in the circuit and on final approach.
Regional Pressure Setting	Altitude	• At or below the **Transition Altitude**, when not in the vicinity of a major aerodrome or under a **CTA** or **TMA**.

Representative PPL - type questions to test your theoretical knowledge of Altimeter Settings.

1.   You are flying above the Transition Altitude with 1013 mb (hPa) set on the altimeter which is reading 6 000 feet. What is your Flight Level (FL)?

     a.   FL6
     b.   FL006
     c.   FL60
     d.   FL600

2.   You are on the apron of an aerodrome and ask ATC for the aerodrome QFE which you then set on the altimeter. Would your altimeter then read zero feet?

     a.   Yes
     b.   Not necessarily, since QFE is measured from a standard pressure setting
     c.   Not necessarily, since QFE is measured from the Aerodrome Reference Point which may not be coincident with the apron
     d.   There is no location on the aerodrome where the altimeter would read zero

3.   You are on the apron of an aerodrome and ask ATC for the aerodrome QNH which you then set on the altimeter. Which of the following should your altimeter reading indicate?

     a.   Height
     b.   Vertical distance above the SPS
     c.   Zero feet
     d.   The aerodrome elevation

4.   What is the Standard Pressure Setting?

     a.   QNH
     b.   QFE
     c.   Zero feet
     d.   1013.2 millibars or 1013.2 hectopascals

5.   You fly from an aerodrome of a given atmospheric pressure to a destination aerodrome where the atmospheric pressure is significantly lower than at your point of departure. If you fly the route at a constant altimeter reading on the departure aerodrome QNH, what would be the path of your aircraft in terms of its vertical separation from the ground?

     a.   It would climb as you approach your destination
     b.   It would descend as you approach your destination
     c.   It would remain at the same height above the ground
     d.   It would remain at the same vertical distance above mean sea-level

6.   What is QFE?

a.   The pressure setting at the aerodrome reference point, normally the highest point on the landing area
b.   The pressure setting at the aerodrome reference point, reduced to sea level
c.   The pressure setting of the altimeter in the ATC Tower
d.   The pressure setting at the lowest point on the aerodrome

7.   What is the Transition Altitude at most aerodromes in the United Kingdom?

a.   2 000 feet
b.   3 000 feet
c.   5 000 feet
d.   18 000 feet

8.   If a pilot is to carry out circuit practice at an aerodrome, what is the most practical and appropriate pressure setting for the altimeter?

a.   QFE
b.   1013 mb (hPa)
c.   The Standard Pressure Setting
d.   The Regional Pressure Setting

9.   If you are to fly a cross-country route below the transition altitude, what is the most appropriate pressure setting for your altimeter when you have left the immediate vicinity of your departure aerodrome?

a.   QFE
b.   Regional Pressure Setting provided you are not still beneath a CTA or TMA
c.   Standard Pressure Setting
d.   1013 mb (hPa)

10.   You are flying en-route below the Transition Altitude. How must you report your aircraft's vertical position to an Air Traffic Service Unit?

a.   As a Flight Level
b.   As a height
c.   As an altitude
d.   As an elevation

11.   What is defined as the "first available Flight Level above the Transition Altitude"?

a.   Transition Layer
b.   Transition Elevation
c.   Transition Level
d.   Transition Height

12. What is the Transition Layer?

    a. The vertical distance between a given Flight Level and the Transition Level

    b. The vertical distance between the Transition Altitude and the Transition Level

    c. The vertical distance from the ground to the Transition Altitude

    d. The vertical distance from the Aerodrome Reference Point (ARP) to the Transition Altitude

13. An altimeter reading from an aircraft in the air, based on aerodrome QFE is reported as:

    a. Elevation
    b. Altitude
    c. Height
    d. Flight Level

14. The reading of an altimeter, in flight, with QNH set on its subscale is known as:

    a. Flight Level
    b. Altitude
    c. Height
    d. Elevation

15. Which of the four options below gives the most accurate definition of "transition altitude"?

    a. The altitude at or above which the vertical position of an aircraft is monitored by reference to altitude

    b. The altitude at or below which the vertical position of an aircraft is monitored by reference to altitude

    c. The altitude at or above which the vertical position of an aircraft is monitored by reference to height

    d. The altitude at or below which the vertical position of an aircraft is monitored by reference to height

16. What pressure setting should be entered on the altimeter subscale of an aircraft which is descending to below the transition level prior to commencing a visual approach to a non-military aerodrome?

    a. The Regional Pressure Setting
    b. The Standard Pressure Setting
    c. The Aerodrome QFE
    d. The Aerodrome QNH

17. Complete the following sentence. While passing through the transition layer, vertical separation from the appropriate pressure datum level should be expressed as _____ when climbing and _____ when descending.

    a. Flight Level   Altitude
    b. Height   Altitude
    c. Flight Level   Height
    d. Height   Flight Level

18. A VFR pilot is cruising, en-route, in level flight, above the transition level of FL35. His magnetic heading is 355°, and he sees that by having allowed for 8° of starboard drift he is exactly on track. What would be an appropriate Flight Level for the pilot to choose in accordance with the Quadrantal Rule?

    a. FL40
    b. FL45
    c. FL50
    d. FL55

19. A pilot setting off on a cross-country route in a cruise climb over a part of the country where the transition altitude is 3000 feet, has just been given a Regional Pressure Setting of 970 mb (hPa), from a local ATSU. His magnetic track is 260°. What will be the transition level and what will be lowest available Flight Level that the pilot can use, in accordance with the Quadrantal Rule? (Note: assume that pressure falls with increasing height by 1 mb every 30 feet)

    a. FL 45   FL 60
    b. FL 40   FL 55
    c. FL 30   FL 30
    d. FL 45   FL 55

20. A pilot, who has just left the ATZ of the departure aerodrome and has set off on a cross-country route, is flying beneath a Terminal Control Area (TMA). What pressure setting should he have on his altimeter subscale?

    a. The destination aerodromes QFE
    b. The Regional Pressure Setting
    c. The departure aerodrome's QFE
    d. The QNH of an aerodrome beneath the TMA

21. You are flying above the transition level, on a VFR cross-country flight in a light aircraft, following a magnetic track of 180°. You refer to the Quadrantal Rule to decide what Flight Level to cruise at. With your altimeter subscale set at 1013 mb (hPa), you should choose:

    a. Odd thousands of feet
    b. Even thousands of feet
    c. Even thousands of feet plus 500
    d. Odd thousands of feet plus 500

22.   The transition altitude for civil aerodromes in the United Kingdom is:

    a.   5 000 feet amsl
    b.   3 000 feet amsl unless otherwise notified, for example for the
            Scottish, Manchester and London TMAs
    c.   4 500 feet amsl
    d.   3 000 feet amsl

Question	1	2	3	4	5	6	7	8	9	10	11	12
Answer												

Question	13	14	15	16	17	18	19	20	21	22
Answer										

The answers to these questions can be found at the end of this book.

ANNEX A
GENERAL LIGHTS
AND SIGNALS

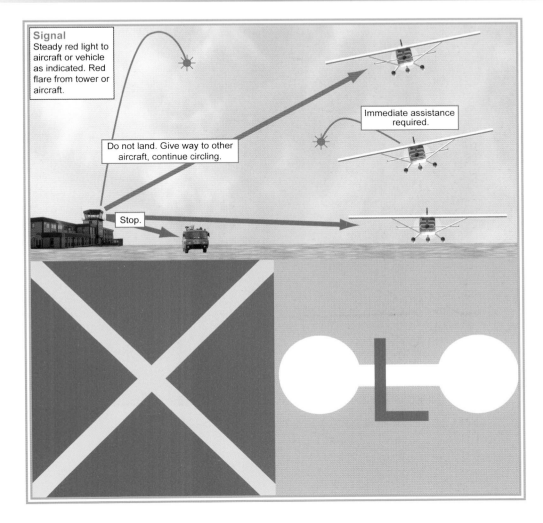

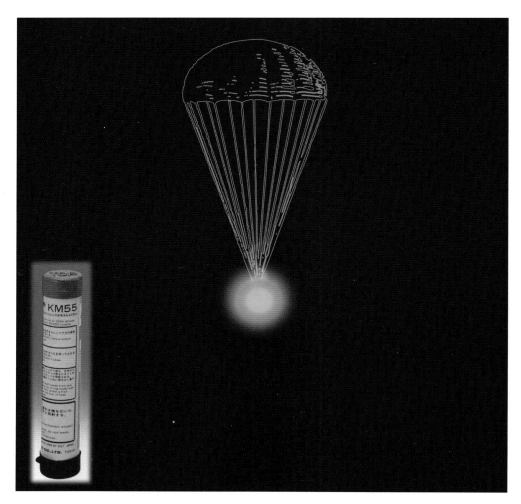

Figure A-1 A Parachute Flare.

INTRODUCTION.

Even when flown for recreation and/or sport, most aircraft today, however basic their instrument fit, carry radios. Radiotelephony is, of course, by far the most efficient method for aircraft and Air Traffic Service Units to communicate. Indeed, for several decades past, most large aerodromes and airfields have insisted that aircraft operating into or out of them be equipped with standard VHF radios.

Nowadays, then, it is routine for a pilot to obtain information and instructions for the safe conduct of his flight over the radio. Consequently, if a pilot suffers radio failure, he is likely immediately to find himself hindered in the progress of his flight. If either he or his aircraft is in trouble, the absence of radio may make the situation extremely critical.

Questions may be asked on any of the lights and signals in this Chapter. All must be known.

It is, therefore, vitally important for the pilot to be able to understand the various forms and meanings of the signals that may be made by Air Traffic Control Services, or for that matter by anyone else, for the attention of aircraft. The pilot may also need to signal to people on the ground concerning his own situation and/or intentions.

It is the aim of this Annex to describe the different type of signals that are used for air-ground and ground-air communications. For the most part, the signals are visual signals in the form of lights or pictograms. Distress messages passed by Radiotelephony are dealt with fully in Volume 7 of this series: **'Radiotelephony'**.

Signals will be presented in this Annex which cover the following situations:

*   Distress & Urgency Signals.
*   Signals For Use in the Event of Interception.
*   Signals Pertinent to Restricted, Prohibited and Danger Areas.
*   Light Signals Between Aircraft and Air Traffic Service Units.
*   Acknowledgement Signals by Aircraft in the Air.
*   The Signals Square.
*   Marshalling Signals – Marshaller to Pilot.
*   Marshalling Signals – Pilot to Marshaller.

DISTRESS & URGENCY.

When an aircraft which is airborne is in distress or urgency, the situation is tense and a pilot often needs to think primarily about flying the aircraft. If he is also experiencing radio failure, the situation is made even more critical.

The following methods of signalling distress and urgency may seem to be desperate measures and, in the case of pyrotechnics and flares, to offer a highly impractical solution to the light aircraft pilot. However, a pilot who can signal an emergency to the ground by any means whatsoever may just manage to create the conditions which prevent disaster. Therefore, the following signals are included in this Annex.

Of course, a pilot may be on the ground when he needs to make a distress or urgency signal; or else someone on the ground may wish to signal to an aircraft. In this case, a difficult situation is made slightly easier.

Even if the radio is working, it is desirable, in an emergency, that the pilot should express his predicament, at least partially, in a simple-to-understand and unambiguous code. And, of course, the pilot's top priority in an emergency situation is to fly the aircraft, not to worry about the words he is using on the radio.

Distress Signals.

The following signals, used either together or separately, mean that grave and imminent danger threatens, and immediate assistance is requested:

- Visually signalling, or signalling by any other method, the letters SOS in the Morse Code (. . . — — — . . .).

- A series of red pyrotechnic lights, fired one at a time at short intervals.

- A parachute flare showing a red light *(see Figure A-1, page 346)*.

- If your radio has failed, but you suspect that the radio's carrier wave is still transmitting, signal the letters SOS with your microphone switch.

- Select the SSR Code 7700 on your transponder

Urgency Signals.

The following signals, used either together or separately, mean that an aircraft wishes to give notice of difficulties which compel it to land, without requiring immediate assistance:

- The repeated switching on and off of the landing lights.

- The repeated switching on and off of the navigation lights in such a manner as to be distinct from flashing navigation lights.

- In order to indicate an urgency situation regarding your own aircraft or regarding another vessel, vehicle or aircraft, signal the letters XXX (— . . —   — . . —   — . . —) with your landing lights.

Ground-Air Signals for use by Survivors of a Downed Aircraft.

Ground to air signals for use by survivors of a downed aircraft, or for use by rescue teams, may be constructed by any means available. These signals are depicted below. The minimum length of the arms of a signal should be 8 feet (2.5 metres).

Ground - air visual signal code for use by survivors

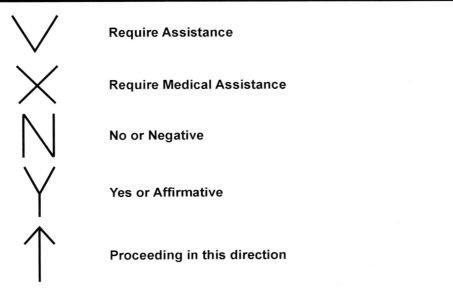

V   **Require Assistance**

X   **Require Medical Assistance**

N   **No or Negative**

Y   **Yes or Affirmative**

↑   **Proceeding in this direction**

Figure A-2 Distress Signals - Ground to Air, for use by survivors.

Ground - air visual signal code for use by rescue teams

LLL   **Operation completed**

LL   **We have found all personnel**

++   **We have found only some personnel**

XX   **We are not able to continue. Returning to base.**

    We have divided into two groups. Each proceeding in the direction indicated.

→ →   **Information received that aircraft is in this direction.**

NN   **Nothing found. Will continue search.**

Figure A-3 Distress Signals - Ground to Air, for use by rescue teams.

SIGNALS FOR USE IN THE EVENT OF INTERCEPTION.

Introduction.

The United Kingdom Air Navigation Order stipulates that on international flights all aircraft must carry a copy of **'Signals for Use in the Event of Interception'**. These are detailed in the **UK AIP ENR 1– 12**.

The table below summarises the signals and procedures to be used, but the important point is that the law requires the pilot to carry the appropriate documentation with him.

The reason why a pilot needs to know these interception signals when flying internationally is that each ICAO contracting state reserves the right, for reasons of military necessity or public safety, to restrict or prohibit the aircraft from other states from flying over certain areas of its territory. A state may , therefore, wish to investigate the identity of aircraft and perhaps lead the intercepted aircraft away from a particular area or require it to land at a particular aerodrome.

Signals Initiated by Intercepting Aircraft and Responses by Intercepted Aircraft.

INTERCEPTING Aircraft Signals	Meaning	INTERCEPTED Aircraft Responds	Meaning
1. DAY or NIGHT Rocking aircraft and flashing navigation lights at irregular intervals (and landing lights in the case of a helicopter) from a position slightly above and ahead of, and normally to the left of, the intercepted aircraft (or to the right if the intercepted aircraft is a helicopter) and, after acknowledgement, a slow level turn, normally to the left, (or to the right in the case of a helicopter) onto the desired heading.	You have been intercepted. Follow me.	**DAY or NIGHT** Rocking aircraft, flashing navigation lights at irregular intervals and following.	Understood, will comply.
2. DAY or NIGHT An abrupt break-away manoeuvre from the intercepted aircraft consisting of a climbing turn of 90 degrees or more without crossing the line of flight of the intercepted aircraft.	You may proceed.	**DAY or NIGHT** Rocking the aircraft.	Understood, will comply.
3. DAY or NIGHT Lowering landing gear (if fitted), showing steady landing lights and over-flying runway in use or, if the intercepted aircraft is a helicopter, over-flying the helicopter landing area. In the case of helicopters, the intercepting helicopter makes a landing approach, coming to hover near to the landing area.	Land at this aerodrome.	**DAY or NIGHT** Lowering landing gear, (if fitted), showing steady landing lights and following the intercepting aircraft and, if, after over-flying the runway in use or helicopter landing area, landing is considered safe, proceeding to land.	Understood, will comply.

Signals Initiated by the Intercepted Aircraft and Responses by Intercepting Aircraft.

INTERCEPTED Aircraft Signals	Meaning	INTERCEPTING Aircraft Responds	Meaning
4. DAY or NIGHT Raising landing gear (if fitted) and flashing landing lights while passing over runway in use, or helicopter landing area, at a height exceeding 300 m (1 000 ft) but not exceeding 600 m (2 000 ft) (in the case of a helicopter, at a height exceeding 50 m (170 ft) but not exceeding 100 m (330 ft)) above the aerodrome level, and continuing to circle runway in use or helicopter landing area. If unable to flash landing lights, flash any other lights available.	aerodrome you have designated is inadequate.	**DAY or NIGHT** If it is desired that the intercepted aircraft follow the intercepting aircraft to an alternate aerodrome, the intercepting aircraft raises its landing gear (if fitted) and uses the Series 1 signals prescribed for intercepting aircraft. If it is decided to release the intercepted aircraft, the intercepting aircraft uses the Series 2 signals prescribed for intercepting aircraft.	Understood, follow me. Understood, you may proceed.
5. DAY or NIGHT Regular switching on and off of all available lights but in such a manner as to be distinct from flashing lights.	Cannot comply	**DAY or NIGHT** Use Series 2 signals prescribed for intercepting aircraft.	Understood.
6. DAY or NIGHT Irregular flashing of all available lights.	In distress.	**DAY or NIGHT** Use Series 2 signals prescribed for intercepting aircraft.	Understood.

SIGNALS FROM RESTRICTED, PROHIBITED OR DANGER AREAS.

By day and by night, a series of projectiles discharged from the ground at intervals of 10 seconds, each showing, on bursting, red and green lights or stars will indicate to an unauthorized aircraft that it is flying in, or about to enter, a restricted, prohibited or danger area, and that the aircraft is to take such remedial action as may be necessary.

LIGHT SIGNALS BETWEEN AIRCRAFT AND AIR TRAFFIC SERVICE UNITS.

The following signals may be made between an Air Traffic Services Unit (ATSU) and aircraft in the air or on the ground. The meaning of signals between an ATSU and vehicles on the aerodrome is also given.

A continuous red light directed from the tower to an aircraft in flight means "Give way to other aircraft and continue circling".

A continuous red light directed from the tower to an aircraft or vehicle on the ground means "stop".

A flashing red light directed from the tower to an aircraft in flight means "Do not land, the aerodrome is unavailable for landing".

A flashing red light directed from the tower to an aircraft or vehicle on the ground means "Move clear of the landing area".

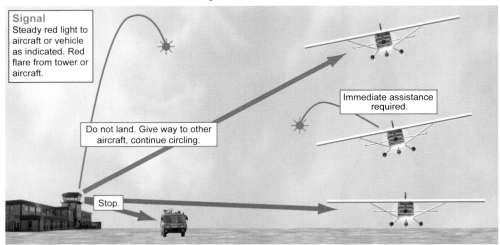

Signal
Steady red light to aircraft or vehicle as indicated. Red flare from tower or aircraft.

Do not land. Give way to other aircraft, continue circling.

Immediate assistance required.

Stop.

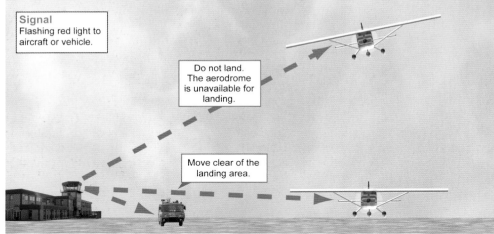

Signal
Flashing red light to aircraft or vehicle.

Do not land. The aerodrome is unavailable for landing.

Move clear of the landing area.

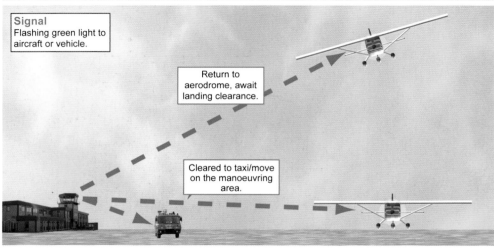

Signal
Flashing green light to aircraft or vehicle.

Return to aerodrome, await landing clearance.

Cleared to taxi/move on the manoeuvring area.

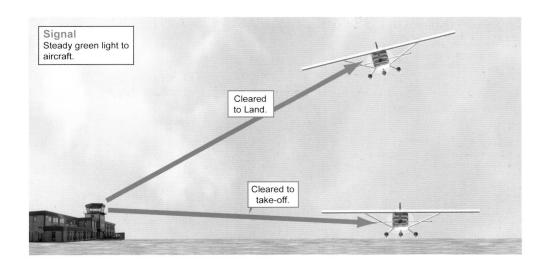

Signal
Steady green light to aircraft.

Cleared to Land.

Cleared to take-off.

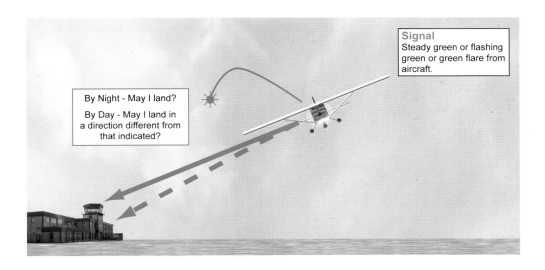

Signal
Steady green or flashing green or green flare from aircraft.

By Night - May I land?

By Day - May I land in a direction different from that indicated?

Signal
White flashes to aircraft or vehicle.

Land here on receipt of steady green and await further instructions.

Return to the starting point on the aerodrome.

A series of white flashes from the tower to an aircraft in flight means "Land at this aerodrome after receiving a continuous green light, and await further instructions".

A series of white flashes from the tower to an aircraft or vehicle on the ground means "Return to the starting point on the aerodrome".

ACKNOWLEDGEMENT BY AN AIRCRAFT.

When an ATSU has passed a signal to an aircraft in the air or on the ground, by lights or pyrotechnics, the aircraft will acknowledge the signal in the following manner.

When in flight:

•   During the hours of daylight: by rocking the aircraft's wings.

(**NB:** This signal should not be expected on the base and final legs of the approach.)

•   During the hours of darkness: by flashing on and off **twice** the aircraft's landing lights or, if not so equipped, by switching on and off twice its navigation lights.

When on the ground:

•   During the hours of daylight: by moving the aircraft's ailerons or rudder.

•   During the hours of darkness: by flashing on and off **twice** the aircraft's landing lights or, if not so equipped, by switching on and off twice its navigation lights.

GROUND SIGNALS.

At those aerodromes where there is a significant number of general aviation movements, and which allow the operation of non-radio traffic, two basic types of ground **signal** are employed. These are:

•   **The Signals Square**.

•   **A Signal Mast**.

THE SIGNALS SQUARE.

Where provided, the Signals Square is 12 metres square and bounded by a white border. The Signals Square is located in a position from which it can be seen by aircraft joining the circuit. (*See Figure A-4*).

Figure A-4 A Signals Square located near the tower.

The signals displayed in the signals square include the following:

Prohibition of Landing.
A horizontal, red, square panel with yellow diagonal lines indicates that landings are prohibited and that the prohibition is liable to be prolonged.

Need for Special Precautions while Approaching or Landing.
A horizontal, red, square panel with one yellow diagonal indicates that owing to the bad state of the manoeuvring area, or for any other reason, caution must be observed in approaching to land or in landing.

Use of Runways and Taxiways.

A horizontal white dumb-bell when displayed in a Signals Square indicates that aircraft are required to land, take off and taxi on runways and taxiways only.

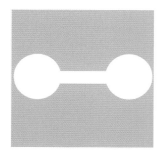

A horizontal white dumb-bell, with a black bar placed perpendicular to the shaft across each circular portion of the dumb-bell, indicates that aircraft are required to land and take off on runways only, but other manoeuvres need not be confined to runways and taxiways.

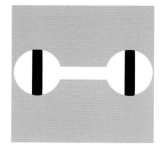

Closed Runways or Taxiways.

Crosses of a single contrasting colour, yellow (taxiways) or white (runways), displayed horizontally on runways and taxiways, or parts thereof, indicate an area unfit for the movement of aircraft.

Directions for Landing or Take-off.

A horizontal white or orange landing **T** indicates the direction to be used by aircraft for landing and take-off, which shall be in a direction parallel to the shaft of the **T** towards the cross arm.

Note: When used at night, the landing **T** is either illuminated or outlined in white coloured lights.

A white disc displayed alongside the cross arm of the **T** signifies that the directions of take-off and landing do not necessarily coincide.

This signal displayed on the Signals Square has the same meaning as a single black ball hoisted on a mast.

A set of two digits displayed vertically at or near the aerodrome control tower indicates to aircraft on the manoeuvring area the runway in use. Normally, the lettering is black on a yellow background. This signal indicates that Runway 12 is in use.

Right-Hand Traffic.
When displayed in a Signals Square, or horizontally at the end of the runway or strip in use, a right-hand arrow of conspicuous colour (normally yellow and red stripes) indicates that a right-hand circuit is in force and that turns are to be made to the right before landing and after take-off.

This signal displayed on the Signals Square has the same meaning as a green flag hoisted on a mast.

Air Traffic Services Reporting Office.
The letter **C** displayed vertically in black against a yellow background indicates the location of the **A**ir **T**raffic **S**ervices reporting office.

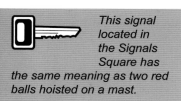

This signal located in the Signals Square has the same meaning as two red balls hoisted on a mast.

Glider Flights in Operation.

A double white cross displayed horizontally indicates that the aerodrome is being used by gliders and that glider flying is in progress.

Helicopter Operations.

A large white **H** signifies that helicopters shall take off and land within the area designated by the letter **H**, and that the area is to be used for take-off and launching of helicopters only.

Light Aircraft Operations.

A red **L** displayed on a white dumb-bell signifies that light aircraft are permitted to take off and land either on a runway or on the area designated, usually a grass area marked with a large white letter **L** (see below).

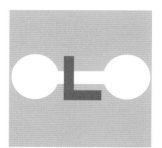

Area Reserved for Take-Off and Landing of Light Aircraft.

A large white **L** may be located on a part of the manoeuvring area to be used only for the take-off and landing of light aircraft.

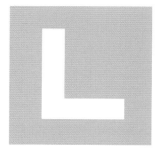

Dropping Operations.

A yellow marker in the shape of a St. George's cross indicates an area reserved for the dropping of tow ropes or similar articles.

SIGNALS DISPLAYED ON THE SIGNALS MAST.

A Single Black Ball.
A single black ball hoisted on a mast, as shown, indicates that the directions for take-off and landing are not necessarily the same.

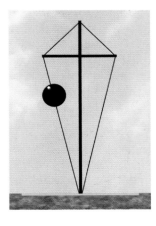

Two Red Balls.
Two red balls signify that glider flying is in progress at the aerodrome.

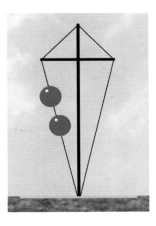

A Rectangular Green Flag.
Indicates that a right-hand circuit is in force.

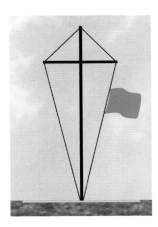

MISCELLANEOUS SIGNS.

Taxi According to ATC Instructions.
A panel or flag made up of red and yellow squares indicates that aircraft may taxi only in accordance with ATC instructions. If it is a flag, it is flown on the signals mast. If it is the form of a panel, it is displayed and located on the Control Tower.

Boundaries.
Orange and white striped markers are used to delineate the boundary of an airfield where the natural boundary is insufficiently conspicuous.

MARSHALLING SIGNALS - MARSHALLER TO PILOT.

To assist aircraft to manoeuvre on the ground, especially on the apron, a standard system of signals has been developed for use between an aircraft marshaller and the pilot. These signals are shown here. The marshaller uses a high-visibility bat during the day (or he may signal without a bat), and illuminated batons after dark.

"Proceed under guidance of another marshaller."
Point both arms upward,move and extend arms outward to sides of body and point with wands to direction of next signalman or taxi area.

"Straight ahead."

Bend extended arms at elbows and move wands up and down from chest height to head.

"Open up starboard engine" or "turn to port."

Right arm horizontal, the left arm repeatedly moved upwards and backwards. The speed of the arm movement indicates the rate of turn.

"Open up port engine" or "turn to starboard."

Left arm horizontal, the right arm repeatedly moved upwards and backwards. The speed of the arm movement indicates the rate of turn.

"Normal Stop."

Fully extend arms and wands at a 90º angle to sides and slowly move to above head until wands close.

"Start engine."

Raise right arm to head level with wand pointing up and start a circular motion with hand; at the same time, with left arm raised above head level, point to engine to be started.

"Emergency Stop."

Abruptly extend arms and wands to top of head, crossing wands.

Numbering of Aircraft Engines
Note: *The engines of multi-engined aircraft are numbered, with the marshaller facing the aircraft, from right to left (i.e. No.1 engine being the port outer engine).*

"Chocks inserted."

Arms extended above head, with hands or wands pointing inwards, then swung sharply inwards until they touch

"Chocks away."

Arms extended above head, with hands/wands pointing outwards, then swung sharply outwards.

"Cut engine(s)."

Extend arm with wand forward of body at shoulder level; move hand and wand to top of left shoulder and draw wand to top of right shoulder in a slicing motion across throat.

"Slow down."

Move extended arms downwards in a "patting" gesture, moving wands up and down from waist to knees.

"Slow down engine(s) on side indicated by moving arm."

Arms placed down, with palms towards the ground, then appropriate arm moved up and down several times.

"Fire."

Move right-hand wand in a "fanning" motion from shoulder to knee, while at the same time pointing with left-hand wand to area of fire.

"All clear – marshalling finished."

The right arm raised at the elbow, with the palm facing forward.

Note: Sometimes this meaning is indicated by the right arm raised at the elbow with thumb erect.

"Release brakes."

Raise hand just above shoulder height with hand closed in a fist. Ensuring eye contact with flight crew, open palm. Do not move until receipt of "thumbs up" acknowledgement from crew.

"Engage brakes."

Raise arm and hand with fingers extended, horizontally in front of body, then clench fist.

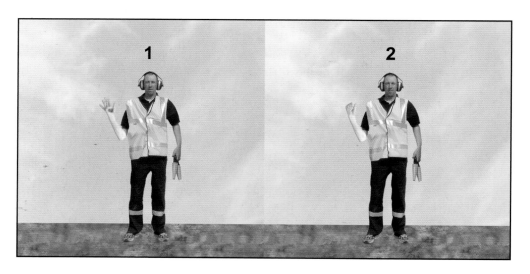

ALL AIRCRAFT EXCEPT HELICOPTERS.

"Back aircraft tail to starboard."

Point left arm with wand down and bring right arm from overhead vertical position to horizontal forward position, repeating right-arm movement.

"Back aircraft tail to port."

Point right arm with wand down and bring left arm from overhead vertical position to horizontal position, repeating left-arm movement.

PILOT TO MARSHALLER.

"Brakes engaged."

Raise arm and hand with fingers extended horizontally in front of face, then clench fist.

"Brakes released."
Raise arm and hand with fist clenched horizontally in front of face, then extend fingers.

"Insert chocks."
Arms extended palms facing outwards, move hands inwards to cross in front of face.

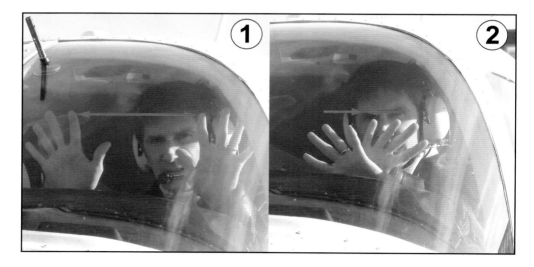

"Remove chocks."
Hands crossed in front of face, palms facing outwards, move arms outwards.

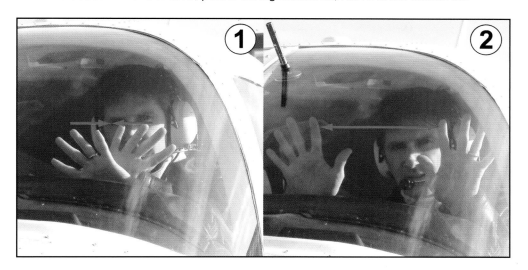

"Ready to start engine indicated."
Raise the number of fingers on one hand indicating the number of the engine to be started.

Representative PPL - type questions to test your theoretical knowledge of Flight and Ground Limitations.

1. What is the meaning of a continuous red light directed from the tower to an aircraft in flight?

    a. Return to the aerodrome.
    b. Land immediately.
    c. Do not land. Airfield unavailable for landing.
    d. Give way to other aircraft and continue circling.

2. What is the meaning of a series of white flashes directed at an aircraft in flight or on the ground?

	In Flight	On the Ground
a.	Do not land, the airfield is unavailable for landing.	Move clear of the landing area.
b.	Give way to other aircraft. Continue circling.	Stop.
c.	Land at this aerodrome after receiving a continuous green and await further instructions.	Return to the starting point on the aerodrome.
d.	Land immediately.	Clear the runway.

3. What ground sign do the survivors construct to indicate that they require medical assistance?

    a. **X**
    b. **N**
    c. **Y**
    d. ↑

4. What ground sign do the survivors construct to indicate that they require assistance?

    a. **X**
    b. **N**
    c. **Y**
    d. **>**

5. What is the meaning of a black ball hoisted on a signals mast or a white Ṫ with a white disc placed in the middle of a cross-bar?

    a. Glider flying in progress
    b. Direction of take-off and landing may differ
    c. Movement of aircraft and gliders confined to hard surface areas.
    d. Landing prohibited.

6.   What is the meaning of a flashing red light directed from the tower to an aircraft in flight?

   a.   Do not land. Aerodrome is unavailable for landing.
   b.   Give way to other aircraft and continue circling.
   c.   Land immediately
   d.   Return to aerodrome.

Question	1	2	3	4	5	6
Answer						

The correct answers to these questions can be found at the end of this book.

ANNEX B
THE JAR - FCL
PRIVATE PILOT'S LICENCE

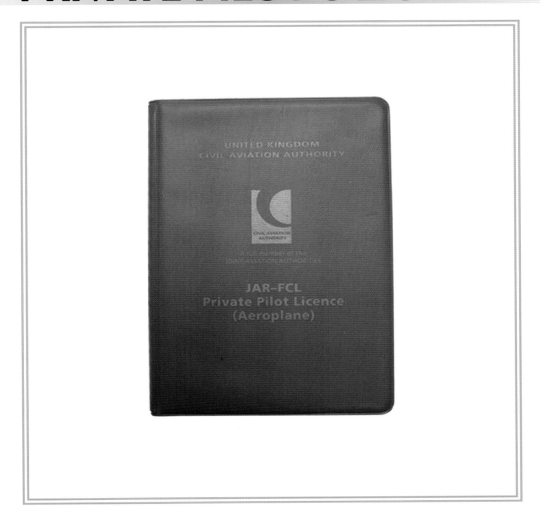

THE JAR-FCL PRIVATE PILOT'S LICENCE .

INTRODUCTION.

It is a requirement of the JAR-FCL Private Pilot's Licence (JAR-FCL PPL) theoretical knowledge syllabus for Air Law that students should learn about the regulations and conditions attached to the training for, and issue of, a JAR-FCL PPL, and that they should understand the privileges and limitations of the Licence.

Full details of flying training, theoretical knowledge training, the corresponding tests and examinations, and the privileges and limitations pertaining to the JAR-FCL PPL (Aeroplanes) are contained in the Joint Aviation Authorities (JAA) publication, **'JAR–FCL 1 (A)' SUBPART C – PRIVATE PILOT LICENCE (Aeroplanes) – PPL(A).**

Though this chapter deals principally with the JAR-FCL PPL (Aeroplanes), general information contained in this chapter will normally apply also to the JAR-FCL PPL (Helicopters). Full details of the JAR-FCL (Helicopters) is contained in the JAA publication JAR-FCL A, Subpart C.

You will sometimes find that the JAR-FCL PPL is referred to as the JAA PPL. Both terms refer to the same licence.

JAR-FCL stands for Joint Aviation Requirements – Flight Crew Licensing. In terms of flight crew licensing, the terms JAA and JAR-FCL are mostly interchangeable. As mentioned in the Foreword to this series of books, the titles

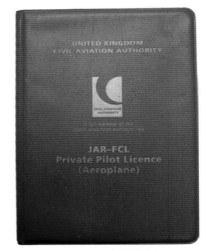

Fig B1 JAR-FCL PPL Licence.

of licences are likely to change again when the European Aviation Safety Agency takes over general responsibilities for licence issue. Do not allow the nomenclature to concern you over much.

*(For students based in the United Kingdom, full details of JAR-FCL PPL training and examinations can be found in the CAA publication **Licensing Administration Standards Operating Requirements Safety (LASORS).**)*

THE JAA PPL GENERAL.

In order to qualify for a JAA PPL a candidate must:

•   Meet the flying experience requirements and flying theoretical knowledge training requirements.

•   Obtain a pass in the skill test conducted on the same class/type of aircraft as that in which he has received flying instruction.

•   Hold either a valid Class 1 or valid Class 2 Medical Certificate

If the holder wishes to fly at night, an additional night qualification is required.

AGE.

There is no minimum age prescribed for the commencement of dual instruction for a JAR-FCL PPL(A), but dual instruction received before the age of 14 years does not count towards the flying experience requirements for the issue of a licence.

A candidate for a JAR-FCL PPL may not fly solo before the age of 16. A candidate may not apply for the licence to be issued until he or she has attained the age of 17 years.

PRIVILEGES AND CONDITIONS.

The privileges pertaining to a JAR-FCL PPL issued by the United Kingdom Civil Aviation Authority (UK CAA) are detailed in Schedule 8 of the Air Navigation Order, and summarised in LASORS.

Revenue & Non-Revenue Flights

Once the licence has been issued, the holder of a JAR-FCL PPL may fly as the pilot-in-command, or the co-pilot, of any aeroplane for which he holds a type/class rating, on non-revenue flights.

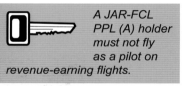
A JAR-FCL PPL (A) holder must not fly as a pilot on revenue-earning flights.

Effectively this means that a PPL holder cannot earn money by exercising the privileges of his licence. The laws surrounding 'revenue flights' or flights for 'valuable consideration' are complex. Therefore, PPL-holders are advised to be very cautious about accepting money or rewards for flights that they conduct. The authorities treat illegal commercial operations extremely seriously. Cost sharing between a PPL holder and his passengers is permitted in accordance with certain conditions. The Air Navigation Order contains details of these conditions.

In order to carry passengers, a PPL-holder must have carried out 3 take- offs and landings as the pilot operating the controls of an aeroplane of the same class/type (or in a flight simulator of the same type/class) in the preceding 90 days.

Carriage of Passengers.

The holder of a JAA PPL(A) is permitted to carry passengers. However, JAR-FCL1.026 requires that a pilot should not operate the controls of an aeroplane with passengers on board unless he has carried out at least three take-offs and landings as the pilot operating the controls of an aeroplane of the same type/class (or in a flight simulator of the same type/class) in the preceding 90 days. If the pilot holds a Night Qualification, 1 of the 3 take-offs and landings must be at night, if passengers are to be carried at night.

TRAINING FOR THE JAR-FCL PPL (A).

Appendix 1 to JAR-FCL 1.125 lays down the syllabus of training that must be completed before a JAR-FCL PPL(A) licence may be issued.

An applicant for a JAR-FCL PPL (A) must undergo the prescribed syllabus of training at an approved Flying Training Organisation (FTO) or at a registered training facility acceptable to the national authority.

Training for the JAR-FCL PPL (A) consists of flying instruction and theoretical knowledge instruction.

Fig B2 A Flying Training Organisation (FTO) - Oxford Aviation Academy, Oxford Airport.

On completion of training, a candidate's flying proficiency is tested in a skills test conducted by an examiner authorised by the national authority. Candidates are also required to pass theoretical knowledge examinations in the subjects stipulated by the syllabus *(see below)*.

Flying Training.

An applicant for a JAR-FCL PPL (A) must have completed a minimum of 45 hours total flight time as a pilot of aeroplanes.

The 45 hours total experience must be made up of:

a. Not less than 25 hours dual instruction.

b. At least 10 hours supervised solo flight time which must include at least 5 hours of solo cross-country flight time, of which 1 flight must be of at least 270 km (150 nm) during which full-stop landings are made at two aerodromes different from the aerodrome of departure.

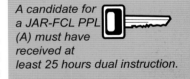

A candidate for a JAR-FCL PPL (A) must have received at least 25 hours dual instruction.

A candidate for a JAR-FCL PPL (A) must have completed at least one solo cross-country flight of at least 270 km (150 nm) during which 2 full stop landings are made at two aerodromes other than the aerodrome of departure.

Of the 45 hours total flying time, 5 hours may be completed on a flight navigation procedures trainer (FNPT) or flight simulator. Holders of a pilot's licence or equivalent privileges for aircraft other than aeroplanes (but excluding balloon and airship licences) may be credited with 10% of the flight time logged on those aircraft (subject to a maximum credit of 10 hours) towards the flying experience required for the issues of a JAR-FCL PPL (A).

If an applicant for a JAR-FCL PPL (A) has been credited with pilot-in-command flight time on an aircraft other than aeroplanes, the dual instruction requirement is reduced to a minimum of 20 hours.

Night Qualification.

If a night qualification is to be added to the JAR-FCL PPL (A), 5 hours flying must be completed at night, consisting of 3 hours dual instruction, including 1 hour night cross-country navigation and 5 solo night take-offs and full-stop landings.

(Training for a Night Qualification (Aeroplanes) may be included within the 45 hours required for the issue of a JAR-FCL PPL (A), provided the minimum dual and supervised solo requirements are satisfied.)

Recording Flying Experience.

The flying time to be entered in a pilot's logbook is the time from the aircraft first moving for the purpose of taking off to the time it finally comes to rest at the end of the flight.

All pilots must keep a record of their flying experience in a pilot's log book. The hours recorded in the pilot's log book must be only those defined as flight time.

Flight time is recorded as the total time from the moment an aircraft first moves for the purpose of taking off until it finally comes to rest at the end of the flight.

A pilot is required to log the flying activity he is carrying out, as well as the flight time. For example, if a student pilot flies 1 hour dual on a cross-country flight he would log:

•   1 hour total.

and, under the appropriate sub-headings in his logbook:

•   1 hour dual

•   1 hour cross-country

Relevant flight simulator time is also recorded in the pilot's log book.

The pilot's log book is a pilot's own personal record of his flying experience. Complete your log book neatly and legibly; you will be glad you did so in later years. If you are required to submit your log book to a national aviation authority, take a photocopy of the latest entries.

Flying Skill Test.

Following completion of the specified PPL(A) flying training, a student pilot has a period of 6 months in which to take and pass the necessary flying skill test. This will require the student to demonstrate his ability as pilot-in-command of an aeroplane, to the satisfaction of a Flight Examiner (FE). Full details of the JAR-FCL PPL (A) **Skills Test** are given in **Appendix 1 and 2 to JAR-FCL 1 1.135**.

The skill test may be flown on a single or (subject to the experience requirements in JAR-FCL 1.255 or 1.260 of 70 hours flight time as Pilot-in-Command) on a multi-engined aircraft.

An applicant for a JAR-FCL PPL (A) may not take the skills test until <u>all</u> of the theoretical knowledge examinations have been passed.

Theoretical Knowledge Examinations.

The training requirements for issue of a JAR-FCL PPL (A) are not confined to flying training. In order to qualify as a private pilot, a student must also demonstrate that he has acquired the theoretical knowledge required of a qualified pilot by passing ground examinations in the following subjects:

•   Air Law.

•   Operational Procedures.

•   Aircraft General Knowledge.

- Principles of Flight.

- Meteorology.

- Navigation and Radio Aids.

- Human Performance and Limitations.

- Flight Performance and Planning (including Mass and Balance).

- Radiotelephony Communications.

The examinations consist of multiple-choice questions, and are normally conducted by the Flying Training Organisation or registered training facility at which the student has undergone training. Examination papers may cover several subjects. In the United Kingdom, the examination papers currently bear the following titles:

- Air Law and Operational Procedures.

- Human Performance and Limitations.

- Navigation and Radio Aids.

- Meteorology.

- Aircraft (General) and Principles of Flight.

- Flight Performance and Planning (including Mass and Balance).

The pass mark in all papers is 75%.

An applicant for a JAR-FCL PPL (A) is deemed to have successfully completed the theoretical knowledge examinations when he has achieved a pass mark in all subjects within a period of 18 months of taking the first examination. For the purposes of licence issue, a candidate will be credited with successful completion of the theoretical knowledge examinations for a period of 24 months after having obtained a pass in all subjects.

RADIOTELEPHONY (RTF) LICENCE.

A JAR-FCL PPL may be issued without the holder needing to possess a **Flight Radiotelephony Operator's Licence (FRTOL)**. But if the PPL holder wishes to operate his aircraft's radio, he must have obtained a FRTOL. In order to obtain an FRTOL, pilots must pass the practical radiotelephony test and apply for the FRTOL separately from the JAR-FCL PPL. You should note that the Radiotelephony paper in the PPL theoretical knowledge examinations does not contribute towards obtaining an FRTOL. The FRTOL remains a national licence, so the PPL and the FRTOL are distinct licences issued under different legislation.

Student pilots are permitted to use an aircraft's radio without an FRTOL while undergoing flights for the purpose of gaining a pilot's licence.

Student pilots are permitted to operate the aircraft's radio, without having obtained a FRTOL, during flights for the purpose of gaining a pilot's licence, provided the flight is authorised by a qualified flying instructor.

STATE OF LICENCE ISSUE.

General.

Applicants for a JAR-FCL PPL must complete the requirements for licence issue to the satisfaction of the national aviation authority of the state under whose authority the training and testing for the licence were carried out. That State, on issuing the licence, then becomes the State of Licence Issue.

The State of Licence Issue is the country in which the aviation authority which authorises you to act as a pilot is headquartered.

Despite the multinational nature of the JAA, each nation's aviation authority (NAA) acts under the authority of the legislature of that nation. Hence, the Civil Aviation Authority is the licence-issuing authority for the United Kingdom.

Training in Different JAA Countries.

It is permitted for a student pilot to commence his training in one State and complete it in another State. In this case, the NAAs of the states concerned will agree which state is to act as the State of Licence Issue.

If the holder of a licence requires additional ratings or authorisations, in accordance with JAR-FCL, these may be obtained in any JAA State and subsequently be entered in the licence by the State of Licence Issue.

TRANSFER OF STATE OF LICENCE ISSUE.

A JAR-FCL PPL (A) licence holder may apply to transfer his licence from one state to another if he is normally resident in the new State (at least 185 days per year) or if he has taken up employment there.

It is permitted for a licence holder to make a request for his licence to be transferred from one JAA State to another if there is an administrative need to do so. For instance, if the holder changes his State of normal residency (the place where he normally lives for at least 185 days in any year) or if he takes up employment in the new state, the new state may become the State of Licence Issue.

Validity of Licences and Ratings.

A JAR-FCL PPL (A) is valid for a period of 5 years.

A JAR-FCL PPL (A) is valid for 5 years.

Providing that a pilot has renewed his medical certificate (see below) and has not had the licence revoked or suspended by the NAA, a PPL will be reissued, at the end of the 5 years validity period, on submission of the necessary paperwork and fees to the NAA.

TYPE AND CLASS RATINGS.

General Requirements.

In addition to his pilot's licence, a pilot will also be required to hold a valid Class Rating for any aeroplane that he wishes to fly.

Aeroplanes are divided into Classes and, further, into Types. Generally, Class Ratings are for simple aircraft and a Type Rating is required for a more sophisticated aircraft.

THE SKILL TEST AND CLASS RATING.

If the Skill Test for the JAR-FCL PPL (A) is taken in a simple light aircraft, the PPL Skill Test also counts as the Class Rating Test for the class of aeroplane in question, most commonly the Single-Engine Piston (Land) Class.

If a pilot wishes to fly other classes or types of aeroplanes he will be required to pass a separate skill test on each class or type of aeroplane he intends to fly.

Class Rating.

A Class Rating qualifies a pilot to fly as Pilot-in-Command of any aeroplane within that Class.

Aeroplanes are divided into classes and types.

Class Ratings are issued for the following classes of aeroplanes:

- All single-engine piston aeroplanes (land).

- All single-engine piston aeroplanes (sea).

- All touring motor gliders.

In addition to a pilot's licence, a pilot must also hold a valid class or type rating, and a current medical certificate.

- Each manufacturer of single-engine turbo-prop aeroplanes (land).

- Each manufacturer of single-engine turbo-prop aeroplanes (sea).

- All multi-engine piston aeroplanes (land).

- All multi-engine piston aeroplanes (sea).

There is no limitation on the number of class or type ratings that a pilot may hold at any one time.

Differences Training.

Although a class rating, in general, qualifies a pilot to fly any aeroplane within that class, differences training may be required in order that he may pilot a variant of aircraft within the class which has markedly different flying characteristics and technical and performance specifications.

For the Single-Engine Piston (Land) pilot, a category which encompasses the majority of PPL holders, differences training is required when changing from the simple, light, fixed tricycle-undercarriage, fixed-pitch propeller aeroplane to aeroplanes displaying any of the following features, often referred to as complex singles:

- Variable-pitch propellers.

- Retractable undercarriage.

- Turbo/super-charged engine.

- Cabin pressurisation.

- Tail wheel.

Whether or not differences training is a formal requirement, pilots should always arrange to undergo instruction with an appropriately qualified flying instructor when considering flying an aeroplane which has significantly different flying characteristics from the aircraft they are used to.

The Type Rating.

In general, type ratings are required for:

- Each type of multi-pilot aeroplane.

- Each type of single-pilot, multi-engine aeroplane fitted with turbo-prop or turbojet engines.

- Each type of single-pilot, single-engine aeroplane fitted with turbojet engines

- Any other type of aeroplane considered necessary by the National Aviation Authority.

To obtain a type rating, a pilot will need to:

- Attend a type rating course for the relevant type, consisting of both theoretical knowledge and flying instruction.

- Pass a theoretical knowledge examination.

- Pass a skill test on the aircraft type, conducted by a Type Rating Examiner (TRE).

VALIDITY OF CLASS AND TYPE RATINGS.

The validity of a pilot's licence is dependent on the validity of the ratings it contains and the currency of the associated medical certificate.

Single-Pilot, Single-Engine Class Ratings.

A single-pilot, single-engine piston Class Rating is valid for 2 years.

Single-pilot, single-engine Class Ratings (including Touring Motor Glider ratings) are valid for 2 years. In order to be re-validated for this type of rating, the pilot must either:

- Pass a proficiency check with an authorised examiner within the 3 months preceding the expiry date of the Rating,

or

- Within 12 months of the expiry date of the rating, have flown 12 hours on an aircraft of the relevant class, to include:

    - 6 hours as Pilot-in-Command.

    - 12 take-offs and 12 landings.

    - A training flight of at least 1 hour's duration with a Flight Instructor or a Class Rating Instructor.

Note: The one hour dual flight with an Instructor can be replaced with any JAR-FCL Skills Test or Proficiency Check or by an IMC Rating flight Test.

Type Ratings and Multi-Engine Class Ratings.

Type Ratings and Multi-Engine Class Ratings are valid for a period of 1 year from the date of issue. To revalidate a Type Rating, or a Multi-Engine Class Rating, a pilot must pass a proficiency test with an authorised examiner within the 3 months immediately preceding the date of expiry of the Rating. If the qualification is revalidated within the period of validity, the new Rating will be valid from the date of expiry of the old rating.

To renew a single-pilot, single-engine piston Class Rating, a pilot must have passed a proficiency check within 3 months of the expiry of the rating, or have renewed the rating by virtue of flying experience.

Failure of a Proficiency Check.

If a pilot fails any part of a proficiency check for a class rating or type rating, he must not exercise the privileges of that rating until all the parts of the proficiency check have been successfully completed.

Consequently, if during the last 3 months of a PPL (A) Single-Engine Piston Class Rating, a pilot takes and fails a revalidation proficiency check, his current class rating becomes invalid until the proficiency check has been successfully completed.

EXPIRY OF A CLASS OR TYPE RATING.

If a pilot allows his class or type rating to expire the rating will have to be renewed, if the pilot again wishes to exercise the privileges of the rating. Renewal <u>may</u> entail refresher training, and <u>will</u> entail having to re-take the appropriate skill test.

To renew a single-pilot, single-engine piston Class Rating by experience, a pilot must, within 12 months of the rating expiring, have completed 12 hours flying, of which 6 hours is as pilot-in-command, have completed 12 take-offs and landings, and a flight of at least one hour's duration with a qualified instructor.

For an expired single-pilot single-engine class rating to be renewed, a pilot must successfully complete the initial skill test in accordance with **Appendix 3** to **Paragraph 1.240** of **Section** 1 of **JAR-FCL 1 (A)**.

ADDITIONAL RATINGS.

As the holder of a JAR-FCL PPL (A), a pilot is entitled to fly as pilot-in-command or co-pilot of an aeroplane of any of the types and classes specified in his licence. Normally, the licence holder may exercise the privileges of his licence in any JAA member state, while flying an aircraft registered in a JAA member state.
A basic JAR-FCL PPL (A) holder may not normally, however:

- fly for remuneration.

- give flying instruction for remuneration.

- conduct flying tests.

- fly as pilot-in-command in uncontrolled airspace when the flight visibility is less than 3 km.

- fly as pilot-in-command within a Control Zone on a Special VFR Clearance, when the flight visibility is less than 10 km.

- fly out of sight of the surface.

- fly as pilot-in-command in controlled airspace in circumstances which require compliance with the Instrument Flight Rules.

- fly at night.

Various ratings can be added to the basic JAR-FCL PPL (A) which bestow extended privileges on the licence holder. Each rating has its own regulation pertaining to revalidation and renewal. Here is a summary of additional ratings that a PPL (A) holder may add to his licence: Full details may be found in **LASORS**.

- **IMC Rating (Aeroplanes)**. The IMC Rating is a United Kingdom national rating which may be added to a UK-issued pilot's licence only. The IMC Rating entitles the holder to fly as pilot-in-command in weather minima below those with which the basic PPL holder must comply. The holder of an IMC Rating may also fly in accordance with IFR in Class D and E airspace, with the necessary ATC clearances. (See OAAmedia's interactive CD-ROM 'The IMC Rating and Instrument Flying.') The privileges of the IMC Rating may not be exercised in any other country than the United Kingdom, unless permission to do so has been given by the appropriate authority of that country.

- **Instrument Rating (Aeroplanes)**. The holder of a full Instrument Rating may fly as pilot-in-command without being subject to VFR or IMC Rating weather minima, and fly IFR in controlled airspace.

- **Night Qualification (Aeroplanes)**. The Night Qualification (Aeroplanes) allows the holder to fly as pilot-in-command of an aeroplane, at night.

- **Flying Instructor Rating**. A Flying Instructor's Rating entitles the holder to give instruction in flying.

THE UNITED KINGDOM NATIONAL PRIVATE PILOT'S LICENCE.

In the United Kingdom, in order to make it easier for the recreational flyer to obtain a PPL than it would be if the requirements of the standard JAR-FCL PPL had to be met, the **United Kingdom National Private Pilot's Licence (UK NPPL)** has been introduced.

Full details of the regulations governing the training for, issue of and privileges of the UK NPPL may be found by consulting LASORS and the Air Navigation Order. Most flying club websites give details of the NPPL. The NPPL also has its own medical requirements.

The NPPL is a "sub-ICAO" licence and the holder of a UK NPPL (A) is restricted to flight in a simple, UK-registered, single-engine piston aeroplane (including motor gliders and microlights) whose Maximum Authorized Take-off Weight does not exceed 2000 kg. Flight is normally permitted in UK airspace only, by day, and in accordance with the Visual Flight Rules.

Flying Training.
Currently 32 hours of flying training are required for the issue of a UK NPPL (A), of which 22 hours are to be dual instruction, and 10 hours to be supervised solo flying time.

There are separate general and navigation skills tests.

Theoretical Knowledge Examinations.
The UK NPPL theoretical knowledge syllabus and ground examinations are the same as for the JAA PPL (A).

MEDICAL REQUIREMENTS.

- An applicant for a JAR-FCL PPL must hold a valid JAA Class 1 or Class 2 Medical Certificate issued within the provisions of JAR-FCL 3.

- A student pilot must hold a valid Medical Certificate before he will be permitted to fly solo.

A Class 1 or Class 2 medical certificate must be held by a candidate for a JAR-FCL PPL (A) licence.

General Requirements.
Private Pilots must be mentally and physically fit to exercise the privileges of their licence. This is a continuing requirement and places the onus on the pilot to maintain fitness to fly. If a pilot does not feel fit to fly, he should seek professional advice preferably from an aeromedical practitioner, to determine his medical fitness.

N.B. If a pilot allows his medical certificate to expire, his licence becomes invalid immediately. Consequently, it is most important to arrange medical examinations early to ensure that this does not happen.

If you allow your medical certificate to expire, your pilot's licence becomes invalid immediately.

The regulations governing medical fitness are different for the **UK NPPL (A)** and the **JAR-FCL PPL (A)**.

MEDICAL EXAMINATIONS.

Class Two Initial and Revalidation Examinations.

A Class 2 medical examination must be conducted either:

- At an Aeromedical Centre (AMC). In the UK this is at the CAA Aeromedical Centre at Gatwick,
or
- By an Authorised Medical Examiner (AME). A list of AMEs can be found on the CAA Website.

For the issue of a JAR-FCL PPL in the United Kingdom, the initial JAR-FCL Class 2 medical examination may be obtained from a UK CAA AME or from an AME in a mutually recognised JAA member state.

MEDICAL CERTIFICATE.

General.
A pilot's Medical Certificate is regarded as an integral part of his licence.
The issue of the certificate will follow a successful initial medical examination conducted by an Authorised Medical Examiner. Once the medical certificate has been issued, its continuing validity will depend upon the pilot passing a periodical medical examination.

Validity of a Class 2 Medical Certificate.
The intervals between required medical examinations depend on the age of the pilot. The intervals are as follows:

Up to the age of 40 years: every 60 months.

40 years and up to 49 years: every 24 months.

50 years and over: every 12 months.

Note: A **medical certificate** issued before a pilot's 40th birthday will not be valid after his 42nd birthday. (In other words as soon as a pilot attains the age of 40, his Medical Certificate can only be valid for a maximum of 2 further years.)

Validity of a Class 2 medical certificate for the JAR-FCL PPL (A):

Up to 40 years of age:
60 months

40 years and up to 49 years:
24 months

50 years and over:
12 months

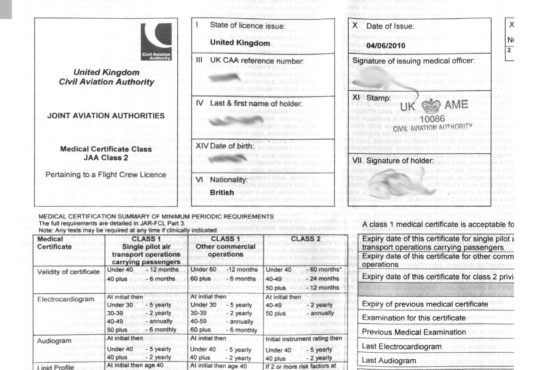

Fig B3 A Class 2 Medical Certificate.

If the revalidation of a medical certificate takes place within 45 days prior to the expiry date, the validity of the new medical certificate extends from the expiry date of the previous certificate.

Decrease in Medical Fitness.
The holder of a medical certificate who becomes aware of any of the circumstances below must inform the National Aviation Authority of the condition, in writing, immediately, or after a period of 21 days for illness.

If the holder of a JAR-FCL pilot's licence suffers from a condition which affects his ability to act as a flight crew member, he must inform the National Aviation Authority, in writing, either immediately or, in the case of illness, within a period of 21 days.

- A hospital or clinic admission for more than 12 hours.

- Any surgical operation or invasive procedure (this includes eye laser surgery). The reader is strongly recommended to contact his/her AME prior to undergoing eye laser surgery and to seek advice.

- The need for regular use of medication.

- The regular need to wear correcting lenses.

- An incapacitating injury.

- Any illness which incapacitates a pilot and prevents him from flying as a pilot throughout a period of 21 days or more.

- Pregnancy.

A pilot's medical certificate (and, therefore, his licence) will be deemed to be suspended during the period of incapacity. The suspension will be lifted after a medical examination passes a pilot fit once more.

In the case of pregnancy, the suspension may be temporarily lifted during the early months of the pregnancy and finally lifted after the end of the pregnancy when the pilot has been declared fit to resume flying.

Representative PPL - type questions to test your theoretical knowledge of JAA Licensing.

1.　Of the total hours requirement for the issue of a JAA PPL(A), how many may be flown in a FNPT or Flight Simulator?

    a.　5
    b.　10
    c.　15
    d.　2

2.　Which of the following statements applies to the carriage of passengers by the holder of a JAR-FCL PPL(A) licence?

    a.　Any money you receive must be given to charity
    b.　You cannot carry passengers with a JAA PPL(A)
    c.　You must have made 3 take-offs and landings in the last 90 days
    d.　You must receive special clearance to carry passengers

3.　Which of the following does a pilot require in addition to his licence in order to fly an aeroplane?

    a.　A Medical certificate issued in accordance with JAR-FCL 3
    b.　A valid type rating only
    c.　A radiotelephony licence
    d.　An MCC certificate

4.　The flying experience that you record in your pilot's log book must be only:

    a.　Actual airborne time
    b.　Flight time only (as defined as the total time from when the aircraft first moves for the purpose of taking off until it finally comes to rest at the end of the flight)
    c.　Flight time, as defined in b, above, but also to include relevant simulator and flight navigation procedure trainer (FNPT) hours
    d.　Flight time and taxi time only

5.　In addition to your pilot licence, what else is required before you can exercise the privilege of the licence?

    a.　A valid medical certificate and a valid Class Rating or Type Rating
    b.　A valid medical certificate, a valid Class Rating or Type Rating and a valid Instrument Rating
    c.　A valid medical certificate and a valid Class Rating or Type Rating and recent experience consisting of 3 take-offs and landings in the past 90 days
    d.　A valid medical certificate and an MCC Certificate for dual operations

6.   What does a student pilot require in order to fly a solo training sortie?

    a.   A Class or Type Rating
    b.   A certificate of proficiency signed by his instructor
    c.   To have attained 17 years of age
    d.   A valid medical certificate, be at least 16 years of age, and have the authorisation of a qualified flying instructor.

7.   The JAA document dealing with matters relating to the training for and issue of pilots' licences for flying aeroplanes is:

    a.   JAR OPS-3
    b.   JAR FCL-3
    c.   JAR FCL-2
    d.   JAR FCL-1

8.   For how long is the Class Rating for a single-pilot, single-engine aircraft valid?

    a.   1 year
    b.   2 years
    c.   3 years
    d.   5 years

9.   A pilot gained his JAR-FCL PPL (A) on a single piston-engine, fixed tricycle-undercarriage aircraft, fitted with a constant speed propeller. For which of the following types of aircraft would he be required to undergo differences training?

    a.   Any aircraft of similar handling characteristics
    b.   A similar aircraft fitted with a Global Positioning Navigation System
    c.   A tail wheel aeroplane
    d.   A similar aircraft fitted with electrically operated flaps

10.   You are the holder of a JAR-FCL PPL(A). If your optician tells you that you now need to use spectacles to read, do you need to tell the Licensing Authority?

    a.   No
    b.   Yes, immediately
    c.   Yes, but only if you cannot read the instruments without the spectacles
    d.   Not if contact lenses solve your problem

11.   As part of the flying experience a student pilot needs for the issue of a JAR-FCL PPL (A), he must undertake a solo cross-country flight. At least one cross-country flight must exceed a stated minimum distance. What is this distance?

    a.   100 nm
    b.   150 nm
    c.   200 nm
    d.   270 nm

12. For which of the following aircraft types would a pilot require a Type Rating?

   a. An aeroplane with dual controls
   b. A single-pilot aeroplane with a variable-pitch propeller
   c. A single-pilot aeroplane fitted with a turbo-prop or gas-turbine engine
   d. A touring motor glider

13. Can the Class Rating for a single-engine piston aeroplane (land) be revalidated by a proficiency check?

   a. Yes, but the check must be completed within the 3 months prior to the expiry date of the current rating
   b. No, the rating is experience dependent only
   c. Yes, but there is also an experience requirement which must also be achieved
   d. No

14. Can a student pilot 'log' all dual instructional time towards the 45 hours experience he needs to gain his licence?

   a. No, he can only log half the dual time
   b. No, he cannot log any instruction hours, it must all be solo hours
   c. Yes, provided he has attained the age of 14
   d. Only if it is VMC time

15. For how long is a Class 2 Medical Certificate for a JAR-FCL PPL (A) valid for a pilot who is 34 years of age?

   a. 60 months
   b. 24 months
   c. 12 months
   d. 6 months

16. One of the requirements permitting the retention of a current single-engine piston class rating for a JAR-FCL PPL (A) holder is that, preceding the expiry of the rating, a pilot must fly:

   a. 20 hours flight time in the relevant Class of aeroplane within the preceding 2 years
   b. 4 hours as Pilot-in-Command within the preceding 12 months
   c. 10 take-offs and 10 landings within the preceding 12 months
   d. A training flight of at least 1 hour's duration with a qualified Flying Instructor or a Class Rating Instructor within the preceding 3 months

17. In order to exercise the privileges of a flying licence, the holder must hold a Medical Certificate issued in accordance with the provisions of:

   a.   JAR-FCL 1
   b.   JAR-FCL 2
   c.   JAR-FCL 3
   d.   JAR-FCL 4

18. The definitive privileges of licences and ratings issued by the United Kingdom Civil Aviation Authority (UK CAA) are contained in:

   a.   The appropriate UK CAA Safety Sense Leaflet
   b.   Schedule 8 of the Air Navigation Order.
   c.   The United Kingdom Aeronautical Information Publication
   d.   In the appropriate AIC.

19. If the holder of a JAR-FCL PPL (A) has discovered that he has a medical condition for which he needs surgery, he should:

   a.   Consult an authorised medical authority as soon as possible
   b.   Continue to fly as normal but, not fly as pilot-in-command during the 24 hours preceding the surgery
   c.   Continue to fly as normal until admitted to hospital
   d.   Not fly until 6 months after the surgery has been performed

20. In order to be able to carry passengers, the holder of a JAR-FCL PPL (A) must have met the following currency requirements:

   a.   3 take-offs and 3 landings within the preceding 28 days
   b.   3 take-offs and 3 landings within the preceding 90 days
   c.   5 take-offs and 5 landings within the preceding 28 days
   d.   5 take-offs and 5 landings within the preceding 90 days

21. The flying hours that the holder of a JAR-FCL licence enters in his pilot's log book are defined as:

   a.   The time from lift-off to touch down
   b.   Airborne time only
   c.   The time from engine start to engine shutdown
   d.   The time from the aircraft's first moving under its own power to its coming to rest at the end of the flight

22. What are the options open to the holder of a JAR-PCL PPL (A) for revalidating a single-pilot, single-engine piston Class Rating?

    a. Complete a proficiency check within 3 months preceding the expiry of the Class Rating, and also, within 12 months of its expiry, have completed 12 hours flying time, including 6 hours as pilot-in-command, with 12 take-offs and landings, and to include a flight of at least one hour's duration with a qualified flying instructor or class rating instructor.

    b. Complete a proficiency check within 12 months preceding the expiry of the Class Rating, or, within 24 months of its expiry, have completed 12 hours flying time, including 6 hours as pilot in command, with 12 take-offs and landings, and to include a flight of at least one hour's duration with a qualified flying instructor or class rating instructor.

    c. Complete a proficiency check within 3 months preceding the expiry of the Class Rating, or, within 12 months of its expiry, have completed 12 hours flying time, including 6 hours as pilot-in-command, with 12 take-offs and landings, and to include a flight of at least one hour's duration with a qualified flying instructor or class rating instructor.

    d. Complete a proficiency check within 3 months preceding the expiry of the Class Rating, and also, within 24 months of its expiry, have completed 12 hours flying time, including 5 hours as pilot-in-command, with 10 take-offs and landings, and to include a flight of at least one hour's duration with a qualified flying instructor.

23. The holder of a medical certificate issued in accordance with JAR-FCL 3 must inform the appropriate National Aviation Authority, in writing, of any condition which affects his ability to act as a flight crew member if:

    a. In the case of sickness, the condition makes him unfit to act as a flight crew member for 21 days or more

    b. The condition will make him unfit to act as a flight crew member beyond the date of expiry of his medical certificate

    c. He is advised to do so by his flying instructor

    d. A visit to a doctor has been necessary

24. The holder of a JAR-FCL pilot's licence is entitled to act as pilot-in-command of an aircraft only if:

    a. He holds at least a valid class rating for the aircraft he is to fly

    b. He holds at least a valid medical rating

    c. He also holds an Instrument Rating or Night Qualification for the aircraft he is to fly

    d. He also holds a valid medical certificate for his licence and a valid class or type rating for the aircraft he is to fly

25. The period of validity of a JAR-FCL PPL (A) is

    a. 3 years

    b. Life

    c. 5 years

    d. 10 years

26. For the purposes of obtaining a JAR-FCL PPL (A), flying hours accumulated towards the issue of the licence must have been carried out in an aircraft:

    a. Of the same type as that for which the basic licence is to be issued
    b. Of the same class as that for which the basic licence is to be issued
    c. Of the same performance category as that for which the basic licence is to be issued
    d. With the same type of propeller as that for which the basic licence is to be issued

27. An injury which incapacitates the holder of a JAR-FCL pilot's licence:

    a. Renders the associated medical certificate invalid as soon as the National Aviation Authority is informed in writing of the injury
    b. Automatically renders invalid the associated medical certificate
    c. Does not affect the validity of the medical certificate but the licence-holder must not fly as pilot while he remains incapacitated
    d. Will prevent a valid medical certificate from being revalidated

28. A pilot who does not hold a Flight Radiotelephony Operator's Licence (FRTOL) may operate an aircraft's radio:

    a. Provided he does not seek a full air traffic control service
    b. Provided he remains clear of controlled airspace
    c. If flying as a student pilot with the authorisation of a qualified flying instructor for the purposes of obtaining a pilot's licence
    d. Provided he is accompanied by a qualified pilot who is an FRTOL holder

29. The minimum number of dual instructional hours to be completed by a candidate for a JAR-FCL PPL (A) is:

    a. 25 hours
    b. 45 hours
    c. 10 hours
    d. 30 hours

30. A JAR-FCL PPL (A) holder may:

    a. Not fly in controlled airspace
    b. Not operate as a pilot on a revenue-earning flight or flight for "valuable consideration"
    c. Not operate above the transition level
    d. Not fly in accordance with the Instrument Flight Rules

31.   In order to transfer a JAR-FCL pilot's licence from the State of Licence Issue to another JAA member state the licence holder must:

     a.   Be normally resident in the new State (for at least 185 days per year) or have taken up full-time employment within that State

     b.   Have resided in the new State for at least 30 consecutive days.

     c.   Reside in the new State for a minimum of 30 days annually.

     d.   Must have become a citizen of the new State

Question	1	2	3	4	5	6	7	8	9	10	11	12
Answer												

Question	13	14	15	16	17	18	19	20	21	22	23	24
Answer												

Question	25	26	27	28	29	30	31
Answer							

The answers to these questions can be found at the end of this book.

ANNEX C
AIR LAW DEFINITIONS

ANNEX C: DEFINITIONS

DEFINITIONS.

Accident: An occurrence associated with the operation of an aircraft which takes place between the time any person boards the aircraft with the intention of flight until such time as all such persons have disembarked, in which :

a.   A person is fatally or seriously injured as a result of :

•   being in the aircraft,

                              or

•   direct contact with any part of the aircraft, including parts which have become detached from the aircraft,

                              or

•   direct exposure to jet blast,

      except when the injuries are:

                  -      from natural causes, or

                  -      self-inflicted, or

                  -      inflicted by other persons, or

                  -      to stowaways hiding outside the areas normally available to passenger or crew,

                              or

b.   the aircraft sustains damage or structural failure which:

•   adversely affects the structural strength, performance or characteristics of the aircraft and

•   would normally require major repair or replacement of the affected part except for engine failure or damage, when the damage is limited to the engine, its cowlings or accessories; or for damage limited to propellers, wing tips, antennas, tyres, brakes, fairings, small dents or puncture holes in the aircraft skin .

                              or

c.   the aircraft is missing or is completely inaccessible

Advisory Airspace: An airspace of defined dimensions, or designated route, within which an air traffic advisory service is available.

Advisory Route (ADR): A designated route along which an air traffic advisory service is available.

Aerial Work: Any purpose (other than public transport) for which an aircraft is flown if valuable consideration is given or promised in respect of the flight or the purpose of the flight. Examples of this would be agriculture, construction, photography, surveying, observation and patrol, search and rescue, aerial advertisement, etc.

Aerobatic Flight: Manoeuvres intentionally performed by an aircraft involving an abrupt change in its attitude, an abnormal attitude, or an abnormal variation in speed and includes loops, spins, rolls, bunts, stall turns, inverted flying and any other similar manoeuvre.

Aerodrome: A defined area on land or water (including any buildings, installations and equipment) intended to be used either wholly or in part for the arrival, departure and surface movement of aircraft.

Aerodrome Beacon: An Aerodrome Beacon is used to indicate the location of an aerodrome from the air.

Aerodrome Control Service: An air traffic control service for aerodrome traffic.

Aerodrome Control Tower: A unit established to provide an air traffic control service to aerodrome traffic.

Aerodrome Elevation: The elevation of the highest point of the landing area.

Aerodrome Operating Minima: The limits of usability of an aerodrome for:

- Take-off, expressed in terms of runway visual range (RVR) and/or visibility and, if necessary, cloud conditions.

- Landing in precision approach and landing operations with vertical guidance expressed in terms of visibility and/or runway visual range and decision altitude/height (DA/DH).

- Landing in non-precision approach and landing operations, expressed in terms of visibility and/or runway visual range, minimum descent altitude/height (MDA/H) and if necessary cloud conditions.

Note: The basic difference between a precision and a non-precision approach is that in a precision approach the pilot will receive vertical as well as horizontal guidance.

Aerodrome Reference Point (ARP): The designated geographical location of an aerodrome.

Aerodrome Traffic: All traffic on the manoeuvring area of an aerodrome and all aircraft flying in the vicinity of an aerodrome.

Note: An aircraft is in the vicinity of an aerodrome when it is in, entering or leaving an aerodrome traffic circuit.

Aerodrome Traffic Circuit: The specified path to be flown by aircraft operating in the vicinity of an aerodrome.

Aerodrome Traffic Zone: An airspace of defined dimensions established around an aerodrome for the protection of aerodrome traffic.

Aeronautical Information Publication (AIP): A publication issued by or with the authority of a State and containing aeronautical information of a lasting character essential to air navigation.

Aeronautical Station: A land station in the aeronautical mobile service. In certain instances, an aeronautical station may be located on board ship or on a platform at sea.

Aeroplane: A power-driven heavier-than-air aircraft, deriving its lift chiefly from aerodynamic reactions on surfaces which remain fixed under given conditions of flight.

Aircraft: Any machine that can derive support in the atmosphere from the reactions of the air other than the reactions of the air against the earth's surface.

Aircraft Stand: A designated area on an apron intended to be used for parking an aircraft.

Air-ground Control Radio Station: An aeronautical telecommunication station having primary responsibility for handling communications pertaining to the operation and control of aircraft in a given area.

AIRMET Information: Information issued by a meteorological watch office concerning the occurrence or expected occurrence of en-route weather which may affect the safety of low-level aircraft operations and which was not already included in the forecast issued for the region.

AIRPROX: The code word used in an air traffic incident report to designate aircraft proximity.

Air Traffic: All aircraft in flight or operating on the manoeuvring area of an aerodrome.

Air Traffic Advisory Service: A service provided within advisory airspace to ensure separation, insofar as practical, between aircraft which are operating in accordance with IFR flight plans.

Air Traffic Control Clearance: Authorisation for an aircraft to proceed under conditions specified by an Air Traffic Control Unit.

Note 1:- For convenience, the term "air traffic control clearance" is frequently abbreviated to "clearance" when used in appropriate contexts.

Note 2:- The abbreviated term "clearance" may be prefixed by the words "taxi", "take-off", "departure", "en route", "approach" or "landing" to indicate the particular portion of flight to which the air traffic control clearance relates.

Air Traffic Control Service: A service provided for the purpose of :
a) preventing collisions:

1) between aircraft,

and

2) on the manoeuvring area between aircraft and obstructions, and

b) expediting and maintaining an orderly flow of air traffic.

Air Traffic Control Unit: A generic term referring to a unit responsible for the control of air traffic, meaning variously: Area Control Centre, Approach Control Centre or Aerodrome Control Tower.

Air Traffic Flow Management (ATFM): A service established with the objective of contributing to the safe, orderly and expeditious flow of traffic by ensuring that air traffic control service (ATCS) capacity is utilized to the maximum extent possible and that the traffic volume is compatible with the capacities declared by the appropriate ATCS authority.

Air Traffic Service: A generic term meaning variously, flight information service, alerting service, air traffic advisory service, air traffic control service (area control service, approach control service or aerodrome control service).

Air Traffic Services Airspace: Airspaces of defined dimensions, alphabetically designated, within which specific types of flights may operate and for which air traffic services and rules of operation are specified.

Note:- Air Traffic Services Airspace is classified as Class A to G, inclusive.

Air Traffic Services Reporting Office: A unit established for the purpose of receiving reports concerning air traffic services and flight plans submitted before departure.

Note:- An Air Traffic Services Reporting Office may be established as a separate unit or combined with an existing unit, such as another Air Traffic Services Unit, or a unit of the Aeronautical Information Service.

Air Traffic Services Unit:- A generic term meaning variously, Air Traffic Control Unit, Flight Information Centre or Air Traffic Services Reporting Office.

Airway: A control area or portion thereof established in the form of a corridor.

Alerting Post: A unit designated to receive information from the general public regarding aeroplanes in an emergency and to forward the information to the associated Rescue Coordination Centre (RCC).

Alerting Service: A service provided to notify appropriate organisations regarding aircraft in need of search and rescue aid, and assist such organizations as required.

Alert Phase: A situation wherein apprehension exists as to the safety of an aircraft and its occupants.

Alternate Aerodrome: An aerodrome to which an aircraft may proceed when it becomes either impossible or inadvisable to proceed to or to land at the aerodrome of intended landing. Alternate aerodromes include the following :

> **Take-off Alternate:** An alternate aerodrome at which an aircraft can land should this become necessary shortly after take-off when it is not possible to use the aerodrome of departure.

> **En-route Alternate:** An aerodrome at which an aircraft would be able to land after experiencing an abnormal or emergency situation while en-route.

> **Destination Alternate:** An alternate aerodrome to which an aircraft may proceed should it become either impossible or inadvisable to land at the aerodrome of intended landing.

Note:- The aerodrome from which a flight departs may also be an en-route or a destination alternate aerodrome for that flight.

Altitude: The vertical distance of a level, a point or an object considered as a point, measured from mean sea level (MSL).

Approach Control Office: A unit established to provide an Air Traffic Control Service to controlled flights arriving at, or departing from, one or more aerodromes.

Approach Control Service: An Air Traffic Control Service for arriving or departing controlled flights.

Appropriate ATS Authority: The relevant authority designated by the State responsible for providing air traffic services in the airspace concerned.

> **Appropriate authority:-**

> a) Regarding flight over the high seas: The relevant authority of the State of Registry.

> b) Regarding flight other than over the high seas: The relevant authority of the State having sovereignty over the territory being overflown.

Apron: A defined area, on a land aerodrome, intended to accommodate aircraft for the purposes of loading or unloading passengers, mail or cargo, fuelling, parking or maintenance.

Area Control Centre: A unit established to provide an Air Traffic Control Service to controlled flights in control areas under its jurisdiction.

Area Control Service: An Air Traffic Control Service for controlled flights in control areas.

ATS Route: A specified route designed for channeling the flow of traffic as necessary for the provision of air traffic services.

Note:- The term "ATS Route" is used to mean variously: airway, advisory route, controlled or uncontrolled route, arrival or departure route, etc.

Automatic Terminal Information Service (ATIS): The automatic provision of current, routine information to arriving and departing aircraft throughout 24 hours or a specific time period.

Blind Transmission: A transmission from one station to another station in circumstances where two-way communication cannot be established but where it is believed that the called station is able to receive the transmission.

Ceiling: The height above the ground or water of the base of the lowest layer of cloud below 6 000 metres (20 000 feet) covering more than half the sky.

Clearance Limit: The point to which an aircraft is granted an air traffic control clearance.

Clearway: A defined rectangular area on the ground or water, under the control of the appropriate authority, selected or prepared as a suitable area over which an aeroplane may make a portion of its initial climb to a specified height.

Common Mark: A mark assigned by I.C.A.O. to the common mark registering authority registering an aircraft of an international agency on other than a national basis.

Congested Area: in relation to a city, town or settlement, means any area which is substantially used for residential, industrial, commercial or recreational purposes.

Contracting State: Any State which is party to the Chicago Convention.

Control Area (CTA): A controlled airspace extending upwards from a specified limit above the earth.

Controlled Aerodrome: An aerodrome at which air traffic control service is provided to aerodrome traffic.

Controlled Airspace: An airspace of defined dimensions within which an Air Traffic Control Service is provided in accordance with the airspace classification system.

Note:- Controlled airspace is a generic term which covers ATS airspace Classes A, B, C, D and E, inclusive.

Controlled Flight: Any flight which is subject to an Air Traffic Control Clearance.

Control Zone (CTR): A controlled airspace extending upwards from the surface of the earth to a specified upper limit.

Cruising level: A level maintained during a significant portion of a flight.

Danger Area: An airspace of defined dimensions within which activities dangerous to the flight of aircraft may exist at specified times.

Dangerous Goods: Articles or substances which are capable of posing a risk to health, safety, property, or the environment and which are shown in the list of dangerous goods in the Technical Instructions or which are classified according to the Instructions.

Decision Altitude (DA) or Decision Height (DH): A specified altitude or height during a precision approach at which a missed approach must be initiated if the required visual reference to continue the approach has not been established.

Declared Distances:
a.   Take-Off Run Available (TORA). The length of runway declared available and suitable for the ground run of an aircraft taking-off.

b.   Take-Off Distance Available (TODA). The length of the take-off run available plus the length of the clearway, if provided.

c.   Accelerate-Stop Distance Available (ASDA). The length of the take-off run available plus the length of the stopway, if provided.

d.   Landing Distance Available (LDA). The length of runway which is declared available and suitable for the ground run of an aeroplane landing.

Displaced Threshold: A threshold not located at the extremity of a runway.

Distress Phase: A situation where there is reasonable certainty that an aircraft and its occupants are threatened by grave and imminent danger or require immediate assistance.

Ditching: The forced landing of an aeroplane on water.

Elevation: The vertical distance of a point or a level, on the surface of the earth, measured from mean sea level.

Emergency Phase: A generic term meaning, as the case may be, Uncertainty Phase, Alert Phase or Distress Phase.

Estimated Elapsed Time: The estimated time required to proceed from one significant point to another.

Estimated Off-Block Time: The estimated time at which the aircraft will commence movement associated with departure.

Estimated Time of Arrival: For IFR flights, the time at which it is estimated that the aircraft will arrive over that designated point, defined by reference to navigation aids, from which it is intended that an instrument approach procedure will be commenced, or, if no navigation aid is associated with the aerodrome, the time at which the aircraft will arrive over the aerodrome. For VFR flights, the time at which it is estimated that the aircraft will arrive over the aerodrome.

Expected Approach Time: The time at which ATC expects that an arriving aircraft, following a delay, will leave the holding point to complete its approach for a landing.

Flight Information Centre (FIC): A unit established to provide flight information service and alerting service.

Flight Information Region (FIR): An airspace of defined dimensions within which a Flight Information Service and an Alerting Service are provided.

Flight Information Service (FIS): A service provided for the purpose of giving advice and information useful for the safe and efficient conduct of flights.

Flight Level: A surface of constant atmospheric pressure which is related to a specific pressure datum, 1 013.2 hectopascals (hPa), and is separated from other such surfaces by specific pressure intervals.

Flight Plan: Specified information provided to Air Traffic Services Units, relative to an intended flight or portion of a flight of an aircraft.

Flight Time – Aeroplanes: The total time from the moment an aeroplane first moves for the purpose of taking off until the moment it finally comes to rest at the end of the flight.

Flight Time – Helicopters: The total time from the moment a helicopter's blades start turning until the moment the helicopter finally comes to rest at the end of the flight, and the rotor blades have stopped.

Flight Visibility: The visibility forward from the cockpit of an aircraft in flight.

Ground Visibility: The visibility at an aerodrome, as reported by an accredited observer.

Heading: The direction in which the longitudinal axis of an aircraft is pointed, usually expressed in degrees from North (true, magnetic, compass or grid).

Height: The vertical distance of a level, a point or an object considered as a point, measured from a specified datum.

Identification Beacon: An aeronautical beacon emitting a coded signal by means of which a particular point of reference can be identified.

IFR: Abbreviation for Instrument Flight Rules.

IFR Flight: A flight conducted in accordance with the instrument flight rules.

IMC: Abbreviation for Instrument Meteorological Conditions.

Incident: An occurrence, other than an accident, associated with the operation of an aircraft which affects or could affect the safety of operation.

Instrument Flight Rules: The Instrument Flight Rules require an aircraft to be flown:

a)   in controlled airspace:

(i) in accordance with stipulated minimum heights; a flight plan must also be filed, and the aircraft flown in accordance with ATC clearances, departure and approach procedures.

(ii) in accordance with the flight plan; position and level reports must be submitted to ATC as required.

(iii) in accordance with the semi-circular rule.

b) outside controlled airspace:

(i) in accordance with stipulated minimum heights.

(ii) in accordance with the quadrantal or semi-circular rules.

Instrument Meteorological Conditions (IMC): Meteorological conditions expressed in terms of visibility, distance from cloud, and ceiling, less than the minima specified for Visual Meteorological Conditions.

Instrument Runway: One of the following types of runway intended for the operation of aircraft using instrument approach procedures :

a) Non-precision approach runway.

b) Precision approach runway.

Landing Area: That part of a movement area intended for the landing or take-off of aircraft.

Landing Direction Indicator: A device to indicate visually the direction currently designated for landing and for take-off.

Level: A generic term relating to the vertical position of an aircraft in flight and meaning variously, height, altitude or flight level.

Maintenance Release: A document which contains a certification confirming that the maintenance work to which it relates has been completed in a satisfactory manner, either in accordance with the approved data and the procedures described in the maintenance organisation's procedures manual or an equivalent system.

Manoeuvring Area: That part of an aerodrome to be used for the take-off, landing and taxiing of aircraft, excluding aprons.

Marker: An object displayed above ground level in order to indicate an obstacle or delineate a boundary.

Missed Approach Procedure: The procedure to be followed if the approach cannot be continued.

Movement Area: That part of an aerodrome to be used for the take-off, landing and taxiing of aircraft, consisting of the manoeuvring area and the apron(s).

Night - I.C.A.O: The hours between the end of evening civil twilight and the beginning of morning civil twilight or such other period between sunset and sunrise, as may be prescribed by the appropriate Authority.

Night - UK: The UK Air Navigation Order (ANO) defines night as : the time from half an hour after sunset until half an hour before sunrise (both times inclusive), sunset and sunrise being determined at surface level.

NOTAM: A notice distributed by means of telecommunication containing information concerning the establishment, condition or change in any aeronautical facility, service, procedure or hazard, the timely knowledge of which is essential to personnel concerned with flight operations.

Obstacle: All fixed (whether temporary or permanent) and mobile objects which are located on an area intended for the surface movement of aircraft or which extend above a defined surface intended to protect aircraft in flight.

Operator: A person, organisation or enterprise engaged in or offering to engage in an aircraft operation.

Pilot-In-Command - ICAO: The pilot designated by the operator, or, in the case of general aviation, the owner as being in command of and charged with the safe conduct of the flight. The Pilot-in-Command is responsible for the operation and safety of the aircraft.

Pilot-In-Command - UK: A person who for the time being is in charge of the piloting of the aircraft without being under the direction of any other pilot in the aircraft.

Pressure Altitude: An altitude based on the ISA mean sea level pressure of 1013.2 mb/hPa, used in the calculation of aircraft performance; it is equivalent to a Flight Level in value, but expressed in feet.

Prohibited Area: An airspace of defined dimensions, above the land areas or territorial waters of a State, within which the flight of aircraft is prohibited.

Radar Vectoring: Provision of navigational guidance to aircraft in the form of specific headings, based on the use of radar.

Radiotelephony: A form of radio communication primarily intended for the exchange of information in the form of speech.

Reporting Point: A specified geographical location in relation to which the position of an aircraft can be reported.

Rescue Coordination Centre (RCC): A unit responsible for promoting efficient organisation of search and rescue services and for coordinating the conduct of search and rescue operations within a Search and Rescue Region.

Restricted Area: An airspace of defined dimensions, above the land areas or territorial waters of a State, within which the flight of aircraft is restricted in accordance with certain specified conditions.

Runway: A defined rectangular area on a land aerodrome prepared for the landing and take-off of aircraft.

Runway Holding Position: A designated position intended to protect a runway or an ILS/MLS critical/sensitive area at which taxiing aircraft and vehicles shall stop and hold, unless otherwise authorised by the aerodrome control tower.

Runway Visual Range (RVR): The range over which the pilot of an aircraft on the centre line of a runway can see the runway surface, markings or the lights delineating the runway or identifying its centre line.

Search and Rescue Region: An area of defined dimensions within which search and rescue services are provided.

Shoulder: An area adjacent to the edge of a pavement so prepared as to provide a transition between the pavement and the adjacent surface.

SIGMET Information: Information used by a meteorological watch office concerning the occurrence or expected occurrence of specified significant en-route weather which may affect the safety of aircraft operations.

Signals Square: An area on an aerodrome used for the display of ground signals.

Special VFR Flight: A VFR flight cleared by an Air Traffic Control Unit to operate within a control zone in meteorological conditions below VMC.

State of Manufacture: The State having jurisdiction over the organisation responsible for the final assembly of the aircraft.

State of Occurrence: The State in the territory of which any accident or incident occurs.

State of Registry: The State on whose register an aircraft is entered.

Stopway: A defined rectangular area on the ground at the end of the Take-Off Run Available prepared as a suitable area in which an aircraft can be stopped in the case of an abandoned take-off.

Taxiing: Movement of an aircraft on the surface of an aerodrome under its own power, excluding take-off and landing.

Taxiway: A defined path on a land aerodrome established for the taxiing of aircraft and intended to provide a link between one part of the aerodrome and another.

Taxiway Intersection: A junction of two or more taxiways.

Terminal Control Area (TCA or TMA): A control area normally established at the confluence of ATS routes in the vicinity of one or more major aerodromes.

Threshold: The beginning of that portion of the runway usable for landing.

Touchdown Zone: The portion of a runway, beyond the threshold, where it is intended that landing aeroplanes first contact the runway.

Track: The projection on the Earth's surface of the path of an aircraft, the direction of which path at any point is usually expressed in degrees from North (true, magnetic or grid).

Traffic Information: Information issued by an Air Traffic Services Unit to alert a pilot to other known or observed air traffic which may be in proximity to the position or intended route of flight and to help the pilot avoid a collision.

Transition Altitude: The altitude at or below which the vertical position of an aircraft is controlled by reference to altitudes.

Transition Layer: The airspace between the Transition Altitude and the Transition Level.

Transition Level: The Transition Level is the lowest available Flight Level above the Transition Altitude.

Uncertainty Phase: A situation wherein uncertainty exists as to the safety of an aircraft and its occupants.

VFR: Abbreviation for Visual Flight Rules.

VFR Flight: A VFR Flight is a flight during which the prevailing weather conditions enable a pilot to conduct the flight, and to navigate, by reference to ground features. VMC must prevail for a flight to be conducted in accordance with the Visual Flight Rules.

Visibility: The ability, as determined by atmospheric conditions and expressed in units of distance, to see and identify prominent, unlighted objects by day, and prominent lighted objects by night.

Visual Flight Rules: The Visual Flight Rules require an aircraft to be flown in accordance with the VMC minima appropriate to the classification of airspace in which it is flying.

Visual Meteorological Conditions (VMC): Meteorological conditions expressed in terms of visibility, distance from cloud, and ceiling equal to or better than specified minima.

Waypoint: A specified geographical location used to define an area navigation route or the flight path of an aircraft employing area navigation.

JAR-FCL PPL THEORETICAL KNOWLEDGE SYLLABUS

AIR LAW

The table below contains the principal topics and subtopics from the current outline syllabus for the theoretical examination in Air Law for the Private Pilot's Licence, as published in **JAR-FCL 1**. Syllabuses may be modified, so always check the latest examination documentation from your national civil aviation authority, or from **JAR-FCL/EASA**.

AIR LAW
LEGISLATION
The Convention on International Civil Aviation
The International Civil Aviation Organisation

Articles of the Convention	Sovereignty; Territory; Flight over territory of Contracting States; Landing at customs airports; Applicability of air regulations; Rules of the air; Entry and clearance regulations of Contracting States; Search of aircraft; Facilitation of formalities; Customs and immigration procedures; Customs duty; Documents to be carried in aircraft; Use of aircraft radio equipment; Certificate of airworthiness; Licences of personnel; Recognition of certificates and licences; Journey log books; Cargo restrictions; Restrictions on use of photographic equipment; Adoption of international standards and procedures; Endorsement of certificates and licences; Validity of endorsed certificates and licences.

ANNEXES TO THE CONVENTION

Aircraft nationality and registration marks:	Definitions; Aircraft registration marks; Certificate of Registration; Identification plate.
Airworthiness	Definitions; Certificate of Airworthiness (C of A); Continuing airworthiness; Validity of C of A; Instruments and equipment; Aircraft limitations and information.
Rules of the air:	Definitions; Applicability; General rules; Visual Flight Rules; Signals; Interception of civil aircraft.

Air traffic regulations and Air Traffic Services:	Definitions; Objectives of air traffic services; Classification of airspace; Flight Information Regions, Control Areas and Control Zones; air traffic control services; Flight Information Service; Alerting Service; Visual Meteorological Conditions; Instrument Meteorological Conditions; in-flight contingencies.
Aerodrome data:	Definitions; Conditions of the movement area and related facilities; Visual aids for navigation; Indicators and signalling devices; Markings; Lights; Signs; Markers; Signal area; Visual aids for denoting obstacles; Marking of objects; Lighting of objects; Visual aids for denoting restricted use of areas; Emergency and other services; Aerodrome ground lights and surface marking colours; Colours for aeronautical ground lights; Colours for surface markings.
PROCEDURES FOR AIR NAVIGATION SERVICES - AIR TRAFFIC MANAGEMENT	
General provisions:	Definitions; ATS operating practices; Flight plan, clearances and information; Control of air traffic flow; Altimeter setting procedures; Wake turbulence information; Meteorological information; Air reports (AIREP).
Area Control Service:	Separation of controlled traffic in the various classes of airspace; pilots, responsibility to maintain separation in VMC; Emergency and communications failure procedures by the pilot; Interception of civil aircraft.
Approach Control Service:	Departing and arriving aircraft procedures in VMC.
Aerodrome Control Service:	Function of aerodrome control towers; VFR operations; Traffic and circuit procedures; Information to aircraft; Control of aerodrome traffic.
Flight Information and Alerting Service	Air traffic advisory service; Objectives and basic principles.

JAA REGULATIONS	
General requirements:	1.025 – Validity of licences and ratings; 1.035 – Medical fitness; 1.040 – Decrease in medical fitness; 1.050 – Crediting of flight time; 1.065 – State of licence issue.
Student pilots:	1.085 – Requirements; 1.090 – Minimum age; 1.095 – Medical fitness.
Private pilot licences:	1.100 – Minimum age; 1.105 – Medical fitness; 1.110 – Privileges and conditions; 1.115 – Ratings for special purposes; 1.120 – Experience and crediting; 1.125 – Training courses; 1.130 – Theoretical knowledge examinations; 1.135 – Skill tests.
Instrument Rating:	1.175 – Circumstances in which an instrument rating is required
Type and Class Ratings:	1.215 – Division of Class Ratings; 1.225 – Circumstances in which type or class ratings are required; 1.245 – Validity, revalidation and renewal.
Instructor ratings:	1.300 – Instruction – general.

ANSWERS TO
AIR LAW QUESTIONS

Chapter 1   *Aviation Law (ICAO)*

Question	1	2	3	4	5	6	7	8	9	10	11	12
Answer	b	a	c	d	a	a	b	a	b	a	c	d

Question	13	14	15	16	17	18	19	20	21	22	23
Answer	c	b	c	d	b	c	a	d	b	c	c

Chapter 2   *Rules of the Air (ICAO)*

Question	1	2	3	4	5	6	7	8	9	10	11	12
Answer	a	c	d	b	b	a	b	c	d	d	b	b

Question	13	14	15	16	17	18	19	20	21	22	23	24
Answer	a	a	b	a	a	d	b	d	b	b	b	b

Question	25	26	27	28	29	30	31	32	33
Answer	c	a	b	b	b	a	c	c	b

Chapter 3   *Registration (ICAO)*

Question	1	2	3	4	5	6	7
Answer	b	c	c	d	d	c	d

Chapter 4   *Airworthiness (ICAO)*

Question	1	2	3	4	5	6	7	8	9
Answer	b	d	c	d	c	c	a	b	b

Chapter 5   *Airspace Division and Air Traffic Services (ICAO)*

Question	1	2	3	4	5	6	7	8	9	10	11	12
Answer	b	c	c	c	a	c	c	b	d	b	b	a

Question	13	14	15	16	17	18	19	20	21	22	23	24
Answer	a	d	d	a	a	d	b	b	a	d	b	d

Question	25	26
Answer	b	b

Chapter 6   *Flight Plans and Clearances (ICAO)*

Question	1	2	3	4	5	6	7	8	9	10	11	12
Answer	c	b	d	c	a	a	a	b	c	d	d	d

Question	13	14
Answer	b	b

Chapter 7   *Aeronautical Information (ICAO)*

Question	1	2	3	4	5
Answer	c	d	d	a	b

Chapter 8   *Separation (ICAO)*

Question	1	2	3	4	5	6	7	8	9	10
Answer	c	d	a	c	b	a	c	b	b	c

Chapter 9   *Aerodromes (General)*

Question	1	2	3	4	5	6	7	8	9	10	11	12
Answer	d	a	c	b	b	c	a	d	d	c	d	b

Question	13	14	15	16	17	18	19	20	21
Answer	a	a	b	c	d	c	b	a	b

Chapter 10   *Air Law (UK)*

No Questions.

Chapter 11   *Rules of the Air (UK)*

Question	1	2	3	4	5	6	7	8	9	10	11	12
Answer	c	b	d	a	c	a	a	d	c	a	d	c

Question	13	14	15	16	17	18	19	20	21	22	23	24
Answer	a	d	c	b	d	b	b	a	c	d	b	c

Question	25	26	27
Answer	b	c	b

Chapter 12 **Registration**

Question	1	2	3	4	5	6	7	8	9	10
Answer	b	a	c	d	d	b	a	c	c	d

Chapter 13 **Airworthiness**

Question	1	2	3	4	5	6	7	8	9	10
Answer	d	a	c	d	b	b	c	d	a	c

Chapter 14 **Airspace Division and Air Traffic Services (CAA)**

Question	1	2	3	4	5	6	7	8	9	10	11	12
Answer	c	d	c	b	b	a	c	c	c	c	d	d

Question	13	14	15	16	17	18	19	20	21	22	23	24
Answer	b	c	a	c	b	d	c	c	c	d	b	d

Question	25	26	27	28
Answer	b	d	b	d

Chapter 15 **Flight Planning and Clearances**

Question	1	2	3	4	5	6	7	8	9	10	11	12
Answer	b	a	b	a	d	a	c	d	d	d	b	c

Question	13
Answer	d

Chapter 16 **Aeronautical Information (CAA)**

Question	1	2	3	4	5	6	7	8	9	10	11	12
Answer	a	d	c	b	d	b	c	d	a	b	b	c

Question	13	14	15	16	17	18	19
Answer	c	b	b	d	c	b	a

Chapter 17   *Separation (CAA)*

Question	1	2	3	4	5	6	7	8	9	10	11	12
Answer	d	a	d	c	b	b	c	a	b	c	d	b

Question	13	14	15
Answer	d	c	c

Chapter 18   *Obstacles (General)*

Question	1	2	3	4	5	6	7	8	9	10	11	12
Answer	b	a	c	c	b	b	b	c	a	d	c	b

Question	13	14	15	16	17	18	19	20
Answer	a	b	d	b	d	c	c	b

Chapter 19   *Altimeter Setting and Procedures (General)*

Question	1	2	3	4	5	6	7	8	9	10	11	12
Answer	c	c	d	d	b	a	b	a	b	c	c	b

Question	13	14	15	16	17	18	19	20	21	22
Answer	c	b	b	d	a	c	a	d	b	b

Annex A   *General Lights and Signals*

Question	1	2	3	4	5	6
Answer	d	c	a	d	b	a

Annexe B   *JAA Licensing*

Question	1	2	3	4	5	6	7	8	9	10	11	12
Answer	a	c	a	c	a	d	d	b	c	b	b	c

Question	13	14	15	16	17	18	19	20	21	22	23	24
Answer	a	c	a	d	c	b	a	b	d	c	a	d

Question	25	26	27	28	29	30	31
Answer	c	b	b	c	a	b	a

For your convenience the ICAO Air Law and United Kingdom Air Law sections have been indexed separately

International (ICAO) Air Law Index.

A

Aerodrome Beacon	151
Aerodrome Control	99
Aerodrome Control Service	98
Aerodrome Lighting	151
Aerodrome Markings	146
Aerodrome Obstacles	159
Aerodromes	143
Aeronautical Information Service	127
Aeronautical Information Services	127
- Aeronautical Information Circulars	129
- Aeronautical Information Publication	128
Aiming Point	148
Aircraft Lights	71
Aircraft Operating Limitations	72
Air Navigation Order (ANO)	15
Air Traffic Clearances	119
Air Traffic Control Service	98
Air Traffic Control Units	97
Air Traffic Services	96, 97
Air Traffic Service Units	97
Airways	86
Airworthiness of Aircraft	69
- Temporary Loss Of Airworthiness	69
Alerting Service	98
Applicability of Air Regulations	5
Approach Slope Indicators	153
Apron Management Service	164
Articles Of The ICAO Convention	4

C

Cargo Restrictions	10
Certificate Of Airworthiness (C of A)	69
Certificate Of Registration (C of R)	63
Chicago Convention	3
Classification Of Airspace	79
- Classification Of Airspace By Letter	89
Communications Failure	40
Control Areas	85
Controlled Airspace	80
Control Zones	84
Cruising Levels	25
Customs And Immigration Procedures	7
Customs Duties	7

D

Documents Carried In Aircraft   7
Dropping And Spraying   25

E

Emergency Phases   104
European Aviation Safety Authority (EASA)   14

F

Fire & Rescue Services   163
Flight Information Regions   81
Flight Information Service   101
Flight Manual   73
Flight Plans   115
  - Abbreviated Flight Plan   115
  - Adherence to Flight Plan - Controlled Flights   117
  - Changes to a Flight Plan   117
  - Closing a Flight Plan   118
  - Contents of a Flight Plan   116
  - Contents of an Arrival Report   119
  - Full Flight Plan   115
  - Submission of Flight Plans   116
Flight Rules And Airspace Classification   92
Formation Flying   26

G

Ground Movement Controller   99

I

ICAO Annexes   14
Instrument Flight Rules (IFR)   24
Integrated Aeronautical Information Package   127
international Air Law   3
International Civil Aviation Organisation (ICAO)   3, 13

J

Joint Aviation Authorities (JAA)   13

L

Landing   30
Licences Of Personnel   9
Lighting (Aerodrome)   151
Lighting Of Objects/Obstacles   159
Lights To Be Displayed By Aeroplanes   33
Location Signs   157
Log Book   10

M

Markings and Placards 73
Minimum Heights 25
Minimum Heights Low Flying 49

N

Nationality Marks
  - *Classification of Aircraft ICAO* 64
  - *Common Mark* 61
  - *Dispensation from Markings* 62
  - *Identification Plate* 64
  - *Size of Markings* 62
Non-load bearing surfaces. 161
NOTAM 128

O

Overtaking in the Air 30

P

Parachute Descents and Aerobatic Flights 26
Position Reports by Aircraft Under Air Traffic Control 27
Precision Approach Path Indicator (PAPI) 154
Pre-flight Information Bulletins 128
Prohibited Areas 26

R

Recognition of Certificates and Licences 9
Registration Mark 61
Right- of- Way - Aircraft in the Air 28
Rules of the Air 23
  - *Applicability of Rules of the Air* 24
  - *Avoidance of Collisions* 27
  - *Operation on and in the Vicinity of an Aerodrome* 26
Runway Approach Lights 155
Runway Designator 146
Runway End Lights 153
Runway Holding Position & Stop Bars 39
Runway Lights 153
Runway Markings 146

S

Safety & Survival Equipment 71
Separation (ICAO) 133
  - *Horizontal Separation* 133
  - *Lateral Separation* 134
  - *Longitudinal Separation* 133
Service, Aeronautical Information 127
Servicing and Maintenance of Aircraft 73
Signalling Lamp 145
Signal Square 145

Sovereignty	4
Standards and Recommended Practices (SARPS)	11
Surface Movement of Aircraft	32

T

Taking Off	31
Taxiway Center-Line Lights	156
Taxiway Lighting	156
Taxiway Edge Lights	156
Territorial Airspace	4
Territory	4
Threshold Lighting	153
Threshold Marking	148
Towing	25
Transverse Stripe & Displaced thresholds	148
Types of Separation	133

U

U.K. Aeronautical Information Publication (AIP)	15
Uncontrolled Airspace	80
Unlawful Interference - (Hijack)	41
Upper Information Region (UIR)	81
Use of Aircraft Radio Equipment	8

V

Validity of Endorsed Certificates and Licences	13
Visual Aids for Navigation	144
Visual Approach Slope Indictor (VASI)	153
Visual Circuit	50
Visual Flight Rules (VFR)	45
Visual Meterorological Conditions (VMC)	44

W

Water on a Runway	144
Windsocks	144

CAA United Kingdom Air Law Index

A

Aerials and Tall Communication Masts	308
Aerial Tactics Areas	312
Aerobatics	192
Aerodrome Control	245
Aerodrome Obstacles	307
Aerodrome Traffic Zones	238
Aeronautical Information (CAA)	279
Aeronautical Information Regulation And Control (AIRAC)	281
Age	378
AIC	282
Air Navigation Order	173
Airspace Division And Air Traffic Services In The UK	221
Air-to-Air Refueling Areas (AARA)	313
Air Traffic Services	242
Airways	226
Airworthiness	213
- Aircraft, Engine and Propeller Logbooks	215
- Insurance	217
Altimeter	323
Altimeter Setting Procedures	336
Altimeter Setting Regions	328
Altimeter Subscale Setting	323
Approach and Landing	337
Approach Control	243
Areas of Intense Air Activity (AIAA)	311
Automatic Terminal Information Service (ATIS)	246

B

Banners & Towropes etc.	194
Briefing of Passengers	194

C

Captive and Free Flight Manned Balloon Sites & Kite Flying	315
Carriage of Passengers	378
Certificate of Airworthiness	213
Class A Airspace	184
Class Rating	383
Communications Failure	194
Control Area (CTA)	226
Controlled Airspace	225
Control Zone (CTR)	226
Cross-Country Flying	326
Crossing an Airway	238

D

Danger Area Activity Information Service (DAAIS)	255, 311
Danger Area Crossing Service (DACS)	311
Danger Areas	310

Display of Lights by Aircraft   190
Diversion   270
Dropping Articles   188

E
En-route Obstacles   307
Exceptions to low flying prohibitions   187

F
Failure of a Proficiency Check   385
Flight Manual / Pilot's Operating Handbook   216
Flight Plan   263
Flying Displays   188
Flying Experience and crediting (towards the PPL)   379
Flying Over Open Air Assemblies   186
Flying Skill Test   380

G
Gas and Oil Operations   314
Gliders   188

H
Hectopascals   323
High-tension Masts and Cables   308

I
ICAO Standard Atmosphere (ISA)   323
Instrument Flight Rules (IFR)   181
Insurance   217

L
Land-based Air Navigation Obstacles   307
Land Clear Rule   186
Landing and Taking-off   187
Lighting of En-route Obstacles   308
London and Scottish FIRs   223
London and Scottish UIRs   223
Lower Airspace   223
Low Flying Rule (Rule 5)   185

M
Markings & Registration   205
- Certificate of Registration (C of R)   205
- Change of Ownership   207
- Classification of UK Aircraft   205
- Identification Plate   207
- Nationality & Registration Marking   207
Medical Certificate   387
Medical Examinations   387
Microlight Flying Sites   315

Military Aerodrome Traffic Zones (MATZ)   240
Millibars   323

N
Noise Certificate   216
Non-controlled Airfields   247

O
Obstacles   307
Offshore Obstacles   307
One Thousand Foot Rule   186

P
Permit to Fly   214
Pilot's Licence (UK National PPL)
- Medical Requirements   387
Pilot's Licence (UK NPPL)   386
Pre-Flight Information Bulletins (PIB)   285

Q
QFE   324
QFE and QNH   324
QNH   325
Quadrantal Rule   182

R
Radiosonde Balloon Ascents   313
Regional Pressure Setting   328
Repetitive Flight Plan (RPL)   263
Right-hand Rule   193
Right of Way on the Ground (Vehicles and Aircraft)   192
Rights of Way in the Air and on Take-off and Landing   191
RT Phraseology   326
Rules of the Air   177

S
Saving Life   188
Semi-Circular Rule   183
Separation (CAA)   295
Signals For Aerodrome Traffic   352
Simulated Instrument Flights   189
Special VFR (SVFR)   184
Speed Restriction   184
Standard Pressure Setting of 1013.2 Millibars   330
State of Licence Issue   382

T
Take-off, Climb and Cruise   336
Technical Log   215
Terminal Control Area   227

Terminal Manoeuvring Area   227
Transition Altitude   323, 330
Transition Level   333
"Trigger" NOTAM   284
Two-way Radio Communication Failure   194
Type Rating   382, 384
Types of NOTAM   284
Types of Separation   295

U

UK AIP   280
UK Flight Information Service   250
- *Basic Service*   251
- *Deconfliction Service*   251
- *Procedural Service*   252
- *Traffic Service*   251
UK Military Low Flying System   312
UK Obstacles To Air Navigation, Prohibited, Restricted & Danger Areas   307
Upper Airspace   223
Upper Information Region   223
Use of Transponders   184

V

Validity of Class 2 Medical Certificate for JAA PPL(A)   388
Validity of Class and Type Ratings   384
VFR Flight in the Aerodrome Circuit Pattern   248
VFR Flight Plans   269
Visual Flight Rules   178
VMC Minima for Flights Outside Controlled Airspace   179
VMC Minima for Flights Within Controlled Airspace   180

W

Wake Turbulence   297
Weather Minima   190
Weather Reports   190
Weight Schedule   216

SKILLS · FOR · FLIGHT

Operational Procedures

Oxford
aviation academy

1

<u>OPERATIONAL PROCEDURES</u>

CHAPTER 1: FLIGHT PREPARATION AND IN-FLIGHT PROCEDURES   1

CHAPTER 2: AEROPLANE INSTRUMENTS AND EQUIPMENT   21

CHAPTER 3: WINDSHEAR   27

CHAPTER 4: CONTROLLED FLIGHT INTO TERRAIN   33

CHAPTER 5: SEARCH AND RESCUE   39

OPERATIONAL PROCEDURES QUESTIONS   49

OPERATIONAL PROCEDURES SYLLABUS   57

ANSWERS TO THE OPERATIONAL PROCEDURES QUESTIONS   59

OPERATIONAL PROCEDURES INDEX   63

CHAPTER 1
FLIGHT PREPARATION
AND IN - FLIGHT PROCEDURES

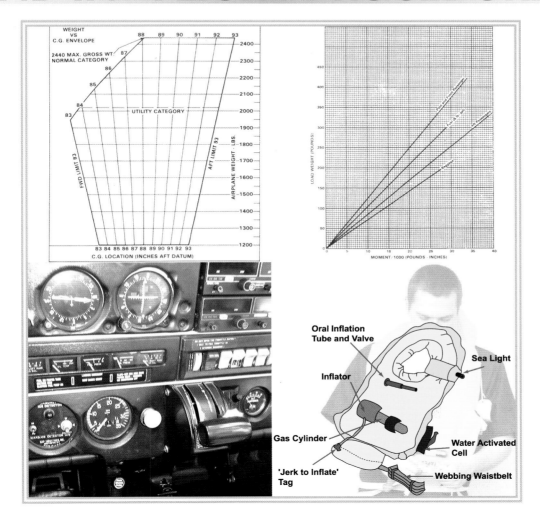

INTRODUCTION.

All holders of a pilot's licence are required to have knowledge of basic aircraft Operational Procedures, based on both national and international regulations.

The basis for this requirement is contained within International Civil Aviation Organisation (ICAO) publication Annex 6 Part 2. In addition, the following subjects are required to be studied and are included in the JAA Operational Procedures theoretical knowledge examination:

- ICAO Annex 12 (SEARCH AND RESCUE).

- ICAO Annex 13 (AEROPLANE ACCIDENT INVESTIGATION).

- NOISE ABATEMENT.

- CONTRAVENTION OF AVIATION REGULATIONS.

THE RESPONSIBILITY OF THE PILOT IN COMMAND (PIC).

The Pilot in Command must not commence a flight unless he is satisfied that the flight can be operated safely according to the following requirements:

If a light aircraft is hired from a flying club for a private flight, the PIC is responsible for planning the flight and ensuring the weather is suitable.

Figure 1.1 Flight Preparation.

- The ground and aeroplane communication facilities are adequate.

- The ground and aeroplane Navigation Aids are adequate.

- The nature of the terrain to be over-flown has been fully taken into account.

- The required aeroplane instruments and equipment are adequate and serviceable.

- The aeroplane is airworthy, accompanied with supporting documentation.

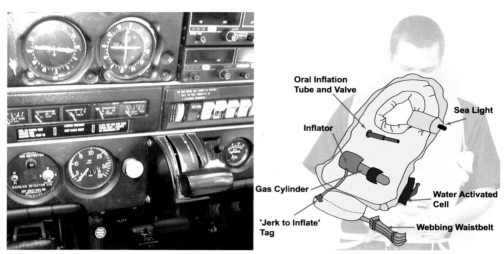

Figure 1.2 Flight Preparation - Instruments and equipment must be serviceable.

- The aircraft is appropriately insured.

- The aeroplane is registered.

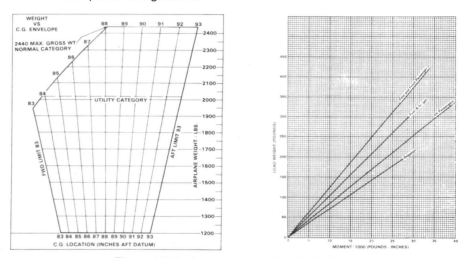

Figure 1.3 Performance operating limitations.

- The mass and centre of gravity are within limits.

- Any load carried is properly distributed and safely secured.

- The calculated performance ensures that any limitations in the Flight Manual will not be exceeded for take-off, climb, cruise, descent and landing *(see Figure 1.3)*.

- The aeroplane will not be flown to or from an aerodrome using operating minima lower than appropriate limits.

- The PIC is familiar with all available meteorological information appropriate to the intended flight *(see Figure 1.4)*.

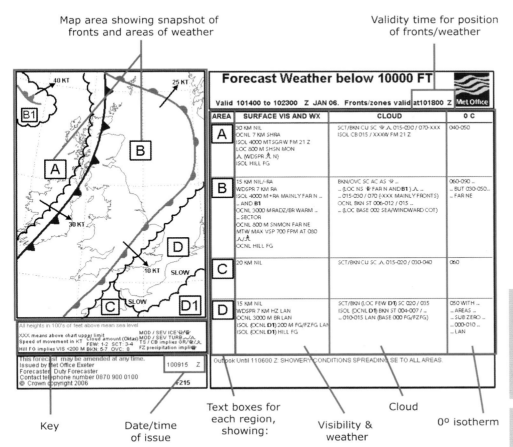

Map area showing snapshot of fronts and areas of weather

Validity time for position of fronts/weather

Key

Date/time of issue

Text boxes for each region, showing:

Visibility & weather

Cloud

0° isotherm

Figure 1.4 UK and European low-level Significant Weather Charts (F215 and F415).

If a pilot is unsure as to whether the aircraft is suitably equipped for a flight, he should consult the aircraft's Pilot's Operating handbook.

The Pilot -in-Command has the sole responsibility to carry out the pre-flight checks.

- Sufficient fuel, lubricants and other fluids are carried for the flight.

- The appropriate pre -flight checks have been accomplished.

If the use of Air Traffic Services (ATS) is planned, the aeroplane must be equipped with a serviceable radio and transponder with both modes 'A' and 'C'. If any part of the flight is to be VFR or Special VFR (SVFR) within controlled airspace, VHF radio must be carried.

The PIC is solely responsible for all of the actions above being completed correctly. In certain circumstances he may delegate some of the actions, but if an action is missed or incorrectly performed, the responsibility for the action remains with the PIC.

PRE-FLIGHT PASSENGER SAFETY BRIEFING OF CREW AND PASSENGERS.

Prior to commencing a flight the PIC shall ensure that all crew members and passengers are fully briefed on the location and use of the following items:

• Seat belts and harnesses.

• Emergency exits.

• Life Jackets.

• Oxygen dispensing equipment.

• First Aid Kit and Fire Extinguisher.

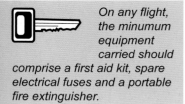

The Pilot - in - Command must brief passengers on:

SEAT BELTS

SURVIVAL EQUIPMENT

EMERGENCY EXIT

OXYGEN

FIRST AID KIT

FIRE EXIT

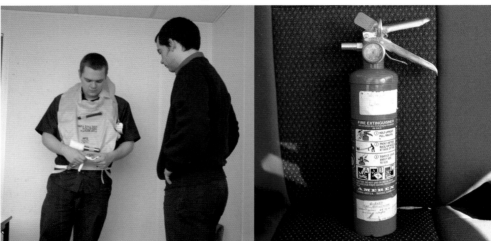

Figure 1.5 Emergency equipment.

On any flight, the minumum equipment carried should comprise a first aid kit, spare electrical fuses and a portable fire extinguisher.

There are a number of other general points that passengers should be made aware of, including availability of sick bags and the necessity of not interfering with the operation of the aeroplane or causing a distraction to the pilot in flight.

PRE-FLIGHT PASSENGER BRIEFINGS ON EMERGENCY SITUATIONS.

No matter what type of aircraft, large or small, whenever passengers are carried it is essential they receive a detailed safety briefing before flight. The pilot-in-command (PIC) is responsible for ensuring that passengers are adequately briefed. Amongst other things, the briefing must include instruction in the location and use of applicable emergency equipment.

All commercial transport operators are required by law to carry out appropriate passenger briefings before flight commences. The briefing may include verbal advice and instructions by the cabin crew, the showing of safety videos, and/or the distribution of printed cards available to individual passengers.

A PPL holder, as commander of his aircraft, also has a legal duty to ensure that his passengers are properly briefed on use of emergency equipment, and how to exit the aircraft in an emergency. This is most likely to be done verbally and might also include advising your front seat passenger not to handle the controls unless briefed and asked. Remind them not to rest their feet on the rudder pedals and any toe brakes!

Although emergencies are rare, airborne emergencies may develop into a situation where it becomes imperative to abandon further flight. If this is the case a pilot's reaction to the emergency should be carried out with minimum risk to passengers and in such a way as to protect the integrity of the airframe. It would obviously be impractical and ineffective for a pilot to brief passengers on actions to take in an emergency, while the emergency is occurring. Therefore, appropriate briefings must be given on the ground before flight.

If the nature of the emergency is such that an en-route alternate aerodrome has to be selected, the ATSU with which the pilot is in contact must be informed of the nature of the emergency and assistance required using emergency RT communication procedures (Mayday/Pan Pan). Instructions from ATC should be complied with regarding necessary routeing and communications. An emergency situation may rapidly deteriorate, forcing an emergency landing or a ditching. It is the responsibility of the ATSU to alert the ground emergency services and to render all possible assistance to the commander of the aircraft suffering the emergency.

INSTRUCTIONS TO PASSENGERS DURING AN EMERGENCY.

Instructions to passengers during the emergency itself must be concise. The onset of fear amongst passengers is probable in an emergency situation, and this may easily lead to panic. Passengers will be reassured by calm words from the pilot about what has happened, what is being done and what the likely outcome will be.

1. Check harness is tight and locked.

2. Unlock doors before touchdown but do not open them.

3. Adopt the braced position.

DIRECTION OF AIRCRAFT

Figure 1.6 Passenger emergency briefing.

CERTIFICATES AND DOCUMENTATION.

Part of the PIC's pre flight procedures will include checking that the aeroplane has the following documents to support the registration, maintenance and airworthiness requirements.

- Certificate of Registration.

- Certificate of Airworthiness.

- Certificate of Maintenance Review.

- Certificate of Maintenance Inspection of Release to Service.

- Technical Log.

Figure 1.7 JAR-FCL Pilots Licence.

- Noise Certificate (If applicable).

- Aeroplane Radio Licence.

- Third Party Insurance Certificate.

- Individual Crew Member Licence with appropriate rating *(see Figure 1.7).*

UK DIFFERENCES - AIR NAVIGATION ORDER (ANO).

Operation of Aeroplanes.
The following paragraphs cover some of the rules contained in the Air Navigation Order (ANO) and applicable in the United Kingdom.

Operations Manual.
For any public transport aeroplane registered in the UK an operator shall make available to each member of the operating staff an operations manual. The manual shall contain all such information and instructions as may be necessary to enable the operating staff to perform their duties.

Operator's Responsibility.
The operator of an aeroplane registered in the UK must designate a pilot to be the commander of the aeroplane. In addition, the operator must satisfy himself that the following conditions are met:

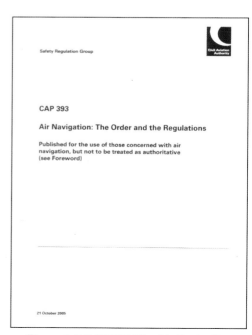

Figure 1.8 CAP 393 The Air Navigation Order.

- That the aeronautical radio stations and navigation aids for the planned route and any diversions are adequate for safe navigation of the aeroplane.

- That every place at which it is intended to take off or land are suitable for the purpose and must be manned and suitably equipped to ensure a safe operation at the time of use.

- That no person is permitted to be a member of the crew on a public transport flight unless that person has had the training, experience, practice and periodical tests in order to perform that duty using the equipment provided in the aeroplane.

- That no member of the flight crew is permitted to simulate emergency manoeuvres and procedures which would adversely affect the flight characteristics of the aeroplane.

Operation of Radio in Aeroplanes.

The radio equipment in an aeroplane must only be operated by persons holding an appropriate R/T licence or when otherwise permitted under the law of the country of registration or the State of the operator.

Towing of Gliders.

An aeroplane shall not tow a glider in flight unless its Certificate of Airworthiness allows it. The length of the combination of towing aeroplane, tow rope and glider in flight shall not exceed 150 metres. Before take-off the commander of the towing aeroplane shall ensure that its performance in the actual conditions is safe and that the tow rope is in good

Figure 1.9 Ensure all radio equipment functions.

condition and of sufficient strength. The commanders of the towing aeroplane and the glider must agree emergency signals and procedures should it be necessary to discontinue the tow or if the tow cannot be released.

Towing, Picking Up and Raising of Persons and Articles.

An aeroplane in flight shall not, by means external to the aeroplane, tow any article, other than a glider, or pick up any animal or article unless allowed to do so in accordance with the Certificate of Airworthiness. An aeroplane shall not launch or pick up tow ropes, banners or similar articles other than at an aerodrome.

An aeroplane in flight shall not tow any article, other than a glider, at night or when the flight visibility is less than one nautical mile. The length of the combination of towing aeroplane, tow rope, and article in tow, shall not exceed 150 metres.

A helicopter shall not fly at any height over a congested area of a city, town or settlement at any time when an article, person or animal is suspended from the helicopter.

Nothing shall prohibit picking up or raising of any person in an emergency or for the purpose of saving life (e.g. a helicopter on a rescue operation).

Dropping of Articles and Animals.

Any article or animal (whether or not attached to a parachute) shall not be dropped, or permitted to drop, from an aeroplane in flight so as to endanger persons or property. In certain circumstances, with the approval of the CAA and authority of the aeroplane commander, some tasks are exempt from this restriction e.g. dropping of articles for the purpose of saving life, emergency jettisoning of fuel, dropping of ballast in the form of water or sand and the dropping at aerodromes of tow ropes, banners or similar articles towed by aeroplanes.

Dropping of Persons.

A person shall not drop, be dropped, be permitted to drop or jump from an aeroplane in flight so as to endanger persons or property. The CAA may grant written permission or under the terms of a Police Air Operators Certificate for persons to be dropped or jump from an aeroplane to the ground in the UK. Parachuting may be permitted by the CAA providing the Certificate of Airworthiness includes provision for it and a parachuting manual is available to every employee or person who is or may be engaged in parachuting activities conducted by the operator.

Carriage of Weapons and of Munitions of War.

Except with the written permission of the CAA, munitions of war must not be carried on aeroplanes. Where permission is granted, severe restrictions apply to the type of article carried and where it is positioned on the aeroplane. Permission is also required for the carriage of sporting weapons.

Munitions of war means any weapon, ammunition or article containing an explosive, noxious liquid or gas, including parts or components for such weapon, ammunition or article. Munitions, weapons of war or sporting weapons must be carried in parts of the aeroplane which cannot be accessed by passengers and any firearms must be unloaded.

Carriage of Dangerous Goods.

Certain articles and substances which pose a significant risk to health, safety or property are classified as Dangerous Goods. Aeroplane operators have to obtain State approval if they intend carrying Dangerous Goods by air. Severe restrictions apply when carrying dangerous goods and it is the operator's responsibility to ensure that all personnel are trained and informed of the necessary procedures.

ICAO Annex 18 and the Technical Instructions contain the standards and recommended practices for the transport of dangerous goods by air.

It is extremely important that all dangerous articles and substances be classified, identified, packed, marked, labelled *(Figure 1.10),* and accompanied with a dangerous goods transport document. The PIC must always be informed if Dangerous Goods are to be carried on his aeroplane. Some articles are allowed to be carried in the cargo compartments of passenger carrying aeroplanes. Others are restricted to cargo aeroplanes only.

Prior to travelling, passengers are to be informed of the restrictions when carrying articles and substances classified as dangerous goods on their person or in any accompanying luggage.

Figure 1.10 Dangerous goods labels.

The following are examples of forbidden items: corrosive chemicals, radioactive material, explosives, liquids having vapour inhalation toxicity, infected live animals, mercury based products and ignition elements for lighters etc. Certain hazardous items may be "hidden" inside other items, e.g. aeroplane spares containing oxygen cylinders or compressed gases, tyre assemblies, paint, adhesives, aerosols, life saving appliances, first aid kits, fuel and wet or lithium batteries. Certain instruments may conceal barometers, manometers, mercury switches or magnetic materials which can affect compasses.

Passenger baggage must not contain such items as fireworks, flammable household liquids, corrosive oven or drain cleaners, flammable gas or liquid lighter refills or camping gas stove cylinders, matches and bleaching powders.

Some examples of goods which may be included in crew or passenger hand luggage, or carried on the person are: non-radioactive medicinal or toilet articles (including aerosols), cardiac pacemakers, medical/clinical thermometer, carbon dioxide, solid carbon dioxide (dry ice), alcoholic beverages, hydrocarbon powered gas curlers and safety matches or a lighter with fuel/fluid fully absorbed in a solid for individual use.

The full list of dangerous goods which are prohibited from carriage in aircraft is too extensive for PPL licence study but it is very important to pay close attention to what you are carrying on your aeroplane and to be aware that dangerous goods could prove to be more dangerous in a light aeroplane than in a commercial jet. Particular attention must be paid to the carriage and use of a number of electronic devices such as games, personal stereos, radios, laptop and computers. Anything which has a transmitting capability, such as a mobile phone or wireless laptop, must be prohibited from usage in an aircraft at any time.

Methods of Carriage of Persons.

No person shall be in or on any part of an aeroplane in flight that is not designed to accommodate people, in particular they shall not be on the wings or undercarriage. The exception to this is that a person may have temporary access to any cargo compartment in flight which is designed for access or to any other area for reasons of safety.

Endangering Safety of Aeroplanes.

No person carried in an aeroplane shall behave recklessly or negligently in a way that is likely to endanger the aeroplane or any other person in it.

Endangering Safety of any Person or Property.

A person shall not recklessly or negligently cause or permit an aeroplane to endanger any person or property. Low flying over buildings or people is an example of a breach of this article.

Drunkenness in Aeroplanes.

A person must not enter an aeroplane when drunk, or be in a state of drunkenness on any aeroplane. A person acting as an aeroplane crew member must not be under the influence of alcohol or drugs such that his capacity to perform their duty is impaired. For pilots and crew members, JAR OPS specifies a maximum blood-alcohol limit of 20 milligrams of alcohol per 100 millilitres of blood (the UK driving limit is 80 milligrams per 100 millilitres).

Smoking in Aeroplanes.

A notice displaying when and where smoking is prohibited shall be exhibited in every aeroplane registered in the UK so as to be visible from each passenger seat. Illuminated "No Smoking" signs must be obeyed at all times and no person shall smoke in any compartment where smoking is prohibited.

Figure 1.11 No Smoking Sign.

Authority of the Commander and Members of Crew of an Aeroplane.

All persons in an aeroplane shall obey any lawful command of the commander for the purpose of securing the safety of the aeroplane, and of those aboard, and for the safety, efficiency or regularity of air navigation.

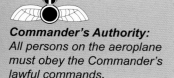

Commander's Authority:
All persons on the aeroplane must obey the Commander's lawful commands.

Acting in a Disruptive Manner.

No person in an aeroplane shall:

- Use any threatening, abusive or insulting words towards a member of the crew of the aeroplane.

- Behave in a threatening, abusive, insulting or disorderly manner towards a member of the crew of the aeroplane.

- Intentionally interfere with the performance of crew duties.

This regulation may not seem relevant to the type of flying undertaken by the holder of a PPL but disruptive behaviour remains a possibility. Therefore awareness and vigilance should always be exercised.

Stowaways.
An operator of any aeroplane shall take all necessary precautions to prevent a person from stowing away on the aeroplane.

Flying Displays.
The Civil Aviation Authority (CAA) must be consulted and their written permission given before any person organises a flying display. Any pilot who participates in a flying display must hold a display authorisation and ensure that the necessary permission has been granted for the display. The pilot must comply with any conditions subject to which the authorisation was given.

Flying Displays:

The CAA must be consulted.

Pilot requires authorisation/ permission.

AEROPLANE PERFORMANCE AND OPERATING LIMITATIONS.

During flight, the PIC must ensure that the aeroplane is operated in compliance with the terms of its Airworthiness Certificate or within any operating limitations imposed by the certificating authority of the State of Registry.

Prior to flight, the PIC must be satisfied that the aeroplane is loaded correctly and that the mass is within the constraints of the performance envelope contained within the mass and balance schedule *(see Figure 1.12)*.

Pilot - in - Command Checks:

Prior to departure, the aeroplane must not exceed any structural limitations or constraints given within the performance envelope.

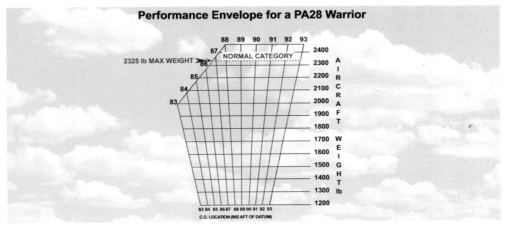

Figure 1.12 C of G envelope for a typical light aeroplane.

The PIC is responsible that the mass of the aeroplane, calculated prior to start-up, does not exceed any structural limitations or performance limitations for the aeroplane. In making the calculations, the following factors must be taken into account:

- The mass (weight).

- The Centre of Gravity (C of G) must be within the operating limits of the aircraft.

- The elevation of the aerodrome.

- The temperature.

- The wind direction and velocity.

- The gradient of the runway.

- The runway length at departure and destination aerodromes.

- The condition of the runway. (Presence of slush, water or ice).

Where there is an aircraft operating limitation to be complied with, this limitation must be displayed to the pilot in the cockpit in the form of a placard or a list, or included in the instrument display. It is vitally important that no limitation should be exceeded.

If appropriate, noise abatement regulations must be considered prior to departure so this may be properly included in aircraft performance planning.

NOISE ABATEMENT.

General Principles.
All aircraft except certain classes of exempted aircraft e.g. certain STOL aircraft, require a noise certificate to certify that they comply with applicable standards in relation to noise pollution.

Noise generated by aeroplanes of any size, power or mass has the potential to seriously affect the environment. It is, therefore, necessary for pilots of any licence category to be aware of this factor and to keep the noise nuisance to a minimum while ensuring safe flight operations. There are numerous noise sensitive areas containing such institutions as hospitals, schools, nursing homes and private residences etc. which should be avoided where possible. Large and frequent changes of engine power contribute to significant noise levels distributed over long distances. An aerodrome with numerous traffic movements, including circuit training flights will constitute a significant noise nuisance to the surrounding area. Training flights involving manoeuvres such as stalling and aerobatics will require frequent changes of engine power, thus increasing intrusive noise levels.

There are strict recommendations and procedures for commercial jet transport designed to address the reduction of noise levels at aerodromes and in surrounding areas.

Light aircraft must observe the low flying rules and should keep training circuits within the required boundaries. Training flights may be restricted to certain hours during which aircraft noise would have least impact. Take-off and landing procedures may also be adapted to reduce noise pollution. *Figure 1.13* shows an example of noise abatement procedures for circuit flying at an airfield.

NOT FOR FLIGHT PLANNING USE

CHICHESTER (Goodwood)
Noise Abatement and Circuits

2006

Rwys 10/28 and 14/32

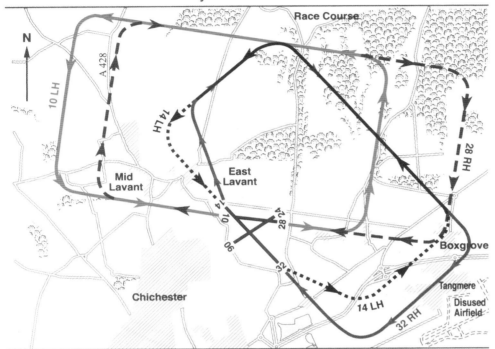

Rwy 06/24

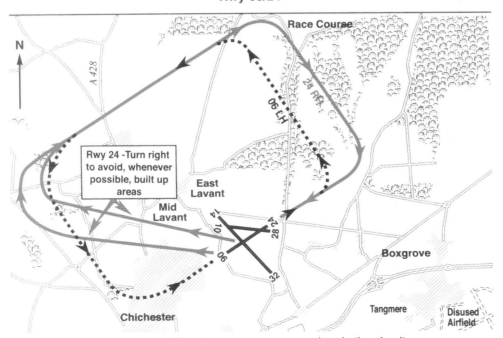

Figure 1.13 VFR noise abatement procedure in the circuit.

Take-off, Approach and Landing.

Aeroplane operators are required to establish noise abatement procedures for take-off, landing, departure and arrival routes. The PIC must be aware of such routings and apply them in order to avoid any noise violations.

An aerodrome operator will establish and publish noise abatement procedures applicable to the environmental factors at that location. The procedures may comprise one or more of the following measures:

- Use of noise preferential runways to direct the initial and final approach paths away from any noise sensitive areas.

- Use of noise preferential routes to assist aeroplanes in avoiding noise sensitive areas on departure and arrival.

- Use of procedures for take-off and approach to minimise the exposure of noise sensitive areas to noise, while at the same time, maintaining the required level of flight safety. The State in which aerodrome operations take place must approve any noise abatement procedures developed by the operator.

In the United Kingdom, if noise abatement procedures are in force at an aerodrome, details of the procedures will be published in the UK AIP (Air Pilot), and in commercially produced flight guides such as those published by Pooleys and A.F.E. Pilots should ensure that they use these publications (only the AIP is authoritative) to brief themselves on the noise abatement procedures in force at airfields they are planning to visit.

Pilots must be aware that the PIC has at all times the authority to decide not to execute a noise abatement procedure if to do so would endanger his aircraft or persons or property on the ground.

Pilots should especially bear in mind that on specific routes for the take-off and climb, they should not be required to execute turns until the aircraft has reached 500 feet above terrain, or above the highest obstacle under the flight path.

On noise-preferential routes, when a turn is executed, pilots should limit bank angles to 15° except where adequate provision is made for an acceleration phase, permitting the aircraft to attain a flying speed at which it is safe to select a bank angle greater than 15°.

MAINTENANCE.

Responsibilities.

The Certificate of Airworthiness (C of A) must be valid and current before an aircraft can to operated.

It is the responsibility of the owner or, if the aircraft is leased, the operator, to ensure that the aeroplane is maintained in an airworthy condition in accordance with a system acceptable to the Authority of the State in which the aircraft is registered. All operational and emergency equipment necessary for any intended flight must be serviceable and all maintenance must be carried out in accordance with a maintenance programme accepted by the authority.

The aeroplane cannot be operated unless it has a valid and current Certificate of Airworthiness, and is maintained and released to service in accordance with a maintenance system acceptable to the responsible Authority (See Figure 1.14).

Maintenance Records.

It is vitally important that records of all maintenance carried out on an aircraft should be recorded and documented as recommended by ICAO. The relevant documentation includes records of the total service hours of the aeroplane and all life-limited components and details of all modifications and repairs made to the aircraft.

The current status of compliance with the maintenance programme and all mandatory matters affecting the airworthiness must be shown.

Aeroplane component parts must have their total hours in service recorded, as well as the date of last inspection and frequency of inspection cycles.

Any modifications and repairs must be acceptable to the State of Registry and must be recorded.

Figure 1.14 Certificate of Airworthiness.

Maintenance Release.

Before a flight can commence, maintenance documentation release must be completed and signed certifying that any required maintenance work has been completed satisfactorily. Maintenance release documentation should include:

- The basic details of the work carried out.

- The date the work was completed.
- The identity of the approved organisation carrying out the work.

- The identity of the person signing the maintenance release.

CONTRAVENTION OF AVIATION REGULATIONS.

The CAA document CAP 393 - the Air Navigation Order (ANO) contains offences and penalties concerning Aviation Law applicable in the United Kingdom. Contravention of a requirement in the ANO is a criminal offence subject to prosecution.

Many offences are related to documentation. Examples of such offences are:

- Use of any certificate, licence, approval or other documents required or issued by the authority which has been forged, altered, revoked or suspended or to which a person is not entitled.

- Lending or allowing any certificate, licence, approval or other document required by the ANO to be used by any unauthorised person.

- Making any false representation for the purpose of obtaining the grant, issue, renewal or variation of any certificate, licence, approval or other document required by the CAA.

This latter offence particularly applies to destroying, causing damage to, or altering log books and records during the period that they are required to be preserved.

There are many other penalties referred to in the ANO Schedules e.g. failure to keep log books, flight in unfit condition, requirement for the pilot to remain at the controls of an aircraft, requirement for passenger briefing, carriage of persons in or on any part of an aeroplane not registered for that purpose, breach of

Figure 1.15 Serious breaches of aviation regulations may result in licence revocation.

Rules of the Air, requirement to comply with an air traffic direction etc.

In the UK, an aeroplane shall not fly unless it carries certain documents required by the ANO. Specific documents must be produced by an aeroplane commander within a reasonable time, if requested by an authorised person. The documents include:

- The Certificate of Registration and Airworthiness.

- The Flight Crew licences.

- Any other documents required by the ANO.

Under the ANO pilots are required to keep a personal flying log book and may be required to produce it within a reasonable time to an authorised person within 2 years of the last entry in the log book.

These regulations and offences may seem a bit daunting. Bear in mind however, that the CAA is not looking to prosecute pilots unnecessarily but to protect against neglect and recklessness by those who fly in, or are associated with, aeroplanes.

OFFENCES.

The ANO, in Article 241 and Schedule 13, lists the offences (over 100) which can be committed for breaches of the Order.

There are three levels of seriousness, reflected by the gravity of the sentence. For example, if a pilot fails to keep accurate logbooks under Article 22 of the ANO, he is guilty of an offence which has a maximum penalty of a £2500 fine. Flying without a current licence can attract imprisonment of up to 2 years. Endangering an aircraft carries a penalty of up to 5 years imprisonment. Conviction of any of these offences could lead to the loss of one's licence.

CHAPTER 2
AEROPLANE INSTRUMENTS
AND EQUIPMENT

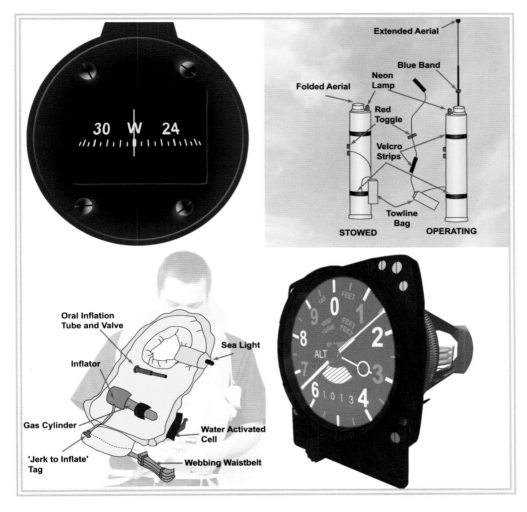

AEROPLANE INSTRUMENTS AND EQUIPMENT.

This chapter contains details of the minimum instrumentation with which an aircraft should be fitted, and the minimum equipment to be carried in the aircraft. In general, the instruments and equipment fit dealt with in this chapter is the minimum required for the issue of a Certificate of Airworthiness (C of A). The official regulations for the issue of a C of A must be consulted, and complied with at all times.

We should remind ourselves that the minimum equipment fit is the ICAO recommended minimum, and that, ultimately, the operator must comply with instrument and equipment regulations approved and accepted by the State of Registry.

INSTRUMENTS.

An aeroplane's instrument fit must enable the flight crew to operate the aeroplane within the constraints of the operating limitations, in the expected operating conditions.

EQUIPMENT.

It is recommended that all aeroplanes on all flights shall be equipped with the following equipment, charts and documents:

•	An accessible first aid kit.

•	A portable non-air-contaminating fire extinguisher, one to be located in the pilot's compartment, and one in any passenger compartment that is separated and not readily accessible to the pilots.

•	A seat for each person over an age to be determined by the State of Registry.

•	A seat belt or harness for each seat and a child-restraint device for every child under the age of 2 years.

•	Survival equipment appropriate for the flight to be undertaken.

•	A Flight Manual and/or such other documents required by the certificating authority concerning operating limitations.

•	Current and suitable charts must be carried for each flight, including charts relevant to any possible diversion.

•	Interception procedures.

•	Visual signals for use by intercepting/intercepted aeroplanes.

•	Spare electrical fuses of the appropriate rating for replacing fuses accessible in flight.

Note: It is recommended by ICAO that all aeroplanes should be equipped with ground-air signal codes for search and rescue purposes.

EMERGENCY BREAK-IN MARKING.

Whilst it is unlikely that aeroplanes flown by PPL holders will require break-in areas, it is a requirement that the holder has knowledge of this provision. ICAO states that, if, following an accident or incident, normal access into the interior of the aeroplane is prevented, an area must be identified through which access can be gained. This area is to be identified as an externally marked break in area, on the fuselage with rectangular lines coloured red or yellow and with a white outline. If the corners of the rectangle are more than 2m apart, intermediate lines of 9cm x 3cm shall be inserted, coloured red or yellow with a white outline.

VFR FLIGHTS.

All aeroplanes on flights in accordance with Visual Flight Rules (VFR) shall be equipped with:

• A magnetic compass.

• An accurate timepiece showing the time in hours, minutes and seconds.

• A sensitive pressure altimeter.

• An airspeed indicator (ASI).

• Any additional instrumentation which may be prescribed by the State of Registry.

IFR FLIGHTS.

If the intention is to operate in accordance with the Instrument Flight Rules (IFR), or in Instrument Meteorological Conditions (IMC) the aeroplane shall be equipped with:

• A magnetic compass.

• An accurate timepiece, indicating time in hours, minutes and seconds.

• A sensitive pressure altimeter (not drum pointer type).

• An airspeed indicating system with anti-icing facility.

• A turn and slip indicator.

• A heading indicator (Directional Gyroscope).

• A power failure indicating system for Gyro instruments.

• An outside air temperature indicator.

• A rate of climb and descent indicator (RCDI/VSI).

- Any additional instruments or equipment which may be prescribed by the appropriate authority.

FLIGHTS OVER WATER.

Lifejackets.
If a single engine aeroplane is operated over water beyond gliding distance from the shore, it should be equipped with a lifejacket for each person on board. A lifejacket should be stowed in a position which is easily accessible from the seat of the person who will use it.

EXTENDED FLIGHTS OVER WATER.

Lifejackets.
All aeroplanes operated over water at a distance of more than 93 km (50 nm) away from land shall be equipped with a lifejacket for each person on board stowed in a position easily accessible from their occupied position.

Liferafts.
Life saving rafts able to carry all persons on board must be carried when a single engine aeroplane is intended to be operated more than 185 km (100 nm) from land, or a multi-engined aeroplane is more than 370 km (200 nm) from land. The rafts must be equipped with pyrotechnic distress signals and survival equipment.

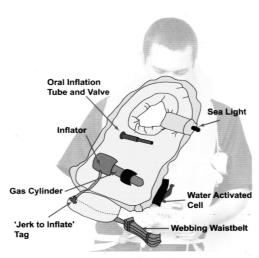

Figure 2.1 Life Jacket.

DIFFICULT SEARCH AND RESCUE AREAS.

Where a state has designated a land area as one in which search and rescue would be especially difficult, an aeroplane shall be equipped with such signalling devices and life saving equipment appropriate to the area overflown, e.g. polar and desert areas.

HIGH ALTITUDE FLIGHTS.

All aeroplanes intended to be operated at altitudes exceeding 10 000 feet shall be equipped with appropriate oxygen equipment to satisfy the requirements outlined in JAR-OPS 1.770.

If an aeroplane is a pressurised aeroplane, operated at flight altitudes higher than 25 000 feet, it should be equipped with a warning device to indicate to the flight crew any dangerous loss of pressurisation.

NIGHT OPERATION.

When an aeroplane is operated at night it shall be equipped with all of the equipment detailed for flight in IFR (above) plus a landing light, illumination for all essential flight instruments and equipment, lights in the passenger compartment and an electric torch at each crew member's station.

EMERGENCY LOCATOR TRANSMITTER.

It is recommended that all aeroplanes should carry an automatic Emergency Locator Transmitter *(see Figure 2.2)*, if the aircraft is to be operated on extended flights over water and when operated on flights over certain designated land areas.

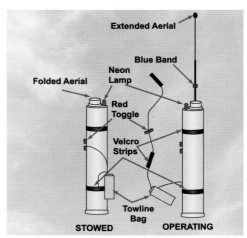

Figure 2.2 Example of an Emergency Locator Transmitter.

UK DIFFERENCES AS DESCRIBED IN THE AIR NAVIGATION ORDER (ANO).

The Air Navigation Order (ANO) (Schedules 4 and 5) contains details of minimum equipment fit in respect of aeroplanes registered in the UK which vary according to aircraft mass, type of operations and C of A category.

For PPL holders, requirements for unpressurised aeroplanes are the most relevant. As an example, when flying below flight level 100 - there is no requirement for pilots of light aircraft to be supplied with supplementary Oxygen, but when flying above FL 100 but not exceeding FL 120 there must be a supply of Oxygen for all members of the flight crew for any period.

The UK ANO also stipulates that aeroplanes flying for purposes other than public transport are to carry a number of spare fuses for all electrical circuits. The requirement is for 10% of the number of fuses of each rating or three of each rating, whichever is the greater.

Maps, charts, codes and any other documents and navigation equipment required for a sortie, including any diversions, must be carried in the aircraft.

Before any flight, it is the PIC's responsibility to ensure that the aircraft is properly equipped for the planned flight. If there is any doubt, the PIC should consult the minimum equipment list.

On any flight, the minimum safety equipment that must be carried is: a first-aid kit, a fire extinguisher, and spare electrical fuses.

CHAPTER 3
WINDSHEAR

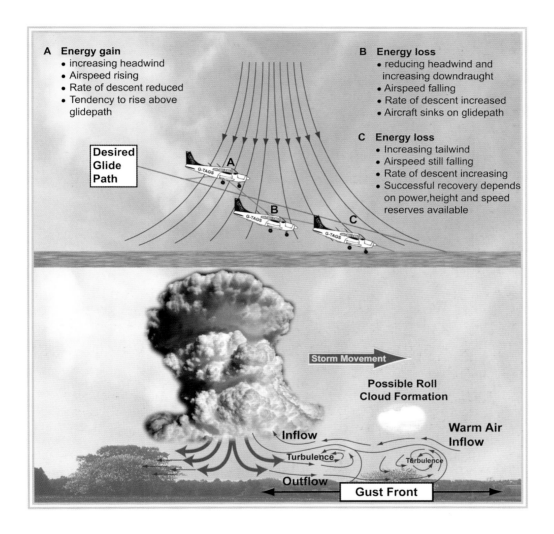

A Energy gain
- increasing headwind
- Airspeed rising
- Rate of descent reduced
- Tendency to rise above glidepath

B Energy loss
- reducing headwind and increasing downdraught
- Airspeed falling
- Rate of descent increased
- Aircraft sinks on glidepath

C Energy loss
- Increasing tailwind
- Airspeed still falling
- Rate of descent increasing
- Successful recovery depends on power, height and speed reserves available

Desired Glide Path

Storm Movement

Possible Roll Cloud Formation

Inflow

Warm Air Inflow

Turbulence

Turbulence

Outflow

Gust Front

WINDSHEAR.

Low altitude windshear is a major hazard to light aircraft. The effects of windshear in the take-off, approach and landing phases of flight have been responsible for numerous accidents to light aircraft.

The aim of this chapter is that the pilot should learn the definitions of windshear, where and when to expect windshear, and what actions should be taken to avoid or counter windshear.

DEFINITIONS.

Windshear may be defined as variations in wind speed and/or direction along an aircraft's flight path which may displace an aircraft abruptly from its flight path and which may require substantial control inputs to counter it.

Low Altitude Windshear is defined as windshear on the final approach path or along the runway, and on the take-off and initial climb-out flight paths.

Windshear is defined as a change in wind speed and/or direction over a relatively short distance.

| Figure 3.1 Vertical Windshear. | Figure 3.2 Horizontal Windshear. |

Vertical Windshear is defined as a change of wind speed and/or direction with height. *(See Figure 3.1.)*

Horizontal Windshear is a change of wind speed and/or direction over a horizontal distance. *(See Figure 3.2.)*

THE EFFECTS OF WINDSHEAR.

The effect of an aircraft flying into windshear is basically that the aircraft's indicated airspeed will either decrease or increase momentarily. Because the lift generated by an aircraft's wings is heavily dependent on its airspeed, the effect of windshear is also to increase or decrease lift sharply.

Whenever an aircraft flies into or through windshear, its airspeed will be affected. This is especially hazardous on take-off and landing.

An aircraft in flight, because it possesses mass and is flying at a given speed, will also possess a certain amount of momentum by virtue of its mass and speed. (momentum = mass × velocity). Because of the associated property of inertia, an aircraft flying at a given velocity will, therefore, tend to continue flying at that velocity, even when a force intervenes to change its velocity. In other words, it will always take a finite amount of time for an aircraft to change speed.

So, if an aircraft is approaching to land at an indicated airspeed of 75 knots against a 30 knot headwind, its speed over the ground will be 45 knots. But, if vertical windshear is present on the approach, and the windspeed suddenly drops to 10 knots *(see Figure 3.3)*, the aircraft will be descending through decelerating air, and the aircraft's momentum will cause it to continue, momentarily, to travel at 45 knots relative to the ground. Consequently, for a very short period of time, the aircraft's airspeed will fall to 55 knots. More importantly, however, the lift generated by the aircraft's wings will suddenly decrease, too, and the aircraft will sink below the pilot's desired approach path. (Remember that the lift force acting on the aircraft varies with the <u>square</u> of the True Airspeed (V): **Lift = ½rC$_L$V²S**) If there is sufficient loss of airspeed through loss of headwind, the aircraft may even stall. If the pilot is unprepared for such situations, height loss can be significant.

If the aircraft is close to the ground, a heavy landing or undershoot, or both, can occur. In extreme cases, such a situation may lead to a serious impact with the ground.

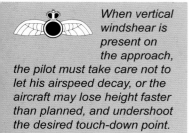

When vertical windshear is present on the approach, the pilot must take care not to let his airspeed decay, or the aircraft may lose height faster than planned, and undershoot the desired touch-down point.

APPROACH ATTITUDE

Height	300 ft
Indicated Air Speed	75 kt
Ground Speed	45 kt

30 kt

PLANNED APPROACH PATH

SHEAR LINE

10 kt

AIRCRAFT DROPS BELOW APPROACH PATH

Height	100 ft
Indicated Air Speed	55 kt
Ground Speed	45 kt

Figure 3.3 Vertical windshear on the approach and its possible effect on an aircraft approaching to land.

The pilot must, therefore, always be aware of weather and wind conditions which may give rise to windshear. He must also know the symptoms of windshear, and how to react to the effects of windshear if he has been unsuccessful in avoiding it.

The main problem facing a pilot whose aircraft encounters low-level windshear is the very fact that he may be low with little height in which to recover, if things go badly wrong. And, of course, the average light aircraft does not have a lot of power to counter the effects of windshear. Consequently, it is of supreme importance that airspeed be constantly monitored, and not allowed to decay.

Let us now look at some of the causes of windshear:-

CAUSES OF WINDSHEAR.

Thunderstorms.

Cumulonimbus thunderclouds can create conditions which will produce windshear, because of severe turbulence and precipitation associated with such clouds.

The Gust Front.

Some cumulonimbus thunder clouds have a well-defined area of cold air flowing out from downdraughts, which are called gust fronts, and which extend up to 15 nautical miles ahead of an approaching storm. These gust fronts are regions of great turbulence which give little or no warning of their approach. *(See Figure 3.4.)*

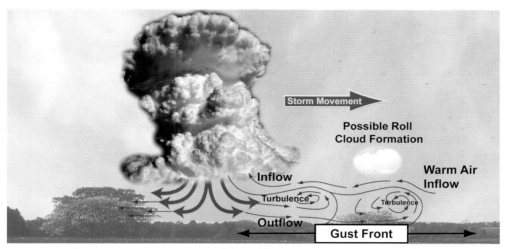

Figure 3.4 A gust front associated with a cumulonimbus thundercloud.

Microburst.

A microburst is a highly concentrated and powerful downdraught of air, typically less than 2 nautical miles across, which lasts for about 1 to 5 minutes. Microbursts are the most lethal form of windshear with downdraught speeds of 60 knots or more. There have been a number of fatal accidents to large commercial aircraft caused by microbursts on the final approach.

Figure 3.5 depicts how a light aircraft on approach to land, caught in the windshear from a microburst, may be forced below the planned glide-path, because of the effects of windshear on airspeed and rate of descent.

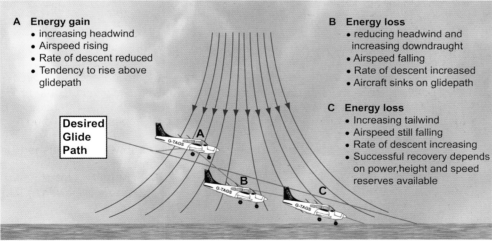

If a pilot is caught unawares by severe windshear on the approach, an unplanned impact with the ground may result.

Figure 3.5 Windshear on the approach caused by a microburst.

Frontal Passage.

Fronts vary in strength. It is normally only well-developed, active fronts, with narrow frontal zones and marked temperature differences, which are likely to carry the risk of windshear.

On a weather chart, a pilot should look for fronts with sharp changes in wind direction across the front. The pilot should also note that temperature differences of 5°C or more across a front, or a front moving with a speed of 30 knots or more, may indicate a potential windshear hazard.

Inversion.

A low-level temperature inversion may develop and separate the stronger upper air-flow from slower moving air near the surface, giving rise to windshear at the inversion boundary. These inversions tend to form on clear nights.

Low-Level Turbulence.

Low-level turbulence within the friction layer can lead to windshear because of:

- Strong surface winds leading to pronounced gusts and lulls.

- Thermal turbulence caused by intense solar heating.

Topographical Windshear.

Topographical windshear is of two principal types. It may be caused by friction between the lower wind and the ground, leading to a marked decrease in wind speed as the surface is approached through the lower 1 000 feet, or so. *(See Figure 3.3.)* Topographical windshear is also caused by natural or man-made features, such as hills or buildings, which change the direction and speed of the wind blowing over them; under certain conditions, 'rotor streaming' (vortices) may occur downwind of ridges or large hills, sometimes visible as roll cloud. Larger airport buildings adjacent to runways, as well as lines of trees, can create local windshear during both the final approach and initial departure.

TECHNIQUES TO COUNTERACT EFFECTS OF WINDSHEAR.

For the pilot of a light aircraft, the best way to deal with windshear is to use his knowledge and understanding of the subject to avoid severe windshear altogether, if at all possible, and consider diverting to an alternate aerodrome. However, should a pilot encounter windshear, the following actions may be considered. *(N.B. This is not a flying instructional manual, and you must, above all, deal with windshear in the manner recommended by your flying instructor.)*

- Increase power (to full power, if needed).

- Maintain or increase airspeed appropriately (attitude control).

- Co-ordinate pitch and power correctly.

- Be prepared to carry out a go-around or missed approach.

- If the pilot is on the ground, he should stay there until the windshear has abated.

In order to counteract windshear effect, be prepared to make pronounced control inputs.

If you wish to learn more about low-level windshear, the United Kingdom CAA currently produces an **Aviation Information Circular** on the subject, **AIC Number 19/2002 (pink 28)**.

CHAPTER 4
CONTROLLED FLIGHT
INTO TERRAIN

Image used by kind permission of Jedrzej Wiler

DEFINITION.

The expression "Controlled Flight Into Terrain" (CFIT) describes a situation in which an airworthy aircraft, under the control of the pilot, is inadvertently flown into terrain, water or obstacles with the pilot, at all times, being unaware of the approaching disaster. CFIT can theoretically occur during most phases of flight, but is more common during the approach and landing phase.

From the previous definition, you will see that CFIT is a category of aircraft accident which would mainly involve a pilot flying on instruments in Instrument Meteorological Conditions (IMC), when there are no external visual references. However, a VFR pilot who becomes disorientated in low visibility Visual Meteorological Conditions (VMC), or who inadvertently flies into IMC, will also run the risk of a CFIT accident; therefore we have judged that the inclusion on CFIT is relevant for the private VFR pilot.

CONTRIBUTORY ERRORS.

There are three main errors which contribute to CFIT accidents gathered from statistical data, they are:-

CFIT Linked Errors	
Decision Errors	**Cause 50% of accidents**
Skill Based Errors	**Cause 30% of accidents**
Errors of Perception	**Cause 20% of accidents**

DECISION ERRORS.

Decision errors occur because of poor decision making or lack of appropriate knowledge. Decision errors fall into four main sub-categories:

• Improper flight planning.

• Improper altitude or clearance.

• Weather evaluation inadequate.

• Improper remedial action.

SKILL BASED ERRORS.

Skill based errors can occur because of lapses in basic flying skills, such as:

• Lack of instrument flying training or practice.

• Not complying with clearance.

• Not maintaining airspeed.

- Not keeping a good lookout.

- Not maintaining the correct glidepath.

- Poor emergency procedures.

- Not maintaining altitude or correct separation.

ERRORS OF PERCEPTION.

Errors of perception occur if sensory input is degraded. Examples of errors of perception are:

- Spatial disorientation/vertigo.

- Misjudged altitude.

- Misjudged manoeuvre or procedure.

- Visual illusion.

- Misjudged distance or descent.

EXAMPLES OF CONTRIBUTORY ERRORS TO CFIT.

To highlight some of the errors which contribute to CFIT, the following summaries are offered for your consideration.

- A pilot encounters weather conditions that are worse than forecast and, in an attempt to maintain or regain visual contact with the ground, in an area of low cloud and dense fog, descends, and the aircraft strikes the ground.

- A pilot loses situational awareness while flying over snow-covered terrain under a low overcast ceiling and flies into the ground because of the lack of external visual references.

- A pilot flying in marginal weather conditions with poor external visual references is over-reliant on his GPS, and, despite the weather, continues to follow the GPS routing. While attempting to remain VMC, he strikes the ground.

CFIT AVOIDANCE.

The means used to avoid CFIT can be grouped into two main categories: aircraft equipment and education/training. Investigations of CFIT accidents indicated that many of them would have been avoided if some form of terrain warning system or improved navigation systems had been available.

EQUIPMENT - THE GROUND PROXIMITY WARNING SYSTEM.

The Ground Proximity Warning System (GPWS) is designed to warn a pilot if there is a danger that his aircraft may fly into the ground.

The GPWS monitors an aircraft's height above the ground based on information from a radio altimeter. The GPWS computer constantly interprets this information, calculates trends, and will if the aircraft arrives in a dangerous position, or if its rate of descent is excessive, the GPWS will issue visual and audio warnings.

The various situations in to which the GPWS will respond, with typical warning messages, are:

- Excessive descent rate ("PULL UP", "SINKRATE").

- Excessive terrain closure rate ("TERRAIN", "PULL UP").

- Altitude loss after take-off ("DON'T SINK").

- Unsafe terrain clearance ("TOO LOW - TERRAIN", "TOO LOW - GEAR", "TOO LOW - FLAPS").

- Excessive deviation below the glideslope ("GLIDESLOPE").

The basic GPWS does have limitations, though. Being based on readings from a radio altimeter, the system can gather data only from directly below the aircraft. Distant terrain features can not be recognised. Therefore if the nature of terrain changes abruptly, for instance if terrain elevation were to increase suddenly, basic GPWS may not detect aircraft closure rate until it is too late for the pilot to take evasive action.

A new GPWS system known as Enhanced GPWS (EGPWS) is able to overcome the limitations of basic GPWS by combining a digital terrain database with a Global Positioning Navigation System, Inertial Navigation System, or the like. Computers can then compare the aircraft's present position with the terrain database. With the EPGWS pilots receive early warnings of ground proximity hazards.

TRAINING.

Training is a very important factor in raising awareness of the dangers of CFIT. A constant reminder of where we are and the hazards surrounding us must remain high on the list of priorities. Private Pilots, like professional pilots, should be permanently aware of the importance of knowing where they are, where the track that they are following will lead them, and what hazards threaten them.

How can we best help ourselves? Before setting out on any flight, pilots should:

- Prepare thoroughly.

- Assess the weather accurately, en-route, and at the destination and alternate aerodromes.

- Know their minimum safe altitudes (MSA's) and adhere to them.

- Know and remain within their own limitations of qualifications and skill.

- Allow for contingencies.

- Ensure that they have enough fuel for the sortie, including all contingency fuel.

- Be prepared to divert if there is any doubt about their being able to land safely at the destination aerodrome.

- Not take risks.

- Use their judgement responsibly.

CFIT accidents can be prevented. The key to prevention is situational awareness.

KNOW WHERE YOU ARE AT ALL TIMES.

CHAPTER 5
SEARCH AND RESCUE

SEARCH AND RESCUE.

Organisation.
Under ICAO recommended practices, it is a requirement that a contracting state should provide and establish search and rescue services within their own territory on a 24 hour basis. The territorial boundaries should, where possible, coincide with the corresponding Flight Information Regions (FIR). There will be some areas which are not so easily defined, in which case the rescue services will be determined on the basis of any regional air navigation requirements. Where assistance is provided it must be provided to all aircraft and survivors of any accident regardless of the state of origin of the aircraft.

A state-established search and rescue region will provide a Rescue Coordination Centre, whose responsibility is to coordinate any rescue effort in that region.

DEFINITIONS.

The following definitions are used in search and rescue operations:

Alerting Post.
A unit designated to receive information from the general public regarding aeroplanes in distress or urgency, and to forward the information to the associated Rescue Coordination Centre.

Uncertainty Phase.
A situation wherein uncertainty exists as to the safety of an aeroplane and its occupants.

Alert Phase.
A situation wherein apprehension exists as to the safety of an aeroplane and its occupants.

Distress Phase.
A situation wherein there is a reasonable certainty that an aeroplane and its occupants are threatened by grave and/or imminent danger or require medical assistance.

Ditching.
The forced landing of an aeroplane on water.

Emergency Phase.
A generic term referring to the uncertainty phase, alert phase or distress phase.

Rescue Coordination Centre.
A unit responsible for promoting the efficient organisation of search and rescue services and for coordinating the conduct of search and rescue operations within a search and rescue region.

Search and Rescue Region.
An area of defined dimensions within which search and rescue services are provided.

The Uncertainty Phase is a situation wherein uncertainty exists as to the safety of an aeroplane and its occupants.

The Alert Phase is a situation wherein apprehension exists as to the safety of an aeroplane and its occupants.

The Distress Phase is a situation wherein there is a reasonable certainty that an aeroplane and its occupants are threatened by grave and imminent danger or require medical assistance.

Ditching is the term used for the forced landing of an aircraft on water.

ALERTING PHASES.

Alert Phases:

• *Uncertainty.*

• *Alert.*

• *Distress.*

There are three phases of alert used where there is concern for the safety of an aeroplane and its occupants. They are known as Uncertainty, Alert and Distress phase.

One or more of the Alerting Phases may be declared when there is reason for concern about the safety of an aircraft or of its occupants. PICs should, however, always be aware that an Alerting Phase may be declared unnecessarily if pilots omit to close a flight plan on arrival at their destination, to inform Air Traffic Control that they have diverted from their flight plans, or even failed to report a change of radio frequency. The main factors of the three alerting phases are summarised here.

UNCERTAINTY PHASE.

An uncertainty phase can be declared when

• No communication has been received from an aeroplane within a period of thirty minutes after the time a communication should have been received, or thirty minutes from the time an unsuccessful attempt to establish communications with the aeroplane was first made, which ever is the earlier,

or when

• An aeroplane fails to arrive within thirty minutes of the estimated time of arrival last notified to, or estimated by ATCU's, whichever is the later.

ALERT PHASE.

An Alerting Service is provided for all aircraft being given an air traffic control service and, in so far as is practicable, to all other aircraft having filed a flight plan, and to any aircraft known to be the subject of unlawful interference.

When an Alert Phase is declared, responsibility for alerting the necessary Search and Rescue Units lies with the Rescue Coordination Centre.

An alert phase is declared when:

• Following the uncertainty phase, subsequent attempts to establish communication with the aeroplane or inquiries of other relevant sources have failed to reveal any news of the aeroplane,

or when

• An aeroplane has been cleared to land and fails to land within five minutes of the estimated time of landing and communications have not been established with the aeroplane,

or when

• Information has been received which indicates that the operating efficiency of the aeroplane has been impaired, but not to the extent that a forced landing is likely,

or

• An aeroplane is known or believed to be the subject of unlawful interference.

DISTRESS PHASE.

The distress phase is declared when:

- following the alert phase, further unsuccessful attempts to establish communication with the aeroplane and more widespread unsuccessful inquiries point to the probability that the aeroplane is in distress,

  or when

- the fuel on board is considered to be exhausted, or to be insufficient to enable the aeroplane to reach safely,

  or when

- information is received which indicates that the operating efficiency of the aeroplane has been impaired to the extent that a forced landing is likely,

  or when

- information is received or it is reasonably certain that the aeroplane is about to make or has made a forced landing.

Operating Procedures.

When an aeroplane is believed to be in distress, or when an alert phase exists, the Rescue Coordination Centre (RCC) shall initiate a predetermined action plan. This will involve trying to locate the aeroplane, conveying and reporting developments of operations to the operator, notifying associated air traffic services and adjacent RCC's, and notifying the State of Registry and accident investigation authorities. Additionally, the RCC will inform any nearby aeroplanes or vessels of the situation and request them to listen out on the emergency frequency and to assist where possible. When the first aeroplane to reach the scene is not a Search and Rescue aeroplane the PIC will take charge of any on-scene activity until such time as a Search and Rescue Unit arrives.

Whilst pilots of civil aeroplanes are not generally involved in Search and Rescue operations, it is a requirement that the procedures by which help and assistance may be given to an aircraft in distress should be understood by all parties.

Pilot-In-Command Procedures when Observing a Case of Distress.

The actions to be taken by professional pilots when observing a distress incident or interpreting a distress message are complex. The actions mentioned here are those the authors think appropriate for a private pilot to take. These actions have been adopted from SAR operational procedures documentation. For the full text, see JAR-OPS Annex 12, Chapter 5. Also see Document 7333 Search and Rescue.

When the PIC of an aeroplane observes that another vehicle, vessel or aircraft is in distress he should keep it in sight as long as it is practicable and safe to do so. Where possible the PIC should report details to the RCC or the ATSU with which he is in contact, and then act as instructed by them. The important details to report are the type of craft in distress, its identification, condition, geographical position and the time of observation. The PIC should also report on any observed survivors who have abandoned the craft including, if possible, their physical condition.

If the PIC of an aeroplane intercepts a distress signal and/or message he should record the position of the craft in distress and if possible take a bearing on the transmission.

Procedures for PIC Intercepting a Distress Transmission.

If a PIC of an aeroplane intercepts a distress signal and/or message he should record the position of the craft in distress and if possible take a bearing on the transmission.

All available information should be given to the appropriate RCC or ATSU with which the PIC is in contact and whilst awaiting instructions the PIC should, at his discretion, proceed to the position of the craft in distress.

GROUND - AIR VISUAL SIGNAL CODE.

In order to assist aeroplanes in Search and Rescue operations a knowledge of the Search and Rescue symbols and their meaning is required. The following Ground-Air signals for use by survivors and Ground-Air signals for use by rescue units can be constructed by any means disposable, e.g. strips of fabric, parachute material, pieces of wood, stones or by marking the surface by tramping or staining with oil. If the surface is snow, it can be trampled or marked by shovelling or dragging. Symbols constructed should be 2.5 meters (8 feet) long and be as conspicuous as possible. These symbols are shown in *Figures 5.1a* and *Figure 5.1b*.

Ground - air visual signal code for use by survivors
V — **Require Assistance**
X — **Require Medical Assistance**
N — **No or Negative**
Y — **Yes or Affirmative**
↑ — **Proceeding in this direction**

Figure 5.1a Distress signals - ground to air for use by survivors.

AIR-TO-GROUND SIGNALS.

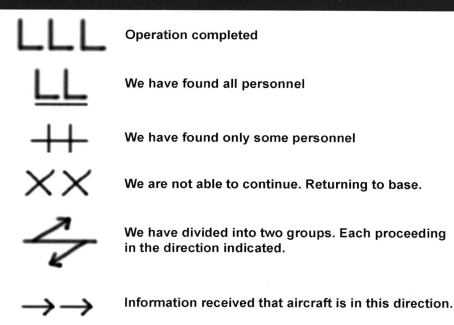

LLL	**Operation completed**
LL	**We have found all personnel**
++	**We have found only some personnel**
XX	**We are not able to continue. Returning to base.**
(arrows)	**We have divided into two groups. Each proceeding in the direction indicated.**
→ →	**Information received that aircraft is in this direction.**
NN	**Nothing found. Will continue search.**

Ground - air visual signal code for use by rescue teams

Figure 5.1b Distress signals - ground to air for use by rescue teams.

To convey that any ground signals have been understood the following signals are used by aeroplanes:

- During the hours of daylight by rocking the aeroplane's wings

- During the hours of darkness by flashing on and off, twice, the aeroplane's landing lights or, if not equipped with landing lights, by switching on and off, twice, its navigation lights.

AEROPLANE ACCIDENT INVESTIGATION.

DEFINITIONS.

Accident to Person.

The ICAO defines an accident as an occurrence associated with the operation of an aeroplane, which takes place between the time any person boards the aeroplane with the intention of flight until such time as all such persons have disembarked, in which a person is fatally or seriously injured as a result of being in or in direct contact with any part of the aeroplane. Included in this definition is death or serious injury as a result of parts becoming detached from the aeroplane or from direct exposure to jet blasts. Not included in this definition are death from natural causes, self inflicted

If a component detaches from an aircraft in flight and seriously injures someone on the ground, this event would still be defined as an aircraft accident.

A person's death from natural causes while on board an aircraft is NOT classified as an accident.

The ICAO definition of an aircraft accident includes death or serious injury to persons on the ground as a result of parts becoming detached from the aeroplane, or from direct exposure to jet blasts.

If an aircraft accident occurs in the United Kingdom, it must be reported by the quickest means available to the local Police and the Chief Inspector of Air Accidents.

injuries, injuries caused by other persons, or injuries to stowaways who are outside of normal areas reserved for passengers and crew.

If an aircraft accident occurs in the United Kingdom, it must be reported by the by the quickest means available to the local Police and the Chief Inspector of Air Accidents. If an aircraft has an accident at a licensed airfield, it is the responsibility of the Pilot in Command to report the accident.

Accident to Aircraft.

An accident to an aircraft is defined as the aeroplane sustaining damage or structural failure which will adversely affect the structural strength, performance or the flight characteristics of the aeroplane. The consequence of such an accident may be that major repair or replacement of aeroplane structure or components are required.

Not included in this definition are engine failures or damage limited to the engine, cowlings or accessories, propellers, wing tips, antennas, tyres, brakes and small holes or dents in the aeroplane skin. An accident is also defined as the aeroplane being missing or completely inaccessible.

Aircraft Incident.

An incident is defined as an occurrence, other than an accident, associated with the operation of an aircraft which affects, or could affect, the safety of operation of the aircraft.

Some examples of serious incidents are:

- Landings or attempted landings on a closed or engaged runway.

- Aborted take-offs on an engaged runway.

- Take-off or landing incidents:- incidents such as undershooting, overrunning or running off the sides of runways.

- Running short of fuel, requiring the declaration of an emergency by the pilot.

AEROPLANE ACCIDENT AND INCIDENT INVESTIGATION.

Objective of Accident Investigation.

The sole objective of the investigation of an accident or incident shall be the prevention of accidents and incidents. It is not the purpose of an investigation to apportion blame or liability.

PROTECTION OF EVIDENCE, CUSTODY AND REMOVAL OF AEROPLANE.

Responsibility of the State in which the Occurrence Takes Place.

It is the responsibility of the state in which an occurrence takes place to protect the evidence and maintain safe custody of the aeroplane and its contents for the period of the investigation. The evidence may be protected by photographing anything that may be removed, obliterated, lost or destroyed.
Further damage, pilfering, deterioration or unauthorised access must be prevented.

REQUEST FROM STATE OF REGISTRY, STATE OF THE OPERATOR, STATE OF DESIGN OR STATE OF MANUFACTURE.

The State of Occurrence should comply with any request submitted by the State of Registry, Design or Manufacture that the aeroplane's contents and any other evidence be left undisturbed pending inspection. Such request will not prevent the aeroplane being moved in the event that persons, animals, mail or valuables have to be removed, or if there is a danger of fire, or if the aeroplane is causing an obstruction to air navigation or to the public.

Release from Custody.
Following the completion of the investigation, the State of Occurrence shall release the aeroplane, its contents or any aircraft parts as soon as they are no longer required, to the State of Registry or the State of the Operator, as appropriate.

NOTIFICATION.

Responsibility of the State of Occurrence.
The State of Occurrence shall forward a notification of an accident, or serious incident, as soon as possible by the most suitable and quickest means available to the following:

*   The State of Registry.

*   The State of the Operator.

*   The State of Design.

*   The State of Manufacture.

*   The ICAO, when the aeroplane involved is of maximum mass of over 2 250 kg.

RESPONSIBILITY OF THE STATE OF REGISTRY, STATE OF THE OPERATOR, STATE OF DESIGN AND STATE OF MANUFACTURE.

The appropriate states (listed above) should acknowledge receipt of notification of a report of an accident or serious incident and provide the State of Occurrence with any information available to them regarding the aeroplane or flight crew involved in the accident or serious incident. The states must also provide information regarding any dangerous goods carried on board the aeroplane. The applicable states have the right, or may be requested, to provide an accredited representative to participate in the investigation.

INVESTIGATION.

RESPONSIBILITY FOR INSTITUTING AND CONDUCTING THE INVESTIGATION.

State of Occurrence.
When there is an accident or serious incident, the State of Occurrence is responsible for instituting an investigation or delegating part or all of the investigation to another state, by mutual arrangement and consent. When the whole investigation is delegated to another state, that state is to conduct the whole investigation including the issuance of a final report. If only part of the investigation is delegated, the State of Occurrence is responsible for the investigation and final report.

Responsibility of the State Conducting the Investigation.
The state carrying out the investigation will have complete independence and unrestricted authority over the conduct of the investigation. The investigation must include the following elements:

• Gathering, recording and analysing of all available information on the accident or incident.

• Drawing conclusions, including the determination of causes.

• Making safety recommendations.

• Where appropriate, the issuing of safety recommendations.

• Completion of the final report.

OPERATIONAL PROCEDURES
QUESTIONS

Representative PPL - type questions to test your theoretical knowledge of Operational Procedures.

1.   Complete the following wording with one of the options at a, b, c or d below to give the most correct statement.

A pilot in command of a flight during which an aircraft enters the sovereign airspace of a foreign state with the intention of landing:

a.   must ensure before departure that his pilot's licence has been validated by the foreign state
b.   must be satisfied that the aircraft's Certificate of Airworthiness is current and that he holds a type rating for the aircraft
c.   must have ensured that all necessary and relevant documentation is carried on board the aircraft, including the Certificate of Airworthiness, that the aircraft is in an airworthy condition and that it is correctly registered
d.   must be satisfied that the aircraft's Certificate of Airworthiness is current, that he holds a type rating for the aircraft, and that he has passed an Air Law examination set by the foreign state

2.   In level flight at night, from your aircraft, you see an anti-collision beacon and a red navigation light. The lights are at the same altitude as yourself and are steady at 2 o' clock and closing. This indicates that there is:

a.   an airship which should give way to you
b.   a flying machine which should give way to you
c.   a flying machine to which you should give way
d.   no threat

3.   In establishing noise preferential routes, turns during take-off and climb should not be required unless the aircraft has reached:

a.   1 000 feet above terrain or the highest obstacles under the flight path
b.   500 feet above terrain or the highest obstacles under the flight path
c.   1 500 feet above terrain or the highest obstacles under the flight path
d.   2 000 feet above terrain or the highest obstacles under the flight path

4.   The Air Navigation Order states that a person shall not recklessly or negligently act in a manner likely to endanger an aircraft or any person therein. To whom does this apply?

a.   Only to airline crew
b.   Only to cabin staff
c.   Only to the pilot in command
d.   To every person

5. Which of the following documents is not required to be carried in an aircraft of an ICAO member state?

a. Certificate of Registration
b. Certificate of Airworthiness
c. Flight crew licences
d. Flight crew birth certificates

6. A light aircraft is hired from a flying club for a private flight; the person responsible for planning the flight and ensuring that the weather is suitable is:

a. the CFI
b. the Operations Manager
c. the PIC
d. the duty instructor

7. In the UK, an aircraft accident must be reported without delay to:

a. the nearest ATCU and the local police
b. the CAA and the Air Investigation Branch
c. the flight safety officer at the base airfield
d. the Chief Inspector of the Air Investigation Branch and the local police

8. In establishing noise preferential routes, bank angles for turns after take-off should be limited:

a. to 20 degrees except where adequate provision is made for an acceleration phase permitting attainment of safe speeds for bank angles greater than 20 degrees
b. to 10 degrees except where adequate provision is made for an acceleration phase permitting attainment of safe speeds for bank angles greater than 10 degrees
c. to 15 degrees except where adequate provision is made for an acceleration phase permitting attainment of safe speeds for bank angles greater than 15 degrees
d. to 25 degrees except where adequate provision is made for an acceleration phase permitting attainment of safe speeds for bank angles greater than 25 degrees

9. Which of the following is not a Search & Rescue Alerting phase?

a. Urgency phase
b. Uncertainty phase
c. Alert phase
d. Distress phase

10.   An Alerting Service is:

   a.   provided for all aircraft being given an air traffic control service and,
          insofar as is practicable, to all other aircraft having filed a flight plan
          or otherwise known to the air traffic services, and also to any aircraft
          known to be the subject of unlawful interference
   b.   the provision of navigation and weather warnings to pilots in flight
   c.   specifically for the provision of search and rescue services
   d   only provided for aircraft on an IFR flight plan

11.   Which of the following is not an SAR ground to air signal?

   a.   V
   b.   N
   c.   R
   d.   Y

12.   At the scene of an aircraft accident, a survivor has made a ground signal
        showing a large cross with angles of 90° between the arms of the cross.
        What does this mean?

   a.   Require medical assistance
   b.   Require assistance
   c.   This is our position
   d.   All survivors are uninjured

13.   Before departure the commander of an aircraft must brief all passengers on
        the:

   a.   location of all exits and the procedure to be followed in the event of
          ditching or forced landing
   b.   the operation of the seat belts and life jackets
   c.   location of all exits and the operation of any safety equipment that is
          carried
   d.   the weather en-route and at the destination

14.   Which of the following cases constitutes a reportable accident?

   a.   A lightning strike on an aircraft in flight
   b.   The injury of a person on the ground after being struck by any part
          of an aircraft which had detached from the aircraft while it was
          airborne, but where the safety of the aircraft was not necessarily
          compromised
   c.   An engine failure in flight
   d.   A burst main gear or tailwheel tyre during the take off or landing roll

15. If an aircraft has an accident, involving injury to persons or damage to the aircraft, at a licensed airfield, who is responsible for reporting the accident to the appropriate authority?

    a. The ATC watch officer
    b. The ATC supervisor
    c. The pilot in command
    d. The police

16. Which one of the following statements is false?

    An accident must be reported if, between the time that anyone boards an aircraft to go flying and until everyone has left it:

    a. anyone is killed or seriously injured while in or on the aircraft
    b. the aircraft incurs damage or structural failure
    c. the aircraft is completely inaccessible or missing
    d. a passenger dies from natural causes

17. Following an aviation accident in the United Kingdom, to which of the following must the accident be reported as expeditiously as possible?

    a. The home airfield of the aircraft involved in the accident
    b. The Civil Aviation Authority and the local police
    c. The Chief Inspector of the Air Accident Investigation Branch (AAIB) and to the local police
    d. The nearest Air Traffic Control Unit

18. It is the pilot's responsibility to ensure that the aircraft is properly equipped for the planned flight. If there is any doubt the pilot should consult the:

    a. Certificate of Airworthiness
    b. Certificate of Maintenance Review
    c. Minimum Equipment List
    d. Pilot's Operating Handbook

19. On any flight the minimum safety equipment that must be carried is:

    a. first aid kit, fire axe, portable oxygen for all on board and a fire extinguisher
    b. first aid kit, spare electrical fuses and a portable fire extinguisher
    c. first aid kit, life jackets for all on board and a fire extinguisher
    d. first aid kit, smoke hoods and a fire extinguisher

20. Which of the following is correct with reference to which aircraft require a noise certificate and which are exempt?

    a. All aeroplanes except certain STOL aircraft require a noise certificate
    b. Non-public transport aircraft are exempt
    c. All aircraft which can take off from a hard dry runway in less than 610 metres are exempt
    d. Training aircraft are exempt

21.   The definition of a forced landing on water is:

    a.   Hydroplaning
    b.   Ditching
    c.   Surfing
    d.   Skimming

22.   A situation wherein uncertainty exists as to the safety of an aircraft and its occupants is:

    a.   Distress phase
    b.   Alert phase
    c.   Uncertainty phase
    d.   Emergency phase

23.   The definition of 'Distress' is:

    a.   the aircraft has an urgent message to transmit concerning the safety of persons on board or within sight
    b.   the aircraft has an immediate message to transmit concerning the safety of persons on board or within sight
    c.   the aircraft is in serious and/or imminent danger and requires immediate assistance
    d.   a crew member is distressed and requires medical assistance

24.   If a pilot intercepts an RT distress message, he should, if no acknowledgement is heard, relay it and then:

    a.   standby to receive further instructions whilst holding in present position
    b.   endeavour to guide other aircraft to the location of the aircraft in distress
    c.   at his discretion, proceed to the location of the aircraft in distress
    d.   proceed on flight plan route

25.   In a situation where concern for the safety of an aircraft and its occupants exists (alert phase), responsibility for alerting the necessary search and rescue units lies with:

    a.   the ATCU which received the distress message on the international distress frequency
    b.   the appropriate responsible person
    c.   the rescue coordination centre
    d.   the pilot in command

26.   To indicate that assistance is required, survivors would use which of the following signals from the Ground to Air Emergency Code?

    a.   X
    b.   V
    c.   g
    d.   R

27.   If a component becomes detached from an aircraft in flight, seriously injuring someone on the ground, but not affecting the continuation of the aircraft's flight, how would ICAO define this occurrence?

a.   An aircraft accident
b.   An aircraft incident
c.   An occurrence to be reported
d.   A fortuitous occurrence

Question	1	2	3	4	5	6	7	8	9	10	11	12
Answer												

Question	13	14	15	16	17	18	19	20	21	22	23	24
Answer												

Question	25	26	27
Answer			

The answers to these questions can be found at the end of this book.

JAR-FCL PPL THEORETICAL KNOWLEDGE SYLLABUS

OPERATIONAL PROCEDURES

The table below contains the principal topics and subtopics from the current outline syllabus for the theoretical examination in **Operational Procedures** for the **Private Pilot's Licence**, as published in **JAR-FCL 1**. Syllabuses may be modified, so always check the latest examination documentation from your **national civil aviation authority**, or from **JAR-FCL/EASA**.

OPERATIONAL PROCEDURES	
ICAO Annex 6, Part II – Operation of aircraft:	foreword; definitions; general statement; flight preparation and in-flight procedures; performance and operating limitations; instruments and equipment; communications and navigation equipment; maintenance; flight crew; lights to be displayed.
ICAO Annex 12 – Search and rescue:	definitions; alerting phases; procedures for pilot-in-command (para 5.8 and 5.9); search and rescue signals (para 5.9 and Appendix A).
ICAO Annex 13 – Aircraft accident investigation:	definitions; national procedures.
Noise abatement:	general procedures; application to take-off and landing.
Contravention of aviation regulations:	offences; penalties.

ANSWERS TO THE OPERATIONAL PROCEDURES QUESTIONS

ANSWERS TO THE OPERATIONAL PROCEDURES QUESTIONS

Question	1	2	3	4	5	6	7	8	9	10	11	12
Answer	c	c	b	d	d	c	d	c	a	c	c	a

Question	13	14	15	16	17	18	19	20	21	22	23	24
Answer	c	b	c	d	c	d	b	a	b	c	c	c

Question	25	26	27
Answer	a	b	a

Index

A
Aeroplane Instruments and Equipment ... 23
Air-to-Ground Signals ... 44
Alerting Post ... 41
Alert Phase ... 41
Authority of the Commander ... 12

C
Carriage of Dangerous Goods ... 10
Carriage of Weapons ... 10
Certificates and Documentation ... 8
Contravention of Aviation Regulations ... 18
Controlled Flight Into Terrain ... 35

D
Distress Phase ... 41
Ditching ... 41
Dropping of Articles and Animals ... 10
Dropping of Persons ... 10

E
Emergency Break-in Marking ... 24
Emergency Locator Transmitter (ELT) ... 26
Emergency Phase ... 41
Endangering Safety of Aeroplanes ... 12
Endangering Safety of any Person or Property ... 12
Equipment ... 23

F
Flight Preparation ... 3
Flying Displays ... 13

G
Ground- Air Visual Signal Code ... 44

I
IFR Flights ... 24
Instruments ... 23

L
Lifejackets ... 25
Liferafts ... 25

M
Maintenance ... 16
Maintenance Release ... 17

O

Operation of Radio   9
Operator's Responsibility   8

P

Performance and Operating Limitations   13
Pre-flight Passenger Briefings   6
Pre-flight Passenger Safety Briefing   6

R

Rescue Coordination Centre   41

S

Search and Rescue   41
Search and Rescue Region   41
Smoking in Aeroplanes   12
Stowaways   13

T

Towing of Gliders   9

U

Uncertainty Phase   41

V

VFR Flights   24

W

Windshear   29